Palgrave Explorations in Workplace Stigma

Series Editor
Julie Gedro
Empire State College
Rochester, NY, USA

This series is a call to action for organizations to not only recognize but include, support, and value employees of all walks of life, regardless of the social stigmas that might create material, affective, or psychological divisions between them and their ostensibly "normal" counterparts. It fills the gap in scholarship surrounding the difficult issues employees or job seekers might face based on their demographics, life events, or other factors. The series explores issues such as mental illness and wellness; and alcohol and drug addiction and recovery. It explores the complex and often times nuanced issues that face sexual minorities, or those who are formerly incarcerated, or military veterans in the context of employment or career decision making.

Through rigorous research and contributions from the foremost scholars in human resources, books in the series will provide an in-depth exploration of each population and challenge HR scholars and practitioners to effectively consider and embrace these explorations and consider expanding their own awareness. The series speaks on behalf of anyone who has ever been affected–directly or indirectly–by discrimination or exclusion in the context of work, and promotes a positive, productive, and purposeful working environment for employees at all levels.

More information about this series at
http://www.palgrave.com/gp/series/15458

Cong Liu · Jie Ma
Editors

Workplace Ostracism

Its Nature, Antecedents, and Consequences

palgrave
macmillan

Editors
Cong Liu
Hofstra University
Hempstead, NY, USA

Jie Ma
Jinan University
Guangzhou, Guangdong, China

ISSN 2662-3625 ISSN 2662-3633 (electronic)
Palgrave Explorations in Workplace Stigma
ISBN 978-3-030-54378-5 ISBN 978-3-030-54379-2 (eBook)
https://doi.org/10.1007/978-3-030-54379-2

This Palgrave Macmillan imprint is published by the registered company Springer Nature Switzerland AG
The registered company address is: Gewerbestrasse 11, 6330 Cham, Switzerland

Contents

Notes on Contributors

Adrienne R. Carter-Sowell, Ph.D. is a jointly appointed Associate Professor in the Psychological and Brain Sciences Department and the Africana Studies Program at Texas A&M University. She is leading an interdisciplinary research team addressing the costs of being "socially invisible." Dr. Carter-Sowell serves as a member of multiple External Advisory Boards, as Co-Principal Investigator on several Collaborative Research projects, and an Ad Hoc Reviewer for multiple programs at the National Science Foundation. Dr. Carter-Sowell was honored as an ADVANCE Diversity Champion by the Office of the Dean of Faculties in May 2020, because of her demonstrated commitment to diversity, equity, and inclusion (DEI) efforts to improve the workplace environment at Texas A&M University.

Xinxuan Che, Ph.D. is an Assistant Professor in the Industrial and Organizational Psychology program at Florida Institute of Technology. Prior to joining FIT, Dr. Che gained her Ph.D. from University of South Florida and has worked for Johns Hopkins University. Her research mainly focuses on occupational health psychology and leadership in teams.

Maayan Dvir, Ph.D. is an Assistant Professor in the Departments of Behavioral Sciences and Education at the Max Stern Yezreel Valley College. Maayan received her Ph.D. in Social Psychology from Purdue University. She studies social exclusion and sexual harassment, and the interplay between social exclusion and sexual objectification.

Sally D. Farley, Ph.D. is an experimental social psychologist whose research typically falls at the intersection between nonverbal behavior and relationship science. Because she explores relational variables that influence power and affiliation, she has been interested in ostracism and social exclusion for many years.

Asha Ganesan, Ph.D. is a Postdoctoral Research Associate at the Department of Psychological and Brain Sciences at Texas A&M University. Her research focuses on gender, intergroup relations, and culture. Other research interests include cultural evolution, gender-based power, and health-related cognition.

Sharon Glazer, Ph.D. primarily studies occupational stress from a cross-cultural lens. She was a Fulbright and Erasmus Mundus 3rd Country scholar, a visiting professor at universities around the globe, editor for the *International Journal of Stress Management*, co-editor of two book series related to culture and IO Psychology, and elected Fellow of SIOP, IAIR, and IAAP.

Xixi Gu is a Ph.D. candidate in the Department of Psychology at Hofstra University, USA. Her research interests include workplace mistreatment, such as workplace ostracism and abusive supervision, emotion regulation, employee's harmony value, and entrepreneurship.

David J. Howard is a doctoral candidate in the Industrial and Organizational Psychology program at the University of South Florida. He is a statistical consultant for the Doctor of Business Administration program in the Muma College of Business. His research interests encompass technology-related counterproductive work behavior, research methods, and study design.

Cong Liu, Ph.D. is a Professor in the Department of Psychology at Hofstra University. She received her B.S. from Beijing Normal University, China, and her Ph.D. from University of South Florida, USA. She studies workplace ostracism, workplace conflict, and interpersonal harmony values in China and the USA. She is the Associate Editor for the *International Journal of Stress Management*.

Jie Ma, Ph.D. is an Associate Professor at School of Management, Jinan University, China. His research interests include cognitive appraisals of workplace stressors and positive organizational psychology. His current research projects are concerned about how personal factors (e.g., personality traits and motivational orientation) affect employee cognitive appraisals of job demands.

Joshua A. Nagel is a Ph.D. student in Industrial and Organizational Psychology at The Graduate Center and Baruch College, City University of New York. His research interests mainly involve interpersonal relationships at work.

Yisheng Peng, Ph.D. is currently a tenure-track Assistant Professor of Industrial and Organizational Psychology at George Washington University. His primary research interests are workplace mistreatment (e.g., abusive supervision, incivility, ostracism, etc.), stress coping, aging and older worker issues (e.g., aging and occupational health, eldercare, bridge employment).

Tannaz T. Rahman, M.S. is a Senior Research Analyst at IMPAQ International LLC. She has worked on research related to ostracism since her student days at the University of Baltimore. She has been involved in both experimental studies where she explored the relationship between exclusion and affiliative behavior and survey studies where she examined workplace ostracism and psychosocial stressors.

Nicolette A. Rainone is a Ph.D. student studying Industrial and Organizational Psychology at Baruch College and The Graduate Center, CUNY. Her primary interests include diversity in the workplace, as well as how this intersects with a wide variety of topics (e.g., leadership, employee health and well-being, and assessment).

Aditi Rabindra Sachdev, Ph.D. works with the Corporate Talent Management and Organization Development team at PepsiCo, NY, USA. Her current research projects examine biases and discrimination at workplace.

Nicholas P. Salter, Ph.D. is an Assistant Professor of Industrial and Organizational Psychology at Hofstra University. As the director of the WILD (Workplace Inclusion, Leadership, and Diversity) lab, his research explores issues of diversity and inclusion of all kinds in the workplace. Additionally, he has been invited to speak to multiple organizations about this topic.

Kristin L. Sommer, Ph.D. is a Professor of Psychology at Baruch College, City University of New York. She holds appointments on the doctoral faculties in Basic and Applied Social Psychology and Industrial and Organizational Psychology at The Graduate Center. Dr. Sommer's primary research interests lie in workplace ostracism and language-based exclusion.

Paul E. Spector, Ph.D. (pspector@usf.edu) is a courtesy distinguished professor emeritus in the School of Information Systems and Management, Muma College of Business, University of South Florida. One of his main interests is in research methodology, with a particular focus on control variables, method variance, and issues dealing with scientific inference.

Na Tang has recently received her Master's degree in management from Lanzhou University, China. Her research interests focus on work stress, well-being, and proactive work behavior. Her current research project examines how, when, and why employee would behave differently in response to job demand.

Eric D. Wesselmann, Ph.D. is an Associate Professor in the Department of Psychology at Illinois State University. Eric received his Ph.D. in Social Psychology from Purdue University. He studies the various ways that people experience social inclusion and exclusion in daily life.

Kipling D. Williams, Ph.D. is Distinguished Professor of Psychological Sciences at Purdue University, where he has taught since 2004. He earned his B.S. from the University of Washington—Seattle (1975) and his Ph.D. in Social Psychology at The Ohio State University (1981). Prior to coming to Purdue, Williams was on faculties at Macquarie University and University of New South Wales (both in Sydney, Australia), University of Toledo (Ohio), and Drake University (Iowa). His research areas include ostracism, performance motivation in groups, and social influence.

Myia S. Williams, Ph.D. is a Research Industrial and Organizational Psychologist in the Department of Medicine at Northwell Health and Assistant Professor in the Department of Psychiatry at Donald and Barbara Zucker School of Medicine at Hofstra University/Northwell Health. Her research interests include workplace ostracism, immigrant/foreign-born workers, stress, racial/ethnic minorities, and health disparities.

Jun Yang, Ph.D. is an Assistant Professor at University of North Carolina at Greensboro. Her primary area of research is in organizational behavior and human resource management; specifically, her research addresses the social influence and moral reasoning processes in interpersonal relationships, with particular reference to dysfunctional leadership, ostracism, bullying, voice, and social networks.

Zhiqing E. Zhou, Ph.D. is an Assistant Professor in Industrial and Organizational Psychology at Baruch College and The Graduate Center of the City University of New York. His research interests include workplace mistreatment, employee health and well-being, work-nonwork inference, and illegitimate tasks.

Carla A. Zimmerman, Ph.D. is an Assistant Professor of Psychology at Colorado State University, Pueblo with a Ph.D. in Social Psychology and a certificate in gender studies from Texas A&M University. Her research focuses on how people react to and cope with being ignored and excluded by others.

List of Tables

CHAPTER 1

Ostracism Applied to the Workplace

Kristin L. Sommer, Joshua A. Nagel, and Kipling D. Williams

Prior to the 1990s, theoretical and empirical work on ostracism, exclusion, and rejection within the field of psychology was sparse. Developmental psychologists sought to understand reciprocal relationships between peer rejection and aggression in early childhood (Asher & Coie, 1990; Asher & Parker, 1989), and relationship scholars examined ostracism as a response to conflict between romantic partners (Gottman & Krokoff, 1992; Rusbult, Verette, Whitney, Slovik, & Lipkus, 1991). Only a handful of studies on social exclusion appeared in research outside these populations, and they focused primarily on emotional and attitudinal responses to exclusion. Broadly, these experiments revealed that excluded compared to included individuals are less attracted to their groups (Dittes, 1959; Geller, Goodstein, Silver, & Sternberg, 1974; Jones, Knurek, & Regan, 1973; Pepitone & Wilpizeski, 1960) and feel worse about themselves (Craighead, Kimball, & Rehak, 1979; Pepitone & Wilpizeski,

K. L. Sommer (✉) · J. A. Nagel
Baruch College and the Graduate Center, City University of New York, New York, NY, USA
e-mail: Kristin.Sommer@baruch.cuny.edu

K. D. Williams
Purdue University, West Lafayette, IN, USA

C. Liu and J. Ma (eds.), *Workplace Ostracism*,
Palgrave Explorations in Workplace Stigma,
https://doi.org/10.1007/978-3-030-54379-2_1

1960). Little was understood about how people respond behaviorally to exclusion, however, either within or outside of their rejecting groups.

The early to mid-90s brought the publication of a few key papers that gave rise to a groundswell of interest in exclusion and ostracism among social psychologists. Social exclusion theory (Baumeister & Tice, 1990; Leary, 1990), belongingness theory (Baumeister & Leary, 1995), and the need-threat model of ostracism (Williams, 1997; Williams & Sommer, 1997) provided solid theoretical foundations for generating predictions about affective, cognitive, and behavioral responses to exclusion or ostracism. Roughly 15 years later, almost two hundred studies on social exclusion and related phenomena had been conducted (Blackhart, Nelson, Knowles, & Baumeister, 2009), and many more have appeared in the literature since this time.

Perhaps ironically, the wealth of knowledge generated about reactions to exclusion and ostracism underscored the complexities of this phenomenon. If any single theme emerged from the explosion of work on this topic, it was that reactions to being excluded and ignored are anything but consistent. Some studies linked exclusion and ostracism with decrements in mood and self-esteem (Gerber & Wheeler, 2009; Leary, Tambor, Terdal, & Downs, 1995), threatened needs (Gerber & Wheeler, 2009; Williams, Cheung, & Choi, 2000), hurt feelings (Leary, Springer, Negel, Ansell, & Evans, 1998), and higher levels of social pain (Bernstein & Claypool, 2012b; Eisenberger, 2012; MacDonald & Leary, 2005). Others argued for emotional numbness (Twenge, Baumeister, Tice, & Stucke, 2001) and the absence of changes in self-esteem (Blackhart et al., 2009; DeWall & Baumeister, 2006). Exclusion and ostracism sometimes caused decreases in prosocial behavior (Twenge, Baumeister, DeWall, Ciarocco, & Bartels, 2007) or increases in antisocial behavior (Bourgeois & Leary, 2001; Twenge et al., 2001; Warburton, Williams, & Cairns, 2006) and other times caused increases in prosocial behavior (DeWall, 2010; Lakin, Chartrand, & Arkin, 2008; Maner, DeWall, Baumeister, & Schaller, 2007; Williams et al., 2000; Williams & Sommer, 1997). What emerged from the disparate set of findings was the recognition that a full understanding of prosocial, antisocial, and avoidant reactions to social exclusion could only be achieved through the identification of relevant mediators and moderators (Bernstein & Claypool, 2012a; Smart Richman & Leary, 2009; Williams, 2009) and by delineating between relatively automatic (reflexive) responses and controlled responses to ostracism (DeWall, Maner, & Rouby, 2009; Sommer & Bernieri, 2015; Williams,

2009). While more work remains to be done, social psychologists now have a fairly good understanding of the myriad strategies individuals employ to cope with exclusion, ostracism, and rejection and the implications of these processes for relationships with both rejectors and other interaction partners. We briefly summarize the major theoretical models of ostracism and exclusion within the social psychology literature before turning our attention to the literature on workplace ostracism.

Need to Belong

Baumeister and Leary (1995) advanced the belongingness hypothesis which states that all people have a fundamental need to form and maintain interpersonal relationships. This need to belong, thought to have developed out of ancient humans' dependence on belonging to groups for survival, is satisfied through frequent pleasant interactions with a few others characterized by mutual care for each other's welfare. Failure to meet this need, by way of being rejected, excluded, or ignored, will cause negative impacts on thought, emotion, and behavior. The authors cited evidence linking deprivation of belongingness to emotional distress such as anxiety, depression, and loneliness, and higher levels of mental and physical illness. The belongingness hypotheses provided a strong theoretical foundation for the subsequent surge of research on social exclusion and related phenomena.

Temporal Need Threat Model of Ostracism

At about the same time, Williams (1997, 2009) began developing the Temporal Need Threat Model of Ostracism to provide an overarching framework from which to consider the phenomenon of ostracism for both sources (those who ostracize) and targets (those who are ostracized). The full model includes *antecedents* (e.g., target characteristics, source characteristics, situational characteristics), the *motives* for ostracizing (e.g., punitive, defensive, oblivious), the *modalities* in which ostracism can occur (e.g., physical, social, cyber), and the psychological *impact* on targets (and to some extent, sources).

The psychological impact is presented as three distinct temporal stages of target reactions to ostracism. In the first, *reflexive* stage, ostracized individuals experience social pain and immediate threats to four fundamental needs for belonging, self-esteem, control, and meaningful existence.

These pain effects emerge across a wide range of variables, including age, culture, personality, gender, and race; for a range of ostracism sources (pre-programmed computer "players," in-group members, out-group members, and despised others); and in instances in which inclusion would logically seem not to matter, such as when ostracism is more financially rewarding than inclusion. The next, *reflective stage* occurs soon after, and incorporates thoughtful reflection, assessment, sense-making, and coping. The primary goal of this stage is to reduce the pain and fortify the threatened needs. For example, increasing one's bonds with others as a means to fortify belonging and self-esteem could involve being extra nice and agreeable; fortifying a sense of control and meaningful existence might involve being provocative and aggressive. Control could also be fortified by "turtling," or pulling away from others and seeking seclusion so as to minimize future rejection. Individual differences guide the coping responses and recovery rates, and situational factors can prolong the distress or make it fleeting. The final stage is the *resignation* stage, and only applies to targets who face chronic ostracism in their daily lives, including their home, workplace, church, or community. The cognitive and motivational resources required for coping in the reflective stage become depleted, leaving the individual in a state of alienation, depression, helplessness, and unworthiness.

Multimotive Model of Exclusion

Smart Richman and Leary (2009) sought to integrate disparate research findings associated with negative interpersonal events including ostracism, discrimination, and stigmatization. As noted previously, research streams in various disciplines had found myriad, and sometimes contradictory, reactions to rejection experiences in the form of prosocial, antisocial, and withdrawal behaviors. The Multimotive Model starts with the assumption that all rejection experiences primarily threaten individuals' perceived relational value. This arouses simultaneously three distinct motives: a desire for social connections (prosocial), a desire to defend oneself or hurt the source of rejection (antisocial), and a desire to avoid further hurt (withdrawal). Individuals construe the rejection experience in one of six possible ways, and these in turn predict which of the motivations will predominate. These motives then guide individuals' behavioral responses, which can either restore or fail to restore their relational value, with ramifications for psychological and physical well-being. For example, an individual may construe a rejection experience as unfair, which in turn will activate the motivation to hurt the source of rejection, culminating in antisocial behavioral reactions, which may (or may not) restore the individual's sense of belongingness. Satiation of the belongingness need (or lack thereof) will in turn give rise to better (or worse) mental and physical health. Thus, the Multimotive Model provides a framework for describing and explaining the cognitive, emotional, and behavioral reactions to rejection.

Workplace Ostracism

At about the same time that scholars were attempting to consolidate experimental findings on ostracism, interest in workplace ostracism began to build. Two turning points within the I-O and management literatures were the creation of a scale for assessing perceived ostracism in the workplace (Ferris, Brown, Berry, & Lian, 2008) and the integrated model of workplace ostracism proposed by Robinson, O'Reilly, and Wang (2013). These papers sought to operationally and conceptually differentiate ostracism from other forms of workplace deviance, including aggression, social undermining, and bullying. Combined with the rich set of findings from social psychology, they provided the springboard for the spate of work that would follow.

Ferris et al. (2008) defined workplace ostracism as feelings of being ignored or excluded by others at work. The 10-item measure provides respondents with several examples of being ignored in the workplace (e.g., your greetings have gone unanswered at work; others at work did not invite you or ask you if you wanted anything when they went out for a coffee break) and assesses the frequency with which respondents experience these events along 7-point scales ranging from never to always. The measure demonstrates high internal consistency ($\alpha = .89$ to $.96$) and good evidence of construct validity as reflected by confirmatory factor analyses and significant but moderate correlations with social undermining ($r = .56$), interpersonal justice ($r = -.62$), and group cohesion ($r = -.53$).

Robinson et al. (2013) defined *workplace ostracism* as occurring when "an individual or group omits to take actions that engage another organizational member when it is socially appropriate to do so" (p. 206). Ostracism reflects the omission rather than commission of behavior and hence serves to reduce rather than increase social interaction. This emphasis on inaction rather than action serves to further differentiate workplace ostracism from most other forms of workplace mistreatment, including workplace bullying, social undermining, and workplace incivility. The integrated model places strong emphasis on social context by restricting the definition of workplace ostracism to instances in which inclusion is socially appropriate. Excluded from the definition of ostracism are instances in which social contact is neither expected nor normative, such as among strangers in a crowded elevator. Robinson et al. propose that organizational antecedents of purposeful (intentional) workplace ostracism include low task interdependence among coworkers and cultures that discourage overt conflict. Organizational antecedents to nonpurposeful (unintentional) ostracism include stressful work environments and those in which members are geographically dispersed. Impacts of workplace ostracism are differentiated according to their psychological and pragmatic outcomes, the latter of which refers to loss of resources and relationships. According to the model, negative psychological and pragmatic impacts are stronger when employees are aware of and threatened by the ostracism. Negative impacts in turn drive behavioral consequences including declines in job performance and organizational citizenship behaviors, and increases in withdrawal and workplace deviance. Factors that may mitigate or attenuate these impacts include high levels of re-inclusion efficacy, high task interdependence, and high levels of identification with or attachment to the sources of ostracism. Although some aspects of the model remain untested, the paper reflects the strongest effort to date to create a comprehensive framework of predictors and outcomes of ostracism in the workplace.

Before proceeding, it bears mentioning that definitions of workplace ostracism endorsed by organizational scholars (ignoring *or* excluding) differ slightly from the definition of social ostracism endorsed by Williams (1997, 2009) (ignoring *and* excluding) (Ferris et al., 2008; Robinson et al., 2013). For this reason, a broader range of exclusionary behaviors are included within workplace conceptualizations of ostracism. The broader social psychological literature on ostracism, exclusion, and (active) rejection has suffered from construct contamination, with authors failing to acknowledge the limitations of consolidating findings based on substantively different manipulations (cf., Bernstein & Claypool, 2012a, 2012b; Gerber & Wheeler, 2009). We encourage readers to attend to conceptual and operational definitions of ostracism when appraising the overlaps and inconsistencies among studies described in this chapter and elsewhere.

In the forthcoming sections, we provide a brief survey of the existing work on workplace ostracism. We describe different types or manifestations of ostracism in the workplace, identify common targets of workplace ostracism, and summarize major antecedents to and outcomes of workplace ostracism. Comprehensive discussions of these topics appear in the other chapters in this book, so we present them only briefly here. We conclude with a brief discussion of major gaps in the literature and promising areas for future research.

Types of Workplace Ostracism

Ostracism can manifest in a multitude of ways. Collectively these reflect the diversity of means by which an employee might feel ignored or excluded within the organization.

General workplace ostracism. The commonly used operationalization of workplace ostracism by Ferris et al. (2008) assesses feeling ignored or excluded by "coworkers" and "others" but does not make any assumptions about the causes of ostracism. The Workplace Exclusion Scale (WES-R) by Hitlan and Noel (2009) includes subscales for perceived exclusion by supervisors, exclusion by coworkers, and exclusion due to lack of language proficiency and is similarly written broadly enough so as to capture a range of perceived motives for ostracism.

Organizational shunning. Organizational shunning has been defined as "the deliberate, systematic exclusion of a person once included in the rites and everyday rituals that signify organizational membership" (Anderson, 2009, p. 36). Anderson conducted interviews with shunned employees who had blown the whistle on a colleague or been demoted or denied promotion. Respondents reported being gradually excluded from social activities like getting coffee with colleagues, denied voice in decision making, and increasingly "feeling like a piece of furniture." They noted that even allies were careful not to be seen interacting with them for fear that allies' reputations would be damaged by association. Organizational shunning might be thought of as an instance of widespread ostracism that occurs when someone behaves in a way that lowers their status or attractiveness in the eyes of others.

Thwarted belonging. Thwarted belonging refers to unmet needs for belongingness at work. Thau, Aquino, and Poortvliet (2007) measured thwarted belonging by providing individuals with 7 pairs of circles with varying degrees of overlap, and asking them to select the pair that best reflects their (a) desired and (b) perceived closeness with coworkers. Thwarted belonging was higher to the extent that ratings of desired self-other overlap exceeded those of actual self-other overlap. Thau et al. found that higher levels of thwarted belonging were associated with more deviant behaviors and fewer helping behaviors as reported by supervisors. Thwarted belonging and workplace ostracism appear to be relatively distinct, correlating weakly and slightly negatively in working populations (−.07; Sommer, 2019). This suggests that people can experience deficits in emotional closeness at work without perceiving they are being ignored by their coworkers, and can feel ostracized by coworkers without desiring higher levels of closeness or intimacy with them.

General workplace belongingness. Workplace belongingness refers to feeling "personally accepted, respected, included and supported by others in the organisational environment" (Cockshaw & Shochet, 2010, p. 284). It is typically (although not always) operationalized using the Psychological Sense of Organisational Membership (PSOM; Cockshaw & Shochet, 2010). This construct appears primarily in the literature on mental health and emotional well-being. For example, lower levels of belongingness at work are associated with higher levels of depression and anxiety (Cockshaw & Shochet, 2010; Cockshaw, Shochet, & Obst, 2014; Rubin, Paolini, Subašić, & Giacomini, 2019), workplace burnout (Somoray, Shakespeare-Finch, & Armstrong, 2017) and psychological distress (Shakespeare-Finch & Daley, 2017), and lower levels of psychological resilience (Shakespeare-Finch & Daley, 2017).

Out-of-the-loop ostracism. Out-of-the-loop ostracism is a form of partial ostracism that involves not having access to information possessed by others (Jones, Carter-Sowell, Kelly, & Williams, 2009). Being out of the loop threatens psychological needs and negatively impacts trust in and liking for group members even when having the information would confer no tangible benefit (Jones et al., 2009). These deleterious impacts occur primarily when the information loss is perceived as intentional or preventable on the part of group members (Jones & Kelly, 2010), although even unintentional information loss can threaten needs and perceived competence when it prevents individuals from participating in group discussions (Jones, Carter-Sowell, & Kelly, 2011).

Out-of-the-loop ostracism is related to the idea of knowledge hiding. *Knowledge hiding* is defined as intentionally withholding information from others or "playing dumb" by feigning ignorance about a matter (Connelly, Zweig, Webster, & Trougakos, 2012). People who are ostracized are more likely than those who are included to withhold information from group members (Gkorezis & Bellou, 2016), particularly when they are dispositionally high (compared to low) in negative reciprocity (the belief that negative treatment should be reciprocated) or moral disengagement (the tendency to disengage from self-sanctions for behaving unethically) (Zhao, Xia, He, Sheard, & Wan, 2016). These findings point to the possibility of an "out-of-the-loop" loop, or reciprocal relationship between being denied access to information and depriving others of information. Knowledge hiding may allow out-of-the-loop employees to regain a sense of control.

Linguistic ostracism. Linguistic ostracism refers to any instance in which two or more people converse in a language others cannot understand (Dotan-Eliaz, Sommer, & Rubin, 2009; Hitlan, Kelly, Schepman, Schneider, & Zárate, 2006). Dotan-Eliaz et al. (2009) found that participants who were linguistically ostracized (compared to included) by Russian-speaking team members reported higher levels of anger and lower levels of team potency, and worked less hard within their teams if they were low (but not high) in social self-efficacy. Hitlan et al. (2006) found that people who imagined being linguistically ostracized in Spanish reported higher levels of symbolic threat and prejudice against immigrants compared to those who imagined being ostracized in English or socially included.

Linguistic ostracism is a form of *language-based exclusion*, which refers to any instance in which language or linguistic features (e.g., accents, vocabulary) serve as the basis for social exclusion (Kulkarni & Sommer, 2015). Language can trigger ethnic or cultural prejudices, such as when a Mandarin speaker living in Hong Kong is rejected by a Cantonese speaker. Language can also mark perceived deficits in the capacity for complex thought, such as when an expatriate struggles to convey a nuanced idea or interpret an idiomatic expression (e.g., "not playing with a full deck") in her non-native language. Even subtle changes in vocabulary can result in psychological outcomes similar to being outright ignored, such as when male interviewers use gender-exclusive language (e.g., "We know a good employee when we see him") toward a female interviewee.

Cyberostracism. Cyberostracism is defined as being ignored over the Internet. This term was introduced in the context of a web-based experimental manipulation (Cyberball) for manipulating feelings of inclusion and ostracism in an ostensibly on-line environment (Williams et al., 2000; Williams & Jarvis, 2006). Cyberball-based ostracism has large impacts on needs satisfaction which are consistent across samples and structural aspects of the game (Hartgerink, Van Beest, Wicherts, & Williams, 2015). Cyberostracism can occur through other channels as well. For example, feelings of ostracism can occur when people receive no, curt, or delayed responses to email messages or cell phone texts (Smith & Williams, 2004), are ignored in chat rooms (Filipkowski & Smyth, 2012; Williams et al., 2002) or fail to receive a high number of "Likes" or responses to status updates on social media (Hayes, Wesselmann, & Carr, 2018; Schneider et al., 2017; Tobin, Vanman, Verreynne, & Saeri, 2015).

Targets of Ostracism

Although most of the work on ostracism has focused on outcomes of being ostracized, some research has identified factors that increase one's risk of ostracism. We outline these briefly below.

Burdensome, underperforming, or unethical group members. Individuals whose behaviors are burdensome or violate descriptive or injunctive norms are strong candidates for ostracism by their groups (Davis & Johnson, 2015; Scott & Duffy, 2015). For example, Wesselmann, Wirth, Pryor, Reeder, and Williams (2013) showed that individuals will make strong efforts to include a group member who has been unjustifiably ostracized by the group, but will join others in ostracizing that member when the person has been particularly slow to perform a task (creating a burden on the group). Free-riding or loafing behavior is a particularly unattractive quality in a team member. Not only does it objectively decrease the probability that the team will succeed, but it also conveys a lack of concern for others' efforts and personal outcomes associated with team performance. Indeed, the decision to ostracize undercontributing group members is driven more strongly by members' intended contributions than their actual contributions (Liddell & Krusch, 2014). This suggests that groups may continue to include members whose low performance stems more from lack of ability than effort.

Employees may also ostracize coworkers who behave unethically, although this may depend on perceptions of job performance. Quade, Greenbaum, and Petrenko (2017) found that employees' unethical behavior as reported by their supervisors positively predicted employees' experiences with ostracism, but only when their job performance was simultaneously low. High-performing employees were generally buffered from ostracism in the face of unethical behaviors. The authors suggested that individuals may be willing to overlook moral violations among those whose strong job performance contributes to organizational success. In a somewhat different pattern of findings, Quade, Greenbaum, and Mawritz (2019) found that individuals who believed they were more (compared to less) ethical than a coworker reported more negative affect, which in turn predicted a stronger desire to socially undermine and ostracize that coworker. This effect was amplified when employees believed their coworker was outperforming them. Whether strong performance among unethical employees decreases or increases ostracism by coworkers may depend on the implications for coworkers' self-evaluations and perceptions of fairness.

Rate busters and *high performers*. As suggested in the previous section, employees who outperform their coworkers may be more vulnerable to ostracism. Rate busters are workers whose output exceeds injunctive norms for performance within the group. The Hawthorne studies (Roethlisberger & Dickson, 1939; Whitebead, 1938) conducted in the late 20s and early 30s revealed that rate busters were sometimes subjected to social exclusion by group members, presumably because rate busters threatened to increase management's expectations of productivity. In line with the findings of Quade et al. (2019), high-performing employees may also be targeted for ostracism because they threaten feelings of efficacy or esteem in their coworkers. Indeed, targets of threatening upward comparisons (Exline & Lobel, 1999; Schaubroeck & Lam, 2004) are more likely than others to fear or perceive ostracism by their coworkers. Other findings show that employees who feel envied by coworkers for being exceptionally successful at work perceive higher levels of ostracism by coworkers, particularly to the extent employees are high in neuroticism or low on the need to belong (Liu, Liu, Zhang, & Ma, 2019).

Uncivil employees. Like other aversive interpersonal behaviors, incivility is likely to inspire ostracism by others (Sommer & Yoon, 2013). Ostracism as a response to uncivil behavior may depend on other features of the relationship, however. For example, Scott, Restubog, and Zagenczyk (2013) found that employees were less trusting of coworkers who displayed high levels of workplace incivility, and distrust in turn predicted higher levels of coworker-rated ostracism. This effect held primarily when coworkers had a negative or weak exchange relationship with these employees, however, meaning that coworkers tended to underbenefit from these relationships.

Stronger exchange relationships attenuated the impact of distrust on ostracism. Ostracism also may not be a viable response to incivility by those with whom maintaining a positive relationship is critical to one's job or career (e.g., one's supervisor).

Temporary employees. Individuals employed on a temporary or contingent basis may be vulnerable to higher levels of perceived exclusion both in and outside of the organization (Feldman, Doerpinghaus, & Turnley, 1994; McInnes, 1999). A meta-analysis of the antecedents of workplace ostracism by Howard, Cogswell, and Smith (2020) revealed that part-time workers reported experiencing more ostracism than full-time workers. Gundert and Hohendanner (2014) examined the relationship between labor market integration and broader perceptions of social integration. Panel respondents of varying employment levels reported on the extent to which they were participating in social life and felt integrated into society. Compared to permanent employees, temporary employees reported lower feelings of social integration/affiliation. Exclusion was higher among temporary agency workers than fixed-term or contract workers, who enjoy more stable and relatively longer employment in an organization.

In related research, Lapalme, Stamper, Simard, and Temblay (2009) found that temporary agency workers' feelings of "insider status" increased to the extent that they perceived higher levels of support from supervisors and permanently employed coworkers. Insider status in turn predicted higher levels of interpersonally facilitative behaviors and affective commitment to the organization. Stamper and Masterson (2002) revealed that employees with higher self-ratings of insider status were rated by their supervisors as more altruism/helpful and less likely to engage in production deviance (e.g., intentionally working slower). Thus, temporary or contingent workers may be at greater risk of feeling excluded at work and from society in general, but this can be offset by supervisors' and coworkers' expressions of support and acceptance.

Whistleblowers. Whistle-blowing refers to the act of revealing misconduct or wrongdoing to an organizational member who is in a position to do something about it (Bjørkelo, 2013). Early evidence of ostracism as a retaliatory response to whistle-blowing was provided by Miceli and Near (1992), who detailed historical accounts of employees being ignored and excluded after blowing the whistle on another member of the organization. Both qualitative and quantitative studies have corroborated these observations by revealing that ostracism is among several ways in which organizations and their employees may retaliate among those who expose wrongdoing within their ranks. For example, an integrative review of six years of research on whistle-blowing among nurses revealed strong fears or experiences of being silenced or bullied after whistle-blowing (Jackson et al., 2014). In another study of 72 Korean whistle-blowers who had disclosed wrongdoing to the media or authorities outside the organization, 97% reported being "ignored or excluded" by colleagues, and 80% reported having their "opinions or views ignored" by their supervisors (Park, Bjørkelo, & Blenkinsopp, 2018). This was in addition to receiving more active forms of mistreatment, such as being subjected to criticism, gossip, unwarranted allegations, and threats of physical violence. Mistreatment by supervisors was associated with mistreatment by colleagues, suggesting that supervisors may provoke or set norms for ostracism and other "bullying" behaviors by coworkers. This is consistent with earlier research showing that retaliatory responses to whistle-blowing are more severe for whistle-blowers who feel unsupported by their supervisors or upper management (Near & Miceli, 1986).

Related evidence on retaliation can be found on reactions to those who express voice over being unfairly treated in the workplace. In one study (Cortina & Magley, 2003), federal court employees who voiced concerns about workplace mistreatment (workplace incivility or sexual harassment) experienced higher levels of social retaliation, including ostracism, from colleagues to the extent that the source of mistreatment was higher in power. Retaliation was strongest when the victims directly confronted the powerful wrongdoer or sought social support from colleagues. These findings suggest that those who complain about unfair treatment are particularly at risk for ostracism when their actions threaten to destabilize power hierarchies within the organization.

Racial, ethnic, and sexual minorities. Members of minority groups who experience discrimination at work are at increased risk of ostracism. Broadly defined, workplace discrimination includes behaviors that would not be considered illegal per se but nevertheless exert a detrimental effect on employees (Dhanani, Beus, & Joseph, 2018). This includes social exclusion due to one's race, ethnicity, sexual orientation, disability, or other stigmatizing characteristics. Research shows that members of minority groups are at increased risk of bullying and ostracism in the workplace (DeSouza, Wesselmann, & Ispas, 2017; Fox & Stallworth, 2005), and that minority employees may feel excluded even when organizations have formal policies emphasizing diversity and inclusiveness

(Priola, Lasio, De Simone, & Serri, 2014). Priola et al. conducted qualitative interviews of sexual minorities working in Italian social cooperatives. The authors found that, despite working in organizations that prioritized employment of individuals from disadvantaged groups, respondents complained of "heteronormative cultures" and self-silencing with respect to disclosure of their sexual identities.

Older workers. Older employees may be ostracized by younger employees, particularly when older employees' presence in the workforce is perceived as a barrier to employment by younger generations. North and Fiske (2016) examined the interactive effects of perceived resource scarcity and prescriptive age-based stereotypes on intergenerational exclusion of older workers. In three studies, they found that younger workers were less interested in networking with older workers to the extent that older workers were perceived as depleting the available pool of jobs *and* to the extent that older workers violated prescriptive norms for how older individuals should behave. Prescriptive norm violations included delaying retirement, undergoing a resource-intensive healthcare procedure, and trying to "act like" younger generations.

Older work on temporal changes in group socialization suggests that both newcomers and old-timers within an organization may be ostracized, albeit for different reasons. Newcomers need to develop relationships and earn their place in the group, whereas old-timers are no longer valued and are viewed as replaceable (Moreland & Levine, 1982).

Personality. Four of the five Big 5 personality traits have been linked to workplace ostracism. Research by L. Wu, Wei, and Hui (2011) revealed that extraversion and agreeableness were associated with lower perceptions of being ostracized, and neuroticism was associated with higher perceptions of ostracism. Hales, Kassner, Williams, and Graziano (2016) found that people were more likely to ostracize targets who were described as disagreeable compared to agreeable, and this was independent of whether targets behaved prosocially or antisocially. Being ostracized in return reduced one's desire to be agreeable. In multiple studies using a variety of methods, Rudert, Keller, Hales, Walker, and Greifeneder (2020) found that participants reported stronger intentions or were more likely to ostracize targets portrayed as low (compared to high) in conscientiousness or agreeableness. This effect held when controlling for target likeability. The authors suggest that people low in agreeableness and conscientious are ostracized because they violate prosocial norms and are perceived as burdensome to others, respectively.

As a caveat, we note that ascribing personality characteristics to targets or sources of ostracism is appropriate only for sources who habitually employ ostracism (as a first response to any type of annoyance or disagreement), or targets who habitually elicit ostracism from others, across time and domains. In surveys, daily diaries, and interviews, it is quite clear that most people have been ostracized and most people have ostracized others (Nezlek, Wesselmann, Wheeler, & Williams, 2012). By extension, we suggest that most instances of workplace ostracism are not likely to be a direct result of personality but rather a consequence of discrete, changeable, or transient work behaviors or situations (e.g., social loafing or task interdependency).

Reactions to Ostracism

The literature on psychological and behavioral reactions to workplace ostracism is voluminous and discussed in detail in other chapters of this book. We review them only briefly here. A more comprehensive list of relevant citations can also be found in the recent meta-analysis conducted by Howard et al. (2020).

Employee well-being. A number of studies have explored the impact of workplace ostracism on various indicators of well-being. For example, data from a two-wave study of Chinese workers found that workplace ostracism positively related to psychological distress, which the authors operationalized according to self-reported job tension, emotional exhaustion, and depressed mood at work (Wu, Yim, Kwan, & Zhang, 2012). S. Zhang and Shi (2017) demonstrated that workplace ostracism was linked with lower subjective well-being by way of correlating negatively with life satisfaction and positive affect, and positively with negative affect. Hitlan, Cliffton, and DeSoto (2006) found that effects of workplace exclusion on psychological well-being were moderated by gender. Well-being was higher among men compared to women in the face of workplace inclusion, but lower among men compared to women in the face of exclusion. A daily diary study by Pereira, Meier, and Elfering (2013) illustrated that daily workplace exclusion was positively related to sleep fragmentation the following night.

Spillover effects on family life. Although family support can mitigate the adverse impacts of ostracism, family life can also be negatively impacted by workplace ostracism. A three-wave study conducted by J. Liu, Kwan, Lee, and Hui (2013) revealed that workplace ostracism predicted future perceptions of work-to-family conflict, which in turn predicted future declines in family satisfaction. In a large sample of matched employees and their spouses, Thompson, Carlson, Kacmar, and Vogel (2020) found that workplace ostracism predicted higher ratings of family emotional exhaustion (i.e., feeling drained and burned out by family demands) as reported by both employees and their spouses, and that this was mediated by higher levels of psychological distress among employees. These findings suggest that the psychological impacts of ostracism on employees can have negative spillover effects on family members who would otherwise serve as sources of support.

Organizational citizenship behavior. With rare exception, both time-lagged and multi-source data also point to lower levels of prosocial discretionary work behaviors among targets of workplace ostracism. Research on this topic typically involves unique combinations of mediators and moderators and reflects a diverse set of theoretical perspectives. For example, drawing from sociometer theory (Leary et al., 1995), Peng and Zeng (2017) found that the effects of workplace ostracism on citizenship behavior were mediated by declines in self-esteem and strengthened by the presence of 360-degree feedback. Ferris, Lian, Brown, and Morrison (2015) reported that workplace ostracism led to a decline in citizenship behaviors among people for whom job performance *was not* important to self-esteem (consistent with self-verification theory) but not for those for whom performance *was* important to self-esteem (consistent with self-enhancement theory). R. Zhang, Ye, and Ferreira-Meyers (2017) and Zhu, Lyu, Deng, and Ye (2017) analyzed the link between workplace ostracism and citizenship behavior through the lens of conservation of resources theory; in R. Zhang et al., this relationship was mediated by higher levels of work-family conflict and strengthened among employees high compared to low in rumination. In Zhu et al., declines in citizenship behaviors following ostracism were mediated by higher levels of job tension and exacerbated among those with high compared to low levels of need for affiliation. Balliet and Ferris (2013) adopted a social dilemma perspective, proposing and finding that the negative relationship between workplace ostracism and citizenship behaviors was stronger among people who were low (relative to high) in orientation toward future outcomes. C. Wu, Liu, Kwan, and Lee (2016) grounded their predictions in social identity theory, finding that ostracism predicted fewer citizenship behaviors, and that this was mediated by reductions in organizational identification.

The negative relationship between workplace ostracism and organizational identification was stronger when alternative job prospects were high compared to low. Chung (2015) found that lower levels of in-role behavior and citizenship behaviors following ostracism were mediated by perceptions of coworker conflict. Finally, consistent with the conceptualization of workplace ostracism as the absence of positive attention rather than presence of negative attention, Ferris et al. (2019) found that the negative impacts of workplace ostracism on citizenship behaviors were stronger among people with approach temperaments (who are sensitive to the presence/absence of positive stimuli) than those with avoidance temperaments (who are sensitive to the presence/absence of negative stimuli).

In one exception to research linking ostracism with lower levels of citizenship behavior, Xu, Huang, and Robinson (2017) observed a positive relationship between ostracism and prosocial behavior among employees who identified strongly with their organizations but no relationship among those who identified weakly with their organizations. The authors proffered that ostracism impels compensatory responses that affirm ostracized individuals' connections to their organizations. This is consistent with Robinson et al.'s (2013) proposition and past social psychological work (Maner et al., 2007; Williams & Sommer, 1997) linking perceived prospects for re-inclusion with higher levels of prosocial behavior.

Unethical and counterproductive work behaviors. In addition to performing fewer OCBs, targets of ostracism are more likely to exhibit unethical, counterproductive, or "deviant" work behaviors directed toward both other employees (e.g., making fun of others; publicly embarrassing others) and the organization (e.g., taking property, intentionally dragging out work to get overtime, falsifying receipts) (Hitlan & Noel, 2009; Howard et al., 2020). As with the literature on citizenship behaviors, the relationship between ostracism and counterproductive work behaviors is often contingent on other factors. Zhao, Peng, and Sheard (2013) found that the relationship between workplace ostracism and counterproductive work behaviors was strongest among employees low compared to high in proactive personality (defined according to the ability to resist situational forces and bring about change) and low compared to high in political skill (i.e., level of social confidence and influence at work). Corroborating evidence of the mitigating impact of high political skill was observed by Yang and Treadway (2018). Kouchaki and Wareham (2015, Study 2) found that employees who were ostracized were more likely to behave unethically as reported by their supervisors, and that this was mediated by employees' self-reported physiological arousal at work. The authors suggested that negative arousal associated with the prospect of behaving unethically would normally inhibit unethical behavior. In the face of ostracism, however, that negative arousal is instead attributed to being ostracized, which in turn disinhibits the unethical behavior. Other observed mediators of the link between ostracism and supervisor, peer, or self-ratings of deviance include state self-control (Yan, Zhou, Long, & Ji, 2014), emotional exhaustion (Jahanzeb & Fatima, 2018), and self-esteem (Peng & Zeng, 2017), respectively.

Work performance. Declines in overall job performance are also associated with workplace ostracism, and several studies implicate self-esteem as a causal factor. Using a multi-source, multi-wave design, L. Wu et al. (2011) found that the effects of workplace ostracism on future supervisor rated job performance were mediated by organizational self-esteem. Relatedly, Huertas-Valdivia, Braojos, and Lloréens-Montes (2019) reported that perceptions of workplace ostracism among hospitality workers were associated with lower extra-role customer service ratings, and this was mediated by decreases in self-esteem. Ferris et al. (2015) reported that workplace ostracism predicted lower levels of global self-esteem, which predicted lower peer-rated in-role performance. However, this was significant only for employees whose job performance was not important to their self-esteem. For employees whose performance was important to their self-esteem, self-esteem remained uncorrelated with job performance. Other research points to increases in tension or stress as a cause of low performance (Chung, 2018; Zhu, Lyu, Deng, & Ye, 2017). The deleterious impacts of ostracism on job performance are attenuated among those who are high in psychological empowerment (Chung, 2018), are high in self-efficacy (De Clercq, Haq, & Azeem, 2019), or perceive high levels of family support (Feng, Li, Feng, & Jiang, 2019).

Job commitment/turnover. Perhaps not surprisingly, targets of workplace ostracism report lower levels of psychological attachment or commitment to their organizations, which in turn predict higher levels of turnover intentions (Lyu & Zhu, 2019; Zhang et al., 2019; Zheng, Yang, Ngo, Liu, & Jiao, 2016). O'Reilly et al. (2015) found that workplace ostracism predicted actual turnover assessed three years later (whereas experiences with workplace harassment did not) and that this was mediated by decreased feelings of belongingness at work. Psychological resources can buffer the impact of ostracism on intentions to leave the organization. For example, Zheng et al. (2016) found that the negative impacts of workplace ostracism on affective commitment and turnover were attenuated among employees with high compared to low levels of psychological capital, which refers to one's efficacy, optimism, and resilience at work. People with high psychological capital may be better able to "bounce back" from being ostracized.

On the other hand, employee characteristics that normally increase feelings of attachment may cease to be advantageous in the face of ostracism. For example, L. Zhang et al. (2019) found that employees who had high/positive versus low/negative exchange relationships with their supervisors reported higher levels of job embeddedness (i.e., immersion in and attachment to the job), but the benefits of high leader-member exchange (LMX) relationships on embeddedness were eliminated in the face of ostracism. Job embeddedness in turn predicted lower levels of voluntary turnover at work. In a similar set of findings, Lyu and Zhu (2019) reported that ostracism undermined high levels of job embeddedness of highly intrinsically motivated people, in turn reducing their affective commitment to the job and increasing their intentions to quit.

Gaps and Future Directions

We envision five key ways in which future scholars can improve upon the already substantial body of work on workplace ostracism. All five relate back to the methods employed by scholars in this area.

1. *More diverse outcome variables*. The first pertains to the expanse of outcome variables on which scholars have traditionally focused. We began this chapter with a discussion of the mixed social psychological findings on prosocial responses to ostracism. For example, social ostracism has been linked to declines in prosocial behavior (Twenge et al., 2007), but it has also been linked with increases in conformity (Williams et al., 2000), linguistic and behavioral mimicry (Lakin et al., 2008; Sommer & Bernieri 2015), and an interest in meeting people (Maner et al., 2007). By comparison, most work on workplace ostracism points to lower levels of prosocial behavior, with an eye toward understanding the variables that strengthen or weaken these negative relationships. On the face

of it, there is no clear reason why ostracism *in* the workplace should motivate relatively more destructive (versus constructive or reparative) behaviors than ostracism *outside* of the workplace. Indeed, ostracism would not be as ubiquitous as it is, across all social animals including humans, if it always backfired by causing aggression or antisocial behavior (Williams, 2001). We would suggest that organizational scholars have not generally attempted to capture the behaviors that ostracized employees enact to mitigate their ostracism or strengthen bonds with others. We would posit, for example, that some ostracized employees might try to align their interests and conversation topics with those of their peers (Sommer & Bernieri, 2015), contribute more to collective tasks (Williams & Sommer, 1997), conform more to non-ostracizing peers (Williams et al., 2000), and be more welcoming to newcomers when the risk of rejection is low (Maner et al., 2007) or feelings of power are high (Narayanan, Tai, & Kinias, 2013). Conformity might also manifest in the form of being more agreeable or less antagonistic when groups must reach consensus, or (more problematically) suppressing contrarian ideas even when these ideas would lead to an objectively superior outcome. The literature on workplace ostracism would benefit from a more diverse set of outcomes variables so as to better capture the myriad ways in which ostracized employees navigate their interactions at work.

2. *More experiments.* Nearly all the work on workplace ostracism is correlational. Most of it seeks to increase confidence in causal inferences by using appropriate control variables, examining lagged effects of a putative causal factor on the presumed outcome, and soliciting data from multiple sources (typically employees and their coworkers or supervisor) to address the limitations of cross-sectional, single-source data. Although these methods arguably increase one's confidence in causal relationships, they still allow for the possibility that empirical relationships are in practice bidirectional or could be explained by confounding variables. Indeed, results of a recent meta-analysis by Howard et al. (2020) revealed that effect sizes pertaining to outcomes of ostracism did not vary as a function of the order in which ostracism and outcomes were assessed, leading the authors to argue that putative outcomes of workplace ostracism may often be antecedents. Indeed, recent evidence suggests that the relationship between ostracism and

citizenship behavior is bidirectional and that citizenship behaviors protect people from experiencing ostracism (Sommer, Pesner, Gonzalez, & Kern, 2020). Inferences about cause and effect would be greatly strengthened through the use of field experiments in which one or more factors could be manipulated. For example, corroborating evidence that workplace ostracism causes increases in deviant behaviors or decreases in citizenship behavior might come from studies that introduce within random subsets of employees workshops, company retreats, or other mechanisms for increasing feelings of belongingness in the workplace and examining pre-post changes in behavior. As another example, evidence that "flatter" organizational structures give rise to more instances of ostracism (Robinson et al., 2013) might be tested by de-emphasizing hierarchical relationships within a small number of departments or units and comparing rates of ostracism against those in which these structures remain in place.

3. *Expanded operationalizations of ostracism.* The body of work on workplace ostracism relies heavily on the 10-item scale created by Ferris and colleagues (2008). There is good reason for this, as the scale is high in face validity, unidimensional, and easy for respondents to complete. As noted earlier in the chapter, however, ostracism can take many forms, including low or minimal responsivity to email, speaking a non-understood language in the presence of coworkers, omitting or excluding others from computer-mediated communication or meetings, or failing to pass along information to one's colleagues (out-of-the-loop ostracism). These forms of ostracism receive relatively less attention and are ripe for exploration. Organizational scholars would also benefit from studying *threats* or *fears* of ostracism rather than focusing nearly exclusively on past experiences with ostracism, as this is where evidence for prosocial, contributory, or conciliatory behaviors is most likely to emerge. Finally, efforts to distinguish between reactions to relatively short-term or transient ostracism versus long-term or chronic ostracism in the workplace may help to elucidate contradictory findings in the literature (Williams, 2009).
4. *The impact of culture.* Scholars would benefit from giving more attention to how culture shapes reactions to ostracism. Although a substantial number of studies on workplace ostracism draw from

East Asian populations (mostly China and South Korea), little attention has been devoted to understanding if or how culture moderates responses to social ostracism. A growing body of work suggests that people in highly collectivistic cultures may be less negatively impacted by ostracism than those in more individualistic culture (see Uskul & Over, 2017, for a review). This runs contrary to the more intuitive assumption that cultures that emphasize social harmony and interpersonal bonds will be more threatened by ostracism. It appears as though high levels of interdependency serve a protective function, as evidenced by both lower physiological and self-report indicators of distress associated with ostracism (Pfundmair et al., 2015) and faster recovery from ostracism (Ren, Wesselmann, & Williams, 2013).

Interdependency may also have implications for the propensity to use ostracism in reaction to burdensome, free-riding, uncivil, or otherwise aversive team members. Ostracism may be viewed as a less effective means of punishing bad behaviors in interdependent cultures (Over & Uskul, 2016). On the other hand, concerns about direct confrontations and minimizing overt conflict within interdependent cultures may make ostracism a particularly attractive option for dealing with unappealing coworkers (Jahanzeb & Fatima, 2018). Research is needed to shed light on these competing predictions.

5. *A greater focus on actual behaviors.* With rare exception, the I-O and management literatures on ostracism rely on self-reported behavior. Coworker and supervisor reports are extremely valuable in this sense, but even these methods can be contaminated by other factors that characterize working relationships with employees. To take a simplistic example, supervisors may rate employees whom they like as demonstrating higher levels of citizenship behaviors, a sort of halo effect, and perceptions of being liked in turn reduce self-reported experiences of ostracism. Methods that allow researchers to directly observe behaviors in the workplace, or that rely on other non-self-report data, would bolster support for some of the claims made in the literature. Turnover rates, for example, derive from an examination of who is still working in a company and hence do not suffer from the same limitations of self-report. In university settings, discretionary service such as the number of committees for which one volunteers or the number of students one advises could be taken as measures of citizenship behavior. Longitudinal or cross-lagged panel designs could be employed to probe the directionality of these relationships.

Conclusion

Organizational scholars have amassed a great deal of knowledge on the factors that give rise to experiences of workplace ostracism and its impacts on individual functioning. Future research would benefit from greater attention to the various forms that ostracism can take, cultural differences in use of and reactions to ostracism, and practical interventions for reducing both the likelihood of ostracism and the negative impacts of ostracism on employee behavior.

References

Anderson, J. W. (2009). Organizational shunning: The disciplinary functions of 'non-sense'. *Atlantic Journal of Communication, 17*(1), 36–50. https://doi.org/10.1080/15456870802506140.

Asher, S. R., & Coie, J. D. (Eds.). (1990). *Peer rejection in childhood*. New York: Cambridge University Press.

Asher, S. R., & Parker, J. G. (1989). Significance of peer relationship problems in childhood. In B. H. Schneider, G. Attili, J. Nadel, & R. P. Weissberg (Eds.), *Social competence in developmental perspectives* (pp. 5–23). Amsterdam: Kluwer Academic.

Balliet, D., & Ferris, D. L. (2013). Ostracism and prosocial behavior: A social dilemma perspective. *Organizational Behavior and Human Decision Processes, 120*(2), 298–308. https://doi.org/10.1016/j.obhdp.2012.04.004.

Baumeister, R. F., & Leary, M. R. (1995). The need to belong: Desire for interpersonal attachments as a fundamental human motivation. *Psychological Bulletin, 117*(3), 497–529. https://doi.org/10.1037/0033-2909.117.3.497.

Baumeister, R. F., & Tice, D. M. (1990). Anxiety and social exclusion. *Journal of Social and Clinical Psychology, 9*(2), 165–195.

Bernstein, M. J., & Claypool, H. M. (2012a). Not all social exclusions are created equal: Emotional distress following social exclusion is moderated by exclusion paradigm. *Social Influence, 7*(2), 113–130. https://doi.org/10.1080/15534510.2012.664326.

Bernstein, M. J., & Claypool, H. M. (2012b). Social exclusion and pain sensitivity: Why exclusion sometimes hurts and sometimes numbs. *Personality and Social Psychology Bulletin, 38*(2), 185–196. https://doi.org/10.1177/0146167211422449.

Bjørkelo, B. (2013). Workplace bullying after whistleblowing: Future research and implications. *Journal of Managerial Psychology, 28*(3), 306–323. https://doi.org/10.1108/02683941311321178.

Blackhart, G. C., Nelson, B. C., Knowles, M. L., & Baumeister, R. F. (2009). Rejection elicits emotional reactions but neither causes immediate distress nor lowers self-esteem: A meta-analytic review of 192 studies on social exclusion. *Personality and Social Psychology Review, 13*(4), 269–309. https://doi.org/10.1177/1088868309346065.

Bourgeois, K. S., & Leary, M. R. (2001). Coping with rejection: Derogating those who choose us last. *Motivation & Emotion, 25*(2), 101–111. https://doi.org/10.1023/A:1010661825137.

Chung, Y. W. (2015). The mediating effects of organizational conflict on the relationships between workplace ostracism with in-role behavior and organizational citizenship behavior. *International Journal of Conflict Management, 26*(4), 366–385. https://doi.org/10.1108/IJCMA-01-2014-0001.

Chung, Y. W. (2018). Workplace ostracism and workplace behaviors: A moderated mediation model of perceived stress and psychological empowerment. *Anxiety, Stress & Coping, 31*(3), 304–317. https://doi.org/10.1080/10615806.2018.1424835.

Cockshaw, W. D., & Shochet, I. (2010). The link between belongingness and depressive symptoms: An exploration in the workplace interpersonal context. *Australian Psychologist, 45*(4), 283–289. https://doi.org/10.1080/00050061003752418.

Cockshaw, W. D., Shochet, I. M., & Obst, P. L. (2014). Depression and belongingness in general and workplace contexts: A cross-lagged longitudinal investigation. *Journal of Social and Clinical Psychology, 33*(5), 448–462. https://doi.org/10.1521/jscp.2014.33.5.448.

Connelly, C. E., Zweig, D., Webster, J., & Trougakos, J. P. (2012). Knowledge hiding in organizations. *Journal of Organizational Behavior, 33*(1), 64–88. https://doi.org/10.1002/job.737.

Cortina, L. M., & Magley, V. J. (2003). Raising voice, risking retaliation: Events following interpersonal mistreatment in the workplace. *Journal of Occupational Health Psychology, 8*(4), 247–265. https://doi.org/10.1037/1076-8998.8.4.247.

Craighead, W. E., Kimball, W. H., & Rehak, P. J. (1979). Mood changes, physiological responses, and self-statement during social rejection imagery. *Journal of Consulting and Clinical Psychology, 47*(2), 385–396. https://doi.org/10.1037/0022-006X.47.2.385.

Davis, B. J., & Johnson, D. B. (2015). Water cooler ostracism: Social exclusion as a punishment mechanism. *Eastern Economic Journal, 41*(1), 126–151. https://doi.org/10.1057/eej.2014.2.

De Clercq, D., Haq, I. U., & Azeem, M. U. (2019). Workplace ostracism and job performance: Roles of self-efficacy and job level. *Personnel Review, 48*(1), 184–203. https://doi.org/10.1108/PR-02-2017-0039.

DeSouza, E. R., Wesselmann, E. D., & Ispas, D. (2017). Workplace discrimination against sexual minorities: Subtle and not-so-subtle. *Canadian Journal of Administrative Sciences, 34*(2), 121–132. https://doi.org/10.1002/cjas.1438.

DeWall, C. N. (2010). Forming a basis for acceptance: Excluded people form attitudes to agree with potential affiliates. *Social Influence, 5*(4), 449–455. https://doi.org/10.1080/15534511003783536.

DeWall, C. N., & Baumeister, R. F. (2006). Alone but feeling no pain: Effects of social exclusion on physical pain tolerance and pain threshold, affective forecasting, and interpersonal empathy. *Journal of Personality and Social Psychology, 91*(1), 1–15. https://doi.org/10.1037/0022-3514.91.1.1.

DeWall, C. N., Maner, J. K., & Rouby, D. A. (2009). Social exclusion and early-stage interpersonal perception: Selective attention to signs of acceptance. *Journal of Personality and Social Psychology, 96*(4), 729–741. https://doi.org/10.1037/a0014634.

Dhanani, L. Y., Beus, J. M., & Joseph, D. L. (2018). Workplace discrimination: A meta-analytic extension, critique, and future research agenda. *Personnel Psychology, 71*(2), 147–179. https://doi.org/10.1111/peps.12254.

Dittes, J. E. (1959). Attractiveness of group as function of self-esteem and acceptance by group. *Journal of Abnormal and Social Psychology, 59*(1), 77–82.

Dotan-Eliaz, O., Sommer, K. L., & Rubin, Y. S. (2009). Multilingual groups: Effects of linguistic ostracism on felt rejection and anger, coworker attraction, perceived team potency, and creative performance. *Basic and Applied Social Psychology, 31*(4), 363–375. https://doi.org/10.1080/01973530903317177.

Eisenberger, N. I. (2012). The pain of social disconnection: Examining the shared neural underpinnings of physical and social pain. *Nature Reviews Neuroscience, 13*(6), 421–434. https://doi.org/10.1038/nrn3231.

Exline, J. J., & Lobel, M. (1999). The perils of outperformance: Sensitivity about being the target of a threatening upward comparison. *Psychological Bulletin, 125*(3), 307–337. https://doi.org/10.1037/0033-2909.125.3.307.

Feldman, D. C., Doerpinghaus, H. I., & Turnley, W. H. (1994). Managing temps: A permanent HRM challenge. *Organizational Dynamics, 23*(2), 49–63.

Feng, L., Li, J., Feng, T., & Jiang, W. (2019). Workplace ostracism and job performance: Meaning at work and family support as moderators. *Social Behavior & Personality: an International Journal, 47*(11), 1–13. https://doi.org/10.2224/sbp.8244.

Ferris, D. L., Brown, D. J., Berry, J. W., & Lian, H. (2008). The development and validation of the workplace ostracism scale. *Journal of Applied Psychology, 93*(6), 1348–1366. https://doi.org/10.1037/a0012743.

Ferris, D. L., Fatimah, S., Yan, M., Liang, L. H., Lian, H., & Brown, D. J. (2019). Being sensitive to positives has its negatives: An approach/avoidance perspective on reactivity to ostracism. *Organizational Behavior and Human Decision Processes, 152,* 138–149. https://doi.org/10.1016/j.obhdp.2019.05.001.

Ferris, D. L., Lian, H., Brown, D. J., & Morrison, R. (2015). Ostracism, self-esteem, and job performance: When do we self-verify and when do we self-enhance? *Academy of Management Journal, 58*(1), 279–297.

Filipkowski, K., & Smyth, J. (2012). Plugged in but not connected: Individuals' views of and responses to online and in-person ostracism. *Computers in Human Behavior, 28*(4), 1241–1253. https://doi.org/10.1016/j.chb.2012.02.007.

Fox, S., & Stallworth, L. E. (2005). Racial/ethnic bullying: Exploring links between bullying and racism in the US workplace. *Journal of Vocational Behavior, 66*(3), 438–456. https://doi.org/10.1016/j.jvb.2004.01.002.

Geller, D. M., Goodstein, L., Silver, M., & Sternberg, W. C. (1974). On being ignored: The effects of the violation of implicit rules of social interaction. *Sociometry, 37*(4), 541–556.

Gerber, J., & Wheeler, L. (2009). On being rejected: A meta-analysis of experimental research on rejection. *Perspectives on Psychological Science, 4*(5), 468–488. https://doi.org/10.1111/j.1745-6924.2009.01158.x.

Gkorezis, P., & Bellou, V. (2016). The relationship between workplace ostracism and information exchange: The mediating role of self-serving behavior. *Management Decision, 54*(3), 700–713.

Gottman, J., & Krokoff, L. J. (1992). Marital interaction and satisfaction: A longitudinal view. *Journal of Consulting and Clinical Psychology, 57*(1), 47–52.

Gundert, S., & Hohendanner, C. (2014). Do fixed-term and temporary agency workers feel socially excluded? Labour market integration and social well-being in Germany. *Acta Sociologica, 57*(2), 135–152. https://doi.org/10.1177/0001699313496588.

Hales, A. H., Kassner, M. P., Williams, K. D., & Graziano, W. G. (2016). Disagreeableness as a cause and consequence of ostracism. *Personality and Social Psychology Bulletin, 42*(6), 782–797. https://doi.org/10.1177/0146167216643933.

Hartgerink, C. H., Van Beest, I., Wicherts, J. M., & Williams, K. D. (2015). The ordinal effects of ostracism: A meta-analysis of 120 Cyberball studies. *PLoS ONE, 10*(5), e0127002. https://doi.org/10.1371/journal.pone.0127002.

Hayes, R., Wesselmann, E., & Carr, C. (2018). When nobody "likes" you: Perceived ostracism through paralinguistic digital affordances within social media. *Social Media Workplace Ostracism Society, 4*(3), 1–12. https://doi.org/10.1177/2056305118800309.

Hitlan, R. T., Cliffton, R. J., & DeSoto, M. C. (2006a). Perceived exclusion in the workplace: The moderating effects of gender on work-related attitudes and psychological health. *North American Journal of Psychology, 8*(2), 217–235.

Hitlan, R. T., Kelly, K. M., Schepman, S., Schneider, K. T., & Zárate, M. A. (2006b). Language exclusion and the consequences of perceived ostracism in the workplace. *Group Dynamics: Theory, Research, and Practice, 10*(1), 56–70. https://doi.org/10.1037/1089-2699.10.1.56.

Hitlan, R. T., & Noel, J. (2009). The influence of workplace exclusion and personality on counterproductive work behaviours: An interactionist perspective. *European Journal of Work and Organizational Psychology, 18*(4), 477–502. https://doi-org.remote.baruch.cuny.edu/10.1080/13594320903025028.

Howard, M. C., Cogswell, J. E., & Smith, M. B. (2020). The antecedents and outcomes of workplace ostracism: A meta-analysis. *Journal of Applied Psychology, 105*(6), 577–596. https://doi.org/10.1037/apl0000453.

Huertas-Valdivia, I., Braojos, J., & Lloréns-Montes, F. J. (2019). Counteracting workplace ostracism in hospitality with psychological empowerment. *International Journal of Hospitality Management, 76*(Part A), 240–251. https://doi.org/10.1016/j.ijhm.2018.05.013.

Jackson, D., Hickman, L., Hutchinson, M., Andrew, S., Smith, J., Potgieter, I., … Peters, K. (2014). Whistleblowing: An integrative literature review of data-based studies involving nurses. *Contemporary Nurse, 48*(1), 5495–5513. https://doi.org/10.1080/10376178.2014.11081946.

Jahanzeb, S., & Fatima, T. (2018). How workplace ostracism influences interpersonal deviance: The mediating role of defensive silence and emotional exhaustion. *Journal of Business and Psychology, 33*(6), 779–791. https://doi.org/10.1007/s10869-017-9525-6.

Jones, E. E., Carter-Sowell, A. R., & Kelly, J. R. (2011). Participation matters: Psychological and behavioral consequences of information exclusion in groups. *Group Dynamics: Theory, Research, and Practice, 15*(4), 311–325. https://doi.org/10.1037/a0025547.

Jones, E. E., Carter-Sowell, A. R., Kelly, J. R., & Williams, K. D. (2009). 'I'm out of the loop': Ostracism through information exclusion. *Group Processes & Intergroup Relations, 12*(2), 157–174. https://doi.org/10.1177/1368430208101054.

Jones, E. E., & Kelly, J. R. (2010). "Why am I out of the loop?" Attributions influence responses to information exclusion. *Personality and Social Psychology Bulletin, 36*(9), 1186–1201. https://doi.org/10.1177/0146167210380406.

Jones, S., Knurek, D., & Regan, D. (1973). Variables affecting reactions to social acceptance and rejection. *Journal of Social Psychology, 90*(2), 269–284. https://doi.org/10.1080/00224545.1973.9712568.

Kouchaki, M., & Wareham, J. (2015). Excluded and behaving unethically: Social exclusion, physiological responses, and unethical behavior. *Journal of Applied Psychology, 100*(2), 547–556. https://doi.org/10.1037/a0038034.

Kulkarni, M., & Sommer, K. (2015). Language-based exclusion and prosocial behaviors in organizations. *Human Resource Management, 54*(4), 637–652. https://doi.org/10.1002/hrm.21637.

Lakin, J. L., Chartrand, T. L., & Arkin, R. M. (2008). I am too just like you: Nonconscious mimicry as a behavioral response to social exclusion. *Psychological Science, 19*(8), 816–822. https://doi.org/10.1111/j.1467-9280.2008.02162.x.

Lapalme, M., Stamper, C., Simard, G., & Tremblay, M. (2009). Bringing the outside in: Can "external" workers experience insider status? *Journal of Organizational Behavior, 30*(7), 919–940. Retrieved from www.jstor.org/stable/41683874.

Leary, M. R. (1990). Responses to social exclusion: Social anxiety, jealousy, loneliness, depression, and low self-esteem. *Journal of Social and Clinical Psychology, 9*(2), 221–229.

Leary, M. R., Springer, C., Negel, L., Ansell, E., & Evans, K. (1998). The causes, phenomenology, and consequences of hurt feelings. *Journal of Personality and Social Psychology, 74*(5), 1225–1237. https://doi.org/10.1037/0022-3514.74.5.1225.

Leary, M. R., Tambor, E. S., Terdal, S. K., & Downs, D. L. (1995). Self-esteem as an interpersonal monitor: The sociometer hypothesis. *Journal of Personality and Social Psychology, 68*(3), 518–530. https://doi.org/10.1037/0022-3514.68.3.518.

Liddell, T. M., & Krusch, J. K. (2014). Ostracism and fines in a public goods game with accidental contributions: The importance of punishment type. *Judgment & Decision Making, 9*(6), 523–547.

Liu, J., Kwan, H. K., Lee, C., & Hui, C. (2013). Work-to-family spillover effects of workplace ostracism: The role of work-home segmentation preferences. *Human Resource Management, 52*(1), 75–93. https://doi.org/10.1002/hrm.21513.

Liu, F., Liu, D., Zhang, J., & Ma, J. (2019). The relationship between being envied and workplace ostracism: The moderating role of neuroticism and the need to belong. *Personality and Individual Differences, 147*, 223–228. https://doi.org/10.1016/j.paid.2019.04.040.

Lyu, Y., & Zhu, H. (2019). The predictive effects of workplace ostracism on employee attitudes: A job embeddedness perspective. *Journal of Business Ethics, 158*(4), 1083–1095. https://doi.org/10.1007/s10551-017-3741-x.

MacDonald, G., & Leary, M. (2005). Roles of social pain and defense mechanisms in response to social exclusion. *Psychological Bulletin, 131*(2), 237–240.

Maner, J. K., DeWall, C. N., Baumeister, R. F., & Schaller, M. (2007). Does social exclusion motivate interpersonal reconnection? Resolving the "porcupine problem". *Journal of Personality and Social Psychology, 92*(1), 42–55. https://doi.org/10.1037/0022-3514.92.1.42.

McInnes S. (1999). *Ostracism of the invisible worker.* Unpublished Master's thesis, University of New South Wales, Sydney, Australia.

Miceli, M. P., & Near, J. P. (1992). *Blowing the whistle: The organizational & legal implications for companies and employees*. New York: Lexington Books.

Moreland, R. L., & Levine, J. M. (1982). Socialization in small groups: Temporal changes in individual-group relations. *Advances in Experimental Social Psychology, 15,* 137–183.

Narayanan, J., Tai, K., & Kinias, Z. (2013). Power motivates interpersonal connection following social exclusion. *Organizational Behavior and Human Decision Processes, 122*(2), 257–265. https://doi.org/10.1016/j.obhdp.2013.08.006.

Near, J. P., & Miceli, M. P. (1986). Retaliation against whistle blowers: Predictors and effects. *Journal of Applied Psychology, 71*(1), 137–145. https://doi.org/10.1037/0021-9010.71.1.137.

Nezlek, J. B., Wesselmann, E., Wheeler, L., & Williams, K. D. (2012). Ostracism in everyday life. *Group Dynamics: Theory, Research, & Practice, 16*(2), 91–104.

North, M., & Fiske, S. (2016). Resource scarcity and prescriptive attitudes generate subtle, intergenerational older-worker exclusion. *Journal of Social Issues, 72*(1), 122–145. https://doi.org/10.1111/josi.12159.

O'Reilly, J., Robinson, S. L., Berdahl, J. L., & Banki, S. (2015). Is negative attention better than no attention? The comparative effects of ostracism and harassment at work. *Organization Science, 26*(3), 774–793. https://doi.org/10.1287/orsc.2014.0900.

Over, H., & Uskul, A. K. (2016). Culture moderates children's responses to ostracism situations. *Journal of Personality and Social Psychology, 110*(5), 710–724. https://doi.org/10.1037/pspi0000050.

Park, H., Bjørkelo, B., & Blenkinsopp, J. (2018). External whistleblowers' experiences of workplace bullying by superiors and colleagues. *Journal of Business Ethics, 161,* 1–11. https://doi.org/10.1007/s10551-018-3936-9.

Peng, A. C., & Zeng, W. (2017). Workplace ostracism and deviant and helping behaviors: The moderating role of 360-degree feedback. *Journal of Organizational Behavior, 38*(6), 833–855. https://doi.org/10.1002/job.2169.

Pepitone, A., & Wilpizeski, C. (1960). Some consequences of experimental rejection. *Journal of Abnormal and Social Psychology, 60*(3), 359–364.

Pereira, D., Meier, L. L., & Elfering, A. (2013). Short-term effects of social exclusion at work and worries on sleep: Social exclusion, worries, sleep. *Stress and Health, 29*(3), 240–252. https://doi.org/10.1002/smi.2461.

Pfundmair, M., Aydin, N., Du, H., Yeung, S., Frey, D., & Graupmann, V. (2015). Exclude me if you can—Cultural effects on the outcomes of social exclusion. *Journal of Cross-Cultural Psychology, 46*(4), 579–596. https://doi.org/10.1177/0022022115571203.

Priola, V., Lasio, D., De Simone, S., & Serri, F. (2014). The sound of silence: Lesbian, gay, bisexual and transgender discrimination in "inclusive organizations." *British Journal of Management, 25*(3), 488–502. https://doi.org/10.1111/1467-8551.12043.

Quade, M. J., Greenbaum, R. L., & Mawritz, M. B. (2019). "If only my coworker was more ethical": When ethical and performance comparisons lead to negative emotions, social undermining, and ostracism. *Journal of Business Ethics, 159*(2), 567–586. https://doi.org/10.1007/s10551-018-3841-2.

Quade, M. J., Greenbaum, R. L., & Petrenko, O. V. (2017). "I don't want to be near you, unless…": The interactive effect of unethical behavior and performance onto relationship conflict and workplace ostracism. *Personnel Psychology, 70*(3), 675–709. https://doi.org/10.1111/peps.12164.

Ren, D., Wesselmann, E. D., & Williams, K. D. (2013). Interdependent self-construal moderates coping with (but not the initial pain of) ostracism. *Asian Journal of Social Psychology, 16*, 320–326.

Robinson, S. L., O'Reilly, J., & Wang, W. (2013). Invisible at work: An integrated model of workplace ostracism. *Journal of Management, 39*(1), 203–231. https://doi.org/10.1177/0149206312466141.

Roethlisberger, F. J., & Dickson, W. J. (1939). *Management and the worker*. Cambridge: Harvard University Press.

Rubin, M., Paolini, S., Subašić, E., & Giacomini, A. (2019). A confirmatory study of the relations between workplace sexism, sense of belonging, mental health, and job satisfaction among women in male-dominated industries. *Journal of Applied Social Psychology, 49*(5), 267–282. https://doi.org/10.1111/jasp.12577.

Rudert, S. C., Keller, M. D., Hales, A. H., Walker, M., & Greifeneder, R. (2020). Who gets ostracized? A personality perspective on risk and protective factors of ostracism. *Journal of Personality and Social Psychology, 118*(6), 1247–1268. https://doi.org/10.1037/pspp0000271.

Rusbult, C. E., Verette, J., Whitney, G. A., Slovik, L. F., & Lipkus, I. (1991). Accommodation processes in close relationships: Theory and preliminary empirical evidence. *Journal of Personality and Social Psychology, 60*(1), 53–78. https://doi.org/10.1037/0022-3514.60.1.53.

Schaubroeck, J., & Lam, S. S. K. (2004). Comparing lots before and after: Promotion rejectees' invidious reactions to promotees. *Organizational*

Behavior and Human Decision Processes, 94(1), 33–47. https://doi.org/10.1016/j.obhdp.2004.01.001.

Schneider, F. M., Zwillich, B., Bindl, M. J., Hopp, F. R., Reich, S., & Vorderer, P. (2017). Social media ostracism: The effects of being excluded online. *Computers in Human Behavior, 73,* 385–393. https://doi.org/10.1016/j.chb.2017.03.052.

Scott, K. L., & Duffy, M. K. (2015). Antecedents of workplace ostracism: New directions in research and intervention. In P. L. Perrewé, J. R. B. Halbesleben, & C. C. Rosen (Eds.), *Mistreatment in organizations: Research in occupational stress and well-being* (Vol. 13, pp. 137–165). Bingley: Emerald Group. https://doi.org/10.1108/s1479-355520150000013005.

Scott, K. L., Restubog, S. L. D., & Zagenczyk, T. J. (2013). A social exchange-based model of the antecedents of workplace exclusion. *Journal of Applied Psychology, 98*(1), 37–48. https://doi.org/10.1037/a0030135.

Shakespeare-Finch, J., & Daley, E. (2017). Workplace belongingness, distress, and resilience in emergency service workers. *Psychological Trauma: Theory, Research, Practice, and Policy, 9*(1), 32–35. https://doi.org/10.1037/tra0000108.

Smart Richman, L., & Leary, M. R. (2009). Reactions to discrimination, stigmatization, ostracism, and other forms of interpersonal rejection: A multimotive model. *Psychololgy Review, 116*(2), 365–383.

Smith, A., & Williams, K. D. (2004). R U there? Effects of ostracism by cell phone messages. *Group Dynamics: Theory, Research, and Practice, 8*(4), 291–301.

Sommer, K. L. (2019). Ostracism. *Unpublished raw data.*

Sommer, K. L., & Bernieri, F. (2015). Minimizing the pain and probability of rejection: Evidence for relational distancing and proximity seeking within face-to-face interactions. *Social Psychological and Personality Science, 6*(2), 131–139. https://doi.org/10.1177/1948550614549384.

Sommer, K., Pesner, E., Gonzalez, K., & Kern, M. (2020). Being rejected for failing to help: The bidirectional links between workplace ostracism and organizational citizenship behaviors. *Manuscript submitted for publication.*

Sommer, K., & Yoon, J. (2013). When silence is golden: Ego depletion following aversive social interactions. *Journal of Personal and Social Relationships, 30*(7), 901–919. https://doi.org/10.1177/0265407512473006.

Somoray, K., Shakespeare-Finch, J., & Armstrong, D. (2017). The impact of personality and workplace belongingness on mental health workers' professional quality of life: Professional quality of life. *Australian Psychologist, 52,* 52–60.

Stamper, C., & Masterson, S. (2002). Insider or outsider? How employee perceptions of insider status affect their work behavior. *Journal of Organizational Behavior, 23*(8), 875–894. https://doi.org/10.1002/job.175.

Thau, S., Aquino, K., & Poortvliet, P. M. (2007). Self-defeating behaviors in organizations: The relationship between thwarted belonging and interpersonal work behaviors. *Journal of Applied Psychology, 92*(3), 840–847. https://doi.org/10.1037/0021-9010.92.3.840.

Thompson, M. J., Carlson, D. S., Kacmar, K. M., & Vogel, R. M. (2020). The cost of being ignored: Emotional exhaustion in the work and family domains. *Journal of Applied Psychology, 105*(2), 186–195. https://doi.org/10.1037/apl0000433.

Tobin, S., Vanman, E., Verreynne, M., & Saeri, A. (2015). Threats to belonging on Facebook: Lurking and ostracism. *Social Influence, 10*(1), 31–42. https://doi.org/10.1080/15534510.2014.893924.

Twenge, J. M., Baumeister, R. F., DeWall, C. N., Ciarocco, N. J., & Bartels, J. M. (2007). Social exclusion decreases prosocial behavior. *Journal of Personality and Social Psychology, 92*(1), 56–66. https://doi.org/10.1037/0022-3514.92.1.56.

Twenge, J. M., Baumeister, R. F., Tice, D. M., & Stucke, T. S. (2001). If you can't join them, beat them: Effects of social exclusion on aggressive behavior. *Journal of Personality and Social Psychology, 81*(6), 1058–1069. https://doi.org/10.1037/0022-3514.81.6.1058.

Uskul, A., & Over, H. (2017). Culture, social interdependence, and ostracism. *Current Directions in Psychological Science, 26*(4), 371–376.

Warburton, W. A., Williams, K. D., & Cairns, D. R. (2006). When ostracism leads to aggression: The moderating effects of control deprivation. *Journal of Experimental Social Psychology, 42*(2), 213–220. https://doi.org/10.1016/j.jesp.2005.03.005.

Wesselmann, E. D., Wirth, J. H., Pryor, J. B., Reeder, G. D., & Williams, K. D. (2013). When do we ostracize? *Social Psychological and Personality Science, 4*, 108–115. https://doi.org/10.1177/1948550612443386.

Whitehead, T. N. (1938). *The industrial worker, vols. 1 and 2*. Cambridge, MA: Harvard University Press.

Williams, K. D. (1997). Social ostracism. In R. M. Kowalski (Ed.), *Aversive interpersonal behaviors* (pp. 133–170). New York, NY: Plenum Press. https://doi.org/10.1007/978-1-4757-9354-3_7.

Williams, K. D. (2001). *Ostracism: The power of silence*. New York: Guilford.

Williams, K. D. (2009). Ostracism: A temporal need-threat model. *Advances in Experimental Social Psychology, 41*, 275–314. https://doi.org/10.1016/S0065-2601(08)00406-1.

Williams, K. D., Cheung, C. K. T., & Choi, W. (2000). Cyberostracism: Effects of being ignored over the Internet. *Journal of Personality and Social Psychology, 79*(5), 748–762. https://doi.org/10.1037/0022-3514.79.5.748.

Williams, K. D., Govan, C. L., Croker, V., Tynan, D., Cruickshank, M., & Lam, A. (2002). Investigations into differences between social and cyber ostracism. *Group Dynamics: Theory, Research, & Practice, 6*(1), 65–77.

Williams, K. D., & Jarvis, B. (2006). Cyberball: A program for use in research on interpersonal ostracism and acceptance. *Behavior Research Methods, 38*(1), 174–180. https://doi.org/10.3758/BF03192765.

Williams, K. D., & Sommer, K. L. (1997). Social ostracism by coworkers: Does rejection lead to loafing or compensation? *Personality and Social Psychology Bulletin, 23*(7), 693–706.

Wu, C. H., Liu, J., Kwan, H. K., & Lee, C. (2016). Why and when workplace ostracism inhibits organizational citizenship behaviors: An organizational identification perspective. *Journal of Applied Psychology, 101*(3), 362–378. https://doi.org/10.1037/apl0000063.

Wu, L.-Z., Wei, L., & Hui, C. (2011). Dispositional antecedents and consequences of workplace ostracism: An empirical examination. *Frontiers of Business Research in China, 5*(1), 23–44. https://doi.org/10.1007/s11782-011-0119-2.

Wu, L.-Z., Yim, F. H., Kwan, H. K., & Zhang, X. (2012). Coping with workplace ostracism: The roles of ingratiation and political skill in employee psychological distress. *Journal of Management Studies, 49*(1), 178–199. https://doi.org/10.1111/j.1467-6486.2011.01017.x.

Xu, E., Huang, X., & Robinson, S. L. (2017). When self-view is at stake: Responses to ostracism through the lens of self-verification theory. *Journal of Management, 43*(7), 2281–2302. https://doi.org/10.1177/0149206314567779.

Yan, Y., Zhou, E., Long, L., & Ji, Y. (2014). The influence of workplace ostracism on counterproductive work behavior: The mediating effect of state self-control. *Social Behavior and Personality: an International Journal, 42*(6), 881–890. https://doi.org/10.2224/sbp.2014.42.6.881.

Yang, J., & Treadway, D. C. (2018). A social influence interpretation of workplace ostracism and counterproductive work behavior. *Journal of Business Ethics, 148*(4), 879–891. https://doi.org/10.1007/s10551-015-2912-x.

Zhang, L., Fan, C., Deng, Y., Lam, C. F., Hu, E., & Wang, L. (2019). Exploring the interpersonal determinants of job embeddedness and voluntary turnover: A conservation of resources perspective. *Human Resource Management Journal, 29*(3), 413–432. https://doi.org/10.1111/1748-8583.12235.

Zhang, R., Ye, C., & Ferreira-Meyers, K. (2017). Linking workplace ostracism to interpersonal citizenship behavior: A moderated mediation model of work-to-family conflict and rumination. *International Journal of Stress Management, 24*(3), 293–320. https://doi.org/10.1037/str0000056.

Zhang, S., & Shi, Q. (2017). The relationship between subjective well-being and workplace ostracism: The moderating role of emotional intelligence. *Journal of Organizational Change Management, 30*(6), 978–988. https://doi.org/10.1108/JOCM-07-2016-0139.

Zhao, H., Peng, Z., & Sheard, G. (2013). Workplace ostracism and hospitality employees' counterproductive work behaviors: The joint moderating effects of proactive personality and political skill. *International Journal of Hospitality Management, 33*, 219–227. https://doi.org/10.1016/j.ijhm.2012.08.006.

Zhao, H., Xia, Q., He, P., Sheard, G., & Wan, P. (2016). Workplace ostracism and knowledge hiding in service organizations. *International Journal of Hospitality Management, 59*, 84–94. https://doi.org/10.1016/j.ijhm.2016.09.009.

Zheng, X., Yang, J., Ngo, H., Liu, X., & Jiao, W. (2016). Workplace ostracism and its negative outcomes. *Journal of Personnel Psychology, 15*(4), 143–151. https://doi.org/10.1027/1866-5888/a000147.

Zhu, H., Lyu, Y., Deng, X., & Ye, Y. (2017). Workplace ostracism and proactive customer service performance: A conservation of resources perspective. *International Journal of Hospitality Management, 64*, 62–72. https://doi.org/10.1016/j.ijhm.2017.04.004.

CHAPTER 2

Exploring the Overlap Among Workplace Ostracism, Mistreatment, and Related Constructs

Eric D. Wesselmann and Maayan Dvir

Humans are often referred to as "social animals," primarily because of our orientation toward forging (and maintaining) quality interpersonal relationships (e.g., Baumeister & Leary, 1995; Lieberman, 2013) and our tendencies to derive meaning, self-worth, and identity from these relationships (e.g., Ellemers & Haslam, 2012; Leary & Baumeister, 2000). Additionally, having healthy social relationships can provide a variety of benefits for one's psychological and physical health (Cacioppo & Patrick, 2008). In adulthood, people's occupations and workplaces are integral to their lives and incorporate important interpersonal relationships with both colleagues and supervisors. The quality of one's workplace relationships can also impact an individual's physical and psychological health.

E. D. Wesselmann (✉)
Illinois State University, Normal, IL, USA
e-mail: edwesse@ilstu.edu

M. Dvir
Max Stern Yezreel Valley College, Yezreel Valley, Israel

C. Liu and J. Ma (eds.), *Workplace Ostracism*,
Palgrave Explorations in Workplace Stigma,
https://doi.org/10.1007/978-3-030-54379-2_2

For example, the degree to which an employee believes that their organizational members value and care about them generally (i.e., perceived organizational support) positively correlates with job satisfaction and negatively correlates with employee burnout (see Eisenberger, Rhoades Shanock, & Wen, 2020 for a review).

Unfortunately, people do not always treat each other with mutual respect and kindness, and workplace environments are no exception. Diverse research programs examine the variety of ways that employees can harm each other physically and psychologically, assessing the toll that these behaviors take on both the individual employee and the organization. These ways that employees harm each other go by many names: bullying, discrimination, harassment, incivility, ostracism, etc. Collectively, research finds that all these forms of workplace mistreatment (or sometimes called workplace *aggression*) are harmful, but it is unclear whether all of these forms (i.e., constructs) overlap conceptually and empirically, and if so, to what extent (Hershcovis, 2011). These questions cut to the heart of the issue of construct validity—the degree to which measures and experimental manipulations are adequately corresponding to the concepts they purport to be measuring. The issue of construct validity is important not only in organizational sciences but psychological research broadly (e.g., Edwards, 2003; Schwab, 1980). Some researchers have provided opening bids in an attempt to establish some conceptual parameters that can facilitate empirical tests, each acknowledging that their attempts are by no means definitive (e.g., Bowling & Beehr, 2006; Hershcovis, 2011). The importance is to sustain the conversation and inspire future work to map the conceptual terrain more precisely.

It is in the spirit of further exploration that we offer our own perspective to the conversation. First, we will provide a brief overview of ostracism, highlighting its own conceptual overlap debates and discussing the importance that being ignored may have in these debates. Next, we discuss key workplace mistreatment constructs in the organizational literature and highlight their similarities and differences with ostracism and other, more direct forms of social exclusion. Finally, we will raise some remaining questions that future researchers should consider in continuing this conversation, which may help future theory-building and even resolve paradoxes that exist in the empirical literature. These discussions will also help researchers better target their constructs of interest and decide which measure(s) they wish to use, thus increasing measurement accuracy and minimizing redundancy.

Defining Ostracism and Other Forms of Social Exclusion

Ostracism as a psychological construct has been defined differently by various researchers. A common definition focuses on social acts of "ignoring and exclusion" (Williams, Cheung, & Choi, 2000, p. 748). Some researchers focus on the dynamics of ostracism from either the target's *or* the source's perspective (see Wirth & Wesselmann, 2018; Zadro & Gonsalkorale, 2014 for reviews), while sometimes both perspectives are regarded (e.g., Hales, Kassner, Williams, & Graziano, 2016). Research from various social scientific disciplines demonstrate that ostracism is ubiquitous—it occurs commonly across cultures and even across animal species (Williams, 2001).

Even though "ostracism" (as previously defined) has been a popular topic in psychology for only a few decades, aspects of it have been studied in psychology for most of the field's history (Wesselmann & Williams, 2017; Williams, 2007). Part of the difficulty in charting a history of the construct involves how it is defined. Kipling D. Williams was one of the first social psychologists to create a comprehensive program of research investigating this phenomenon, using a variety of empirical methods (i.e., qualitative interviews, cross-sectional surveys, event-contingent diaries, and a variety of experimental paradigms; Williams, 2001). Williams (2007, p. 427) highlighted that being *ignored* (e.g., being denied attention or acknowledgment) is the key component of understanding ostracism as a distinct phenomenon, whereas the *exclusion* component involves "being kept apart from others" which could involve being isolated from others or left out of events. Other authors have further explored the conceptual definition of ostracism as having components involving being ignored and excluded by developing survey items to assess these two aspects (Gilman, Carter-Sowell, DeWall, Adams, & Carboni, 2013). Both sets of items focus on passive *non*-behaviors, rather than active and direct behaviors that someone explicitly does to another person. For example, the *exclusion* items focused on situations in which someone is not included socially, such as when "others don't include me in their plans" or "don't invite me to go out to eat with them." It is important to note that these items involve a passive lack of including someone, rather than explicitly telling them they are unwanted. The *ignoring* items, however, involved situations in which someone was in the presence of others but did not receive the attention or acknowledgment they expected, such as "others treat me as if I am invisible," "others look through me as if I do not exist," and "others ignored me during conversation." Indeed, Robinson, O'Reilly, and Wang (2013) also highlighted the importance of understanding ostracism involves *inaction*, a failure to engage someone when it is socially expected (Leary, 1990, called this *passive* exclusion).

Whereas many of these studies suggest that ostracism involves both being ignored and excluded, other authors have provided definitions suggesting ostracism could involve *either* "ignoring or excluding" (e.g., Ferris, Chen, & Lim, 2017, pg. 136; however, they do note that ignoring is a key component that distinguishes ostracism from other negative workplace experiences). Thus, regardless of the specific nuances between researchers, most of their conceptual definitions of ostracism highlight the importance of being ignored as an integral part of the experience.

One can certainly be "kept apart from others" if they simply are not invited to a social gathering. A non-behavior allows the source of the exclusion plausible deniability; they can say they simply forgot or perhaps suggest the invitation was lost. Sometimes individuals receive a clear, direct communication that they are unwanted—something that has often been termed interpersonal *rejection* (Williams, 2007). Blackhart, Knowles, Nelson, and Baumeister (2009) made a similar assertion about distinguishing rejection as a sub-type of social exclusion, arguing that "its literal meaning refers specifically to a refusal of social connection. The implication is that one person seeks to form and maintain at least a temporary alliance or relationship with someone else, and that other person says no (at least implicitly)" (p. 270). Rejection commonly is manipulated in laboratory studies by providing feedback to participants that someone (or a group) does not want to work with them (e.g., Twenge, Baumeister, Tice, & Stucke, 2001). As Blackhart et al. (2009) noted, the communication of rejection can be subtle or implied; individuals can feel rejected when someone behaves toward them in an angry or cold manner (Wesselmann, Butler, Williams, & Pickett, 2010; Wirth, Bernstein, Wesselmann, & LeRoy, 2017), when someone tells a joke that insults a group they belong to (Wesselmann, Schneider, Ford, & DeSouza, 2018), or when someone laughs at them in a hurtful way (Klages & Wirth, 2014). Some of these even can be used in conjunction, such as a disparaging joke combined with mean-spirited laughter.

Thus, using a hierarchical form of constructs with exclusion as the broadest category of situations in which someone is "kept apart from others" (Williams, 2007, p. 427; see also Riva & Eck, 2016), someone could be excluded by being told explicitly to leave (i.e., given negative attention, aka., rejected) or simply by being ignored altogether (i.e., given no attention, aka., ostracized; Wesselmann et al., 2016). Certainly, both experiences are aversive, but the latter situation involves being treated as if one is not even worth the effort to be treated negatively, as if one does not exist—a form of *social death* (Williams, 2001; see also Hales, 2018). Williams (2001) argued that the experience of being ignored is worse than being excluded via some type of negative attention, channeling William James's (1890/1950) famous quote that to be treated as non-existent would be a "fiendish punishment...from which the cruelest bodily tortures would be a relief" (pp. 293–294).

Potential hyperbole aside, early qualitative interview data suggested that it may be the case that *negative* attention is better than *no* attention, at least for individuals who are facing long-term ostracism (Williams, 2001). Additionally, survey studies of individuals in organizations have found that ostracism has a stronger relationship with negative outcomes (e.g., threatened belonging, employee turnover) than experiences with other forms of negative attention (e.g., insults, teasing; O'Reilly, Robinson, Berdahl, & Banki, 2015). A few experimental studies have supported the general idea that negative attention hurts *less* than being ignored (Rudert, Hales, Greifeneder, & Williams, 2017; Zadro, Williams, & Richardson, 2005). These studies manipulated ostracism by having someone ignored either during an online game of ball-toss (Cyberball; Williams et al., 2000) or during a face-to-face role-playing conversation (O-Train; Zadro & Williams, 2006). In both cases, the researchers compared situations in which someone was ignored or was provided with negative social information via insults or arguments. Even though these preliminary studies suggest being ignored is worse than being rejected via negative attention, we emphasize that the extant data demonstrate that both negative attention and inattention *still* hurt.

Exclusion Hurts. Both types of exclusion share similar negative outcomes for target individuals. Excluded individuals immediately experience pain and negative affect, measured both at the neurological and self-report levels (Eisenberger, Lieberman, & Williams, 2003; Kross, Berman, Mischel, Smith, & Wager, 2011; Wesselmann, Wirth, Mroczek,

& Williams, 2012). When asked to describe exclusion-type events, participants often use visceral language used to describe physical pain, emphasizing their *hurt* feelings (Leary, Springer, Negel, Ansell, & Evans, 1998). Further, individuals can re-experience this pain to a certain degree when they perseverate on the memory of past exclusion events (Chen, Williams, Fitness, & Newton, 2008). In addition to pain, excluded individuals report threats to core psychological needs, such as belonging, control, meaningful existence, and self-esteem (Williams, 2009), and they even experience a threat to their perceived humanity (Bastian & Haslam, 2010).

Further, the initial pain of exclusion can be prolonged by rumination (Hales, Wesselmann, & Williams, 2016; Wesselmann, Ren, Swim, & Williams, 2013), and this may be a key mechanism in understanding why people who are higher in social anxiety take longer to recover from exclusion than those who are lower on that trait (Zadro, Boland, & Richardson, 2006). Because the pain of exclusion can be relived, individuals who may ruminate continuously on an exclusion episode run the risk of being stuck in a vicious cycle of social pain. This cycle may be one of the reasons that individuals who find themselves excluded chronically can develop severe psychological problems, such as feelings of alienation, depression, helplessness, meaninglessness, and suicidal ideation (Riva, Montali, Wirth, Curioni, & Williams, 2017; Van Orden, Witte, Gordon, Bender, & Joiner, 2008; Williams, 2001; 2009).

Organizing Exclusion Constructs. We have been discussing three common terms used to describe situations in which one's interpersonal relationships are threatened in some way. There are other interpersonal phenomena that also can be understood within the context of perceived threats to social connections, such as stigmatization (Kurzban & Leary, 2001), bullying, and many others (Smart Richman & Leary, 2009). Even something like unrequited love (Baumeister, Wotman, & Stillwell, 1993) may be considered a form of exclusion because it involves someone feeling emotionally or physically separated from the person who does not reciprocate their affection. So how do researchers make sense of all these constructs conceptually?

Most researchers would likely agree that many of the aforementioned constructs are not synonymous, even if they share some conceptual—and even empirical—similarities. As such, we argue that researchers should strive not to use the concepts ostracism, rejection, and exclusion as if they are the exact same constructs. This sounds simple enough on the surface, but as we have already noted, different programs of research are using different definitions for the same construct, even if the definitions differ only slightly. Which term should they use? On the one hand, debates about slight linguistic differences such as "and/or" or "exclusion/rejection" could be much ado about nothing in the grand scheme of things. But on the other hand, it may be important if these conceptual differences impact empirical outcomes in theoretically meaningful ways. For example, both studies that use rejection-focused manipulations (i.e., negative attention) and those that use ostracism-focused manipulations (i.e., no attention) find similar effects across various outcome variables (e.g., pain, basic need threat; Wesselmann et al., 2016). However, those ostracism researchers who have emphasized the power of being ignored as being more aversive than direct negative attention would argue that the theoretical distinctions are important if the negative effects are indeed a manner of extremity; some research already supports this idea (Rudert et al., 2017; Williams, 2001; Zadro, Williams, & Richardson, 2005). These conceptual differences may also influence other outcome variables, such as social withdrawal versus attempts to re-engage with others (Molden, Lucas, Gardner, Dean, Knowles, 2009; Ren, Wesselmann, & Williams, 2016), and perhaps even whether one responds to exclusion with affiliative or aggressive behaviors (see Williams, 2009 for review of these paradoxical behavioral responses).

Expanding the Debate to Workplace Mistreatment Constructs

At its core, the conundrum of how and when to use the terms ostracism, rejection, and exclusion is an issue with construct validity, and it is not unique to this area. Research on workplace ostracism can be situated within the broader literature of *workplace mistreatment* or *workplace aggression* (Bowling & Beehr, 2006; Hershcovis, 2011). The crux of the debate on which term to use is that conceptual definitions of aggression often assume that the behaviors in question are both purposeful and intended to do harm to the target (e.g., Anderson & Bushman, 2002), which is not always the case. These nuances can be important when discussing how to understand the causes of these behaviors, as well as practical issues such as determining culpability and legal ramifications. However, individuals who are targets of various forms of mistreatment often experience negative outcomes regardless of the sources's intentions and thus should not be underestimated by researchers, administrators, or policy makers (see discussions by Lilienfeld, 2017; Ong & Burrow, 2017; Sue, 2017). Thus, we elect to use the term mistreatment as a way to remain agnostic to the intentions of the source and instead focus on the target's experiences of their ultimate well-being outcomes. We will only use the term aggression when referring explicitly to negative behaviors purposefully done to cause harm to another person.

Workplace mistreatment has been used as an umbrella term to encapsulate various negative behaviors that colleagues *do* to each other in the workplace. M. Sandy Hershcovis (2011) reviewed this literature to bring the issue of construct validity to the forefront of the discussion, identifying five key constructs that seemed to have overlapping conceptual and empirical aspects: social undermining, incivility, bullying, abusive supervision, and interpersonal conflict. We will discuss Herschovis's assessment of each of these constructs in turn and highlight aspects that we believe are relevant to research on social exclusion (which we continue to use as our preferred umbrella construct). We should note that social exclusion types (e.g., ostracism and rejection) overlap with other forms of workplace mistreatment to some extent, especially in their measurements. Specifically, ostracism involves someone receiving no attention, but other forms of mistreatment can involve both no attention and negative attention (making them blur the lines as to whether they are more related to ostracism or rejection). In our discussion, we will highlight the key conceptual and empirical similarities and differences between these various constructs, which have important implications for researchers who are interested in these constructs.

Social undermining. This construct is defined as behaviors in which someone intentionally attempts to harm a coworker's achievements, social standing, or relationships specifically in the workplace context (Duffy, Ganster, & Pagon, 2002). These behaviors could occur from either a supervisor or a coworker, and involve things like being insulted, being gossiped about, or having one's work sabotaged in some way. Exposure to social undermining has been associated with negative impacts to one's psychological health and feelings of self-efficacy, as well as increasing counter-productive work behaviors (Duffy et al., 2002). Hershcovis (2011) argues that one important aspect that differentiates social undermining from other forms of workplace mistreatment is that the source *intends* the behaviors as harmful, whereas other mistreatment forms do not have to be intentional. From an operational definition perspective, social undermining can also be categorized under the two types of social exclusion: rejection-focused (i.e., negative attention) and ostracism-focused (i.e., lack of attention). A key measure of social undermining (Duffy et al., 2002) involves a survey of how often employees report experiencing different types of behaviors from either supervisors or coworkers. The majority of the items involve negative attention, such as when someone "hurt your feelings," "insulted you," or "made you feel incompetent." Recall that "hurt feelings" is a key psychological outcome for social exclusion (e.g., Leary et al., 1998). Further, hurtful laughter and insulting jokes can make people feel excluded (Klages & Wirth, 2014; Wesselmann et al., 2018). Interestingly, only a few items could be interpreted to involve no attention, such as "gave you the silent treatment," "delayed work to make you look bad or slow you down," and "did not defend you when people spoke poorly of you." Further, it is interesting to note that these passive, lack-of-attention items loaded highest on the coworker undermining factor, whereas they were some of the lowest loading items on the supervisor undermining factor. Thus, future research on the constructs of social undermining and exclusion in the workplace should consider the degree to which they overlap conceptually and empirically, as well as any potential differences between them on whom is the source of the behavior and why. Perhaps it is easier for coworkers to ignore each other due to their hierarchical position, whereas supervisors have to interact with their employees directly due to the nature of their roles. Another possibility is that rejection-focused behaviors (i.e., negative attention) can be observable easily by others and thus documentable, whereas ostracism-focused behaviors are more difficult to substantiate, and thus harder for the institution to punish the sources. Ostracism-focused behaviors are also likely to be seen as more socially acceptable than rejection-focused behaviors (e.g., O'Reilly et al., 2015).

Additionally, the key aspect of intention is one that makes social undermining different from various forms of social exclusion, especially ostracism. Ostracism is not always intentional, and even when it is it can occur for reasons that are not motivated primarily by the desire to harm another person (Nezlek, Wesselmann, Wheeler, & Williams, 2012; Williams, 2001). For example, someone may ostracize another person because social norms dictate it (two people conversing at a restaurant table would not normally include strangers in their conversation; i.e., "role-based ostracism," Williams, 2001). In this case, the conversation partners are purposeful in not talking to the strangers around them, but are not likely to be doing it with a desire to harm them. In the context of ostracism, as in other forms of negative interpersonal interactions, unintended harm still hurts, albeit perhaps less in some cases (e.g., when someone is left out-of-the-loop by accident, as opposed to on purpose; Jones & Kelly, 2010; see also Sommer & Williams chapter in this volume). Regardless of whether one is studying ostracism or other forms of workplace mistreatment, intention (or at least attributions of) should be taken into account in order to understand the potential magnitude of effects. The idea of intent is also important from a practical standpoint when designing organizational interventions. An employee may believe that because they did not intend harm when engaging in some form of mistreatment, they need not take responsibility for their actions or at the least minizine the experience of the injured party because "I didn't mean to hurt them." It is important in these contexts to emphasize that even unintended behaviors can still hurt.

Incivility. Another popular workplace mistreatment construct focuses on the degree to which employees experience incivility, seemingly minor disrespectful behaviors, such as being insulted, talked down to, or even referred to unprofessionally in professional settings. Employees experience these types of behaviors as stressful and exposure to incivility often predicts decreased job satisfaction and higher turnover rates (e.g., Andersson & Pearson, 1999; Cortina, Magley, Williams, & Langhout, 2001). Hershcovis (2011) argues that the ambiguous nature of these behaviors distinguishes the concept of incivility from other workplace mistreatment constructs, at least in terms of understanding their conceptual definitions with reference to the source of the behavior. Whether or not intent matters in terms of the negative impact on the target is a separate question.

In the context of exclusion, intention seems less important for a target's immediate reaction to the treatment—exclusion hurts regardless of why someone does it. However, the attributions a target makes to why they are being excluded may matter in terms of how quickly they recover (Williams, 2009; see also Liu, 2019). From a measurement perspective, this incivility measure has items assessing both negative attention (five items) and no attention (two items; Blau & Andersson, 2005; Cortina et al., 2001), blurring the line between ostracism and rejection-focused forms of social exclusion. In terms of negative attention, the items that seem most applicable to rejection-focused forms of social exclusion involve how often someone recalls a colleague has "put you down or was condescending to you in some way," or "made demeaning, rude or derogatory remarks about you." The other items that involve negative attention may also be experienced as exclusionary, but this is ultimately an empirical question.

In terms of items involving no attention, one item explicitly asks how often someone has been "ignored or excluded" and another involves how much attention someone is paid. Participants report feeling both excluded and *ignored* when someone does not give them eye contact or show much interest in their responses during social interactions (e.g., Wirth, Sacco, Hugenberg, & Williams, 2010; Wirth et al., 2017), so this measure of workplace incivility fits nicely with both rejection- and ostracism-types of social exclusion. A recent measure of incivility adds a third item that also could be interpreted as involving ostracism subtly: being interrupted or spoken over (Matthews & Ritter, 2016). Regardless, future research using this measure should consider separating these items into separate factors to investigate potential differential effects between the incivility that involves negative attention versus incivility involving no attention (i.e., ostracism; see also Ferris et al., 2017).

Bullying and abusive supervision. *Bullying* is a construct that is studied commonly in multiple contexts and often has diverse conceptual definitions. A key conceptual definition in the workplace mistreatment literature defines bullying as repetitive negative behaviors (verbal and non-verbal) that can be perpetrated by coworkers, regardless of their official status in relation to the target's status (Einarsen, 2000). Measures of workplace bullying typically assess a wide range of socially aggressive behaviors (see Hershcovis, 2011, Table 1; also Hoel, Cooper, & Faragher, 2001), such as teasing, rumors, and other forms of verbal abuse. Chronic exposure to bullying in the workplace has been associated with stress responses and other negative mental health outcomes (e.g., Matthiesen & Einarsen, 2001; Mikkelsen & Einarsen, 2001).

Hershcovis (2011) argues that bullying as a construct is unique among other workplace mistreatment constructs in that the persistent nature of the behaviors is a key aspect of the definition. Herschovis further argues that the definition assumes implicitly that there is some type of power differential between the source and the target, but this power difference does not have to be based on the individuals' institutional positions. Rather, power can be construed broadly to involve idiosyncratic social clout or cultural power based on one's demographic characteristics (e.g., gender). The idea of power, at least institutionally, is assessed explicitly in the research on social undermining as well.

Many items used to assess workplace bullying could be considered rejection-focused exclusion, such as assessing individuals' experience with being ridiculed, insulted, or teased. There are other items that assess behaviors characterized by no attention (i.e., ostracism-focused exclusion), such as someone being ignored explicitly or at least having one's opinions ignored. One item even combines these two types of exclusion together ("being ignored or facing hostility when you approach"; Hoel et al., 2001). One way in which the construct of workplace bullying differs from the construct of social exclusion broadly defined is that social exclusion does not assume repetition. Most experimental studies focus on single episodes of exclusion, whereas there are survey-based exclusion studies that have examined prolonged exposure to exclusion in various ways (e.g., Gilman et al., 2013; Nezlek et al., 2012; Riva et al., 2017). Further, social exclusion research does not assume a power differential between the source and the target.

Abusive supervision is similar to bullying in two ways: it involves repetitive negative behaviors and it involves a power differential (in this case, this is an explicit assumption; Hershcovis, 2011; Tepper, 2000). Items for measuring this construct are similar to those measuring bullying, albeit with a few that tap behaviors more likely to occur when there is an explicit institutionalized power differential, such as being able to call someone incompetent explicitly or using power to invade one's privacy. Abusive supervision was related to increased psychological distress and work-family conflict, lower satisfaction with one's job and life overall, decreased organizational citizenship behaviors, and increased turnover (Tepper, 2000; Zellars, Tepper, & Duffy, 2002). Hershcovis (2011) makes it clear that although several of these behaviors may occur among peers, their negative effects will be different qualitatively, and likely more harmful, when they come from a supervisor.

This measure of abuse supervision includes items that involve negative attention, whereas only one item explicitly involves someone being ignored (i.e., "the silent treatment"; Tepper, 2000; see also Table 1 in Hershcovis, 2011). Another item involves situations in which one's supervisor does not give a person credit for their efforts, which may also make someone feel ignored. To our knowledge, the potential connection between being denied credit for one's efforts and feeling ignored has not been examined directly, but is a reasonable hypothesis and a fascinating direction for future research.

Similar to bullying, the conceptual definition of abusive supervision differs from exclusion in the key areas of assumed persistence and power differential. However, the conceptual of definition abusive supervision is more similar to that of exclusion in that both focus on behaviors that do not involve physical contact. These two constructs also are similar in terms of the source's goal for the behavior. Tepper (2007) argues that although the behaviors categorized as abusive supervision are purposeful on the part of the supervisor, they do not necessarily have to be done with the intent to harm per se; the same is the case with exclusion (Nezlek et al., 2012; Williams, 2001).

One broader area that needs further exploration is the potential differential effects of workplace mistreatment between peers and those that involve power differentials. The research on abusive supervision assumes that the effects of mistreatment between peers qualitatively are different from mistreatment perpetrated by a supervisor. Regarding the construct of social exclusion, most research examines the phenomenon within the peer context and is agnostic to power differentials. However, it is reasonable to assume status may be a key moderator in studying both the effects of exclusion and the frequency of use. In some ways, exclusion may be an attractive tool for when individuals who have low status desire to aggress against others because one does not need to be strong physically or have institutional status in order to ignore someone. Qualitative interview data from individuals who experience chronic exclusion in various social situations support this idea (Williams, 2001).

Interpersonal conflict. The interpersonal conflict construct, which focuses on situations in the workplace in which employees disagree (Spector & Jex, 1998), has perhaps the broadest conceptual definition of the workplace mistreatment constructs. It is typically measured with a four-item measure that assesses the degree to which people report being yelled at, get into arguments with others, or are treated in a "nasty" or "rude" manner at work (Spector & Jex, 1998). These experiences are associated with increased psychological distress (e.g., anxiety and depression) as well as decreased job satisfaction and higher intentions to quit (Spector & Jex, 1998). Perhaps because the conceptual definition is so broad, the items used for this measure can be encompassed in the other workplace mistreatment constructs, but without the same level of nuance (likely because of it being such a small number of items). Hershcovis

(2011) argued that there was no clear feature that distinguished this workplace mistreatment construct from the others.

The items for this construct can be examined within the context of social exclusion research. Arguments and being yelled at involve negative attention, but nasty and rude treatment could involve either behaviors consisting of negative attention or no attention, if the latter type of behaviors are interpreted as being hostile. Thus, it is likely that this construct relates to workplace exclusion such that various types of exclusion could be methods by which employees engage in conflict. However, this is just one possible speculation that researchers need to consider when doing work in these area.

The four-item measure is not the only way of assessing interpersonal conflict in the workplace. Another measure categorizes conflicts into three types: task, process, and relationship conflicts (Jehn, 1995; Jehn, Lindred, Levine, & Szulanski, 2008). The items in this measure all assess "disagreements" or fights between employees either on specific tasks, general group decision-making processes, or about personal matters unrelated to work. None of these items are specific about the ways in which employees disagreed (i.e., their behaviors), so there is little conceptual or empirical overlap between this type of conflict measure and the types of social exclusion we have been discussing. It is possible that exclusion-related behaviors, whether direct negative attention or choosing to ostracize someone, may be employed as tools within the conflict. Thus, conflict between employees may not necessarily be counter-productive or psychologically harmful per se; rather, the way in which employees choose to argue may moderate the ultimate outcomes. Researchers interested in this idea could draw inspiration from the research on conflict within romantic relationships which differentiate between constructive ways that couples argue and destructive tactics, which often involve direct negative attention like contempt or even ostracism-type behaviors like giving one's partner the "silent treatment" (e.g., Gottman, 1999; Zadro, Arriaga, & Williams, 2008). Similar dynamics likely occur among coworkers in organizations and offer fruitful avenues for future research.

Expanding the Scope of Both Workplace Mistreatment and Exclusion Constructs

We now extend this discussion of workplace mistreatment constructs and social exclusion by introducing three other concepts we believe are relevant to both research areas: sexual objectification, structural exclusion, and social burden.

Sexual objectification. Sexual objectification is defined as to be treated as merely a body that exists for the use and pleasure of others (Bartky, 1990; Loughnan et al., 2010; Vaes, Paladino, & Puvia, 2011). Sexual objectification can be regarded as an umbrella term that encompasses a wide range of experiences differing in severity, from sexual assault to both explicit and subtle forms of sexual harassment (e.g., inappropriate comments, leering eye gaze; Fredrickson & Roberts, 1997; Gervais, Holland, & Dodd, 2013). In a nationally representative survey conducted in the USA, the majority of women (81%) and many men (43%) reported experiencing some type of sexual objectification, with the workplace being a common location for these incidents (38% women, 13% men; Stop Street Harassment, 2018). Sexual objectification is harmful to one's mental and physical health (Fredrickson & Roberts, 1997; Fredrickson, Roberts, Noll, Quinn, & Twenge, 1998; Hebl, King, & Lin, 2004; Quinn, Kallen, & Cathey, 2006; Martins, Tiggemann, & Kirkbride, 2007; Moradi & Huang, 2008; Swim, Hyers, Cohen, & Ferguson, 2001). Additionally, individuals who experience sexual objectification in the workplace also report with lower organizational commitment, withdrawal from work, decreased job satisfaction, and poor physical and mental health (Willness, Steel, & Lee, 2007).

While sexual objectification is characterized by demeaning *attention* to the individual's body and sexual functions, ostracism traditionally is characterized by *lack of* attention. Thus, sexual objectification and ostracism seem to be contradictory conceptually. However, recent experimental research (Dvir, 2018; Dvir, Kelly, Tyler, & Williams, 2020) demonstrates that sexually objectified women report feeling ostracized (i.e., excluded *and* ignored), as well as experiencing the typical basic need threat found in ostracism research (e.g., Williams, 2009). Using the framework of categorizing social exclusion experiences based on negative attention versus no attention, sexual objectification would be categorized as a *rejection*-type of exclusion. However, participants also reported feeling "ignored," suggesting objectification may also fit in the *ostracism*-type (or no attention type) of exclusion, at least based on their self-reported experiences. This paradox may be reconciled if one considers that objectified individuals may feel that their bodies are the focus of the attention, and thus their thoughts and feelings—key aspects of their identity as persons—are being ignored. Thus, future theorizing on the conceptual aspects of ostracism and other forms of social exclusion need to take the *subjective* experience of participants into account when theorizing how these constructs relate. Some research has already been conducted comparing the differential effects of sexual objectification and other forms of workplace mistreatment (Hershcovis & Barling, 2010). Researchers who are examining ostracism within the workplace should also consider assessing how much sexual objectification may be contributing to employees' feelings of ostracism, and ultimately any potential differential effects on the other negative outcomes being studied.

Structural exclusion. Most research on social exclusion (as well as workplace mistreatment broadly) focuses on interpersonal interactions. However, there may be ways in which environmental cues from the organization itself make individuals feel excluded. As previously described, sexual objectification can make individuals feel excluded. Many examples of sexual objectification are interpersonal, but there are ways in which objectification could occur because of environmental elements. For example, individual employees may post objectifying images in individual cubicles or shared spaces (e.g., an employee breakroom). These posted images could contribute to an overall hostile climate for individuals whose social groups are being objectified. This phenomenon also may be extended to images that involve disparaging humor to various social groups, given the data suggesting hurtful laughter and disparaging humor can cause individuals to feel excluded (Klages & Wirth, 2014; Wesselmann et al., 2018). In addition to the posting of objectifying or disparaging images, a lack of organizational commitment to combating discrimination or efforts to increase diversity and inclusion may also be experienced as exclusion by members of underrepresented groups (e.g., DeSouza, Wesselmann, & Ispas, 2017; Schneider, Wesselmann, & DeSouza, 2017). Research on employees' percpetions of their organizational climate toward various forms of mistreatment (i.e., aggression, bullying, and incivility) suggests that employees who perceive their organization as taking a stand against these behaviors have better psychological and job-related outcomes than employees who perceive less support from their organizations (Yang, Caughlin, Gazica, Truxillo, & Spector, 2014). It is likely that organizational norms opposing exclusion and instead valuing diversity and inclusion would have similar effects on employee outcomes.

There are other ways in which organizational policies may make individuals feel excluded. A recent body of research demonstrates that individuals can experience exclusion based on the language organizations use. For example, a series of laboratory studies found that women are more likely to feel excluded when they read job descriptions that use gendered language (i.e., "he" versus "one"; Stout, & Dasgupta, 2011). Another research program (Gryzbowski, Wesselmann, & Pryor, 2020) examined biased language in politics. Researchers first investigated the terminology used by county boards in two states (IL and WI) to describe their board chairs on their website (e.g., gendered language such as chairman or chairwoman versus neutral language like chairperson or chair). County boards that used gendered language (almost always chair*man*) had fewer women as board members than boards that used gender-neutral titles from the board chair. The researchers conducted a follow-up study by sending online surveys to board members in these two states and found that women board members reported feeling less influence in their board decision and more excluded when their board used gendered language to address the chair than when the language was gender-neutral.

There are likely other examples of environmental cues or polices that may make employees feel excluded because of gender. For example, women may feel excluded if their organization does not provide basic resources such as trash receptacles in restroom stalls or places for nursing mothers to pump breastmilk privately. Men may feel excluded if their organization has policies for maternity leave but not paternity leave. Even if both types of leave options exist, there may be ways that men may be subtly more discouraged from using this option than women. A further form of gender exclusion may occur when organizations do not provide equal numbers of restrooms for women and men, or gender-inclusive restrooms for individuals who identify with a non-binary gender category. These considerations may extend beyond employee impact for organizations that serve the public. Any gendered titles or pronouns used in displays or advertisements may make individuals who do not identify with those terms feel excluded, as if they do not belong in that environment.

A similar pattern may occur for organizations that do not provide gender-inclusive restrooms. Additionally, organizations that provide changing tables in women's restrooms but not men's restrooms may also risk alienating men who are taking care of children. Each of these environmental cues, if they indeed make patrons feel excluded as we suggest, will likely reduce the likelihood of those patrons giving future business to that organization. These are just some examples of potential structural forms of exclusion, and there are likely others that we have not considered. Future research on workplace exclusion should investigate exclusion at multiple levels within the organization, and researchers interested in workplace mistreatment climate should consider assessing organizational policies toward exclusion-related constructs as well.

Social burden. Some employees have a high risk of burnout or other psychological strains due to the nature of their jobs. For example, healthcare workers and mental health professionals often experience burn out because they spend much of their day providing emotional support to traumatized clients (sometimes called *compassion fatigue*; Bride, Radey, & Figley, 2007; Figley, 2002). Most professions do not require their employees to use their compassion resources constantly in such extreme scenarios. That said, coworkers can be an important source of social support when someone is in need. Some individuals may find themselves in occupational environments in which one coworker, or even several, regularly turns to them for social support. Thus the workplace becomes a source of *social burden* and has the potential to be draining psychologically, increasing the risk of burnout and other psychological strains (Yang, Liu, Nauta, Caughlin, & Spector, 2016). Socially burdensome interactions are unpleasant, but they differ from other types of workplace mistreatment (e.g., aggression and incivility) because they generally are not meant to be harmful to the person. Most coworkers who request social support from an employee are not trying to do harm. The occasional request is unlikely to exhaust one's resources for compassion. However, as the popular adage says, "No good deed goes unpunished." Once one establishes themselves as a conscientious, reliable source of social support, repeat requests are likely and may come from an increasing number of coworkers as one's reputation grows.

Whether the source of social burden is a group of coworkers or just one really psychologically needy coworker, it can lead to an emotionally taxing (burdensome) environment. In addition to burnout and psychological stress, social burden may also increase the likelihood of ostracism in the workplace. Research demonstrates that interacting with an obnoxious person can be a psychological drain (Sommer & Yoon, 2013), and these individuals are often targets for ostracism (Hales, Kassner, et al., 2016; see also Wirth & Wesselmann, 2018). Indeed, social burden could lead to a vicious cycle of ostracism, such that a person may ostracize those who are a drain on them, and if the social burden is widespread they may choose instead to seek solitude, thus isolating themselves from their coworkers as much as possible (Ren et al., 2016). Seeking solitude may be a useful stop-gap measure to the problem of social burden, but as a chronic response it will likely cause negative outcomes for both the employee, their coworkers, and the organization broadly.

Conclusion

Humans are social animals and spend most of their day interacting with others, whether it be with family, friends, or coworkers. Sometimes, these interactions can be aversive and involve a variety of types of negative treatment (e.g., interpersonal rejection, bullying, and ostracism) which makes the target feel socially excluded. Psychologists have been investigating these types of experiences as an attempt to understand their negative impacts on individuals. Within the workplace context, a study of social exclusion takes on additional importance because its negative effects can influence not just the individual employees targeted, but also the organization as a whole.

Researchers have begun spear-heading efforts to encorporate a study of social exclusion into the larger area of workplace mistreatment. Such efforts are key for establishing construct validity for each of the individual constructs often considered under this umbrella term (e.g., incivility, abusive supervision; Ferris et al., 2017; Hershcovis, 2011; Hershcovis & Reich, 2013). In this chapter, we have argued that this issue is important to social exclusion research generally, not just within the context of the workplace. The terms exclusion, rejection, and ostracism are often used inconsistently in both the basic and applied literature. For the research on social exclusion to move forward, and for how this research fits into workplace mistreatment broadly, these construct validity issues need to be addressed systematically.

The first step in establishing construct validity in the area of social exclusion research is to examine critically the conceptual definitions used for words such as *exclusion*, *rejection*, and *ostracism*. A "devil's advocate" may argue that debating the usage of these words is not useful ultimately, that maybe they simply amount to the same general psychological experience. Most paradigms using these different terms generally have the same negative outcomes on feelings of pain, mood, and basic need satisfaction (Wesselmann et al., 2016). Participants in rejection-based paradigms also report feeling ignored, even though technically they are not being ignored per se because they are receiving negative attention (e.g., Klages & Wirth, 2014). On the surface, these patterns may suggest the terms are redundant, but without empirical studies directly examining this question it remains speculation.

Perhaps any meaningful conceptual differences between these constructs simply amount to the degree of harm based on the extremity of the exclusion (assuming, of course, that exclusion is an umbrella term). If it is simply a matter of extremity, different theoretical models would at least make testable predictions about how the constructs may compare. For example, Williams (2007, 2009) argued that being ignored would be worse than being rejected (i.e., receiving negative attention) because at least negative attention symbolizes that the target is worth the attention. Mark Leary (1990), however, argued that passive forms of exclusion (e.g., being ignored) are less extreme than active forms of exclusion (e.g., explicitly avoiding people) or the most extreme forms exclusion (e.g., banishment). The types of negative attention we have described as rejection-focused exclusion would likely be considered *active* exclusion in Leary's model, thus being more extreme than being ignored.

Alternatively, understanding different forms of exclusion may be less about general extremity and rather about differential effects on specific outcomes derived from theoretical expectations. For example, some research has already demonstrated that a short-term exclusion manipulation (i.e., ostracism via Cyberball) can cause differential effects than a prospective measure of chronic exclusion (i.e., someone told they likely will spend the rest of their life alone) on measures of pain and basic need satisfaction (Bernstein & Claypool, 2012a, 2012b). Thus, these two exclusion paradigms cannot be considered analogous in terms of their psychological experience, at least in terms of certain outcomes.

It is likely that there are other differences between paradigms that need to be investigated. Williams (2001, 2009) argued that being ignored poses an existential threat, hence the general threat to one's sense of meaningful existence that one would not have—at least to the same degree—during interpersonal rejection (see also Hales, 2018). Perhaps someone who is told directly that no one wants to work with them (i.e., they are rejected) experiences the same threat to belonging as someone who is given the silent treatment (i.e., they are ignored), but the ignored individual experiences a stronger threat to meaningful existence than the rejected individual. These questions can be answered to some degree using extant data by accounting for paradigm usage in a meta-analysis framework (e.g., Blackhart et al., 2009), but the field also needs strong empirical tests using paradigms that can compare rejection-type exclusion against ostracism-type exclusion within the same paradigm (Rudert et al., 2017; Zadro et al., 2005) and broader tests of experimental paradigms against one another (e.g., Bernstein & Claypool, 2012a).

We recognize that these are broad questions with no clear answers. Further, we recognize that forging agreement on conceptual definitions can be a monumental task. There likely will be no consensus in the near future, especially without further empirical investigations such as the ones we have suggested. What do researchers do in the meantime? We certainly have struggled in our own research determining what terms and definitions we prefer, often striving to obtain an optimal balance between conceptual clarity and parsimony. Our current recommendation simply is to pick one's preferred term and define it clearly, and avoid switching back and forth between terms unless one has a specific theoretical reason to do so. As we noted earlier, we prefer using *social exclusion* as an umbrella term and then categorizing related phenomenon based on whether the person is experiencing direct negative attention or being ignored. This approach may work for some theoretical models and research questions, but not others. Each researcher will need to decide which approach best fits their purposes and then be clear about their decisions. Regardless, we hope that these questions inspire researchers to move research on social exclusion to the next theoretical level, integrating these potentially different phenomena in exciting ways that strengthen the field's understanding of how the constructs relate conceptually and empirically.

Acknowledgment We would like to thank Andrew Hales for his developmental feedback on this chapter.

References

Anderson, C. A., & Bushman, B. J. (2002). Human aggression. *Annual Review of Psychology, 53,* 27–51.

Andersson, L. M., & Pearson, C. M. (1999). Tit for tat? The spiraling effect of incivility in the workplace. *Academy of Management Review, 24,* 452–471.

Baumeister, R. F., & Leary, M. R. (1995). The need to belong: Desire for interpersonal attachments as a fundamental human motivation. *Psychological Bulletin, 117,* 497–529.

Baumeister, R. F., Wotman, S. R., & Stillwell, A. M. (1993). Unrequited love: On heartbreak, anger, guilt, scriptlessness, and humiliation. *Journal of Personality and Social Psychology, 64,* 377–394.

Bartky, S. L. (1990). *Femininity and domination: Studies in the phenomenology of oppression.* New York: Routledge.

Bastian, B., & Haslam, N. (2010). Excluded from humanity: The dehumanizing effects of social ostracism. *Journal of Experimental Social Psychology, 46,* 107–113.

Bernstein, M. J., & Claypool, H. M. (2012a). Not all social exclusions are created equal: Emotional distress following social exclusion is moderated by exclusion paradigm. *Social Influence, 7,* 113–130.

Bernstein, M. J., & Claypool, H. M. (2012b). Social exclusion and pain sensitivity: Why exclusion sometimes hurts and sometimes numbs. *Personality and Social Psychology Bulletin, 38,* 185–196.

Blackhart, G. C., Knowles, M. L., Nelson, B. C., & Baumeister, R. F. (2009). Rejection elicits emotional reactions but neither causes immediate distress nor lowers self-esteem: A meta-analytic review of 192 studies on social exclusion. *Personality and Social Psychology Review, 13,* 269–309.

Blau, G., & Andersson, L. (2005). Testing a measure of instigated workplace incivility. *Journal of Occupational and Organizational Psychology, 78,* 595–614.

Bowling, N. A., & Beehr, T. A. (2006). Workplace harassment from the victim's perspective: A theoretical model and meta-analysis. *Journal of Applied Psychology, 91,* 998–1012.

Bride, B. E., Radey, M., & Figley, C. R. (2007). Measuring compassion fatigue. *Clinical Social Work Journal, 35,* 155–163.

Cacioppo, J. T., & Patrick, W. (2008). *Loneliness.* New York: W. W. Norton.

Chen, Z., Williams, K. D., Fitness, J., & Newton, N. C. (2008). When hurt will not heal: Exploring the capacity to relive social and physical pain. *Psychological Science, 19,* 789–795.

Cortina, L. M., Magley, V. J., Williams, J. H., & Langhout, R. D. (2001). Incivility in the workplace: Incidence and impact. *Journal of Occupational Health Psychology, 6,* 64–80.

DeSouza, E. R., Wesselmann, E. D., & Ispas, D. (2017). Workplace discrimination against sexual minorities: Subtle and not-so-subtle. *Canadian Journal of Administrative Sciences, 34,* 121–132.

Duffy, M. K., Ganster, D. C., & Pagon, M. (2002). Social undermining in the workplace. *Academy of Management Journal, 45,* 331–351.

Dvir, M. (2018). *The relation between sexual objectification and ostracism.* Unpublished doctoral dissertation, Purdue University, West Lafayette, IN.

Dvir, M., Kelly, J. R., Tyler, J. M., & Williams, K. D. (2020). I'm up here! Sexual objectification leads to feeling ostracized. *Journal of Personality and Social Psychology.* Advance online publication. https://doi.org/10.1037/pspi0000328.

Edwards, J. R. (2003). Construct validation in organizational behavior research. In J. Greenberg (Ed.), *Organizational behavior: The state of the science* (2nd ed., pp. 327–371). Mahwah, NJ: Lawrence Erlbaum.

Einarsen, S. (2000). Harassment and bullying at work: A review of the Scandinavian approach. *Aggression and Violent Behavior, 5,* 379–401.

Eisenberger, N. I., Lieberman, M. D., & Williams, K. D. (2003). Does rejection hurt? An fMRI study of social exclusion. *Science, 302,* 290–292.

Eisenberger, R., Rhoades Shanock, L., & Wen, X. (2020). Perceived organizational support: Why caring about employees counts. *Annual Review of Organizational Psychology & Organizational Behavior, 7,* 101–124. https://doi.org/10.1146/annurev-orgpsych-012119-044917.

Ellemers, N., & Haslam, S. A. (2012). Social identity theory. In P. A. M. Van Lange, A. W. Kruglanski, & E. T. Higgins (Eds.), *Handbook of theories of social psychology* (pp. 379–399). London, UK: Sage.

Ferris, D., Brown, D. J., Berry, J. W., & Lian, H. (2008). The development and validation of the Workplace Ostracism Scale. *Journal of Applied Psychology, 93,* 1348–1366.

Ferris, D. L., Chen, M., & Lim, S. (2017). Comparing and contrasting workplace ostracism and incivility. *Annual Review of Organizational Psychology & Organizational Behavior, 4,* 315–338.

Figley, C. R. (2002). Compassion fatigue: Psychotherapists' chronic lack of self care. *Journal of Clinical Psychology, 58,* 1433–1441.

Fredrickson, B. L., Roberts, T. A., Noll, S. M., Quinn, D. M., & Twenge, J. M. (1998). That swimsuit becomes you: sex differences in self-objectification, restrained eating, and math performance. *Journal of Personality and Social Psychology, 75,* 269–284.

Fredrickson, B. L., & Roberts, T. (1997). Objectification theory: Toward understanding women's lived experiences and mental health risks. *Psychology of Women Quarterly, 21,* 173–206.

Gervais, S. J., Holland, A. M., & Dodd, M. D. (2013). My eyes are up here: The nature of the objectifying gaze toward women. *Sex Roles, 69,* 557–570.

Gilman, R., Carter-Sowell, A., DeWall, C. N., Adams, R. E., & Carboni, I. (2013). Validation of the ostracism experience scale for adolescents. *Psychological Assessment, 25*, 319–330.

Gottman, J. M. (1999). *The marriage clinic: A scientifically-based marital therapy*. New York, NY: W. W. Norton.

Gryzbowski, M. R., Wesselmann, E. D., & Pryor, J. B. (2020). *Gender-exclusive language: Women's perception of linguistic ostracism, voice, and power in politics*. Manuscript Submitted for Publication.

Hales, A. (2018). Death as a metaphor for ostracism: Social invincibility, autopsy, necromancy, and resurrection. *Mortality, 23*, 366–380.

Hales, A. H., Kassner, M. P., Williams, K. D., & Graziano, W. G. (2016). Disagreeableness as a cause and consequence of ostracism. *Personality & Social Psychology Bulletin, 42*, 782–797.

Hales, A. H., Wesselmann, E. D., & Williams, K. D. (2016). Prayer, self-affirmation, and distraction improve recovery from short-term ostracism. *Journal of Experimental Social Psychology, 64*, 8–20.

Hebl, M. R., King, E. B., & Lin, J. (2004). The swimsuit becomes us all: Ethnicity, gender, and vulnerability to self-objectification. *Personality and Social Psychology Bulletin, 30*, 1322–1331.

Hershcovis, M. S. (2011). "Incivility, social undermining, bullying… oh my!": A call to reconcile constructs within workplace aggression research. *Journal of Organizational Behavior, 32*, 499–519.

Hershcovis, M. S., & Barling, J. (2010). Comparing victim attributions and outcomes for workplace aggression and sexual harassment. *Journal of Applied Psychology, 95*, 874–888.

Hershcovis, M. S., & Reich, T. C. (2013). Integrating workplace aggression research: Relational, contextual, and method considerations. *Journal of Organizational Behavior, 34*(S1), S26–S42. https://doi.org/10.1002/job.1886.

Hoel, H., Cooper, C. L., & Faragher, B. (2001). The experience of bullying in Great Britain: The impact of organizational status. *European Journal of Work and Organizational Psychology, 10*, 443–465.

James, W. (1890/1950). *Principles of psychology* (Vol. 1). New York: Dover.

Jehn, K. A. (1995). A multimethod examination of the benefits and detriments of intragroup conflict. *Administrative Science Quarterly, 40*, 256–282.

Jehn, K. A., Lindred, G., Levine, S., & Szulanski, G. (2008). The effects of conflict types, dimensions, and emergent states on group outcomes. *Group Decision and Negotiation, 17*, 465–495.

Jones, E. E., Carter-Sowell, A. R., Kelly, J. R., & Williams, K. D. (2009). 'I'm out of the loop': Ostracism through information exclusion. *Group Processes & Intergroup Relations, 12*, 157–174.

Jones, E. E., & Kelly, J. R. (2010). "Why am I out of the loop?" Attributions influence responses to information exclusion. *Personality and Social Psychology Bulletin, 36,* 1186–1201.

Klages, S. V., & Wirth, J. H. (2014). Excluded by laughter: Laughing until it hurts someone else. *The Journal of Social Psychology, 154,* 8–13.

Kross, E., Berman, M. G., Mischel, W., Smith, E. E., & Wager, T. D. (2011). Social rejection shares somatosensory representations with physical pain. *Proceedings of the National Academy of Sciences, 108,* 6270–6275.

Kurzban, R., & Leary, M. R. (2001). Evolutionary origins of stigmatization: The functions of social exclusion. *Psychological Bulletin, 127,* 187–208.

Leary, M. R. (1990). Responses to social exclusion: Social anxiety, jealousy, loneliness, depression, and low self-esteem. *Journal of Social and Clinical Psychology, 9,* 221–229.

Leary, M. R., & Baumeister, R. F. (2000). The nature and function of self-esteem: Sociometer theory. In M. P. Zanna (Ed.), *Advances in experimental social psychology* (Vol. 32, pp. 1–62). San Diego, CA: Academic Press.

Leary, M. R., Springer, C., Negel, L., Ansell, E., & Evans, K. (1998). The causes, phenomenology, and consequences of hurt feelings. *Journal of Personality and Social Psychology, 74,* 1225–1237.

Lieberman, M. D. (2013). *Social: Why our brains are wired to connect.* New York, NY: Crown Publishers.

Lilienfeld, S. O. (2017). Microaggressions: Strong claims, inadequate evidence. *Perspectives on Psychological Science, 12,* 138–169.

Liu, C. (2019). Ostracism, attributions, and their relationships with international students' and employees' outcomes: The moderating effect of perceived harming intent. *Journal of Occupational Health Psychology, 24,* 556–571.

Loughnan, S., Haslam, N., Murnane, T., Vaes, J., Reynolds, C., & Suitner, C. (2010). Objectification leads to depersonalization: The denial of mind and moral concern to objectified others. *European Journal of Social Psychology, 40,* 709–717.

Martins, Y., Tiggemann, M., & Kirkbride, A. (2007). Those speedos become them: The role of self-objectification in gay and heterosexual men's body image. *Personality and Social Psychology Bulletin, 33,* 634–647.

Matthews, R. A., & Ritter, K. J. (2016). A concise, content valid, gender invariant measure of workplace incivility. *Journal of Occupational Health Psychology, 21,* 352–365.

Matthiesen, S. B., & Einarsen, S. (2001). MMPI-2 configurations among victims of bullying at work. *European Journal of Work and Organizational Psychology, 10*, 467–484.

Mikkelsen, E. G., & Einarsen, S. (2001). Bullying in Danish work-life: Prevalence and health correlates. *European Journal of Work and Organizational Psychology, 10*, 393–413.

Molden, D. C., Lucas, G. M., Gardner, W. L., Dean, K., & Knowles, M. L. (2009). Motivations for prevention or promotion following social exclusion: Being rejected versus being ignored. *Journal of Personality and Social Psychology, 96*, 415–431.

Moradi, B., & Huang, Y. (2008). Objectification theory and psychology of women: A decade of advances and future directions. *Psychology of Women Quarterly, 32*, 377–398.

Nezlek, J. B., Wesselmann, E. D., Wheeler, L., & Williams, K. D. (2012). Ostracism in everyday life. *Group Dynamics: Theory, Research, & Practice, 16*, 91–104.

Ong, A. D., & Burrow, A. L. (2017). Microaggressions and daily experience: Depicting life as it is lived. *Perspectives on Psychological Science, 12*, 173–175.

O'Reilly, J., Robinson, S. L., Berdahl, J. L., & Banki, S. (2015). Is negative attention better than no attention? The comparative effects of ostracism and harassment work. *Organizational Science, 26*, 774–793.

Quinn, D. M., Kallen, R. W., & Cathey, C. (2006). Body on my mind: The lingering effect of state self-objectification. *Sex Roles, 55*, 869–874.

Ren, D., Wesselmann, E., & Williams, K. D. (2016). Evidence for another response to ostracism: Solitude seeking. *Social Psychological and Personality Science, 7*, 204–212.

Riva, P., & Eck, J. (2016). The many faces of social exclusion. In P. Riva & J. Eck (Eds.), *Social exclusion: Psychological approaches to understanding and reducing its impact* (pp. ix–xv). Switzerland: Springer International Publishing.

Riva, P., Montali, L., Wirth, J. H., Curioni, S., & Williams, K. D. (2017). Chronic social exclusion and evidence for the resignation stage: An empirical investigation. *Journal of Social and Personal Relationships, 34*, 541–564.

Robinson, S. L., O'Reilly, J., & Wang, W. (2013). Invisible at work: An integrated model of workplace ostracism. *Journal of Management, 39*, 203–231.

Rudert, S. C., Hales, A. H., Greifeneder, R., & Williams, K. D. (2017). When silence is not golden: Why acknowledgment matters even when being excluded. *Personality and Social Psychology Bulletin, 43*, 678–692.

Sargis, E. G., & Larson, J. R. (2002). Informational centrality and member participation during group decision making. *Group Processes & Intergroup Relations, 5*, 333–347.

Schneider, K. T., Wesselmann, E. D., & DeSouza, E. R. (2017). Confronting subtle workplace mistreatment: The importance of leaders as allies. *Frontiers in Psychology, 8*, 1051. https://doi.org/10.3389/fpsyg.2017.01051.

Schwab, D. P. (1980). Construct validity in organizational behavior. In L. L. Cummings & B. M. Staw (Eds.), *Research in organizational behavior* (Vol. 2, pp. 3–43). Greenwich, CT: JAI Press.

Smart Richman, L., & Leary, M. R. (2009). Reactions to discrimination, stigmatization, ostracism, and other forms of interpersonal rejection: A multimotive model. *Psychological Review, 116*, 365–383.

Sommer, K. L., & Yoon, J. (2013). When silence is golden: Ostracism as resource conservation during aversive interactions. *Journal of Social and Personal Relationships, 30*, 901–919.

Spector, P. E., Fox, S., Penney, L. M., Bruursema, K., Goh, A., & Kessler, S. (2006). The dimensionality of counterproductivity: Are all counterproductive behaviors created equal? *Journal of Vocational Behavior, 68*, 446–460.

Spector, P. E., & Jex, S. M. (1998). Development of four self-report measures of job stressors and strain: Interpersonal conflict at work scale, organizational constraints scale, quantitative workload inventory, and physical symptoms inventory. *Journal of Occupational Health Psychology, 3*, 356–367.

Stout, J. G., & Dasgupta, N. (2011). When he doesn't mean you: Gender-exclusive language as ostracism. *Personality and Social Psychology Bulletin, 37*, 757–769.

Sue, D. W. (2017). Microaggressions and "Evidence": Empirical or experiential reality? *Perspectives on Psychological Science, 12*, 170–172.

Swim, J. K., Hyers, L. L., Cohen, L. L., & Ferguson, M. J. (2001). Everyday sexism: Evidence for its incidence, nature, and psychological impact from three daily diary studies. *Journal of Social Issues, 57*(1), 31–53.

Tepper, B. J. (2000). Consequences of abusive supervision. *Academy of Management Journal, 43*, 178–190.

Tepper, B. J. (2007). Abusive supervision in work organizations: Review, synthesis, and research agenda. *Journal of management, 33*, 261–289.

Twenge, J. M., Baumeister, R. F., Tice, D. M., & Stucke, T. S. (2001). If you can't join them, beat them: effects of social exclusion on aggressive behavior. *Journal of Personality and Social Psychology, 81*, 1058–1069.

Vaes, J., Paladino, P., & Puvia, E. (2011). Are sexualized women complete human beings? Why men and women dehumanize sexually objectified women. *European Journal of Social Psychology, 41*, 774–785.

Van Orden, K. A., Witte, T. K., Gordon, K. H., Bender, T. W., & Joiner, T. E. (2008). Suicidal desire and the capability for suicide: Tests of the interpersonal-psychological theory of suicidal behavior among adults. *Journal of Consulting and Clinical Psychology, 76*, 72–83.

Wesselmann, E. D., Butler, F. A., Williams, K. D., & Pickett, C. L. (2010). Adding injury to insult: Unexpected rejection leads to more aggressive responses. *Aggressive Behavior, 36*, 232–237.

Wesselmann, E. D., Grzybowski, M. R., Steakley-Freeman, D. M., DeSouza, E. R., Nezlek, J. B., & Williams, K. D. (2016). Social exclusion in everyday life. In P. Riva & J. Eck (Eds.), *Social exclusion: Psychological approaches to understanding and reducing its impact* (pp. 3–23). Switzerland: Springer International Publishing.

Wesselmann, E. D., Ren, D., Swim, E., & Williams, K. D. (2013). Rumination hinders recovery from ostracism. *International Journal of Developmental Science, 7,* 33–39.

Wesselmann, E. D., Schneider, K. T., Ford, T. E., & DeSouza, E. R. (2018, April). *Disparaging humor as a form of social exclusion.* Presentation at the Annual Conference of the Society for Industrial and Organizational Psychology, Chicago, IL.

Wesselmann, E. D., & Williams, K. D. (2017). Social life and social death: Inclusion, ostracism, and rejection in groups. *Group Processes & Intergroup Relations, 20,* 693–706.

Wesselmann, E. D., Wirth, J. H., Mroczek, D. K., & Williams, K. D. (2012). Dial a feeling: Detecting moderation of affect decline during ostracism. *Personality and Individual Differences, 53,* 580–586.

Williams, K. D. (2001). *Ostracism: The power of silence.* New York: Guilford.

Williams, K. D. (2007). Ostracism. *Annual Review of Psychology, 58,* 425–452.

Williams, K. D. (2009). Ostracism: Effects of being excluded and ignored. In M. P. Zanna (Ed.), *Advances in experimental social psychology* (Vol. 41, pp. 275–314). New York: Academic Press.

Williams, K. D., Cheung, C. K. T., & Choi, W. (2000). Cyberostracism: Effects of being ignored over the Internet. *Journal of Personality and Social Psychology, 79,* 748–762.

Willness, C. R., Steel, P., & Lee, K. (2007). A meta-analysis of the antecedents and consequences of workplace sexual harassment. *Personnel Psychology, 60,* 127–162.

Wirth, J. H., Bernstein, M. J., Wesselmann, E. D., & LeRoy, A. (2017). Social cues establish expectations of rejection and affect the response to being rejected. *Group Processes & Intergroup Relations, 20,* 32–51.

Wirth, J. H., Sacco, D. F., Hugenberg, K., & Williams, K. D. (2010). Eye gaze as relational evaluation: Averted eye gaze leads to feelings of ostracism and relational devaluation. *Personality and Social Psychology Bulletin, 36,* 869–882.

Wirth, J. H., & Wesselmann, E. D. (2018). Investigating how ostracizing others affects one's self-concept. *Self and Identity, 17,* 394–406.

Wittenbaum, G. M., Hubbell, A. P., & Zuckerman, C. (1999). Mutual enhancement: Toward an understanding of the collective preference for shared information. *Journal of Personality and Social Psychology, 77,* 967–978.

Yang, L. Q., Caughlin, D. E., Gazica, M. W., Truxillo, D. M., & Spector, P. E. (2014). Workplace mistreatment climate and potential employee and organizational outcomes: A meta-analytic review from the target's perspective. *Journal of Occupational Health Psychology, 19,* 315–335.

Yang, L. Q., Liu, C., Nauta, M. M., Caughlin, D. E., & Spector, P. E. (2016). Be mindful of what you impose on your colleagues: Implications of social burden for burdenees' well-being, attitudes and counterproductive work behaviour. *Stress & Health, 32,* 70–83.

Zadro, L., Arriaga, X. B., & Williams, K. D. (2008). Relational ostracism. In J. P. Forgas & J. Fitness (Eds.), *Social relationships: Cognitive, affective, and motivational processes* (pp. 305–320). New York, NY: Psychology Press.

Zadro, L., Boland, C., & Richardson, R. (2006). How long does it last? The persistence of the effects of ostracism in the socially anxious. *Journal of Experimental Social Psychology, 42,* 692–697.

Zadro, L., & Gonsalkorale, K. (2014). Sources of ostracism: The nature and consequences of excluding and ignoring others. *Current Directions in Psychological Science, 23,* 93–97.

Zadro, L., & Williams, K. D. (2006). How do you teach the power of ostracism? Evaluating the train ride demonstration. *Social Influence, 1,* 81–104.

Zadro, L., Williams, K. D., & Richardson, R. (2005). Riding the "O" Train: Comparing the effects of ostracism and verbal dispute on targets and sources. *Group Processes & Intergroup Relations, 8,* 125–143.

Zellars, K. L., Tepper, B. J., & Duffy, M. K. (2002). Abusive supervision and subordinates' organizational citizenship behavior. *Journal of Applied Psychology, 87,* 1068–1076.

CHAPTER 3

Antecedents of Workplace Ostracism

Cong Liu, Jun Yang, and Xixi Gu

Workplace ostracism happens when organization members fail to include other people at work when it is socially appropriate to include (Robinson, O'Reilly, & Wang, 2013). As a type of workplace aggression (Hershcovis, 2011), workplace ostracism differs from other workplace mistreatments in three major ways. First, workplace ostracism reflects an act of omission rather than an act of commission (Robinson et al., 2013). Rather than engaging in aggressive behaviors, actors of workplace ostracism simply withdraw their social interaction behaviors with the victims. Second, workplace ostracism could be purposeful or non-purposeful (Robinson et al., 2013). An example of purposeful ostracism is the silent treatment, a refusal to communicate verbally with someone who desires to communicate (Williams, Shore, & Grahe, 1998). An example of non-purposeful ostracism is when someone is preoccupied and fails to greet another

C. Liu (✉) · X. Gu
Hofstra University, Hempstead, NY, USA
e-mail: Cong.Liu@Hofstra.edu

J. Yang
University of North Carolina at Greensboro, Greensboro, NC, USA

C. Liu and J. Ma (eds.), *Workplace Ostracism*,
Palgrave Explorations in Workplace Stigma,
https://doi.org/10.1007/978-3-030-54379-2_3

coworker in the hallway. Third, workplace ostracism renders social inappropriateness (Robinson et al., 2013). When the inclusion is deemed as appropriate by the social norm, an exclusion or ignorance would be perceived by the victim as ostracism.

Researchers have predominantly examined the outcomes of workplace ostracism (Howard, Cogswell, & Smith, 2020). A smaller stream focuses on the antecedents of workplace ostracism. Collectively, these research studies have followed a triadic social process examining the actor (Hales, Wesselmann, & Williams, 2016; Nezlek, Wesselmann, Wheeler, & Williams, 2015), the victim (Ng, 2017; Quade, Greenbaum, & Petrenko, 2017), and the work context (Ng, 2017; Zhao, Xia, He, Sheard, & Wan, 2016).

Following the suggestions by Howard et al. (2020), this chapter will examine the holistic dynamics of workplace ostracism by reviewing the antecedent studies from the actor, the victim, and the work context's perspectives. First, we examine individual characteristics that predict the experience of workplace ostracism. This includes the victim's big-five personality traits, positive and negative affects, dark personality traits, approach and avoidance tendencies, warmth and competence, and social abilities and skills. Second, we examine relational factors that predict workplace ostracism. From the victim's perspective, we examine workplace mistreatments such as incivility and interpersonal conflicts as possible antecedents of workplace ostracism. From the actor's perspective, we conclude that others' bad interpersonal and work behaviors elicit workplace ostracism. Third, we examine contextual factors that could incubate workplace ostracism, such as corporative vs. competitive goal interdependence, social interactions based on interdependence theory and game-theoretic models, non-traditional work environments, and language barriers.

Individual Characteristics as Antecedents of Workplace Ostracism

Specific individual characteristics may elicit workplace ostracism, while other stable dispositions may protect one from suffering workplace ostracism. The victim precipitation theory (Curtis, 1974) argues that perpetrators do not randomly attack an individual. There is something in the victim that has elicited the mistreatment (Wu, Wei, & Hui, 2011; Zhang & Dai, 2015). At a minimum, victims may unknowingly become the target of ostracism based on their individual characteristics (e.g., negative affectivity, Aquino, Grover, Bradfield, & Allen, 1999). At a maximum, victims may engage in some emotions or behaviors that provoke ostracism (e.g., aggressiveness, Aquino & Bradfield, 2000). These two types of victims are termed as submissive and provocative victims, respectively (Olweus, 1978).

In their target-centric victimization framework, Aquino and Lamertz (2004) described *submissive victims* as passive, insecure, anxious, and quiet individuals who tend to situate themselves in lower social positions. When being mistreated, they are more likely to blame themselves and less likely to retaliate the actor (Katz, Moore, & Tkachuk, 2007; Tepper, Duffy, Henle, & Lambert, 2006). As such, actors are less likely to refrain themselves from ostracizing submissive victims. In contrast, *provocative victims* are highly aggressive, abusive, and hostile individuals (Aquino & Lamertz, 2004). They provoke hostile treatment from others. Since people behave in groups according to specific social norms and social appropriateness, provocative victims are viewed as violators of social norms. Other members may use retaliatory ostracism as a type of punishment to regulate the violators' undesirable behaviors (Hitlan & Noel, 2009; Renn, Allen, & Huning, 2013; Robinson et al., 2013).

Big-five personality traits. Personality traits reflect a unique way an individual interacts with others (Costa & McCrae, 1992). The most popular model is the big-five personality model: Neuroticism, agreeableness, extraversion, conscientiousness, and openness to experience (Costa & McCrae, 1992).

Neuroticism. Neuroticism refers to people's tendency to experience negative emotions such as anxiety, sadness, and anger (Costa & McCrae, 1992). Individuals high in neuroticism have a tendency to be self-conscious, impulsive, and pessimistic about things happening around them. Based on the victim precipitation theory (Curtis, 1974), high-neurotic employees are susceptible to be either provocative or submissive victims of workplace ostracism (Wu et al., 2011). On the one hand, they may provoke ostracism treatment due to their high impulsiveness and aggressive tendency (Wu et al., 2011). High-neurotic individuals are more suspicious about other's social motives; it is hard for them to trust other people. This distrust may also provoke ostracism because others may feel de-valued (Zhang & Dai, 2015).

On the other hand, the anxious and pessimistic nature will make high-neurotic employees less likely to defend themselves against mistreatment from others, and thus to be submissive victims. High-neurotic individuals tend to interpret normal social interaction as threatening (Langelaan, Bakker, Van Doornen, & Schaufeli, 2006). Research has found that neuroticism was positively related to the sensitivity of social rejection, making high-neurotic employees more easily to perceive workplace ostracism (Brookings, Zembar, & Hochstetler, 2003; Mor & Inbar, 2009). Taken together, research has consistently found that neuroticism is positively related to workplace ostracism (Hitlan & Noel, 2009; Howard et al., 2020; Leung, Wu, Chen, & Young, 2011; Wu et al., 2011; Zhang & Dai, 2015).

Agreeableness. Agreeableness describes the extent to which individuals are people-oriented, friendly, easy-going, and trusting (Costa & McCrae, 1992). High-agreeable individuals have a genuine concern for other people's welfare and are interested in maintaining harmonious interpersonal relationships. At the workplace and team settings, these employees are more cooperative and less defensive about their individual agenda. Therefore, high-agreeable employees are easy to make friends and less likely to be ostracized by other people at work.

In contrast, low-agreeable individuals tend to be stubborn, selfish, and aggressive. They are less empathetic, helpful, and trustworthy (Hales, Kassner, Williams, & Graziano, 2016). When experiencing a negative stimulus, they tend to be antagonistic and argumentative. Low-agreeable individuals are described as provocative victims of workplace ostracism (Wu et al., 2011). Research has shown that agreeableness is negatively related to ostracism (Hales, Kassner, et al., 2016; Howard et al., 2020; Wu et al., 2011). Hales, Kassner, et al. (2016) revealed that the negative relationship between agreeableness and ostracism was mediated by the interpersonal trust toward the target.

Extraversion. Extraversion describes an individual who is social-oriented, outgoing, and energetic (Costa & McCrae, 1992). Individuals high in extraversion seek excitement and external stimuli. These qualities help them get more social attention, be popular, and be more approachable in social settings.

Individuals low in extraversion are described as more reserved, quiet, and passive in social interactions. According to the victim precipitation theory (Curtis, 1974), they could be submissive victims of workplace ostracism because they are perceived as being less able to defend themselves against victimization (Wu et al., 2011). Other people may feel it is less costly to ostracize an introvert individual. In addition, since introvert individuals may withdraw social effort to interact with others, others may form prejudice or misunderstanding about them (Ashton, Lee, & Paunonen, 2002) and consequently avoid them. The research found that high extraversion is negatively related to workplace ostracism (Howard et al., 2020; Wu et al., 2011).

Conscientiousness. Conscientiousness refers to the extent to which an individual is achievement-oriented, self-disciplined, and organized (Costa & McCrae, 1992). High-conscientious employees are featured in two main dimensions: High achievement striving and duty (Moon, 2001). High achievement striving reflects a commitment to accomplishment and personal growth, which motivates proactive behaviors. Duty reflects a commitment to fulfilling one's work responsibilities and maintaining excellent performance which motivates inhibitive tendencies (Moon, 2001). Both qualities help high-conscientious employees to be star performers while not threatening other people's sense of self (Barrick & Mount, 1991).

People evaluate the cost and benefit of their behaviors (Leung et al., 2011; Zimmerman, Carter-Sowell, & Xu, 2016). Since conscientiousness is a highly valued feature, others are less likely to ostracize highly conscientious individuals because doing so will risk their cost-to-benefit ratio. A meta-analysis study found that conscientiousness was negatively related to workplace ostracism (Howard et al., 2020).

Positive affect and negative affect. *Positive affect* (PA) reflects feeling enthusiastic, active, and engaged (Watson & Clark, 1984). The big-five personality trait of extroversion predicts PA (Costa & McCrae, 1995). Since people are drawn to those who are in a positive mood and shed positive light, high PA employees are less likely to be ostracized. In contrast, *negative affect* (NA) co-varies with a host of negative emotions, such as anger, anxiety, and guilt, which are typical emotions experienced by ostracism victims. Aquino and Thau (2009) pointed out that NA is the most consistent predictor of workplace victimization, such as ostracism. High-NA employees are perceived as aggressive and hostile. Based on the victim precipitation theory (Curtis, 1974), they are subjective to be provocative victims. High-NA individuals may also perceive more ostracism from others. Based on the social information processing theory (Salancik & Pfeffer, 1978), employees high in NA may selectively recall more negative information, thus make hostile attributions to ambiguous situations such as workplace ostracism. Finally, people also tend to avoid those who radiate negative emotions, because emotions are contagious. High-NA employees may be socially difficult and thus be ostracized.

Previous research has found that PA is negatively whereas NA is positively related to workplace ostracism (Zhang & Shi, 2017). It worth mentioning that both PA and NA have also been studied as the consequences of ostracism (Hales, Kassner, et al., 2016). Using Cyball experimental manipulation, Hales, Kassner, et al. (2016) found that the ostracized group reported less PA and more NA than the control group.

Dark personality traits. The dark triad traits (psychopathy, narcissism, and Machiavellianism) share many antisocial features. Both psychopathy and narcissism have been studied in the ostracism literature (Greene, Sommerville, Nystrom, Darley, & Cohen, 2001). As far as we know, Machiavellianism has not been studied in the field of workplace ostracism. We focus on a related dark personality trait—paranoia (Spain, Herms, & LeBreton, 2014). A specific paranoid personality trait is one's tendency or *motivation to acquire relationship-threatening information* (MARTI) (Marr, Thau, Aquino, & Barclay, 2012).

Psychopathy and affective empathy. Psychopathy or subclinical psychopathy is characterized as being aloof, cold, and unresponsive to distressed cues, which is caused by under-aroused amygdala (Blair, 1995). The core feature of psychopathy is the lack of affective empathy, which refers to the emotional ability to feel the emotions of another person, such as a feeling of sympathy for unfortunate others (Davis, 1983). People with psychopathy are less able to perceive other people's pain or distress, and consequently, they are less restrained in harm-elicit ostracism. They see others as undeserving so that they use their manipulation (e.g., ostracism) to maximize the gain. Research has found that psychopathy is positively related to ostracism in social dilemmas, such as in situations where protecting group interests also means harming a group member via ostracism (Takamatsu, 2019).

Two constructs related to psychopathy are social dominance orientation and dehumanization beliefs. Individuals who are high in *social dominance orientation* support group-based dominance and inequality (Pratto, Sidanius, Stallworth, & Malle, 1994). They believe that those in superior groups should be more advantaged, have higher status, and possess more resources. Individuals with high social dominance orientation tend to dismiss the well-being of those in inferior groups. Takamatsu

(2019) found that social dominance orientation was positively related to ostracism in social dilemma scenarios. With *dehumanization beliefs*, people think that others have less or no human qualities (Haslam, 2006). Paired with disgust, dehumanization is on the other end of empathy. Takamatsu (2019) found that dehumanization beliefs were positively related to ostracism in social dilemmas.

A common feature across psychopathy, social dominance orientation, and dehumanization beliefs is that they feature a lack of affective empathy. High affective empathy makes one be sensitive to interpersonal harm. Takamatsu (2019) found that affective empathy was negatively related to ostracism in social dilemmas.

Narcissism. Narcissism describes those who have a grandiose evaluation of their self-importance (Judge, LePine, & Rich, 2006). On the one hand, narcissists are self-entitled, arrogant, and dominating. They tend to disrespect, distain, and diminish others (Emmons, 1987; Judge et al., 2006). High narcissism is described as socially aversive and relationally destructive (Colvin, Block, & Funder, 1995). On the other hand, high narcissism is also described as self-assured, energetic, not confirming to obsolete social rules, and visionary (Back, Schmukle, & Egloff, 2010; Paulhus & Williams, 2002). Research has shown a lot of successful leaders scored high on narcissism; narcissists possess some qualities that make them stand out of ordinary people and draw people to their influence (Morf & Rhodewalt, 2001).

Due to the paradoxical nature of narcissism, its relation to workplace ostracism is less clear. Power dependence theory predicts that people are dependent on powerful others (Emerson, 1962). Narcissists may have high dependence power when they are viewed with high expertise status (Van der Vegt, Bunderson, & Oosterhof, 2006). This power dependence is further strengthened with high group goal interdependence (Johnson & Johnson, 1989). When both expertise status and group goal interdependence are high, group members may treat the narcissists as valuable resources. Group members may share the glory shed by the narcissists. They may rationalize and romanticize narcissists' controlling behaviors and high self-regard, and find them to be attractive and charming.

In contrast, when a narcissist is viewed with low expertise status and the group goal interdependence is low, the narcissist would not bring any value to the group and the group members would not benefit from the narcissist's expertise. Under these circumstances, the negative features (e.g., high entitlement, feeling of superiority, arrogance, etc.) related to high narcissism would be salient. Others would tend to ostracize the narcissist.

Based on two studies using the round-robin method, Xu (2012) found that narcissism, expertise status, and group goal interdependence had a joint effect on workplace ostracism enacted by each team member toward the target employee. Specifically, target employee's narcissism was positively related to workplace ostracism when expertise status and group goal interdependence were low. Target employee's narcissism was negatively related to workplace ostracism when expertise status and group interdependence were high.

Paranoid personality traits. Due to the ambiguous nature of workplace ostracism (Robinson et al., 2013), sometimes the victim does not know clearly if other people's social intentions are malevolent or benevolent. According to the motivated social cognition perspective (Kunda, 1990), people select and process social information that is consistent with their motivational goals. Motivation to acquire relationship-threatening information (MARTI) is a goal-driven motivation to find harmful social cues that others have communicated negative information about oneself behind one's back (Marr et al., 2012). Individuals high in MARTI will cognitively select and process social cues that bias toward this goal and commit to paranoid thought patterns, such as sinister attribution error and the self-as-target bias. These motivational goals also channel one's goal-consistent behaviors. Marr et al. (2012) found that MARTI was positive related sinister attribution error, self-as-target bias, and suspicion behaviors such as spying on coworkers' conversations.

Taken together, MARTI presents motivational goals that promote paranoid thought patterns and suspicious behaviors; both signal to other organizational members that they are not trusted. According to the victim precipitation theory (Curtis, 1974), individuals who are high in MARTI are provocative victims of workplace ostracism. Marr et al. (2012) found that people are more likely to exclude individuals in the high MARTI groups than those in the control groups, and group member's anger mediated the relationships.

Approach and avoidance tendencies. The approach-avoidance social motive model (Elliot, 2006; Gable, 2006) predicts that driven by the hope to affiliate, people approach others to establish and maintain positive relationships. Driven by the fear of rejection, people avoid a social relationship that does not seem to go well. Proactive personality and the interpersonal value of harmony enhancement reflect approach social motives. Conflict avoidance and the interpersonal value of disintegration avoidance reflect avoidance motives.

Harmony enhancement and proactive personality. Interpersonal harmony value is the extent to which people value peaceful and concordant interpersonal relationships (Liu, Nauta, Yang, & Spector, 2018). Leung and Brew's (2009) dual model of interpersonal harmony defines two types of social motives in maintaining harmonious interpersonal relationships. *Harmony enhancement* is an approach-oriented social motive. Individuals high in harmony enhancement genuinely care about high-quality interpersonal relationships. They treat others as positively resourceful. When there is any sign of interpersonal infraction, they take an effort to initiate interaction behaviors. Harmony enhancement fosters an open-air forum. Gabhardt (2011) argued that in environments where harmony enhancement is valued by most employees, workplace ostracism is less likely to exist or thrive. Research has found that harmony enhancement is negatively related to workplace ostracism (Gabhardt, 2011; Liu, Li, Bruk-Lee, & Ma, 2019).

Individuals high in harmony enhancement are proactive in social interactions. A related construct is *proactive personality* that describes a personality trait that takes initiatives in social interactions. With proactive personality, people are relatively unconstrained by the situations; they tend to identify those need to be changed in the work context (including relationship problems); they have impulses to change them; and they are more able to affect the environment (Bateman & Crant, 1993; Crant, 2000). On the other hand, individuals low in proactive personality are more likely to endure the interpersonal issues. Zhao, Peng, and Sheard (2013) found that proactive personality was negatively related to workplace ostracism.

Disintegration avoidance and conflict avoidance. *Disintegration avoidance* refers to an avoidance-oriented social motive that guides avoidant behaviors when social relations do not go well. Individuals high in disintegration avoidance care about social relationships, but they are more sensitive to a strained relationship and the associated negative consequences. They tend to avoid a strained relationship because they do not want to disturb it further and hope it will heal on its own. By avoiding, a person who experiences interpersonal infractions will not openly discuss the problem and these interpersonal issues may continue in a cycle. In addition, they may adopt an obliging style in conflict management (Leung et al., 2011). However, they may obey in surface or publicly but disagree inside or privately (Leung & Brew, 2009), and appear to be insincere and distrustful, which causes ostracism from other people (Hales, Kassner, et al., 2016). Gabhardt (2011) argued and found that high disintegration avoidance was positively related to workplace ostracism.

Some related personality traits are categorized as *submissive* personalities, including those individuals who are featured as passive, conflict-avoidant, and quiet in interpersonal relationships (Mao, Liu, Jiang, & Zhang, 2017). Aquino and Bradfield (2000) found that these submissive individuals are more likely to be the target of interpersonal mistreatment.

Warmth and competence. There are certain rules in navigating one's behaviors in group livings. First, group members should add values. The evolutionary theory noted that group animals ostracized conspecifics that were weak, vulnerable, and incompetent for the purpose of group safety, survival, and long-term prosperity (Gruter & Masters, 1986). Similarly, human beings are required to supply materials and resources for group prosperity, such as their skills, knowledge, ability, and expertise. Members who are not motivated or able to add values to the group are considered weak exchange partners and will be shunned by others (Kurzban & Leary, 2001). Social exclusion enables group members to avoid being taken advantage in a dyadic relationship and to enhance group performance.

Second, to survive in social groups, individuals need to abide by *social norms*. Social norms help group members to understand what appropriate behaviors are in maintaining their valuable social membership. Therefore, social norms establish mechanisms through which group members achieve group functions and social goals (Cialdini & Trost, 1998). Social exchange theory (Blau, 1964) and the norm of reciprocity (Gouldner, 1960) supply the norms for healthy social relationships. Group members are expected to be warm, respectful, and kind to other members. Group members who fail to reciprocate favor from another person, or take advantage of others, are deemed to be harmful to social relationships, and consequently, will be ostracized (Kurzban & Leary, 2001). Some examples are those who are needy and routinely require help, fail to reciprocate after receiving favor from others, or talk too much and demand others' time and attention (Scott & Duffy, 2015).

Consistent with the above two lines of reasoning, people's perceptions or judgment of other individuals fall into two Gestalt clusters (Judd, James-Hawkins, Yzerbyt, & Kashima, 2005): The interpersonal dimension of warmth and the task dimension of competence (Judd et al., 2005), which could run as antecedents of workplace ostracism.

Warmth and communion. The warmth dimension is an important component of agreeableness. It comprises traits such as friendliness, cooperativeness, trustworthiness, and helpfulness (Judd et al., 2005). Being cooperative and interpersonal-harmony oriented facilitates group consensus and group cohesion, and helps the group achieve its goals (Graziano & Eisenberg, 1997). Organizational members may judge the warmth of an individual to determine if the individual will be an excellent collaborator. If the individual is too difficult to work with, which will make the accomplishment of the work task impossible, he/she would likely be excluded from further teamwork. Lustenberger (2012) found that participants were more likely to exclude members with low warmth versus those with moderate warmth.

Competence and job performance. The competence dimension comprises traits such as intelligence, industriousness, effectiveness, and skillfulness (Judd et al., 2005). It has both the ability component (e.g., general mental ability) and motivational component (e.g., conscientiousness) (Judd et al., 2005). At work settings, both general mental abilities and conscientiousness are significant predictors of job performance. Therefore, highly competent individuals are top contributors to group goals and performance.

Organizational member judges the competence of a team member to decide if this person makes contribution to the team tasks. If the individual is incompetent, group members may ostracize the poor performer for two reasons. First, they want to let the poor performer know that his/her behavior is out of the norm, and they hope to bring the poor performer back to the line. Second, they want to get rid of the poor performer so that the team can move forward and have a better chance to survive. Research has found that poor performance is positively related to workplace ostracism (Howard et al., 2020; Lustenberger, 2012).

Paradoxically, individuals could also be ostracized as positive deviates (Scott & Duffy, 2015). Being called smart victims (Kim & Glomb, 2010), highly competent individuals may be the targets of victimization due to being envied (Mao et al., 2017; Scott & Duffy, 2015). Based on social comparison theory, comparing oneself against a high standard set by outstanding performers may elicit negative cognitions and feelings (e.g., low self-worth and high competition), and may jeopardize one's reputation at work (Scott & Duffy, 2015). Other group members may struggle with this type of self-concept threat and experience envy and shame, and display hostility and ostracism toward high performers (Kim & Glomb, 2010; Scott & Duffy, 2015).

Social abilities and skills. Social influence theory (Levy & Collins, 1998) provides guidelines to explain why some individuals are less likely to experience workplace ostracism (Cullen, Fan, & Liu, 2012). According to social influence theory, the social nature of the workplace permits employees to influence their workplace relationships to (1) achieve desirable work outcomes (e.g., promotion or pay increase); (2) avoid adverse decisions on their work (e.g., demotion); and (3) reduce mistreatment from others at work, such as workplace ostracism. These social skills include emotional intelligence, political skills, and impression management skills.

Emotional intelligence (EI). EI refers to the social abilities in understanding one's own emotions and others' emotions, which helps an individual to regulate and use his/her emotions to guide thinking and actions (Salovey & Mayer, 1990). EI negatively predicts workplace ostracism for four reasons. First, high-EI individuals have a better ability to mointor and to regulate their emotions so that they are less distressed and more relaxed. Less negative affect and more positive affect will result in less ostracism experience. Second, employees with high EI are more able to control their emotions when dealing with interpersonal infractions (Salovey & Mayer, 1990). They have a better chance to reach conflict resolution than workplace ostracism. Third, employees with high EI are more likely to cultivate good interpersonal relationship at work (Wong & Law, 2002). High-EI employees have been found to engage in helping behaviors and be liked by coworkers (Abraham, 1999). On the contrary, low-EI employees are more likely to engage in deviance behaviors (Brackett & Mayer, 2003). Fourth, high EI has potential to improve job performance and be successful (Wong & Law, 2002), which is valued by organizations. Paired with high EI, these high performers are less likely to be the targets of ostracism. Zhang and Shi (2017) found that EI negatively predicted workplace ostracism measured three months later.

Political skills. Political skills refer to one's ability to understand others at work, and using this knowledge to influence others to act in a way that supports personal and organizational goals (Ahearn, Ferris, Hochwarter, Douglas, & Ammeter, 2004). Because they understand the importance of interpersonal resources, people high in political skills avoid being the victims of workplace ostracism.

Ferris et al. (2005) defined four factors of political skills: *social astuteness*, *apparent sincerity*, *interpersonal influence*, and *networking ability*. With high *social astuteness*, people understand others better and could behave consistently with this knowledge. They are more likely to behave in socially appropriate manner and less likely to offend other people. With high *apparent sincerity*, they are more able to gain trust and enjoy favorable impressions from others (Ferris et al., 2007). With social astuteness and apparent sincerity, they avoid being provocative victims of workplace ostracism. They are better at understanding other people's needs and wants, and how others will react to their behaviors (Ferris et al., 2005). Thus, they can adjust their behaviors to get favorable responses from others; they have the abilities to make other people feel comfortable and approachable (Cullen et al., 2012).

With a high ability in *interpersonal influence*, they have more interpersonal power by gaining support from others. With strong *networking ability*, they can build more interpersonal resources and social capital (Ferris et al., 2005). Their high skills in interpersonal influence and networking ability prevent them from becoming submissive victims. They have the motivation and abilities to build valuable social connections. Being in the center of the social network, they enjoy high popularity and high social exchange value and are less likely to be ostracized by others (Cullen et al., 2012; Scott, Restubog, & Zagenczyk, 2013).

Some research has supported that high political skill is negative related to workplace ostracism (Cullen et al., 2012; Zhao et al., 2013). However, in Howard et al. (2020) meta-analytical study based on five individual samples, political skill was not related to workplace ostracism. More research is needed to understand political skills and workplace ostracism.

Impression management. *Impression management* refers to people's skills in forming a desirable social impression. Governed by a self-regulatory system, an actor of impression management creates and controls an image he/she desires the target to hold (Bozeman & Kacmar, 1997). Therefore, impression management helps people build and maintain a relationship (Leary & Kowalski, 1990; Smart Richman & Leary, 2009). There are three types of impression management: Self-focused impression management, other-focused impression management, and job-focused impression management. With *self-focused impression management*, people try to create self-image with positive personal characteristics such as being friendly, polite, conscientious, and high in integrity (Wayne & Ferris, 1990). With *other-focused impression management*, people try to promote likableness by praising others, doing other people favors, and benefiting others (Wayne & Ferris, 1990). With *job-focused impression management*, people try to enhance their job-related image, such as being an outstanding performer, claiming positive work outcomes, and promoting high achievement at work (Wayne & Ferris, 1990).

According to Bolino, Varela, Bande, and Turnley (2006), the three types of impression management are not equally effective in promoting high-quality interpersonal relationships. They found that only other-focused (i.e., supervisor-focused) impression management positively predicted supervisor liking and organizational citizenship behaviors toward one's supervisor. Similarly, Wu, Kwan, Liu, and Lee (2020) examined other-focused impression management and found it positively predicted popularity (i.e., a collective impression hold by others that the target individual has high social preference and social visibility in a group, Scott (2013)), which negatively predicted workplace ostracism.

Relational Antecedents of Workplace Ostracism

Relational antecedents of ostracism are factors that are embedded in interpersonal relationships that lead to workplace ostracism. Relational factors are different from individual factors, such as personalities or skill sets; rather relational factors emphasize the interpersonal triggers for workplace ostracism. From the victim's perspective, others' unfriendly behaviors or aggressive expressions can lead to a feeling of being left out. Though by definition, workplace ostracism describes a situation that absent of appropriate social actions in a passive-aggressive form (Robinson et al., 2013), the feeling of being excluded can also result from more salient or active types of interpersonal aggression or conflicts via harmed self-esteem or thwarted need to belong. From the perpetrators' perspective, annoying or undesirable behaviors of the victim may also motive the perpetrators to engage in ostracizing behaviors toward the target. We categorize these interpersonal antecedents of workplace ostracism as relational antecedents.

Research on the relational antecedents of workplace ostracism has relied on several theoretical paradigms to develop the frameworks. These theories include sociometer theory and belongingness theory (Baumeister & Leary, 1995; Leary, 2005; Leary & Baumeister, 2000; Schilpzand & Huang, 2018), social identity theory (Penhaligon, Louis, & Restubog, 2009; Schilpzand & Huang, 2018), and social exchange-based models

(Blau, 1964; Scott et al., 2013). We will cover each of the theoretical perspectives and relevant empirical evidence as well as potential future work.

Workplace mistreatment from others: Belongingness theory and sociometer theory. Belongingness theory argues that evolutionarily human beings have a fundamental need to belong and feel included and connected with other humans (Baumeister & Leary, 1995). Individuals strive to have constant, stable, and positive relationships with others. Threats to this need will result in negative affective experience and low evaluations of self-worth. Sociometer theory builds on belongingness theory and extends that because human beings have this fundamental need to belong, they are very sensitive to social signals existed in our social connections (Leary, 2005; Leary, Tambor, Terdal, & Downs, 1995). According to this theory, individuals develop a social monitoring system (i.e., self-esteem) that designed to detect possible deleterious changes in people's inclusionary status, and they continuously seek social cues of potential social rejection and ostracism (Baumeister & Leary, 1995; Leary, 2005; Leary et al., 1995). Sociometer theory also predicts that motivations to keep a good standing of our social status make people behave in ways that maintain their connections with other people and seek to increase their relational value and social acceptance.

In the workplace, others' behaviors including bullying, abuse, aggressive communications, incivility, mobbing, and other forms of aggressive behaviors are likely to hurt individuals' need to belong and signal a risk in social connections easily detected by the victim's socio-monitor in their mind. As predicted by sociometer theory, when these risk factors (any type of mistreatment) are detected, the victims are likely to have a dent on their self-esteem and develop a feeling of social rejection. Workplace ostracism studies under this theoretical umbrella usually derive from the target perspective and argue that mistreatment by team members, unfriendly coworkers, and conflicting work relationships may likely create a feeling of social rejections and distancing in general. For example, Penhaligon and colleagues (2009) found that mistreatment from group members contribute to the target's perceived social rejections and ostracism. They collect information on various types of mistreatment like bullying, social undermining, physical threats, aggressive communications, etc., and found that social rejection acts as the underlying mechanism that mediates the relationships between workgroup mistreatment and depressions/organization-based self-esteem. Similarly, Schilpzand

and Huang (2018) found that team member's incivility lead to a target's feeling of being ostracized. They suggested that workplace incivility is an effective way to indicate social disapproval and exclusionary intention toward unfavorable team members, and it acts as a sign of social unacceptance. When the victims experience their team member's incivility behaviors toward them, their sociometer detected and interpreted this social cue as preludes of potential workplace ostracism.

Feelings of being ostracized or outgrouped: Social identity theory. Social identity theory (Tajfel & Turner, 1979) argues that individuals define themselves with group membership, and social identifications is the perception of oneness with or belongingness to some human groups. Individuals seek memberships in groups that enhance their self-image and self-value. The groups provide the members with a sense of security, a distinct value, and a positive social value (Hogg & Terry, 2000). According to this theory, social disapproval from desired groups at work may likely to provoke the feeling of being ostracized or rejected. Penhaligon et al. (2009) used social identity theory to build their argument of why employees being mistreated (including bullying, social underlying, physical threats, and aggressive communications) by the group members feel ostracized—they feel other group members do not value them.

On the other hand, social identity theory also describes that individuals have preferences over their own group members vs. outsiders, and they may act hostilely or aggressively toward outgroups. Social identity theory helps explain who is chosen to be ostracized in a work environment. This line of reasoning has not been empirically tested in the working environment. Nonetheless, studies on in-group bias, ethnocentrism, or prejudice have highlighted the negative attitudes/behaviors toward outgroup individuals. Future studies may explore how this reasoning would help further understand the precursors of work ostracism toward outgroups.

Social exchange theory and the actor's tendency to ostracize. Social exchange theory suggests that frequent and positive social interactions build favorable treatment between two individuals (Blau, 1964). This relationship-building is governed by the norm of reciprocity (Gouldner, 1960), such as helping individuals who helped themselves. Individuals who fail to reciprocate positively or even harm the others would be viewed as a threat to the relationship and social order in general, and likely become the targets to be avoided or other corrective actions (Gouldner, 1960; Helm, Bonoma, & Tedeschi, 1972). Research using social exchange theory to study workplace ostracism often theorizes from the actors' perspectives and suggests that these actors may choose workplace ostracism as a subtle way to punish or retaliate others, make it even, or get back to those who harm themselves. For example, Scott et al. (2013) used samples of employee-coworker dyads in two organizations and found that employees who engaged in incivility are more likely to activate others' ostracizing behaviors toward them via distrust. Similarly, Quade et al. (2017) found that the target's unethical behaviors ultimately bring workplace ostracism toward themselves via relationship conflicts.

Conservation of resource (COR) and third parties' ostracism behaviors. The COR (Hobfoll, 1989, 2002) theory proposes that individuals maintain and protect different types of resources, including physical objects that are perceived as valuable, conditions (e.g., hierarchical work status, marital status), personal resources that offer resilience to stress (e.g., perceptual orientation, self-esteem, psychological capital), and energies (e.g., money, time). When these resources are lost, threatened by potential loss, or not regained after expenditure, individuals will experience stress. Hobfoll (1989, 2002) assumes that individuals are naturally motivated to accrue resources. Thus, when they experience stress, they will act in ways that conserve their resources and ensure the capacity to generate resources in the future. Research on the third-party (e.g., observers or coworkers) reactions to supervisory abuse in the form of workplace ostracism has been constructed by this theoretical angle. Evidence showed that supervisory abuse leads to the perception of workplace ostracism (Neves & Cunha, 2018). In particular, victims of abusive supervision projected a threat to valuable resources from the third-party perspective (i.e., coworkers), and these coworkers may avoid associations with these victims to prevent any potential resource loss.

Social comparison theory and the initiation of workplace ostracism. Social comparison theory argues that when people have uncertainty about their own ability and opinions, they evaluate themselves by comparing with similar others (Festinger, 1954). Particularly, people socially compare themselves when objective information is not available. Adams (1965) incorporated this basic notion into his well-known equity theory. At the heart of this theory lies the assumption that people pursue a balance between their investments (or "inputs," e.g., time, attention, skills, effort) and the rewards ("outcomes," e.g., status). As predicted by the equity theory, when individuals found the imbalance of his/her own input/output versus others' input/output, they are likely to develop negative attitudes toward others and are motivated to restore balance via actions. In the context of the workplace, if an employee receives rewards/favoritism from the leader that was not considered fair by his/her colleagues, he/she may experience backfires from colleagues such as ostracism. This is interesting because it explores the possibility that the victims of workplace ostracism include not only those who display undesirable behaviors or are viewed as a risk to the group, but also those who receive preferential treatments (e.g., a close relationship with a leader) or doing far better than their cohort in the workplace.

For instance, Wang and Li (2018) found that employees who had a high quality of leader-member exchange (LMX) reported more ostracism from other team members via being envied by these team members. The researchers suggested that according to social comparison theory, employees with better and higher-quality relationships with their supervisors were viewed as superior, that lead to unpleasant envy and jealousy from others. As a way of coping, others attempted to avoid these "in-groups" in order to avoid further emotional distress. Similar to these findings, Ng (2017) found that developmental idiosyncratic deals (e.g., special training opportunities) hurt the employees who received such opportunities because they felt being envied by their colleagues and perceived a greater competitive climate at work, and such perceptions lead to subsequently felt ostracism. It seems that being outstanding sometimes has the downside of being envied, and envious others are likely to use work ostracism as a passive-aggressive strategy to vent their frustrations.

Work Context Antecedents of Workplace Ostracism

Although many scholars realize that work environments are important to workplace ostracism (Robinson et al., 2013; Scott & Duffy, 2015; Williams, 2007), few studies have focused on the environment's influence on ostracism. However, work context per se or combined with other factors (e.g., interpersonal skills, group diversity climate and so on) also predict workplace ostracism.

Cooperative versus competitive goal interdependence. Goal interdependence theory (Deutsch, 1949) explained the nature of the interdependent situation by identifying two types of goal interdependence. *Cooperative goal interdependence* refers to situations wherein the pursuit of one's goals is positively related to another person's goal achievement

(Deutsch, 1949). This may happen when two people have a mutual goal (e.g., two employees need to work together as a team and achieve the same goal) or complementary goals (e.g., Person A wants to sell a product, and Person B need to buy that product) (Tjosvold, 1986). On the contrary, *competitive goal interdependence* refers to situations in which one's goal attainment is negatively related to another individual's goal achievement (Deutsch, 1949). This may happen when two people have a mutually exclusive goal (e.g., two employees are competing for one promotion opportunity) or have non-complementary goals (e.g., an employer wants employees to work longer, while employees want more vacation time) (Tjosvold, 1986).

The two types of goal interdependence differentially impact interpersonal interactions (Deutsch, 1949). Since cooperative goal interdependence represents a situation in which mutual liking, courteous treatment, reliance, and support exist, it is less likely to breed conflict or motivate ostracism (Alper, Tjosvold, & Law, 1998; Johnson & Johnson, 1989; Wu, Ferris, et al., 2015). On the other hand, since competitive goal interdependence represents a situation in which disagreements or incompatible desires exist, it is likely to trigger conflict and motivate ostracism (Jehn & Mannix, 2001; Wu, Ferris, et al., 2015). Wu, Ferris, et al. (2015) found that cooperative goal interdependence negatively related, whereas competitive goal interdependence positively related to workplace ostracism. They also found that low social skills strengthened the negative relationship between employees' cooperative goal interdependence with their supervisor and supervisor ostracism, and high social skills buffered the positive relationship between employees' competitive goal interdependence with their supervisor and supervisor ostracism.

Interdependence theory and game-theoretic models of social interaction. Based on interdependence theory (Kelley et al., 2003; Kelley & Thibaut, 1978) and game-theoretic models to social interaction (Camerer, 2011; Schelling, 1980), most conflict situations can be treated as bargaining situations. As such, scholars have used a two-person bargaining game to mimic the dyadic social interaction, which requires two players to choose between collaborative versus competitive strategies (Halevy, Cohen, Chou, Katz, & Panter, 2014; Zhong, Loewenstein, & Murnighan, 2007).

Based on these theories, scholars proposed these distinct strategies or beliefs to conflict may largely determine their behaviors in social interactions (Kiyonari, Tanida, & Yamagishi, 2000). Halevy et al. (2014)

used two mental models to represent these beliefs. A *competitive mental model* will elicit competitive behaviors that motivate hostile acts toward others, such as rejecting or excluding behaviors. A *cooperative mental model* will lead to more collaborating behaviors that facilitate amicable interactions and reduce interpersonal conflict. The two mental models are further developed into four strategies for people who are in conflict with others: *mutual cooperation* (i.e., both I and others behave cooperatively), *unilateral cooperation* (i.e., I behave cooperatively while others behave competitively), *unilateral competition* (i.e., I behave competitively while others behave cooperatively), and *mutual competition* (i.e., both I and others behave competitively) (Halevy et al., 2014).

Halevy et al. (2014) compared participants with mutual cooperation mental model to those with unilateral competition mental model. They found that the later reported more workplace ostracism, interpersonal hostility, and abusive supervision. Unilateral competition strategy predicted higher ratings on self-interest and aggression by others, and higher intention to ostracize the target by others.

Social identity theory and language-based ostracism. Social identity theory suggests that people try to maintain a positive social identity via group membership (Tajfel & Turner, 1979). Specifically, people may place themselves and others into in-groups or outgroups by some criteria that are prominent in their particular context (Brewer, 1979). Social identification will be enhanced when one's group compares positively to other groups (Hogg, 2001; Kulkarni & Sommer, 2015; Tajfel & Turner, 1979).

Based on the social identity theory, the language may serve as a criterion to identify one as belonging to a specific group, such that people who speak the same language are easily get together and form a group. With the growing linguistic diversity, organizations become an amalgam of various languages and speakers (Kulkarni & Sommer, 2015). Simultaneously, language-related problems appear in organizations. Some researchers argue that employees who cannot fluently use their organizations' dominant language need more time to finish tasks, have reduced access to resources, tend to avoid conferences conducted in the dominant language, and feel less accepted by and less similar to others at work (e.g., Hitlan, Kelly, Schepman, Schneider, & Zárate, 2006). Speaking a different language may threaten one's social identity, and it can be the reason for being rejected or excluded by others (i.e., language-based exclusion) (Dotan-Eliaz, Sommer, & Rubin, 2009; Kulkarni & Sommer, 2015). Therefore, the language barrier could forecast workplace ostracism. Kulkarni and Sommer (2015) indicated that group longevity, group diversity climate, and human resource practice moderated the connection between linguistic diversity and language-based exclusion.

Non-traditional work environments. Traditional work typically has a 9-to-5 schedule, and traditional employees often work at the corporate campus together. Thus, in a traditional work environment, managers can easily and frequently engage in face-to-face contact with their subordinates. The face-to-face communication not only brings recipients immediate feedback and implicit cues (e.g., mood, tone, expression, and body language), but also gives them the sense of social belongingness, resource, and ongoing support (Sacco & Ismail, 2014; Wang & Haggerty, 2009). However, a non-traditional work environment is featured with high work flexibility and autonomy to those who work outside of the traditional office (i.e., virtual workers) or those who work from home (i.e., remote workers). Non-traditional work involves numerous low interdependent tasks, which means fewer interactions and information transferring with others. Non-traditional employees work independently, remotely, and virtually, and they are possibly located in different time zones (Chekwa, 2018). Therefore, their communications largely depend on emails, online meetings, or other forms of virtual technologies.

Some studies support that high reliance on virtual communication and low face-to-face contact may negatively influence work outcomes (Gibson & Gibbs, 2006). For example, non-traditional workers missed a lot of information (e.g., immediate feedback and implicit cues) and lacked access to resources (e.g., supervisor support). Low interdependent task and high dependence on technology may result in high inaction, which could be perceived as workplace ostracism (Wang & Haggerty, 2009). Research has found that the inactions increased employees' feeling of loneliness and isolation (Kenyon, Lyons, & Rafferty, 2002; Wiesenfeld, Raghuram, & Garud, 2001).

Moreover, remote workers, such as those work from home (Staples, 2001), are less likely to be assigned essential roles or tasks due to their long distance from the company. If things continue this way, remote workers may think they are unimportant to their organization, and feel like "outgroup" members. Virtual workers not only may work from home, but also work "on the road" or outside of traditional offices (Wiesenfeld et al., 2001). Different from remote workers, they might not be completely isolated, as they may have interactions with clients or suppliers (Chekwa, 2018). However, these minor differences cannot change the fact that virtual employees are physically separated from other workers, which bring themselves a challenge to coordinate, collaborate, and socialize with other employees (Bartel, Wrzesniewski, & Wiesenfeld, 2012). Therefore, non-traditional work environments may enlarge the physical and social distance between employees and intensify the feeling of being ignored or excluded. In summary, due to the nature of the non-traditional work environment (e.g., shortfall of face-to-face contact, different time zones, and proximity to the office), it can be the antecedent of workplace ostracism and isolation (Bartel et al., 2012; Cooper & Kurland, 2002).

Mediation Mechanism

The research on the mediation mechanism of workplace ostracism has just begun to draw attention from researchers. Ostracism operates as a form of passive-aggressive reactions to others. The great uncharted domain is calling for more research on the underlying mechanism of what leads to workplace ostracism. Several theoretical perspectives such as fairness theory, equity theories, and theories about self (e.g., self-identity theory) may contribute to our further understanding of these mediators.

Based on the fairness theory (e.g., interpersonal justice), people should treat each other in a polite, respectful, and trustworthy way. Interpersonal distrust could be a proximal factor that elicits workplace ostracism from others. For example, Scott et al. (2013) found that workplace incivility activated a sense of distrust from others, which preceded others' avoidance behavior (i.e., workplace ostracism). The authors argued that the disruptive nature of the targets' incivility leads to questions and doubts of their trustworthiness, and the distrust further leads to other organizational members' avoidance of interaction with them because of the potential risk. Interpersonal trust has been found to mediate the relationship between neuroticism and workplace ostracism (Zhang & Dai, 2015). High-neurotic individuals are highly suspicious about other's social motives. Sensing this distrust, others may feel de-valued and consequently ostracize the target. Hales, Kassner, et al. (2016) found that the negative relationship between agreeableness and ostracism was mediated by the interpersonal trust toward the target.

Equity theory has supported envy as a mediator on the relationship preferential treatment and workplace ostracism. At the same time, other attitudes toward unfairness may also play a mediating role, such as anger, retaliation, or even withdrawal of commitment. A possible mechanism through which high cognitive capacity or performance influences workplace ostracism is through envy. Namie and Namie (2000) found that 20% of their survey participants reported that bright people were the target of interpersonal aggression; the perpetrators reported that they envied bright people's competency and abilities. Two studies have highlighted envy as an underlying mechanism that links between antecedents and workplace ostracism (Ng, 2017; Wang & Li, 2018). Ng (2017) found that receiving idiosyncratic deals (i-deals, e.g., special training opportunities) lead to a feeling of being envied, and witnessing coworkers' i-deals lead to a feeling of envy. Both feelings of being envied and envy resulted in a feeling of unfairness and activated negative social dynamics such as competitive climate. These perceptions lead to subsequent workplace ostracism and even turnover. Wang and Li (2018) also found that feeling of being envied mediated the relationship between high LMX and workplace ostracism. Employees who have better relationships with their supervisors are viewed as superior, and this may elicit unpleasant feeling of envy by others. Others will try to reduce the negative feeling of envy by avoiding these cohorts of high LMX. In both studies, envy became a salient motivator to engage in workplace ostracism behaviors, and being envied was a precursor of being ostracized.

As for the theory of self, ostracism presents a subtle and ambiguous experience. Therefore, the state of self may act as an underlying mechanism to link external experience and internal feeling of being ostracized. For instance, self-verification theory proposes that people prefer others to view them the same as their self-views, even these self-images are not positive (Lecky, 1945; Swann Jr., 2011; Swarm Jr., 1983). Based on this theory, people want to maximize coherence and consistency in the surrounding environment, so they know what to expect. Thus, when a person self-views him/herself as a low-valued member in a group, the person anticipates being rejected and excluded on a routine basis. Consequently, ambiguous behaviors by others are more likely to be interpreted as signs of ostracism. This self-verification or consistency with self-view can act as an underlying mechanism.

Moderation Mechanism

Several studies have made an initial effort on investigating the moderators that neutralize the effects of various antecedents on perceived workplace ostracism. These moderators may focus on personalities (e.g., agreeableness and humor) or social skill and social values of the targets. For example, coworker humor (Neves & Cunha, 2018) was found to buffer the effect of abusive supervision on perceived workplace ostracism because humor brings additional resources and alleviates the potential risk of resource loss for the victim. Similar findings on agreeableness suggested that the positive and indirect relationships between LMX and workplace ostracism were buffered by targets' agreeableness (Wang & Li, 2018).

Kim and Glomb (2010) studied the moderating effect of two categories of personality traits, agency and communion, on the relationship between high cognitive capacity and workplace victimization. *Agency* (being self-oriented) refers to individualism within a group and describes achievement, determination, and dominance. *Communion* (being group-oriented) refers to the integration of individuals within a group and describes caring, cooperation, and interpersonal trust. They found that agency exacerbated the positive relationship between cognitive capacity and workplace victimization, whereas communion weakened this relationship. Being smart and focusing on self elicited whereas being smart and focusing on group reduced workplace ostracism. Similarly, Hogg, Fielding, and Darley (2005) noted positive deviates may or may not experience ostracism from group members, depending on how they attribute their success. If they are humble and honor the group for their superiority, they elevate the group status, and other members feel honored and are less likely to ostracize. If they take the full credit themselves, or worse, are egotistical or boastful, their high performance threats other group member's sense of self and status. They are more likely to be the targets of ostracism.

The value or skills of the potential targets of workplace ostracism may also interact with the antecedents in predicting workplace ostracism. For example, Quade et al. (2017) suggested that job performance mitigated the relationship between employees' unethical behaviors and workplace ostracism because high job performance might motivate others to ignore the potential cost of moral violations. Wu, Ferris, et al. (2015) suggested that targets' social skills strengthened the negative impact of cooperative goal interdependence on ostracism and neutralized the positive impact of competitive goal interdependence on ostracism. Another interesting angle is how individuals attribute their success within a group also determine whether they will be ostracized (Hogg et al., 2005). If they are sharing the credit and honor the whole group for their success, they are viewed as helping the group to perform, and this humble gesture may reduce the possibility of ostracism. If they ascribed the success all to themselves, they might face cold shoulders by their cohort because it provokes emotional distress and threatens others' self-image.

The last category of moderators may include perceptions of self. Self-identity orientation theory suggests that belongingness can be recognized at the collective, relational, and individual levels of identity (Brewer & Gardner, 1996; Cooper & Thatcher, 2010; Johnson, Chang, & Yang, 2010). At the collective level, people's self-definition is built on group membership, such that people are driven by the norms and aims supported by the groups they belong to; at the relational level, people define themselves in light of dyadic relationship with particular persons, such that their esteem is increased by having good relationships and satisfied partners; at the individual level, people's self-definition is built on their sense of uniqueness, such that people are driven by being different and a sense of personal value (Brewer & Gardner, 1996; Cooper & Thatcher, 2010). Schilpzand and Huang's study (2018) is based on the self-identity orientation theory. They argued and found that when the targets had a high level of collective or relational identity orientation, they perceived a higher level of workplace ostracism after experiencing work-group incivility. The authors suggested that the identification amplified the impact of group incivility on perceived workplace ostracism.

Closing Remark

Despite the smaller attention devoted to the antecedents of workplace ostracism, researchers have made significant progress in identifying employees who are likely to be ostracized, who tend to engage in ostracism behaviors, and the work context that may foster ostracism among working members. Since workplace ostracism is featured with high level of ambiguity, ranges from purposeful to non-purposeful, and relies on the social norm or social appropriateness to render its meaning (Robinson et al., 2013), it is particularly challenging to study the antecedents and identify motives behind it. Thus, it is crucial to examine both actors and victims in work contexts to understand the dyadic nature of workplace ostracism.

References

Abraham, R. (1999). Emotional intelligence in organizations: A conceptualization. *Genetic, Social, and General Psychology Monographs, 125*(2), 209–224.

Adams, J. S. (1965). Inequity in social exchange. In L. Berkowitz (Ed.), *Advances in Experimental Social Psychology* (Vol. 2, pp. 267–299). New York: Academic Press.

Ahearn, K. K., Ferris, G. R., Hochwarter, W. A., Douglas, C., & Ammeter, A. P. (2004). Leader political skill and team performance. *Journal of Management, 30*(3), 309–327.

Alper, S., Tjosvold, D., & Law, K. S. (1998). Interdependence and controversy in group decision making: Antecedents to effective self-managing teams. *Organizational Behavior and Human Decision Processes, 74*(1), 33–52.

Aquino, K., & Bradfield, M. (2000). Perceived victimization in the workplace: The role of situational factors and victim characteristics. *Organization Science, 11*(5), 525–537.

Aquino, K., Grover, S. L., Bradfield, M., & Allen, D. G. (1999). The effects of negative affectivity, hierarchical status, and self-determination on workplace victimization. *Academy of Management Journal, 42*(3), 260–272.

Aquino, K., & Lamertz, K. (2004). A relational model of workplace victimization: Social roles and patterns of victimization in dyadic relationships. *Journal of Applied Psychology, 89*(6), 1023–1034.

Aquino, K., & Thau, S. (2009). Workplace victimization: Aggression from the target's perspective. *Annual Review of Psychology, 60*(1), 717–741.

Ashton, M. C., Lee, K., & Paunonen, S. V. (2002). What is the central feature of extraversion? Social attention versus reward sensitivity. *Journal of Personality and Social Psychology, 83*(1), 245–252.

Back, M. D., Schmukle, S. C., & Egloff, B. (2010). Why are narcissists so charming at first sight? Decoding the narcissism–popularity link at zero acquaintance. *Journal of Personality and Social Psychology, 98*(1), 132–145.

Barrick, M. R., & Mount, M. K. (1991). The big five personality dimensions and job performance: A meta-analysis. *Personnel Psychology, 44*(1), 1–26.

Bartel, C. A., Wrzesniewski, A., & Wiesenfeld, B. M. (2012). Knowing where you stand: Physical isolation, perceived respect, and organizational identification among virtual employees. *Organization Science, 23*(3), 743–757.

Bateman, T. S., & Crant, J. M. (1993). The proactive component of organizational behavior: A measure and correlates. *Journal of Organizational Behavior, 14*(2), 103–118.

Baumeister, R. F., & Leary, M. R. (1995). The need to belong: Desire for interpersonal attachments as a fundamental human motivation. *Psychological Bulletin, 117*(3), 497–529.

Blair, R. J. R. (1995). A cognitive developmental approach to morality: Investigating the psychopath. *Cognition, 57*(1), 1–29.

Blau, P. (1964). *Power and exchange in social life*. New York, NY: Wiley.
Bolino, M. C., Varela, J. A., Bande, B., & Turnley, W. H. (2006). The impact of impression-management tactics on supervisor ratings of organizational citizenship behavior. *Journal of Organizational Behavior, 27*(3), 281–297.
Bozeman, D. P., & Kacmar, K. M. (1997). A cybernetic model of impression management processes in organizations. *Organizational Behavior and Human Decision Processes, 69*(1), 9–30.
Brackett, M. A., & Mayer, J. D. (2003). Convergent, discriminant, and incremental validity of competing measures of emotional intelligence. *Personality and Social Psychology Bulletin, 29*(9), 1147–1158.
Brewer, M. B. (1979). In-group bias in the minimal intergroup situation: A cognitive-motivational analysis. *Psychological Bulletin, 86*(2), 307–324.
Brewer, M. B., & Gardner, W. (1996). Who is this "We"? Levels of collective identity and self representations. *Journal of Personality and Social Psychology, 71*(1), 83–93.
Brookings, J. B., Zembar, M. J., & Hochstetler, G. M. (2003). An interpersonal circumplex/five-factor analysis of the Rejection Sensitivity Questionnaire. *Personality and Individual Differences, 34*(3), 449–461.
Camerer, C. F. (2011). *Behavioral game theory: Experiments in strategic interaction*. Princeton, NJ: Princeton University Press.
Chekwa, C. (2018). Don't be left out-fostering networking opportunities to reduce workplace isolation among ethnic employees in remote settings. *Journal of Competitiveness Studies, 26*(3/4), 217–235.
Cialdini, R. B., & Trost, M. R. (1998). Social influence: Social norms, conformity and compliance. In D. T. Gilbert, S. T. Fiske, & G. Lindzey (Eds.), *The handbook of social psychology* (4th ed., Vol. 2, pp. 151–192). Boston, MA: McGraw-Hill.
Colvin, C. R., Block, J., & Funder, D. C. (1995). Overly positive self-evaluations and personality: Negative implications for mental health. *Journal of Personality and Social Psychology, 68*(6), 1152–1162.
Cooper, C. D., & Kurland, N. B. (2002). Telecommuting, professional isolation, and employee development in public and private organizations. *Journal of Organizational Behavior, 23*(4), 511–532.
Cooper, D., & Thatcher, S. M. (2010). Identification in organizations: The role of self-concept orientations and identification motives. *Academy of Management Review, 35*(4), 516–538.
Costa, P. T., & McCrae, R. R. (1992). Normal personality assessment in clinical practice: The NEO Personality Inventory. *Psychological Assessment, 4*(1), 5–13.
Costa, P. T., & McCrae, R. R. (1995). Primary traits of Eysenck's PEN system: Three-and five-factor solutions. *Journal of Personality and Social Psychology, 69*(2), 308–317.

Crant, J. M. (2000). Proactive behavior in organizations. *Journal of Management, 26*(3), 435–462.

Cullen, K. L., Fan, J., & Liu, C. (2012). Employee popularity mediates the relationship between political skill and workplace interpersonal mistreatment. *Journal of Management, 40*(6), 1760–1778.

Curtis, L. A. (1974). Victim precipitation and violent crime. *Social Problems, 21*(4), 594–605.

Davis, M. H. (1983). Measuring individual differences in empathy: Evidence for a multidimensional approach. *Journal of Personality and Social Psychology, 44*(1), 113–126.

Deutsch, M. (1949). A theory of co-operation and competition. *Human Relations, 2*(2), 129–152.

Dotan-Eliaz, O., Sommer, K. L., & Rubin, Y. S. (2009). Multilingual groups: Effects of linguistic ostracism on felt rejection and anger, coworker attraction, perceived team potency, and creative performance. *Basic and Applied Social Psychology, 31*(4), 363–375.

Elliot, A. J. (2006). The hierarchical model of approach-avoidance motivation. *Motivation and Emotion, 30*(2), 111–116.

Emerson, R. M. (1962). Power-dependence relations. *American Sociological Review, 27*(1), 31–41.

Emmons, R. A. (1987). Narcissism: Theory and measurement. *Journal of Personality and Social Psychology, 52*(1), 11–17.

Ferris, G. R., Treadway, D. C., Kolodinsky, R. W., Hochwarter, W. A., Kacmar, C. J., Douglas, C., & Frink, D. D. (2005). Development and validation of the political skill inventory. *Journal of Management, 31*(1), 126–152.

Ferris, G. R., Treadway, D. C., Perrewé, P. L., Brouer, R. L., Douglas, C., & Lux, S. (2007). Political skill in organizations. *Journal of Management, 33*(3), 290–320.

Festinger, L. (1954). A theory of social comparison processes. *Human Relations, 7*(2), 117–140.

Gabhardt, S. (2011). *The moderating effect of harmony enhancement and disintegration avoidance on the relationship between workplace ostracism and outcomes* (Unpublished doctoral dissertation). Hofstra University, Hempstead, NY.

Gable, S. L. (2006). Approach and avoidance social motives and goals. *Journal of Personality, 74*(1), 175–222.

Gibson, C. B., & Gibbs, J. L. (2006). Unpacking the concept of virtuality: The effects of geographic dispersion, electronic dependence, dynamic structure, and national diversity on team innovation. *Administrative Science Quarterly, 51*(3), 451–495.

Gouldner, A. W. (1960). The norm of reciprocity: A preliminary statement. *American Sociological Review, 25*, 161–178.

Graziano, W. G., & Eisenberg, N. (1997). Agreeableness: A dimension of personality. In R. Hogan, J. Johnson, & S. Briggs (Eds.), *Handbook of personality psychology* (pp. 795–824). San Diego, CA: Academic Press.

Greene, J. D., Sommerville, R. B., Nystrom, L. E., Darley, J. M., & Cohen, J. D. (2001). An fMRI investigation of emotional engagement in moral judgment. *Science, 293*(5537), 2105–2108.

Gruter, M., & Masters, R. D. (1986). *Ostracism as a social and biological phenomenon*. New York: Elsevier.

Hales, A. H., Kassner, M. P., Williams, K. D., & Graziano, W. G. (2016). Disagreeableness as a cause and consequence of ostracism. *Personality and Social Psychology Bulletin, 42*(6), 782–797.

Hales, A. H., Wesselmann, E. D., & Williams, K. D. (2016). Prayer, self-affirmation, and distraction improve recovery from short-term ostracism. *Journal of Experimental Social Psychology, 64*, 8–20.

Halevy, N., Cohen, T. R., Chou, E. Y., Katz, J. J., & Panter, A. T. (2014). Mental models at work: Cognitive causes and consequences of conflict in organizations. *Personality and Social Psychology Bulletin, 40*(1), 92–110.

Haslam, N. (2006). Dehumanization: An integrative review. *Personality and Social Psychology Review, 10*(3), 252–264.

Helm, B., Bonoma, T. V., & Tedeschi, J. T. (1972). Reciprocity for harm done. *Journal of Social Psychology, 87*(1), 89–98.

Hershcovis, M. S. (2011). "Incivility, social undermining, bullying...oh my!": A call to reconcile constructs within workplace aggression research. *Journal of Organizational Behavior, 32*(3), 499–519.

Hitlan, R. T., Kelly, K. M., Schepman, S., Schneider, K. T., & Zárate, M. A. (2006). Language exclusion and the consequences of perceived ostracism in the workplace. *Group Dynamics: Theory, Research, and Practice, 10*(1), 56–70.

Hitlan, R. T., & Noel, J. (2009). The influence of workplace exclusion and personality on counterproductive work behaviours: An interactionist perspective. *European Journal of Work and Organizational Psychology, 18*(4), 477–502.

Hobfoll, S. E. (1989). Conservation of resources: A new attempt at conceptualizing stress. *American Psychologist, 44*(3), 513–524.

Hobfoll, S. E. (2002). Social and psychological resources and adaptation. *Review of General Psychology, 6*(4), 307–324.

Hogg, M. A. (2001). A social identity theory of leadership. *Personality and Social Psychology Review, 5*(3), 184–200.

Hogg, M. A., Fielding, K. S., & Darley, J. (2005). Fringe dwellers: Processes of deviance and marginalization in groups. In D. Abrams, M. A. Hogg, & J. M. Marques (Eds.), *The social psychology of inclusion and exclusion* (pp. 191–210). New York, NY: Psychology Press.

Hogg, M. A., & Terry, D. I. (2000). Social identity and self-categorization processes in organizational contexts. *Academy of Management Review, 25*(1), 121–140.

Howard, M. C., Cogswell, J. E., & Smith, M. B. (2020). The antecedents and outcomes of workplace ostracism: A meta-analysis. *Journal of Applied Psychology, 105*(6), 577–596. https://doi.org/10.1037/apl0000453.

Jehn, K. A., & Mannix, E. A. (2001). The dynamic nature of conflict: A longitudinal study of intragroup conflict and group performance. *Academy of Management Journal, 44*(2), 238–251.

Johnson, D. W., & Johnson, R. T. (1989). *Cooperation and competition: Theory and research*. Edina, MN: Interaction Books.

Johnson, R. E., Chang, C.-H., & Yang, L.-Q. (2010). Commitment and motivation at work: The relevance of employee identity and regulatory focus. *Academy of Management Review, 35*(2), 226–245.

Judd, C. M., James-Hawkins, L., Yzerbyt, V., & Kashima, Y. (2005). Fundamental dimensions of social judgment: Understanding the relations between judgments of competence and warmth. *Journal of Personality and Social Psychology, 89*(6), 899–913.

Judge, T. A., LePine, J. A., & Rich, B. L. (2006). Loving yourself abundantly: Relationship of the narcissistic personality to self-and other perceptions of workplace deviance, leadership, and task and contextual performance. *Journal of Applied Psychology, 91*(4), 762–776.

Katz, J., Moore, J. A., & Tkachuk, S. (2007). Verbal sexual coercion and perceived victim responsibility: Mediating effects of perceived control. *Sex Roles, 57*(3–4), 235–247.

Kelley, H. H., Holmes, J. G., Kerr, N. L., Reis, H. T., Rusbult, C. E., & Van Lange, P. A. (2003). *An atlas of interpersonal situations*. Cambridge: Cambridge University Press.

Kelley, H. H., & Thibaut, J. W. (1978). *Interpersonal relations: A theory of interdependence*. New York, NY: Wiley.

Kenyon, S., Lyons, G., & Rafferty, J. (2002). Transport and social exclusion: Investigating the possibility of promoting inclusion through virtual mobility. *Journal of Transport Geography, 10*(3), 207–219.

Kim, E., & Glomb, T. M. (2010). Get smarty pants: Cognitive ability, personality, and victimization. *Journal of Applied Psychology, 95*(5), 889–901.

Kiyonari, T., Tanida, S., & Yamagishi, T. (2000). Social exchange and reciprocity: Confusion or a heuristic? *Evolution and Human Behavior, 21*(6), 411–427.

Kulkarni, M., & Sommer, K. (2015). Language-based exclusion and prosocial behaviors in organizations. *Human Resource Management, 54*(4), 637–652.

Kunda, Z. (1990). The case for motivated reasoning. *Psychological Bulletin, 108*(3), 480–498.

Kurzban, R., & Leary, M. R. (2001). Evolutionary origins of stigmatization: The functions of social exclusion. *Psychological Bulletin, 127*(2), 187–208.

Langelaan, S., Bakker, A. B., Van Doornen, L. J., & Schaufeli, W. B. (2006). Burnout and work engagement: Do individual differences make a difference? *Personality and Individual Differences, 40*(3), 521–532.

Leary, M. R. (2005). Sociometer theory and the pursuit of relational value: Getting to the root of self-esteem. *European Review of Social Psychology, 16*(1), 75–111.

Leary, M. R., & Baumeister, R. F. (2000). The nature and function of self-esteem: Sociometer theory. In M. P. Zanna (Ed.), *Advances in Experimental Social Psychology* (Vol. 32, pp. 1–62). New York: Academic Press.

Leary, M. R., & Kowalski, R. M. (1990). Impression management: A literature review and two-component model. *Psychological Bulletin, 107*(1), 34–47.

Leary, M. R., Tambor, E. S., Terdal, S. K., & Downs, D. L. (1995). Self-esteem as an interpersonal monitor: The sociometer hypothesis. *Journal of Personality and Social Psychology, 68*(3), 518–530.

Lecky, P. (1945). *Self-consistency: A theory of personality.* New York, NY: Island Press.

Leung, A. S. M., Wu, L. Z., Chen, Y. Y., & Young, M. N. (2011). The impact of workplace ostracism in service organizations. *International Journal of Hospitality Management, 30*(4), 836–844.

Leung, K., & Brew, F. P. (2009). A cultural analysis of harmony and conflict: Toward an integrated model of conflict styles. In R. S. Wyer, C. Chiu, & Y. Hong (Eds.), *Understanding culture: Theory, research, and application* (pp. 411–428). New York, NY: Psychology Press.

Levy, D. A., & Collins, B. E. (1998). A new model of interpersonal. *Journal of Social Behavior and Personality, 13*(4), 715–733.

Liu, C., Li, H., Bruk-Lee, V., & Ma, J. (2019, August). Supervisor conflict, supervisor ostracism, and employee outcomes: The role of interpersonal harmony. In C. Liu (Chair), *How contextual and dispositional factors predict and interact with workplace ostracism.* Symposium conducted at the Conference of the Academy of Management, Boston, MA.

Liu, C., Nauta, M. M., Yang, L. Q., & Spector, P. E. (2018). How do coworkers "make the place"? Examining coworker conflict and the value of harmony in China and the United States. *Applied Psychology: An International Review, 67*(1), 30–60.

Lustenberger, D. E. (2012). *Targets of social exclusion in teams* (Unpublished doctoral dissertation). Purdue University, West Lafayette, IN.

Mao, Y., Liu, Y., Jiang, C., & Zhang, I. D. (2018). Why am I ostracized and how would I react?—A review of workplace ostracism research. *Asia Pacific Journal of Management, 35*(3), 745–767.

Marr, J. C., Thau, S., Aquino, K., & Barclay, L. J. (2012). Do I want to know? How the motivation to acquire relationship-threatening information in groups contributes to paranoid thought, suspicion behavior, and social rejection. *Organizational Behavior and Human Decision Processes, 117*(2), 285–297.

Moon, H. (2001). The two faces of conscientiousness: Duty and achievement striving in escalation of commitment dilemmas. *Journal of Applied Psychology, 86*(3), 533–540.

Mor, N., & Inbar, M. (2009). Rejection sensitivity and schema-congruent information processing biases. *Journal of Research in Personality, 43*(3), 392–398.

Morf, C. C., & Rhodewalt, F. (2001). Unraveling the paradoxes of narcissism: A dynamic self-regulatory processing model. *Psychological Inquiry, 12*(4), 177–196.

Namie, G., & Namie, R. (2000). *The bully at work*. Naperville, IL: Sourcebooks.

Neves, P., & Cunha, M. P. e. (2018). Exploring a model of workplace ostracism: The value of coworker humor. *International Journal of Stress Management, 25*(4), 330–347.

Nezlek, J. B., Wesselmann, E. D., Wheeler, L., & Williams, K. D. (2015). Ostracism in everyday life: The effects of ostracism on those who ostracize. *The Journal of Social Psychology, 155*(5), 432–451.

Ng, T. W. H. (2017). Can idiosyncratic deals promote perceptions of competitive climate, felt ostracism, and turnover? *Journal of Vocational Behavior, 99*, 118–131.

Olweus, D. (1978). *Aggression in the schools: Bullies and whipping boys*. Washington DC: Hemisphere.

Paulhus, D. L., & Williams, K. M. (2002). The dark triad of personality: Narcissism, Machiavellianism, and psychopathy. *Journal of Research in Personality, 36*(6), 556–563.

Penhaligon, N. L., Louis, W. R., & Restubog, S. L. (2009). Emotional anguish at work: The mediating role of perceived rejection on workgroup mistreatment and affective outcomes. *Journal of Occupational Health Psychology, 14*(1), 34–45.

Pratto, F., Sidanius, J., Stallworth, L. M., & Malle, B. F. (1994). Social dominance orientation: A personality variable predicting social and political attitudes. *Journal of Personality and Social Psychology, 67*(4), 741–763.

Quade, M. J., Greenbaum, R. L., & Petrenko, O. V. (2017). "I don't want to be near you, unless…": The interactive effect of unethical behavior and performance onto relationship conflict and workplace ostracism. *Personnel Psychology, 70*(3), 675–709.

Renn, R., Allen, D., & Huning, T. (2013). The relationship of social exclusion at work with self-defeating behavior and turnover. *Journal of Social Psychology, 53*(2), 229–249.

Robinson, S. L., O'Reilly, J., & Wang, W. (2013). Invisible at work. *Journal of Management, 39*(1), 203–231.

Sacco, D. F., & Ismail, M. M. (2014). Social belongingness satisfaction as a function of interaction medium: Face-to-face interactions facilitate greater social belonging and interaction enjoyment compared to instant messaging. *Computers in Human Behavior, 36*, 359–364.

Salancik, G. R., & Pfeffer, J. (1978). A social information processing approach to job attitudes and task design. *Administrative Science Quarterly, 23*(2), 224–253.

Salovey, P., & Mayer, J. D. (1990). Emotional intelligence. *Imagination, Cognition and Personality, 9*(3), 185–211.

Schelling, T. C. (1980). *The strategy of conflict*. Cambridge, MA: Harvard University Press.

Schilpzand, P., & Huang, L. (2018). When and how experienced incivility dissuades proactive performance: An integration of sociometer and self-identity orientation perspectives. *Journal of Applied Psychology, 103*(8), 828–841.

Scott, B. A. (2013). A conceptual framework for the study of popularity in the workplace. *Organizational Psychology Review, 3*(2), 161–186.

Scott, K. L., & Duffy, M. K. (2015). Antecedents of workplace ostracism: New directions in research and intervention. In P. L. Perrewé, J. R. B. Halbesleben, & C. C. Rosen (Eds.), *Research in occupational stress and well-being: Vol. 13. Mistreatment in organizations* (pp. 137–165). Emerald Group Publishing: Bingley, UK.

Scott, K. L., Restubog, S. L., & Zagenczyk, T. J. (2013). A social exchange-based model of the antecedents of workplace exclusion. *Journal of Applied Psychology, 98*(1), 37–48.

Smart Richman, L., & Leary, M. R. (2009). Reactions to discrimination, stigmatization, ostracism, and other forms of interpersonal rejection: A multimotive model. *Psychololgy Review, 116*(2), 365–383.

Spain, S. M., Harms, P., & LeBreton, J. M. (2014). The dark side of personality at work. *Journal of Organizational Behavior, 35*(S1), S41–S60.

Staples, D. S. (2001). A study of remote workers and their differences from non-remote workers. *Journal of Organizational and End User Computing, 13*(2), 3–14.

Swann, W. B., Jr. (2011). Self-verification theory. In P. A. M. V. Lange, A. W. Kruglanski, & E. T. Higgins (Eds.), *Handbook of theories of social psychology* (Vol. 2, pp. 23–42). London: Sage.

Swarm, W. B., Jr. (1983). Self-verification: Bringing social reality into harmony with the self. *Social Psychological Perspectives on the Self, 2*, 33–66.

Tajfel, H., & Turner, J. C. (1979). The social identity theory of inter-group behavior. In S. Worchel & L. W. Austin (Eds.), *Psychology of intergroup relations* (pp. 94–109). Chicago, IL: Nelson-Hall.

Takamatsu, R. (2019). Personality correlates and utilitarian judgments in the everyday context: Psychopathic traits and differential effects of empathy, social dominance orientation, and dehumanization beliefs. *Personality and Individual Differences, 146*, 1–8.

Tepper, B. J., Duffy, M. K., Henle, C. A., & Lambert, L. S. (2006). Procedural injustice, victim precipitation, and abusive supervision. *Personnel Psychology, 59*(1), 101–123.

Tjosvold, D. (1986). The dynamics of interdependence in organizations. *Human Relations, 39*(6), 517–540.

Van der Vegt, G. S., Bunderson, J. S., & Oosterhof, A. (2006). Expertness diversity and interpersonal helping in teams: Why those who need the most help end up getting the least. *Academy of Management Journal, 49*(5), 877–893.

Wang, Y., & Haggerty, N. (2009). Knowledge transfer in virtual settings: The role of individual virtual competency. *Information Systems Journal, 19*(6), 571–593.

Wang, Z., & Li, G. (2018). You don't actually want to get closer to the star: How LMX leads to workplace ostracism. *Frontiers of Business Research in China, 12*(1), 37–49.

Watson, D., & Clark, L. A. (1984). Negative affectivity: The disposition to experience aversive emotional states. *Psychological Bulletin, 96*(3), 465–490.

Wayne, S. J., & Ferris, G. R. (1990). Influence tactics, affect, and exchange quality in supervisor-subordinate interactions: A laboratory experiment and field study. *Journal of Applied Psychology, 75*(5), 487–499.

Wiesenfeld, B. M., Raghuram, S., & Garud, R. (2001). Organizational identification among virtual workers: The role of need for affiliation and perceived work-based social support. *Journal of Management, 27*(2), 213–229.

Williams, K. D. (2007). Ostracism. *Annual Review of Psychology, 58*, 425–452.

Williams, K. D., Shore, W. J., & Grahe, J. E. (1998). The silent treatment: Perceptions of its behaviors and associated feelings. *Group Processes & Intergroup Relations, 1*(2), 117–141.

Wong, C.-S., & Law, K. S. (2002). The effects of leader and follower emotional intelligence on performance and attitude: An exploratory study. *The Leadership Quarterly, 13*(3), 243–274.

Wu, C. H., Kwan, H. K., Liu, J., & Lee, C. (2020). When and how favour rendering ameliorates workplace ostracism over time: Moderating effect of self-monitoring and mediating effect of popularity enhancement. *Journal of Occupational and Organizational Psychology*. Advance online publication. https://doi.org/10.1111/joop.12328.

Wu, L.-Z., Ferris, D. L., Kwan, H. K., Chiang, F., Snape, E., & Liang, L. H. (2015). Breaking (or making) the silence: How goal interdependence and social skill predict being ostracized. *Organizational Behavior and Human Decision Processes, 131,* 51–66.

Wu, L., Wei, L., & Hui, C. (2011). Dispositional antecedents and consequences of workplace ostracism: An empirical examination. *Frontiers of Business Research in China, 5*(1), 23–44.

Xu, E. (2012). *How am I supposed to live without you: An investigation of antecedents and consequences of workplace ostracism* (Unpublished doctoral dissertation), The Hong Kong Polytechnic University, Hong Kong, China.

Zhang, S., & Shi, Q. (2017). The relationship between subjective well-being and workplace ostracism. *Journal of Organizational Change Management, 30*(6), 978–988.

Zhang, X., & Dai, L. (2015). The relationship between neuroticism and experience of workplace ostracism in new employees. *Open Journal of Social Sciences, 3*(2), 80–87.

Zhao, H., Peng, Z., & Sheard, G. (2013). Workplace ostracism and hospitality employees' counterproductive work behaviors: The joint moderating effects of proactive personality and political skill. *International Journal of Hospitality Management, 33*(1), 219–227.

Zhao, H., Xia, Q., He, P., Sheard, G., & Wan, P. (2016). Workplace ostracism and knowledge hiding in service organizations. *International Journal of Hospitality Management, 59,* 84–94.

Zhong, C.-B., Loewenstein, J., & Murnighan, J. K. (2007). Speaking the same language: The cooperative effects of labeling in the prisoner's dilemma. *Journal of Conflict Resolution, 51*(3), 431–456.

Zimmerman, C. A., Carter-Sowell, A. R., & Xu, X. (2016). Examining workplace ostracism experiences in academia: Understanding how differences in the faculty ranks influence inclusive climates on campus. *Frontiers in Psychology, 7,* 753.

CHAPTER 4

Emotional, Cognitive, and Physiological Responses to Workplace Ostracism

Jie Ma, Aditi Rabindra Sachdev, and Na Tang

As human beings, we have fundamental need to seek social affiliation, belongingness, and inclusion (Baumeister, Twenge, & Nuss, 2002). Children expect consistent love and care from parents to feel secure; partners seek intimacy as a way to validate their love; and students socialize at school to share feelings with others. Work fills a large part of our lives, and interpersonal relationships at the workplace thus carry significant personal implications. Having good relationships in the workplace gives

The first and the second authors contributed equally to this chapter.

J. Ma (✉)
Jinan University, Guangzhou, Guangdong, China

A. R. Sachdev
Corporate Talent Management and Organization Development, PepsiCo Inc., Purchase, NY, USA

N. Tang
School of Management, Lanzhou University, Lanzhou, China

C. Liu and J. Ma (eds.), *Workplace Ostracism*,
Palgrave Explorations in Workplace Stigma,
https://doi.org/10.1007/978-3-030-54379-2_4

employees a sense of support toward personal success and accomplishment of collective goals. Additionally, employees derive esteem at work from the respect, care, and recognition shown by others. More importantly, high-quality relationships at work mean access to greater resources integral to career success. As such, employees attach great importance to building and maintaining high-quality relationships at work.

However, workplace ostracism is ubiquitous. Most employees have experienced some kind of ostracism episodes in the workplace (Ferris, Brown, Berry, & Lian, 2008; Ferris, Chen, & Lim, 2017). Organizations are taking measures to prevent overt aggression such as abusive supervision, conflict, sexual harassment, and bullying. These organizational practices may refrain workers from exhibiting overt aggression. However, workplace ostracism may become even more salient and frequent under these circumstances. This is because workplace ostracism is featured by an act of omission (i.e., no action but neglect is needed to ostracize others). As such, it might be more difficult for organizations to prevent and tackle workplace ostracism. Being ostracized by others hurts the sense of belongingness and generates emotional distress. Besides, social inclusion determines the level of self-esteem or a sense of self-worth, rendering it to hurt self-concept (Williams, 2009). Moreover, workplace ostracism also threatens work-related outcomes and career success that are conditioned partly upon interpersonal relationships. Needless to say, workplace ostracism is a painful and threatening experience deserving much attention from scholars and practitioners.

Research has well documented the harmful effect of workplace ostracism on employee outcomes. This chapter aims to discuss the emotional, cognitive, and physiological consequences of being ostracized. We acknowledge that the negative impact of workplace ostracism on these outcomes is quite apparent and it is relatively straightforward to elucidate why this is the case. That said, this chapter is still valuable and necessary for multiple reasons. First of all, these outcomes demonstrate employees' psychological situations and transitory responses to workplace ostracism. They contribute to employees' work attitudes and well-being at work and function as mechanisms linking workplace ostracism to tangible work outcomes such as job performance. Therefore, a comprehensive discussion regarding why and how workplace ostracism influences employees' emotional, cognitive, and physiological outcomes is the basis for an in-depth knowledge of the overall effect of workplace ostracism. Second, as we will discuss later, multiple theories offer distinct perspectives in explaining the effect of workplace ostracism, suggesting that the processes linking workplace ostracism to those outcomes are more complex than we thought. In this sense, we are less able to obtain enriched understanding of the psychological mechanisms underlying the effect of workplace ostracism until various theoretical perspectives and premises are acknowledged. For the sake of extending theories and advancing research in this literature, it is helpful to attending to these seemingly obvious but in fact complicated topics. Thus, it's the time to synthesize empirical findings and theoretical underpinnings linking workplace ostracism to these outcomes, which would direct organizational interventions and inspire individual coping strategies mitigating the negative effect of workplace ostracism.

The Emotional Impact of Workplace Ostracism

Emotions are an individual's transitory, quick responses to external stimuli (Roseman, 2001). However, an emotion can be prolonged and turn into a global experience (Williams, 2009). By defining one's feelings, emotions are an essential element of subjective well-being (Zhang & Shi, 2017). In the broadest sense, emotions can be distinguished by valence (i.e., positive emotions versus negative emotions) (Barrett & Russell, 1999) and arousal (i.e., high-arousal versus low-arousal) (Bradley, Greenwald, Petry, & Lang, 1992). *Valence* is a hedonic tone that differentiates one's emotions as positive or negative. These two global feelings reflect whether an individual is attending to desirable or undesirable aspects of a stimulus (Barrett, 1998). *Arousal*, on the other hand, is concerned with the intensity of emotion (Barrett & Russell, 1999), which affects the extent to which an individual attends to one's internal sensation. This two-dimensional view categorizes emotions into positive emotions of high-arousal (e.g., enthusiastic and excited), positive emotions of low-arousal (e.g., relaxed and calm), negative emotions of high-arousal (e.g., angry and fearful), and negative emotions of low-arousal (e.g., depressed and anxious) (Remington, Fabrigar, & Visser, 2000).

Workplace ostracism literature has concluded the relationships of workplace ostracism with various types of emotional outcomes, including global negative emotions (e.g., Abubakar, Yazdian, & Behravesh, 2018; Zhang & Shi, 2017), anger (Dotan-Eliaz, Sommer, & Rubin, 2009), depression (Ferris et al., 2008; Liu, 2019), and anxiety (Ferris, Yan, Lim, Chen, & Fatimah, 2016). Meta-analytic results also supported a negative relationship between workplace ostracism and positive emotions and a positive relationship between workplace ostracism and negative emotions (Howard, Cogswell, & Smith, 2020). Additionally, the literature documented the effect of workplace ostracism on a set of emotional distress outcomes, including job tension (Wu, Yim, Kwan, & Zhang, 2012; Zhu, Lyu, Deng, & Ye, 2017), perceived stress (Chung, 2018), and emotional exhaustion (Jahanzeb & Fatima, 2018; Jahanzeb, Fatima, Malik, 2018; Qian, Yang, Wang, Huang & Song, 2019; Wu, Wei, & Hui, 2011). Obviously, being ostracized is emotionally uncomfortable. Emotions carry important evolutionary and adaptive implications. They act as a feedback system that indicates the quality of person-environment interactions and prompts adaptive responses to significant stimuli in the environment (Gil & Droit-Volet, 2012). By experiencing negative emotions, employees are thus very likely to engage in dysfunctional behaviors in response to workplace ostracism (e.g., Ferris, Yan, Lim, Chen, & Fatimah, 2016; Jahanzeb, Fatima, 2018).

Various theoretical perspectives offer different explanations for why a given stimulus elicits a certain emotion (e.g., temporal need-threat model of ostracism, Williams, 2009; conservation of resource theory, Hobfoll, 1989; transactional theory of stress, Lazarus & Folkman, 1984; appraisal theory of emotion, Roseman, 2001; and implicit theory of relationships, Knee, 1998). In this section, we will discuss the theoretical development that links workplace ostracism and a variety type of negative emotions.

Temporal Need-Threat Theory of Ostracism

Temporal need-threat theory (Williams, 2009) seems to be the most prominent framework elucidating the process through which ostracism affects an individuals' emotional, attitudinal, and behavioral outcomes. Past research of workplace ostracism has relied on this theory to hypothesize the effect on emotional outcomes (Jahanzeb et al., 2018). Temporal need-threat theory specifies different stages following ostracism episodes, including ostracism detection, reflexive painful feelings, threatened fundamental needs, need fortification strategies, and the resignation (if ostracism persists too extended periods of time). Once ostracism is detected by victims, they would experience a threat to their fundamental needs, including needs for belonging, self-esteem, control, and meaningful existence (Williams, 2009). Then, the immediate reflexive pain and negative emotions occur, wherein the mitigating circumstances and individual difference cannot alleviate or offset such an undesired effect (Van Beest & Williams, 2006; Williams & Nida, 2011; Zadro, Boland, & Richardson, 2006). In the reflective stage, ostracized individuals reflect on the motivation, meaning, and relevance of ostracism and seek to fortify their needs and regain social acceptance. If ostracism extends to a long period, the prolonged need-threat, depleted resources, and inability to fortify needs would result in feelings of depression, alienation, helplessness, and unworthiness (i.e., resignation stage) (Williams, 2009).

In view of the temporal need-threat theory (Williams, 2009), the emotional impact of workplace ostracism is reflexive and transitory. That is to say, being ostracized will result in negative emotions (e.g., anger) very quickly. Additionally, this emotional impact is partly due to a threat to the four basic needs. On the other hand, this theory differentiates between transitory impact and prolonged/chronic impact on emotions. The negative emotions experienced at the reflexive stage are likely to sustain and stabilize when the employee fails to regain social inclusion after deploying all possible coping strategies (e.g., depression). This is in line with research findings on emotions elicited from lab-induced ostracism (e.g., Van Beest & Williams, 2006) and prolonged emotions after the recovery process (e.g., Zadro et al., 2006).

Notably, the temporal need-threat theory seems to negate personal/situational variations in emotions at the reflexive stage, a notion supported by empirical evidence (e.g., Leary, Haupt, Strausser, & Chokel, 1998; Smith & Williams, 2004; Zadro et al., 2006). Nevertheless, research also acknowledges that there are significant differences in the speed of emotion recovery, which alters the prolonged/chronic impact of workplace ostracism on emotions. For example, social anxiety as a disposition has been found to hinder emotion recovery and sustain negative emotions elicited by ostracism (Zadro et al., 2006). In addition, Williams (2009) noted that group membership significantly affected the emotion recovery process because being ostracized by members of the same group is far more threatening than being ostracized by members of a different group. Although intuitive, these findings were not from organizational samples. Future studies are recommended to uncover work/organization-focused factors to advance this knowledge.

Conservation of Resources Theory (COR)

Conservation of resources theory (COR theory; Hobfoll, 1989, 2001) also helps explain the emotional impact of workplace ostracism. The core principle of COR theory is that individuals have a tendency to protect and gain resources. Stress and negative emotions occur when an individual's resources are at stake or lost. COR theory views resources as "those objects, personal characteristics, conditions, or energies that are valued by the individual or that serve as a means for the attainment of these objects, personal characteristics, conditions or energies" (Hobfoll, 1989, p. 516). That is to say, resources can be any external objects as well as internal factors, which justifies the broad differentiation between psychological resources and instrumental resources, two terms used in our discussion. *Psychological resources* are possessed by an individual, which refer to aspects of self that are either valuable on their own right (e.g., self-esteem) or function to reach desired outcomes (e.g., self-control) (Hobfoll, 2002). It is widely acknowledged that these resources are essential to an individual's integrated psychological functioning and well-being. On the other hand, *instrumental resources* are aspects of a job or work environment that facilitate task completion and attainment of work goals (Hobfoll, 2002; Kwan, Zhang, Liu, & Lee, 2018). Typical examples of instrumental resources include functional support received from coworkers, information/knowledge-exchange, or collaborations among team members (Hobfoll, 2002; Kwan et al., 2018). As can be seen, these resources are partly embedded in social interaction and quality relationship (Hobfoll, 2002).

Workplace ostracism thwarts one's needs for self-esteem and social belongingness (Williams, 2009). Furthermore, being ostracized signals a barrier to task resources and other important input for work completion (Kwan et al., 2018). Therefore, workplace ostracism is likely to consume both job and personal resources, and it is uncertain if employees can regain them. Since these valuable resources are at stake or have been depleted in the context of workplace ostracism, according to COR theory, employees are likely to experience negative emotions. Studies in which COR theory was adopted as the overarching framework have supported the relationship between workplace ostracism with job tension and emotional exhaustion (Jahanzeb & Fatima, 2018; Zhu et al., 2017).

As resource-depletion is quite obvious in the context of ostracism, COR theory has the virtue of simplicity in elaborating the relationship between workplace ostracism and emotions. Because resources include both psychological ones and instrumental ones, COR theory allows for the integration of both psychological and pragmatic influences in developing hypotheses related to emotions. To be specific, the psychological influence is about the harmful impact of workplace ostracism on employee needs, affects, and attitudes (Robinson, O'Reilly, & Wang, 2013). This can be a function of workplace ostracism depleting psychological resources, which subsequently provokes negative emotions. On top of worsening psychological states and hindering need satisfaction, workplace ostracism further shuts the door for social interaction, cuts off the channel for employees sharing essential information and knowledge essential to task completion, and turns functional support inaccessible to those ostracized. That is, workplace ostracism depletes instrumental resources (e.g., information/knowledge-sharing, work collaborations, and functional support from others) embedded in high-quality interpersonal relationships at work (Kwan et al., 2018). This generates the pragmatic influence, namely the detrimental impact of workplace ostracism on practical consequences such as task completion, work success, or one's power and status within an organization (Robinson et al., 2013). For this reason, employees will experience negative emotions due to being less capable of achieving practical consequences. However, COR theory seems unable to effectively predict discrete emotions, simply because resource-conservation is too abstract to measure. Taken together, COR might be suitable for predicting global negative emotions, job tension, and emotional exhaustion in response to workplace ostracism.

Transactional Theory of Stress

As one of the most influential theories of stress, transactional theory highlights the cognitive process through which a stimulus elicits emotions (Lazarus & Folkman, 1984). Its focus on cognitive appraisal offers a clear account of what underlies the emotional impact of workplace ostracism. According to this theory, emotions are a function of cognitive appraisal. When faced with a stressful encounter, employees tend to appraise its meanings to their well-being. As for primary appraisal, employees evaluate if a stressful encounter has already caused personal harm or loss in significant areas (i.e., harm/loss appraisal) or is going to threaten their well-being (i.e., threat appraisal). As for secondary appraisal, employees further evaluate whether they have adequate resources to cope with the encounter. The appraisal of harm/loss or threat becomes more evident if an individual's coping resources are appraised as being insufficient.

We should note that, in transactional theory, cognitive appraisal is concerned with the current or future implications of a stressful encounter (e.g., workplace ostracism). It evaluates "what happened to me?" or "what does a stressful encounter mean to me?" Correspondingly, the harm/loss appraisal indicates the current implications, whereas the threat appraisal is a forward-looking evaluation. We have to highlight this feature because it differentiates transactional theory from other appraisal-oriented theories, such as appraisal theory of emotion (Roseman, 2001) that we are going to discuss later.

Being ostracized entails a loss in social belongingness, self-esteem, and control over social environments (Williams, 2009), and a loss in instrumental resources integral to work completion (Kwan et al., 2018). Employees are likely to make harm/loss appraisal suggesting that they have already lost those valuable resources. Additionally, they can also make threat appraisal for anticipating the future loss of those resources. It is unlike though that employees would appraise workplace ostracism as a challenge that leads to something positive, simply because ostracism is too deleterious to look for a silver lining.

Cognitive appraisal elicits emotions (Lazarus & Folkman, 1984). Specifically, harm/loss appraisal is associated with depression, whereas threat appraisal is associated with anxiety (Bigatti, Steiner, & Miller, 2012). Therefore, transactional theory helps explain why ostracized employees tend to experience these two negative emotions, as reported by previous research (e.g., depression, DeWall, Gilman, Sharif, Carboni, & Rice, 2012; anxiety, Sebastian, Blakemore, & Charman, 2009). Yet, to the best of our knowledge, no published study has explicitly assessed employees' cognitive appraisal of workplace ostracism. For this reason, the appraisal process linking workplace ostracism to emotional experience has not been fully substantiated.

Transactional theory differs from the temporal need-threat theory in the position of individual differences and situational variations in the transitory emotional impact of workplace ostracism. As we noted, the temporal need-threat theory negates the differences in the emotional experience at the reflexive stage, suggesting that the immediate emotional impact is common to most people. In contrast, transactional theory holds that people appraise workplace ostracism differently, partly due to their individual differences or various contextual factors (Lazarus & Folkman,

1984; Ma, Kerulis, Wang, & Sachdev, 2020). Because of such differences in the appraisal process, the emotional impact of workplace ostracism should differ across employees. For example, employees with excellent social skills should appraise ostracism as less threatening and in turn experience lower levels of anxiety because they are better able to manage interpersonal relations and reduce the uncertainty of future resource loss. Employees may also appraise workplace ostracism as more threatening and in turn experience higher levels of negative emotions in a new, novel work environment where they are unfamiliar with the social system (Robinson et al., 2013).

Unfortunately, what personal and situational factors can moderate the relationship between ostracism and cognitive appraisal have been understudied. Other than speculating, we lack solid empirical evidence to substantiate our assertions. Nonetheless, this should be a good avenue for future research. It will be quite interesting to examine if the emotional impact of ostracism at the reflexive stage (wherein people conduct cognitive appraisals) differs across employees and different situations.

Appraisal Theory of Emotion

As an offspring of transactional theory, appraisal theory of emotion also regards cognitive appraisal as a central determinant of one's emotional experience (Roseman, 2001). But, appraisal theory of emotion offers a more comprehensive description of appraisal content with seven dimensions of appraisal outlined (Roseman, 2001): (1) *unexpectedness* evaluates the extent to which an event is unexpected versus expected; (2) *motive-consistency* evaluates whether an event is motive-consistent or motive-inconsistent; (3) *motivational state* evaluates whether an event is associated with one's motive to avoid something negative (i.e., aversive motive) or with one's motive to gain something positive (i.e., appetitive motive), namely the avoidance versus approach tendencies; (4) *uncertainty* assesses whether the motive-relevant outcomes (i.e., avoid something negative or approach something positive) are definite or just possible; (5) *agency or attribution* appraises the causality of an event as being caused by others or by oneself; (6) *control potential* evaluates the extent to which the event is controllable vs. not controllable; and (7) *problem-type* evaluates whether a motive-inconsistent event is unfavorable on its own right or unwanted because it hinders important goals. We present a summary of these appraisal dimensions in relation to workplace ostracism in Table 4.1.

The more detailed explication of an individual's appraisal makes appraisal theory of emotion more effective than transactional theory in predicting discrete emotions in response to stressful encounters. As for transactional theory, cognitive appraisal evaluates only the implications of a stressful encounter, be it a challenge, a threat, or a harm/loss (Lazarus & Folkman, 1984). However, according to appraisal theory of emotion, an individual also appraises the quality/characteristics of a stressful event (e.g., uncertainty; problem-type; agency), which differentiates emotions more specifically. For instance, under harm/loss appraisals, appraising a stressful encounter as inherently unfavorable is likely to stimulate higher levels of disgust, whereas appraising it as being thwarting to important goals is likely to trigger higher levels of frustration (Roseman, Antoniou, & Jose, 1996). Likewise, under threat appraisals, appraising negative consequences associated with a stressful encounter as possible

Table 4.1 Examples of cognitive appraisals of workplace ostracism

Appraisal Dimension	*Examples of Appraisal of Workplace Ostracism*
Unexpectedness	"Ostracism is common in this organization"
	"I never thought I would be ostracized here"
Motive-consistency	"Ostracism is inconsistent with my motive of seeking social inclusion"
	"I don't want to socialize with anyone in this organization, so being ostracized seems ok for me"
Motivational state	"Ostracism hinders my motive to be included by my coworkers" (i.e., appetitive motive)
	"Ostracism hinder my motive to avoid being ignored by my coworkers" (i.e., aversive motive)
Uncertainty	"It is just possible that I will be ostracized by others"
	"I am sure I will be ostracized by most people here"
Agency	"I am ostracized because of my own problems" (i.e., internal attribution)
	"I am ostracized because of others" (i.e., external attribution)
Control potential	"I am (un)able to manage this situation that I am ostracized by others"
Problem-type	"Ostracism is problematic because it is painful"
	"Ostracism is problematic because I am not able to complete work tasks without collaborating with others"

Note These examples are hypothetical based on Roseman's (2001) summary may provoke higher levels of fear, whereas appraising the consequences as definite tends to stimulate higher levels of sadness (Roseman et al., 1996).

The comprehensiveness of appraisal theory of emotion does not sacrifice the simplicity in predicting emotions, because certain emotions can be provoked by only a few appraisal dimensions comparably salient in a given situation (Roseman, 2001). For example, the ambiguity in the causality of ostracism may prompt individuals to appraise the agency. In this sense, Liu (2019) concluded that depression in response to workplace ostracism was predicted by internal attribution (i.e., blaming oneself for ostracism) rather than external attribution (i.e., blaming others for ostracism). In view of Roseman's (2001) discussion of the hypothesized structure of the emotion system, and extending Liu's (2019) study, we may further predict the relationships of workplace ostracism with following discrete emotions. First, appraising ostracism episode as caused by others along with appraising oneself as having a high level of control potential should stimulate *anger* (Roseman, 2001). On the other hand, if the employee appraises it as being caused by others but oneself as having a low level of control potential, he/she will subsequently experience *dislike* (Roseman, 2001). This prediction is consistent with Roseman et al.'s (1996) findings that appraisal of causation by others evoked both anger and dislike, wherein a high level of control potential was associated with anger and a low level of that was associated with dislike. In addition, if an employee appraises an ostracism episode as caused by oneself and perceives a low level of control potential, this employee will experience *shame/guilt*; with a high level of control potential, the employee may instead experience *regret*. Consistently, Roseman et al. (1996) reported that appraisal of causation by oneself stimulated both shame and regret, with regret associated with a high level of control potential and shame associated with a low level of control potential.

Appraisal theory of emotion is a meaningful addition to temporal need-threat theory and transactional theory in explaining the link between workplace ostracism and emotions. First of all, appraisal theory of emotion is concerned with different aspects and implications of workplace ostracism, not only the need-threat or harm/loss, but also the causality, motivational state of employees, and problem-type. The theory helps us to better comprehend employees' psychological experiences when being ostracized. According to Robinson et al. (2013), workplace ostracism may result in negative emotions for both psychological and pragmatic influences. Yet, current research falls short of integrating both forces but rather treats them separately with some studies exclusively focused on the psychological influence (e.g., Ferris, Lian, Brown, & Morrison, 2015) and others on pragmatic influence (e.g., Kwan et al., 2018). The inclusion of motive-consistency and problem-type can help integrate both influences into one picture and establish a comprehensive theory building (Kwan et al., 2018; Robinson et al., 2013). For instance, the psychological influence can manifest into one's appraisal that workplace ostracism is inconsistent with the motive of social belongingness and is problematic for violating the social norm. On the other hand, the pragmatic influence may manifest into one's appraisal that workplace ostracism is inconsistent with the motive of career success and is problematic for excluding one from task resources and information (Kwan et al., 2018).

Implicit Theories of Relationships

The temporal need-threat theory (Williams, 2009) and COR theory (Hobfoll, 1989, 2001) suggest that workplace ostracism increases global negative emotions, while transactional theory of stress (Lazarus & Folkman, 1984) and appraisal theory of emotions (Roseman, 2001) predict discrete emotions in response to workplace ostracism. In a word, these theories are concerned with the valence of emotions and remain relatively silent in predicting the intensity of emotions. Implicit theories of relationships (Knee, 1998) close this gap. This theory was originally developed to understand people's reactions to romantic relationships and has been used in ostracism literature to explain why individuals differ in the intensity of their reactions to ostracism (Chen, DeWall, Poon, & Chen, 2012). According to this theory, people vary in beliefs about interpersonal relationships and thus respond differently to setbacks arisen from social interactions. *Destiny belief* holders assume interpersonal relationships are meant to be fixed, so that they tend to use information from specific events to determine compatibility of relationship partners (Knee, 1998). In contrast, *growth belief* holders think that relationships can be cultivated and the challenge and obstacles from interactions could be overcome (Knee, Patrick, & Lonsbary, 2003).

The difference in relationship beliefs thus significantly affects the intensity of emotions in response to workplace ostracism. For destiny belief holders, being ostracized indicates that both parties are incompatible, and they are not meant to get along. Therefore, victims who are destiny belief holders should experience higher levels of negative emotions due to the perception that no effort would be effective to alter the situation. On the other hand, growth belief holders may perceive ostracism as malleable and manageable, and therefore, they are more likely to regain quality relationships by proactively tackling the problem. These employees should be less psychologically swamped by the ostracism episodes and instead feel more efficacious to address the issue. Therefore, they tend to experience lower levels of negative emotions. Research has supported this speculation such that in the face of ostracism, the intensity of aggressive affect was significantly lower for growth belief holders than for destiny belief holders (Chen et al., 2012). Since implicit theories of relationships endorse the prominence of one's relationship beliefs (Knee et al., 2003), we may find similar results in studying ostracism at workplace.

Summary and Implications for Future Studies

Although it is easy to empirically establish the link between workplace ostracism and emotions, elucidating possible underlying mechanisms are complex. As we discussed above, the emotional impact of workplace ostracism can be understood from various perspectives with distinct theoretical underpinnings. To advance the knowledge of the emotional impact of workplace ostracism, first, future studies should carefully choose the most relevant theoretical framework to guide hypotheses. Transactional theory of stress and appraisal theory of emotions are preferred to study discrete emotions, while the temporal need-threat and COR theory are helpful to argue for the effect on global emotions. Second, studies should explicitly state whether they study transitory and prolonged emotional responses. However, it can be challenging or even impossible to truly capture the transitory effect in field studies dominated by survey designs. To deal with this issue, research may as well employ a combination of various methods such as experiments and dairy designs that allow for assessing transitory experiences. Finally, individual differences and situational contingencies in the emotional impact of workplace ostracism are an important research question but have been poorly studied so far. This significantly constrains our knowledge of boundary conditions of workplace ostracism-emotion relationships and hinders organizations' ability to develop relevant interventions aimed at altering the emotional impact. Given this, future studies are recommended to extend this knowledge.

The Cognitive Impact of Workplace Ostracism

Workplace ostracism influences employees' cognitive reactions (Lyu & Zhu, 2019). Unlike emotions that deal with employees' internal feelings at work, cognitive reactions are concerned about attitudes, evaluations, and beliefs (Thanacoody, Newman, & Fuchs, 2014). It is imperative to summarize the effect of workplace ostracism on reactive reactions because they are essential element of employee work attitudes and well-being and they can formulate certain behavioral reactions significantly impacting an organization's bottom line (Kouchaki & Wareham, 2015).

Research has examined a set of cognitive reactions in response to workplace ostracism. For instance, scholars have been focusing on the deleterious effect of workplace ostracism on employees' judgment of their self-worth (i.e., self-esteem) (Ferris et al., 2017; Peng & Zeng, 2017) and their psychological identity as a member of an organization (Wu, Liu, Kwan, & Lee, 2016). Additionally, employees' beliefs and attitudes toward their job (e.g., job satisfaction, work commitment, and turnover intention) have also drawn much attention (Chung, & Kim, 2017; Fatima, 2016; Lyu & Zhu, 2019). Interestingly, research has further revealed that workplace ostracism, by threatening the need to belong, can lead to a deconstructed cognitive state undermining self-executive functioning including self-awareness, attentional control, logical reasoning, and self-regulation (Baumeister, DeWall, Ciarocco, & Twenge, 2005; Baumeister et al., 2002; Baumeister & Twenge, 2002; Twenge, Catanese, & Baumeister, 2003). Notably, on top of cognitive malfunctioning outcomes, research also suggests that ostracized individuals might become more socially attentive to fulfill the need to belong (Oaten, Williams, Jones, & Zadro, 2008). In this section, we summarize the theoretical frameworks explaining the aforementioned effects of workplace ostracism. The literature has offered numerous theories; however, we focus on the theories that are most relevant to each category of cognitive outcomes.

Sociometer Theory

According to the sociometer theory (Leary & Baumeister, 2000), individuals have the motive to protect and enhance self-esteem (i.e., a sense of self-worth) because it gauges, measures, and monitors relational evaluation that is highly important to individuals. Relational evaluation indicates the degree to which an individual's relationship with other people is perceived as valuable (Leary & Baumeister, 2000). Temporal need-threat theory (Williams, 2009) also considers a threat to self-esteem, however, it deems self-esteem a basic need rather than a gauge of social inclusion and ostracism. Self-esteem, according to sociometer theory, serves as a sociometer that measures the quality of interpersonal relationships. Social inclusion and acceptance indicate that interpersonal relationships are valued by others, which in turn boosts the level of self-esteem. On the contrary, rejection and ostracism denote that one is not eligible to be valued and cared for by others, which diminishes one's level of self-esteem (Blackhart, Nelson, Knowles & Baumeister, 2009).

According to sociometer theory, self-esteem not only responds to immediate ostracism but also one's potential eligibility for social inclusion in the long run (Leary & Baumeister, 2000). The immediate and long-term gauge systems differentiate self-esteem between state and trait. State self-esteem responds to immediate social inclusion or ostracism, whereas trait self-esteem reflects one's general anticipation of being valued by desired others (Leary & Baumeister, 2000).

Furthermore, sociometer theory proposes the idea of a reference group to differentiate the impact of social inclusion/ostracism from different groups on an individual's self-esteem. Simply put, individuals do not expect to be accepted by everyone, but only the group of people whom they desire to interact with. For this reason, being included/ostracized by the desired group is more influential to self-esteem. Research on workplace ostracism has followed principles of sociometer theory, more or less, in arguing for the effect of workplace ostracism on self-esteem (Ferris et al., 2015). Overall, sociometer theory makes it quite easy for us to comprehend this deleterious impact.

Consistent with the tenets of sociometer theory, research has found that individuals with lower trait self-esteem reported increased social pain when being excluded compared to individuals with higher trait self-esteem (Onoda et al., 2010). Furthermore, a series of experiments found that the lower evaluation of individuals' relational value leads to a decrease in their state self-esteem (Leary, 2005). Additionally, sociometer theory proposes that ostracism threatens self-esteem substantially when the relationship with the source of ostracism is instrumental for accomplishing valuable outcomes (Leary & Baumeister, 2000). As such, workplace ostracism is more threatening to self-esteem when 360-degree feedback is used to evaluate employees' job performance as this type of feedback heightens the value of having a good relationship with coworkers (Peng & Zeng, 2017).

Social Identity Theory

Human beings are bonded together through group memberships (Ashforth & Mael, 1989). Social groups or categories to which an individual belongs are integral to his/her self-concept. An individual can belong to various social groups based on distinct characteristics such as age, gender, race, or occupation. Furthermore, workplace represents a subset of unlimited categories that individuals utilize to determine their self-identity and self-concept. According to social identity theory, individuals fulfill their sense of belongingness by forming groups (Tajfel & Turner, 1979), and they subsequently identify with their groups in an attempt to define why they are in social settings (Tajfel, 1978). Therefore, in addition to defining oneself by one's own attributes (e.g., "I am smart"), an individual is likely to define him/herself as a member of the workplace (e.g., "I work for NASA") and identify with the organization. Employees identify with their organization to fulfill the need for belongingness (Tajfel & Turner, 1979).

Social identity theory explains how workplace ostracism can thwart employees' organizational identification (Tajfel, 1978). Organizational identification refers to an individual's perception of oneness with their organization and hence integrating their organizations as a part of their self-concept (Ashforth & Mael, 1989). Social identity theory suggests that organizational identification is strengthened by perceived similarities between the employee and other members within that organization, a strong sense of belongingness derived from the organization, and respect and appreciation received from the organization (Tajfel, 1978; Wu et al., 2016). Ostracism signals a distance between the ostracized employee and others in the workplace (Wu et al., 2016), thwarts the sense of belongingness (Williams, 2009), and communicates the information that the ostracized employee is not worthy of attention (Robinson et al., 2013). As such, the ostracized employees may cease to identify with their organizations. Wu et al. (2016) explicitly followed this framework and reported the negative relationship between workplace ostracism and organizational identification.

A series of time-lagged studies found that ostracized employees are less likely to attach the organization to their self-concept and in turn, identify less with the organization (Wu et al., 2016). This effect is stronger for employees who have high job mobility and access to alternative employment, because these employees are better able to find alternative organizations to work for. Furthermore, Gkorezis, Panagiotou, and Theodorou (2016) found that ostracized nurses indulge in silence and withhold valuable information and ideas as a result of a decrease in organizational identification. Hence, workplace ostracism is a salient organizational problem triggering the de-identification process, psychologically separating an employee's sense of self from an organization.

Affective Priming Theory and Affective Event Theory (AET)

Affective priming theory argues that an individual's affective states in response to encountered external events precede cognitive analysis of environment (Bower, 1981; Klauer, 1997; Klauer & Musch, 2003; Murphy & Zajonc, 1993). Simply put, this theoretical framework maintains the fundamental premises that affective states and cognitive analysis are often congruent, so that negative feelings toward an object are likely to activate negative evaluations and vice versa. Following this rationale, workplace ostracism, an event provoking negative emotions, tends to activate employees' negative evaluations and attitudes toward their job and workplace and in turn worsens their job satisfaction. Furthermore, affective priming framework proposes that affective states also increase the *speed* of processing "valence-congruent" information, so that a happy individual is faster in processing positive information and a unhappy individual is faster in processing negative information (Klauer & Musch, 2003). Therefore, in the face of workplace ostracism, negative attitudes and evaluations toward one's job are made much faster (e.g., job dissatisfaction), leaving less room for an employee to think of positive aspects of the job which may offset those negative thoughts.

Although affective priming theory is persuasive in explaining why workplace ostracism may trigger negative cognition processes, it is rarely cited in organizational psychology literature. Instead, the literature frequently follows affective event theory (AET; Weiss & Cropanzano, 1996) to elucidate how negative workplace events (e.g., workplace ostracism) worsen work attitudes (e.g., job satisfaction). The theory proposes that workplace events are emotionally provocative. On this basis, affective responses to work events tend to prompt valence-congruent attitudinal states, a notion similar to that of affective priming theory (Weiss & Cropanzano, 1996). Hence, those negative-inducing events are likely to elicit negative affect and in turn undermine job satisfaction (Weiss &

Cropanzano, 1996). Following AET, being ostracized is socially painful, which renders it a negative-inducing affective event. When being ostracized, employees are likely to experience negative affect (e.g., anger, anxiety, or hurt feelings) which occupies their attention to the undesirable experience. This process further presages negative thoughts and judgment about one's job, so that employees' job satisfaction suffers.

Chung and Kim (2017) found ostracism to be negatively related to job satisfaction. Furthermore, such an effect is further transmitted into compromised innovation (Chung & Kim, 2017) and increased counterproductive work behavior (Fatima, 2016). Ostracism results in negative experiences allowing individuals to perceive negative cognitive evaluations and negative affect. On the contrary, when individuals are more satisfied, they are more willing to generate new ideas and methods for solving problems. Consequently, job satisfaction mediates the relationship between workplace ostracism and innovative behavior (Chung & Kim, 2017). As such, these findings are consistent with the tenets of affective events theory as negative experiences at work can decrease job satisfaction, which in turn influences cognitive-based behaviors such as innovative behaviors.

Job Embeddedness Theory

Workplace ostracism has been found to decrease organizational commitment and increase turnover intentions (Lyu & Zhu, 2019). Job embeddedness theory is one of the most influential frameworks for understanding why employees become less committed to their organization and eventually quit their job. Job embeddedness theory states that an employee's surroundings and other perceptual factors have a significant influence on the extent to which he or she is embedded in or attached to a job (Halvorsen, Treuren, & Kulik, 2015; Mitchell, Holtom, Lee, Sablynski, & Erez, 2001). Specifically, job embeddedness refers to the extent to which employees are enmeshed in their organization, which is influenced by *links*, *fit*, and *sacrifice* (Mitchell et al., 2001). *Links* indicate the associations between employees and their organization. Being included strengthens the link and gives employees a sense that he/she is closely tied to the organization and other members. However, the perception of ostracism may result in feelings of indifference and apartness (Ferris et al., 2008), hence, weakening the perceived links. *Fit* refers to the employees' compatibility with their surroundings. Social inclusion represents the compatibility between an employee and his/her work environment. In contrast, being ostracized elicits a sense of mismatch and incompatibility with the current work environment (Robinson et al., 2013; Ferris et al., 2015). Finally, *sacrifice* characterizes the potential cost of leaving the job. Leaving an organization with harmonious interpersonal relationships bears a high cost. However, leaving an organization where an employee experiences ostracism bears a much lower cost just because ostracism is such a painful experience that lowers the personal value of the organization (Wu et al., 2012).

When employees are less enmeshed in the organization, they become less committed to their organization and more likely to leave the organization (Mitchell et al., 2001). Researchers have found that workplace ostracism reduced employees' affective commitment and intensified their intention to quit their job (Ferris et al., 2008; Lyu & Zhu, 2019; Ng, 2017; Renn, Allen, & Huning, 2013). After being ostracized, employees will perceive a weak connection with their organization and a reduced cost of leaving. Consistent with the job embeddedness theory, Lyu and Zhu (2019) found negative relationships of workplace ostracism with turnover intention and affective commitment. Using a multi-wave research design, the researchers found that workplace ostracism had a negative effect on employees' job embeddedness, which in turn weakened their affective commitment and induced their turnover intentions. Moreover, Zhang et al. (2019) explicitly assessed job embeddedness among employees and demonstrated the entire chain effect linking workplace ostracism to reduced job embeddedness and then to voluntary turnover. Meta-analysis also reported a positive relationship between workplace ostracism and turnover intention, and negative relationships of workplace ostracism with job satisfaction and work commitment (Howard et al., 2020).

Need to Belong Hypothesis and Executive Functioning

Need to belong hypothesis suggests that need to belong is a fundamental need of human being that sustains social cognition (Baumeister et al., 2002, 2005). On this basis, ostracism, by thwarting one's need to belong, impairs higher-levels cognitive processes such as executive functioning in general or self-regulation in particular (e.g., Bauimester, 1990; Baumeister & Twenge, 2002; Baumeister et al., 2002, 2005; Twenge et al., 2003). Executive functioning is a broad term covering a set of cognitive processes including attention, planning, inhibition, self-regulation, mental monitoring, and working memory (Bradford, Jentzsch, & Gomez, 2015; Goldstein, Naglieri, Princoptta, & Otero, 2014). Need to belong is the ground for the operation of executive functioning, because executive functioning is intertwined with social cognition embedded in social interaction. Baumeister et al. (2002) proposed more detailed reasons for this effect. First, unsatisfied need to belong associated with ostracism triggers emotional distress, and suppression of emotional distress interferes one's cognition system and depletes resources for executive functioning. Additionally, individuals being ostracized are prone to ruminate over the ostracism episodes, which intensifies the attentional load and hinders other important executive activities requiring attention (Baumeister et al., 2002). All in all, workplace ostracism can negatively impact executive functioning and associated cognitive processes, reducing effectiveness in self-regulation, judgment, and reasoning.

These notions are supported by empirical evidence showing that ostracism significantly impaired controlled forms of executive functioning (e.g., thinking, reasoning, and analyzing) that require a substantial amount of executive resources (Baumeister et al., 2002; Lezak, Howieson, & Loring, 2004). Furthermore, Baumeister's (1990) propositions and associated empirical findings (Baumeister & Twenge, 2002; Twenge et al., 2003) also conclude that ostracism prompts individuals to enter the cognitive deconstructive states characterized by less meaningful thought, lethargy, withdraw from self-awareness, and even lack of emotion. Similarly, research also shows that ostracism can substantially impair an individual's capacity to self-regulate his or her responses and produce socially desirable behavior (Baumeister et al., 2005). Then, ostracism was found to impair working memory, decision making, task persistence (but not basic attention) (Buelow, Okdie, Brunell, & Trost, 2015) and increase in riskier decision making (Buelow & Wirth, 2017). Hence, deprivation of the basic need to belong can lead to severe impact on higher levels of cognitive processes.

Social Reconnection Hypothesis

While other theories focus on explaining how negative experiences of ostracism leads to employees' tendency to dismiss oneself from others and the organization, social reconnection hypothesis claims that ostracism can lead to an individual's desire to seek sources of renewed affiliation (Maner,

DeWall, Baumeister, & Schaller, 2007). Excluded individuals may feel a strong desire to form bonds with others and satisfy their drive to belong. The experience of social exclusion increases the motivation to forge social bonds with new sources of potential affiliation (Baumeister & Leary, 1995). Although this hypothesis suggests a potential social reconnection due to exclusion, it is important to note the possible boundary conditions that could restrict the implications (Maner et al., 2007). For instance, excluded individuals are expected to look for new potential pleasant social contacts and avoid the previous perpetrators. Further, the tendencies to evaluate the new connections as a realistic source of positive social connection vary between individuals. For instance, fearful people, in general, will be more hesitant to form new connections (Maddux, Norton, & Leary, 1988) and may not evaluate the new connections a realistic source for positive connection.

Research in general has found that individuals who face social rejection respond prosocially by becoming more socially attentive (Pickett, Gardner, & Knowles, 2004), being compliant or altruistic (Carter-Sowell, Chen, & Williams, 2008; DeWall, Baumeister, Stillman, & Gailliot, 2007), or working harder on group task (Williams & Sommer, 1997). The workplace ostracism literature, however, has not paid adequate attention to this theory. It is highly likely that being ostracized at work should prompt employees to value their family relationships to a higher extent. Future research is recommended to uncover related questions.

Summary and Implications for Future Studies

The cognitive impact of workplace ostracism takes many forms, which entails various theoretical frameworks to understand each of them. The theories we summarized in this section are only a part of plausible frameworks. Other theories can complement what we discussed here. For example, the stress-as-offense-to-self (SOS) model (Semmer, Jacobshagen, Meier, & Elfering, 2007) also argues that workplace ostracism is a stressor that threatens self-esteem. Additionally, identity theory that focuses on one's social roles argues that workplace ostracism may threaten role-based identities including job identity and group identity (Burke & Stets, 2009; Welbourne & Paterson, 2017). Therefore, various identities other than organizational identification can be introduced into workplace ostracism research for an expanded investigation.

Cognitive reactions are an important process linking workplace ostracism to distal outcomes such as work behaviors. However, other than a few exceptions (e.g., Wu et al., 2016), most research only focused on a single cognitive variable in studying how workplace ostracism affects distal outcomes via this process. We deem it necessary for future studies to test competing mechanisms that involve multiple types of cognitive variables in one model. For example, perhaps workplace ostracism affects task performance primarily through job identity and affects organizational citizenship behavior primarily through organizational identity. It is also interesting to compare the effects between multiple cognitive variables and sort out the most influential mechanism for a given distal outcome. On the other hand, cognitive process measures lead to a risk of contaminating behavioral data (Warburton, Williams, & Cairns, 2006); hence, future research may also focus on including indirect measures of cognition to replicate existing findings.

Physiological Outcomes

The effect of workplace ostracism can further manifest into an employee's physiological responses, such as heart rate, blood pressure, cardiac activities. (Tomaka, Blascovich, Kibler, & Ernst, 1997). By capturing one's subtle, physical reactions, studying physiological outcomes could supplement the psychological responses (e.g., emotions and cognitions) in elaborating an individual's experiences of workplace ostracism. These are considered to be the strongest mechanism through which perceptions of exclusion impacts behavior because they are less likely to be within an individual's control (Kouchaki & Wareham, 2015).

Research has shown that emotional distress elicited by ostracism is related to enhanced activation of the limbic system (Eisenberger, 2012; Kross, Berman, Mischel, Smith, & Wagner, 2011), which results in increased sympathetic arousal of the autonomic nervous system (Cavanagh & Allen, 2009). Studies utilizing sophisticated measures such as functional magnetic resonance imaging have shown that the same brain structures activated during physical pain were activated after an individual experienced social rejection (Eisenberger, Lieberman, & Williams, 2003; MacDonald & Leary, 2005). These findings suggest that ostracism causes a sense of "social pain." Other studies have shown that ostracized individuals have greater levels of salivary cortisol—a biomarker of increased physiological arousal and stress reactivity to negative emotion—following a period of exclusion (Blackhart et al., 2007; Stroud, Tanofsky-Kraff, Wilfley, & Salovey, 2000).

An experimental study of social exclusion has shown an increase in heart rate (Williamson, Thomas, Eisenberger, & Stanton, 2018). Kouchaki and Wareham (2015) conducted two studies to reveal the physiological impact of social exclusion and how it further translates into unethical behaviors. The first experimental study showed that participants who were socially excluded were more likely to engage in unethical behavior to make money playing cyberball than participants who were in the inclusion condition. The level of physiological arousal experienced during exclusion—indicated by galvanic skin response—intervened the effects of exclusion on unethical behavior. The following survey study consisting of a sample of supervisor-subordinate dyads revealed a positive relationship between the experience of workplace ostracism and unethical behaviors as rated by the immediate supervisors. This relationship was again mediated by employees' reports of experienced physiological arousal (Kouchaki & Wareham, 2015).

Another study utilized Yale Interpersonal Stressor (YIPS), which is a live interpersonal interaction stressor that involves one or two interactions with two same-sex confederates who actively exclude participants using non-verbal and verbal cues, to examine the effects of rejection. Interpersonal rejection leads to an increase in blood pressure and cortisol levels (Stroud et al., 2000). The increase in blood pressure due to YIPS was similar in males and females; however, the cortisol level increase was significantly higher in females. Physiological responses are immediate underlying outcomes that could explain the behavioral consequences that follow in response to ostracism.

It is commonly held that ostracism arouses physiological responses because it is a social pain that stems from a threat to social belongingness. Many theories emphasize the importance of social belongingness for physical health and well-being (e.g., the belongingness hypothesis, Baumeister & Leary, 1995). Temporal need-threat theory states the social pain hypothesis and maintains that reflexive responses to workplace ostracism include physiological reactions (Williams, 1997, 2007). In this theory, the threat to the basic needs: self-esteem, control, belongingness, and meaningful existence, leads to immediate pervasive negative reaction to ostracism that arouse one's physiological responses to prepare for subsequent coping. As such, it is important to examine how certain physiological responses prime certain emotional, cognitive, and behavioral reactions. However, other than temporal need-threat theory, to the best of our knowledge, there is no solid framework to exclusively explain and predict physiological responses to ostracism. We expect more theories can gain a foothold in this area in the near future.

Summary and Implications for Future Studies

So far, the physiological impact of workplace ostracism has not received sufficient research attention. Researchers should leverage the advances in technology and utilize multiple physiological measures such as electroencephalogram, electromyography, and so on to gather more objective and nuanced understanding of employees' physiological and neural states elicited as a result of ostracism. Utilizing multiple methods and sources to understand the impact of ostracism will not only provide uncontaminated results but will also address the concerns of common method bias (Podsakoff, MacKenzie, & Podsakoff, 2003). The theoretical underpinnings are centered around the reflexive stage of ostracism. Yet, we believe the study of physiological impact could also help us validate the basic assumptions of other theories we have discussed in this chapter. For example, it will be interesting to examine physiological reactions and cognitive reactions together, so that we can understand how physiological responses prompt certain cognitive activities.

Conclusion

Organizations tend to underestimate the effects of workplace ostracism because it is an act of omission rather than commission (O'Reilly, Robinson, Berdahl, & Banki, 2015). The review of the existing literature, although not comprehensive, emphasizes the need to focus on this issue. Emotional outcomes, cognitive processes, and physiological reactions to ostracism are not only important consequences of ostracism; they are also important determinants of negative behavioral consequences (e.g., unethical behavior) in organizations (Warburton et al., 2006; Kouchaki & Wareham, 2015). Hence, it is extremely important to understand these consequences. We demonstrated empirical findings showing the deleterious impact of workplace ostracism on emotional, cognitive, and physiological outcomes in an attempt to remind organizations and employees that "silence still hurts."

We also discussed the theoretical frameworks that can parsimoniously explain these outcomes of workplace ostracism. Some of the theories (e.g., temporal need-threat theory) have been widely used in research (Williams, 2009), whereas some (e.g., appraisal theory of emotions) have not. The review of the existing literature indicates the plethora of research conducted to examine ostracism. However, more research needs to be done to gauge the complexity of this phenomenon. We hope that researchers will use the theories and review of the past studies in this chapter as a guideline to understand the emotional, cognitive, and physiological responses to ostracism. We are eager to see new methods and theoretical reasoning to explain the effect of workplace ostracism. Additionally, more research needs to be conducted using the framework discussed in this chapter to extend knowledge of boundary conditions for the effect of workplace ostracism, so that we will have a better knowledge about when ostracism could be more or less harmful.

References

Abubakar, A. M., Yazdian, T. F., & Behravesh, E. (2018). A riposte to ostracism and tolerance to workplace incivility: A generational perspective. *Personnel Review, 47,* 441–457.

Ashforth, B. E., & Mael, F. (1989). Social identity theory and the organization. *Academy of Management Review, 14,* 20–39.

Barrett, L. F. (1998). Discrete emotions or dimensions? The role of valence focus and arousal focus. *Cognition and Emotion, 12,* 579–599.

Barrett, L. F., & Russell, J. A. (1999). The structure of current affect: Controversies and emerging consensus. *Current Directions in Psychological Science, 8,* 10–14.

Baumeister (1990). Suicide as escape from self. *Psychological Review, 97,* 90–113.

Baumeister, R. F., DeWall, C. N., Ciarocco, N. J., & Twenge, J. M. (2005). Social exclusion impairs self-regulation. *Journal of Personality and Social Psychology, 88,* 589–604.

Baumeister, R. F., & Leary, M. R. (1995). The need to belong: Desire for interpersonal attachments as a fundamental human motivation. *Psychological Bulletin, 117,* 497–529.

Baumeister, R. F., Twenge, J. M., & Nuss, C. K. (2002). Effects of social exclusion on cognitive processes: Anticipated aloneness reduces intelligent thought. *Journal of Personality and Social Psychology, 83,* 817–827.

Bigatti, S. M., Steiner, J. L., & Miller, K. D. (2012). Cognitive appraisals, coping and depressive symptoms in breast cancer patients. *Stress and Health, 28,* 355–361.

Blackhart, G. C., Eckel, L. A., & Tice, D. M. (2007). Salivary cortisol in response to acute social rejection and acceptance by peers. *Biological Psychology, 75*, 267–276.

Blackhart, G. C., Nelson, B. C., Knowles, M. L., & Baumeister, R. F. (2009). Rejection elicits emotional reactions but neither causes immediate distress nor lowers self-esteem: A meta-analytic review of 192 studies on social exclusion. *Personality and Social Psychology Review, 13*, 269–309.

Bower, G. H. (1981). Mood and memory. *American Psychologist, 36*, 129–148.

Bradford, E. E., Jentzsch, I., & Gomez, J. C. (2015). From self to social cognition: Theory of mind mechanisms and their relation to executive functioning. *Cognition, 138*, 21–34.

Bradley, M. M., Greenwald, M. K., Petry, M. C., & Lang, P. J. (1992). Remembering pictures: Pleasure and arousal in memory. *Journal of Experimental Psychology. Learning, Memory, and Cognition, 18*, 379–390.

Buelow, M. T., & Wirth, J. H. (2017). Decisions in the face of known risks: Ostracism increases risky decision-making. *Journal of Experimental Social Psychology, 69*, 210–217.

Buelow, M. T., Okdie, B. M., Brunell, A. B., & Trost, Z. (2015). Stuck in a moment and you cannot get out of it: The lingering effects of ostracism on cognition and satisfaction of basic needs. *Personality and Individual Differences, 76*, 39–43.

Burke, P., & Stets, J. (2009). *Identity theory*. New York, NY: Oxford University Press.

Carter-Sowell, A. R., Chen, Z., & Williams, K. D. (2008). Ostracism increases social susceptibility. *Social Influence, 3*, 143–153.

Cavanagh, J. F., & Allen, J. B. (2009). The behavioral activation system. In D. Sander & K. R. Scherer (Eds.), *Oxford companion to affective sciences* (pp. 72–73). Oxford, United Kingdom: Oxford University Press.

Chen, Z., DeWall, C. N., Poon, K. T., & Chen, E. W. (2012). When destiny hurts: Implicit theories of relationships moderate aggressive responses to ostracism. *Journal of Experimental Social Psychology, 48*, 1029–1036.

Chung, Y. W. (2018). Workplace ostracism and workplace behaviors: A moderated mediation model of perceived stress and psychological empowerment. *Anxiety Stress and Coping, 31*, 304–317.

Chung, Y. W., & Kim, T. (2017). Impact of using social network services on workplace ostracism, job satisfaction, and innovative behaviour. *Behaviour & Information Technology, 36*, 1235–1243.

DeWall, C. N., Baumeister, R. F., Stillman, T. F., & Gailliot, M. T. (2007). Violence restrained: Effects of self-regulation and its depletion on aggression. *Journal of Experimental Social Psychology, 43*, 62–76.

DeWall, C. N., Gilman, R., Sharif, V., Carboni, I., & Rice, K. G. (2012). Left out, sluggardly, and blue: Low self-control mediates the relationship between ostracism and depression. *Personality and Individual Differences, 53*, 832–837.

Dotan-Eliaz, O., Sommer, K. L., & Rubin, Y. S. (2009). Multilingual groups: Effects of linguistic ostracism on felt rejection and anger, coworker attraction, perceived team potency, and creative performance. *Basic and Applied Social Psychology, 31*, 363–375.

Eisenberger, N. I. (2012). The pain of social disconnection: Examining the shared neural underpinnings of physical and social pain. *Nature Reviews Neuroscience, 13*, 421–434.

Eisenberger, N. I., Lieberman, M. D., & Williams, K. D. (2003). Does rejection hurt? An fMRI study of social exclusion. *Science, 302*, 290–292.

Fatima, A. (2016). Impact of workplace ostracism on counter productive work behaviors: Mediating role of job satisfaction. *Abasyn University Journal of Social Sciences, 9*, 388–408.

Ferris, D. L., Brown, D. J., Berry, J. W., & Lian, H. (2008). The development and validation of the Workplace Ostracism Scale. *Journal of Applied Psychology, 93*, 1348–1366.

Ferris, D. L., Chen, M., & Lim, S. (2017). Comparing and contrasting workplace ostracism and incivility. *Annual Review of Organizational Psychology and Organizational Behavior, 4*, 315–338.

Ferris, D. L., Lian, H., Brown, D. J., & Morrison, R. (2015). Ostracism, self-esteem, and job performance: When do we self-verify and when do we self-enhance? *Academy of Management Journal, 58*, 279–297.

Ferris, D. L., Yan, M., Lim, V. K., Chen, Y., & Fatimah, S. (2016). An approach–avoidance framework of workplace aggression. *Academy of Management Journal, 59*, 1777–1800.

Gil, S., & Droit-Volet, S. (2012). Emotional time distortions: The fundamental role of arousal. *Cognition and Emotion, 26*, 847–862.

Gkorezis, P., Panagiotou, M., & Theodorou, M. (2016). Workplace ostracism and employee silence in nursing: The mediating role of organizational identification. *Journal of Advanced Nursing, 72*, 2381–2388.

Goldstein, S., Naglieri, J. A., Princoptta, D., & Otero, T. M. (2014). Introduction: A history of executive functioning as a theoretical and clinical construct. In S. Goldstein & J. A. Naglieri (Eds.), *Handbook of executive functioning* (pp. 3–13). New York, NY: Springer.

Halvorsen, B., Treuren, G. J. M., & Kulik, C. T. (2015). Job embeddedness among migrants: Fit and links without sacrifice. *International Journal of Human Resource Management, 26*, 1298–1317.

Hobfoll, S. E. (1989). Conservation of resources: A new attempt at conceptualizing stress. *American Psychologist, 44*, 513–524.

Hobfoll, S. E. (2001). The influence of culture, community, and the nested-self in the stress process: Advancing conservation of resources theory. *Applied Psychology, 50,* 337–421.

Hobfoll, S. E. (2002). Social and psychological resources and adaptation. *Review of General Psychology, 6,* 307–324.

Howard, M. C., Cogswell, J. E., & Smith, M. B. (2020). The antecedents and outcomes of workplace ostracism: A meta-analysis. *Journal of Applied Psychology, 105,* 577–596.

Jahanzeb, S., & Fatima, T. (2018). How workplace ostracism influences interpersonal deviance: The mediating role of defensive silence and emotional exhaustion. *Journal of Business and Psychology, 33,* 779–791.

Jahanzeb, S., Fatima, T., & Malik, M. A. R. (2018). Supervisor ostracism and defensive silence: A differential needs approach. *European Journal of Work and Organizational Psychology, 27,* 430–440.

Klauer, K. C. (1997). Affective priming. *European Review of Social Psychology, 8,* 67–103.

Klauer, K. C., & Musch, J. (2003). Affective priming: Findings and theories. In J. Musch & K. C. Klauer (Eds.), *The psychology of evaluation: Affective processes in cognition and emotion* (pp. 7–50). Mahwah, NJ: Erlbaum.

Knee, C. R. (1998). Implicit theories of relationships: Assessment and prediction of romantic relationship initiation, coping, and longevity. *Journal of Personality and Social Psychology, 74,* 360–370.

Knee, C. R., Patrick, H., & Lonsbary, C. (2003). Implicit theories of relationships: Orientations toward evaluation and cultivation. *Personality and Social Psychology Review, 7,* 41–55.

Kouchaki, M., & Wareham, J. (2015). Excluded and behaving unethically: Social exclusion, physiological responses, and unethical behavior. *Journal of Applied Psychology, 100,* 547–556.

Kross, E., Berman, M. G., Mischel, W., Smith, E. E., & Wager, T. D. (2011). Social rejection shares somatosensory representations with physical pain. *PNAS: Proceedings of National Academy of Sciences of the United States of America, 108,* 6270–6275.

Kwan, H. K., Zhang, X., Liu, J., & Lee, C. (2018). Workplace ostracism and employee creativity: An integrative approach incorporating pragmatic and engagement roles. *Journal of Applied Psychology, 103,* 1358–1366.

Lazarus, R. S., & Folkman, S. (1984). *Stress, appraisal, and coping.* New York, NY: Springer.

Leary, M. R. (2005). Sociometer theory and the pursuit of relational value: Getting to the root of self-esteem. *European Review of Social Psychology, 16,* 75–111.

Leary, M. R., & Baumeister, R. F. (2000). The nature and function of self-esteem: Sociometer theory. In *Advances in experimental social psychology* (Vol. 32, pp. 1–62). San Diego, CA: Academic Press.

Leary, M. R., Haupt, A. L., Strausser, K. S., & Chokel, J. T. (1998). Calibrating the sociometer: The relationship between interpersonal appraisals and state self-esteem. *Journal of Personality and Social Psychology, 74,* 1290–1299.

Lezak, M. D., Howieson, D. B., & Loring, D. W. (2004). *Neuropsychological assessment* (4th ed.). Oxford: Oxford University Press.

Liu, C. (2019). Ostracism, attributions, and their relationships with international students' and employees' outcomes: The moderating effect of perceived harming intent. *Journal of Occupational Health Psychology, 24,* 556–571.

Lyu, Y., & Zhu, H. (2019). The predictive effects of workplace ostracism on employee attitudes: A job embeddedness perspective. *Journal of Business Ethics, 158,* 1083–1095.

Ma, J. Y., Kerulis, A. M., Wang, Y., & Sachdev, A. R. (2020). Are workflow interruptions a hindrance stressor? The moderating effect of time-management skill. *International Journal of Stress Management, 27,* 252–261.

MacDonald, G., & Leary, M. R. (2005). Why does social exclusion hurt? The relationship between social and physical pain. *Psychological Bulletin, 131,* 202–223.

Maddux, J. E., Norton, L. W., & Leary, M. R. (1988). Cognitive components of social anxiety: An investigation of the integration of self-presentation theory and self-efficacy theory. *Journal of Social and Clinical Psychology, 6,* 180–190.

Maner, J. K., DeWall, C. N., Baumeister, R. F., & Schaller, M. (2007). Does social exclusion motivate interpersonal reconnection? Resolving the 'porcupine problem'. *Journal of Personality and Social Psychology, 92,* 42–55.

Mitchell, T. R., Holtom, B. C., Lee, T. W., Sablynski, C. J., & Erez, M. (2001). Why people stay: Using job embeddedness to predict voluntary turnover. *Academy of Management Journal, 44,* 1102–1121.

Murphy, S. T., & Zajonc, R. B. (1993). Affect, cognition, and awareness: Affective priming with optimal and suboptimal stimulus exposures. *Journal of Personality and Social Psychology, 64,* 723–739.

Ng, T. W. (2017). Can idiosyncratic deals promote perceptions of competitive climate, felt ostracism, and turnover?. *Journal of Vocational Behavior, 99,* 118–131.

O'Reilly, J., Robinson, S. L., Berdahl, J. L., & Banki, S. (2015). Is negative attention better than no attention? The comparative effects of ostracism and harassment at work. *Organization Science, 26,* 774–793.

Oaten, M., Williams, K. D., Jones, A., & Zadro, L. (2008). The effects of ostracism on self-regulation in the socially anxious. *Journal of Social and Clinical Psychology, 27,* 471–504.

Onoda, K., Okamoto, Y., Nakashima, K. I., Nittono, H., Yoshimura, S., Yamawaki, S., ... & Ura, M. (2010). Does low self-esteem enhance social pain? The relationship between trait self-esteem and anterior cingulate cortex activation induced by ostracism. *Social Cognitive and Affective Neuroscience, 5*, 385–391.

Peng, A. C., & Zeng, W. (2017). Workplace ostracism and deviant and helping behaviors: The moderating role of 360 degree feedback. *Journal of Organizational Behavior, 38*, 833–855.

Pickett, C. L., Gardner, W. L., & Knowles, M. (2004). Getting a cue: The need to belong and enhanced sensitivity to social cues. *Personality and Social Psychology Bulletin, 30*, 1095–1107.

Podsakoff, P. M., MacKenzie, S. B., Lee, J. Y., & Podsakoff, N. P. (2003). Common method biases in behavioral research: A critical review of the literature and recommended remedies. *Journal of Applied Psychology, 88*, 879–903.

Qian, J., Yang, F., Wang, B., Huang, C., & Song, B. (2019). When workplace ostracism leads to burnout: The roles of job self-determination and future time orientation. *The International Journal of Human Resource Management, 30*, 2465–2481.

Remington, N. A., Fabrigar, L. R., & Visser, P. S. (2000). Reexamining the circumplex model of affect. *Journal of Personality and Social Psychology, 79*, 286–300.

Renn, R., Allen, D., & Huning, T. (2013). The relationship of social exclusion at work with self-defeating behavior and turnover. *The Journal of Social Psychology, 153*, 229–249.

Robinson, S. L., O'Reilly, J., & Wang, W. (2013). Invisible at work an integrated model of workplace ostracism. *Journal of Management, 39*, 203–231.

Roseman, I. J. (2001). A model of appraisal in the emotion system. In *Appraisal processes in emotion: Theory, methods, research*, 68–91. New York, NY: Oxford University Press.

Roseman, I. J., Antoniou, A. A., & Jose, P. E. (1996). Appraisal determinants of emotions: Constructing a more accurate and comprehensive theory. *Cognition and Emotion, 10*, 241–277.

Sebastian, C., Blakemore, S. J., & Charman, T. (2009). Reactions to ostracism in adolescents with autism spectrum conditions. *Journal of Autism and Developmental Disorders, 39*, 1122–1130.

Semmer, N., Jacobshagen, N., Meier, L., & Elfering, A. (2007). Occupational stress research: The "stress-as-offense-to-self" perspective. In J. Houdmont & S. McIntyre (Eds.), *Occupational health psychology: European perspectives on research, education and practice* (Vol. 2, pp. 43–60). Castelo da Maia, Portugal: ISMAI Publishing.

Smith, A., & Williams, K. D. (2004). R U there? Ostracism by cell phone text messages. *Group Dynamics: Theory, Research, and Practice, 8*, 291–301.

Stroud, L. R., Tanofsky-Kraff, M., Wilfley, D. E., & Salovey, P. (2000). The Yale Interpersonal Stressor (YIPS): Affective, physiological, and behavioral responses to a novel interpersonal rejection paradigm. *Annals of Behavioral Medicine, 22,* 204–213.

Tajfel, H. (1978). Social categorization, social identity, and social comparison. In H. Tajfel (Ed.), *Differentiation between social groups: Studies in the social psychology of intergroup relations* (pp. 61–76). London: Academic Press.

Tajfel, H., & Turner, J. (1979). An integrative theory of intergroup conflict. In W. G. Austin & S. Worchel (Eds.), *The Social Psychology of Intergroup Relations* (pp. 33–47). Pacific Grove, CA: Brooks/Cole.

Thanacoody, P. R., Newman, A., & Fuchs, S. (2014). Affective commitment and turnover intentions among healthcare professionals: The role of emotional exhaustion and disengagement. *International Journal of Human Resource Management, 25,* 1841–1857.

Tomaka, J., Blascovich, J., Kibler, J., & Ernst, J. M. (1997). Cognitive and physiological antecedents of threat and challenge appraisal. *Journal of Personality and Social Psychology, 73,* 63–72.

Twenge, J. M., Catanese, K. R., & Baumeister, R. F. (2003). Social exclusion and the deconstructed state: Time perception, meaninglessness, lethargy, lack of emotion, and self-awareness. *Journal of Personality and Social Psychology, 85,* 409–423.

Van Beest, I., & Williams, K. D. (2006). When inclusion costs and ostracism pays, ostracism still hurts. *Journal of Personality and Social Psychology, 91,* 918–928.

Warburton, W. A., Williams, K. D., & Cairns, D. R. (2006). When ostracism leads to aggression: The moderating effects of control deprivation. *Journal of Experimental Social Psychology, 42,* 213–220.

Weiss, H. M., & Cropanzano, R. (1996). Affective events theory: A theoretical discussion of the structure, causes and consequences of affective experiences at work. *Research in Organizational Behavior, 18,* 1–74.

Welbourne, T. M., & Paterson, T. A. (2017). Advancing a richer view of identity at work: The role-based identity scale. *Personnel Psychology, 70,* 315–356.

Williams, K. D. (1997). Social ostracism. In R. M. Kowalski (Ed.), *Aversive interpersonal behaviors* (pp. 133–170). New York, NY: Plenum.

Williams, K. D. (2007). *Ostracism. Annual Review of Psychology, 58,* 425–452.

Williams, K. D. (2009). Ostracism: A temporal need-threat model. *Advances in Experimental Social Psychology, 41,* 275–314.

Williams, K. D., & Nida, S. A. (2011). Ostracism: Consequences and coping. *Current Directions in Psychological Science, 20,* 71–75.

Williams, K. D., & Sommer, K. L. (1997). Social ostracism by one's coworkers: Does rejection lead to loafing or compensation? *Personality and Social Psychology Bulletin, 23,* 693–706.

Williamson, T. J., Thomas, K. S., Eisenberger, N. I., & Stanton, A. L. (2018). Effects of social exclusion on cardiovascular and affective reactivity to a socially evaluative stressor. *International Journal of Behavioral Medicine, 25,* 410–420.

Wu, C. H., Liu, J., Kwan, H. K., & Lee, C. (2016). Why and when workplace ostracism inhibits organizational citizenship behaviors: An organizational identification perspective. *Journal of Applied Psychology, 101,* 362–378.

Wu, L., Wei, L., & Hui, C. (2011). Dispositional antecedents and consequences of workplace ostracism: An empirical examination. *Frontiers of Business Research in China, 5,* 23–44.

Wu, L. Z., Yim, F. H. K., Kwan, H. K., & Zhang, X. (2012). Coping with workplace ostracism: The roles of ingratiation and political skill in employee psychological distress. *Journal of Management Studies, 49,* 178–199.

Zadro, L., Boland, C., & Richardson, R. (2006). How long does it last? The persistence of the effects of ostracism in the socially anxious. *Journal of Experimental Social Psychology, 42,* 692–697.

Zhang, S., & Shi, Q. (2017). The relationship between subjective well-being and workplace ostracism. *Journal of Organizational Change Management, 30,* 978–988.

Zhang, L., Fan, C., Deng, Y., Lam, C. F., Hu, E., & Wang, L. (2019). Exploring the interpersonal determinants of job embeddedness and voluntary turnover: A conservation of resources perspective. *Human Resource Management Journal, 29,* 413–432.

Zhu, H., Lyu, Y., Deng, X., & Ye, Y. (2017). Workplace ostracism and proactive customer service performance: A conservation of resources perspective. *International Journal of Hospitality Management, 64,* 62–72.

CHAPTER 5

Workplace Ostracism and Employee Prosocial and Antisocial Organizational Behaviors

Zhiqing E. Zhou, Xinxuan Che, and Nicolette A. Rainone

As a specific type of workplace mistreatment and workplace incivility (Ferris, Chen, & Lim, 2017; Howard, Cogswell, & Smith, 2020), workplace ostracism has gained increasing research attention given its potential negative effects on employees. For example, in a recent meta-analysis, Howard et al. (2020) found that workplace ostracism has strong negative relationships with employee well-being outcomes, organizational perceptions such as job satisfaction and justice, and performance outcomes (i.e., in-role performance, deviance, helping, and voice). These findings call for more in-depth reviews of the existing literature and directions for future research. In this chapter, we will focus on employees' behavioral reactions to workplace ostracism that fall into the categories of prosocial organizational behaviors (Brief & Motowidlo, 1986) and antisocial organizational behaviors (Greenberg & Giacalone, 1997).

Z. E. Zhou (✉) · N. A. Rainone
Baruch College and The Graduate Center, CUNY, New York, NY, USA
e-mail: Zhiqing.Zhou@baruch.cuny.edu

X. Che
Florida Institute of Technology, Melbourne, FL, USA

C. Liu and J. Ma (eds.), *Workplace Ostracism*,
Palgrave Explorations in Workplace Stigma,
https://doi.org/10.1007/978-3-030-54379-2_5

This chapter's structure is as follows: We will first briefly introduce the concepts of workplace ostracism adopted in this chapter (for a detailed discussion on its origin, theory, and definitions, as well as the comparison between workplace ostracism and similar workplace mistreatment constructs, see Chapters 1 and 2, respectively), prosocial organizational behaviors, and antisocial organizational behaviors. Second, we will discuss some of the main theoretical frameworks that have been employed in the existing literature to explain the relationship between workplace ostracism and prosocial organizational behaviors, and review the existing findings for the main effects, mediators, and moderators. We will follow the same structure for antisocial organizational behaviors. Finally, we will discuss potential directions for future studies in this line of research.

Introduction to Workplace Ostracism

There are two main approaches to define workplace ostracism. Ferris, Brown, Berry, and Lian (2008) defined workplace ostracism as "the extent to which an individual perceives that he or she is ignored or excluded by others at work" (p. 1348), while Robinson, O'Reilly, and Wang (2013) defined workplace ostracism as "when an individual or group omits to take actions that engage another organizational member when it is socially acceptable to do so" (p. 206). These two definitions suggest that workplace ostracism can be studied as actions (being excluded by someone) or lack of actions (failing to include someone) and can be examined as victims' perceptions or perpetrators' behaviors (Howard et al., 2020). As suggested by Howard et al. (2020), employees' reactions to workplace ostracism are mainly affected by their perceptions of workplace ostracism. Thus, consistent with the definition presented in Chapter 2 of this volume, as well as Howard et al.'s (2020) suggestion, we focus on the experience of being ignored or excluded as workplace ostracism experience and discuss how employees' prosocial and antisocial organizational behaviors might be affected by their workplace ostracism experiences.

Workplace ostracism shares several conceptual similarities with workplace mistreatment and workplace incivility (Ferris et al., 2017; Howard et al., 2020). Similar to workplace incivility, workplace ostracism reflects behaviors employees can perceive as harmful and counternormative, and ostracism behaviors are usually of low intensity (e.g., covert and nonphysical) and the perpetrators' intention is usually ambiguous (victims are not always sure if the perpetrators are intentional or not). Yet, Robinson et al.

(2013) suggest that workplace ostracism is conceptually different from workplace incivility due to its omission of action nature; Ferris et al. (2017) also suggest that workplace ostracism is conceptually different from workplace incivility because workplace ostracism has a noninteractive component as the perpetrators do not interact with the victims in a positive or negative manner. Thus, while workplace ostracism can be considered as a specific and narrower type of workplace incivility, not all incivility behaviors can be considered as ostracism (Ferris et al., 2017; Howard et al., 2020). Thus, in our review, we excluded studies on general workplace incivility or other types of workplace mistreatment and only include studies that specifically focused on workplace ostracism.

Introduction to Prosocial and Antisocial Organizational Behaviors

Rotundo and Sackett (2002) suggest that the performance domain consists of three components: task performance, citizenship performance, and counterproductive performance. Task performance includes "behaviors that contribute to the production of a good or the provision of a service" (p. 67), citizenship performance includes behaviors that contribute to the social and psychological environment, and counterproductive performance includes voluntary behaviors that negatively affect organizations and employees in the organizations.

Prosocial organizational behaviors, defined as employee behaviors toward organizations and the members of the organizations with an intention to promote their welfare (Brief & Motowidlo, 1986), overlap with the citizenship performance component in Rotundo and Sackett (2002). They also share strong conceptual similarities with organizational citizenship behaviors (OCBs; Organ & Konovsky, 1989) and have been operationalized as specific behaviors such as helping (Balliet & Ferris, 2013) and proactive behaviors (Belschak & Den Hartog, 2010) in the workplace ostracism literature. OCBs have been traditionally divided into OCB toward organizations (OCB-O) and OCB toward individuals (OCB-I). Given the conceptual overlap between OCB-I and helping behaviors (Whiting, Podsakoff, & Pierce, 2008), in the current chapter we will review the relevant literature together for these two constructs. Specifically, we will discuss whether and how workplace ostracism affects employees' OCB-O, OCB-I and helping behaviors, and proactive behaviors, respectively.

Antisocial organizational behaviors refer to "any behavior that brings harm, or is intended to bring harm, to an organization, its employees, or its stakeholders" (Greenberg & Giacalone, 1997, p. vii). They overlap with the counterproductive performance component in Rotundo and Sackett (2002) and have been studied as specific types of behaviors, such as counterproductive work behaviors (CWBs; Spector & Fox, 2002), workplace deviance (Bennett & Robinson, 2000), and social loafing (Xu, Huang, & Robinson, 2017) in the workplace ostracism literature. Because both CWBs and workplace deviance concern employee voluntary behaviors that can harm organizations and their members (Berry, Carpenter, & Barratt, 2012), in this chapter we will review studies on CWBs against organizations (CWB-O) and organizational deviance together, and studies on CWBs against individuals (CWB-I) and interpersonal deviance together.

Workplace Ostracism and Prosocial Organizational Behaviors

Theoretical Frameworks

Social identity theory (Tajfel & Turner, 1979) has been used to study the effect of workplace ostracism on prosocial organizational behaviors (e.g., Chung, 2015, 2017; Wu, Liu, Kwan, & Lee, 2016). Social identity theory posits that individuals strive to maintain a positive social identity, which is largely reflected by being favorably identified as an in-group, as compared to out-group, members. When a positive social identity is not achieved, individuals are more likely to leave the group or withdraw their efforts. Thus, when employees perceive ostracism at work, they are less likely to perceive a favorable in-group/out-group distinction, less likely to experience a favorable social identity, and less likely to engage in extra-role behaviors benefiting the organization or individuals within the organization. Some example mediators examined based on this theory include person-organization fit (Chung, 2017) and organizational identification (Wu et al., 2016).

Sociometer theory (Leary, 2005; Leary & Baumeister, 2000) has also been used to explain the effect of workplace ostracism on employee prosocial organizational behaviors (e.g., Peng & Zeng, 2017; Schilpzand & Huang, 2018). Sociometer theory is based on humans' inherent need to belong to social settings and groups, and proposes that individuals constantly monitor their social settings and their self-esteem reflects a measure (sociometer) of whether they are perceived to be "relationally valued and socially accepted by other people" (Leary, 2005, p. 146). When individuals experience a social event, they tend to evaluate the potential inclusion or exclusion threat; when they perceive a threat for exclusion, they are likely to perceive lower self-esteem and experience subsequent outcomes. Workplace ostracism signals a threat for social exclusion and disapproval in interpersonal interaction, and can potentially negatively affect employees' self-esteem and subsequent outcomes such as reduced prosocial organizational behaviors through decreased self-esteem. An important mediator examined based on this theory is self-esteem (Peng & Zeng, 2017).

Conservation of resources theory (COR; Hobfoll, 1989) was also adopted to explain the relationship between workplace ostracism and employee prosocial organizational behaviors (e.g., Zhang, Ye, & Ferreira-Meyers, 2017; Zhu, Lyu, Deng, & Ye, 2017). COR theory posits that individuals strive to conserve, protect, and obtain resources, defined here as things that employees perceive as helpful in achieving important goals and coping with demands (Halbesleben, Neveu, Paustian-Underdahl, & Westman, 2014). When experiencing workplace ostracism, employees tend to allocate personal resources to cope with this stressful experience, and thus experience resource depletion. As a consequence, they will have fewer resources to engage in extra-role efforts such as prosocial organizational behaviors. Example mediators examined under this framework include job tension (Zhu et al., 2017) and work-family conflict (Zhang et al., 2017).

Empirical Findings

Supporting the above two theories, studies have generally found a negative relationship between workplace ostracism and prosocial organizational behaviors (e.g., Mok & De Cremer, 2016; Peng & Zeng, 2017), but findings also differ depending on the type of prosocial organizational behavior being examined. For example, all nine studies we located on the relationship between workplace ostracism and OCB-O found that this relationship was significantly negative. For OCB-I, while eight studies have found this relationship significantly negative, two studies found non-significant relationships. For helping behaviors, seven studies have found that this relationship was negative, while three studies found that this relationship was non-significant. For proactive behaviors, four studies found that this relationship was negative, and one study found that this relationship was non-significant. Several moderators and mediators of these relationships have been identified, including organizational factors (e.g., person-organization fit), social factors (e.g., social support), and variables related to psychological well-being (e.g., self-esteem). Next, we will summarize the empirical findings separately for OCB-O, OCB-I and helping behaviors, and proactive behaviors, along with mediators and moderators examined for their correspondent relationships.

OCB-O. The research reviewed is mostly studied with samples consisting participants from various industries. Further, while two studies were conducted in the North America (e.g., Fiset, Al Hajj, & Vongas, 2017), others were from non-US countries (e.g., Korea: Chung, 2017; China: Wu et al., 2016). Lastly, all of them used data collected from multiple waves to reduce concerns of common method variance. Findings from these studies have consistently found a negative relationship between workplace ostracism and OCB-O (e.g., Ferris et al., 2008), suggesting that victims of workplace ostracism tend to engage in less extra-role behaviors that might benefit the organizations.

Mediators and Moderators. Researchers have also identified several variables that explain the effect of workplace ostracism on OCB-O. Some have found that organizational and social factors explain this relationship. For example, based on social identity theory (Tajfel & Turner, 1979), Chung (2015) found that coworker conflict mediated the relationship between workplace ostracism and OCB-O. The authors suggest that the experience of workplace ostracism represents a divergence in values, needs, and goals, which might result in disagreement among employees. These conflicts can further lead to negative emotions and subsequently fewer OCB-O. Using the same theory, Chung (2017) found that person-organization fit mediated the effect of workplace ostracism on OCB-O, such that ostracism decreased perceptions of fit and subsequently decreased OCB-O.

Also based on the social identity theory (Tajfel & Turner, 1979), Wu et al. (2016) found that organizational identification, defined as one's perception that he/she belongs to an organization and is a member of the organization, mediated the effect of workplace ostracism on OCB-O. The authors suggested that this is because victims of workplace ostracism are less likely to form an organizational identity, or identify with their organization; the lack of organizational identification leads to reduced efforts and fewer extra-role behaviors to contribute to the social and psychological environment in the organizations. Additionally, the indirect effect of ostracism on this form of citizenship behavior through organizational identification was stronger when the individual perceived themselves as having high job mobility. This is because those with high job mobility usually have higher expectations for favorable treatment and can potentially secure other jobs for their identity needs; thus, their organizational identification and OCB-O can be more negatively affected by workplace ostracism experiences.

Based on the sociometer theory (Leary, 2005; Leary & Baumeister, 2000), self-esteem has also been found to mediate the relationship between workplace ostracism and OCB-O. Ferris, Lian, Brown, and Morrison (2015) found that global self-esteem mediates the relationship between workplace ostracism and OCB-O. Further, the authors examined the importance of performance to self-esteem (IPSE), or contingent self-esteem, defined as the extent to which one determines his/her self-worth based on the outcomes in a given domain, as a moderator of the relationship between global self-esteem and OCB-O. It was argued that the mediated relationship between ostracism and OCB-O would be weaker among those whose self-esteem is contingent on demonstrating good job performance because these individuals would prioritize demonstrating their competence in that domain regardless of self-esteem levels. The authors found support for this rationale.

OCB-I and Helping Behavior. Four of the studies on the relationship between workplace ostracism and OCB-I/helping behaviors were conducted in Asia while three of them were conducted in North America (the USA and Canada). The majority of them consisted of participants from various industries, while some of them recruited participants from specific industries such as oil and gas (Wu et al., 2016), telecommunication (Xu et al., 2017), and manufacturing (Zhang et al., 2017). All of these studied used data collected from multiple waves which help address the concern of common method variance. The findings from these studies have been less inconsistent. For example, Ferris et al. (2008) found that workplace ostracism was not significantly related to OCB-I, while other studies have found a negative relationship between workplace ostracism and OCB-I (Fiset et al., 2017; Zhang et al., 2017). Additionally, while some existing research has found that workplace ostracism is negatively related to helping behaviors (Balliet & Ferris, 2013; Peng & Zeng, 2017; Scott, Tams, Schippers, & Lee, 2015), others have found that this relationship is not significant (Peng & Zeng, 2017; Xu et al., 2017).

Mediators. Previous research has identified factors that might explain the relationship between workplace ostracism and OCB-I/helping behaviors. Several mediators of the effect of workplace ostracism on OCB-O were also found to mediate the effect of ostracism on OCB-I. For example, based on social identity theory (Tajfel & Turner, 1979), Chung (2015) found that coworker conflict mediated the relationship between workplace ostracism and OCB-I. The previously discussed study by Wu et al. (2016) found that organizational identification also mediated the effect of workplace ostracism on OCB-I. Additionally, Chung (2017) found that person-organization fit mediated the effect of workplace ostracism on OCB-I.

Based on the sociometer theory (Leary, 2005; Leary & Baumeister, 2000), self-esteem has been a commonly studied mediator of this effect. For example, Chung and Yang (2017) found that organization-based self-esteem (OBSE) fully mediated the effect of workplace ostracism on helping behavior. Additionally, Peng and Zeng (2017) found that state self-esteem mediated the effect of workplace ostracism on helping behavior when 360 feedback was used by the participant's organization. The previously discussed study by Ferris et al. (2015) also found that global self-esteem mediates the effect of workplace ostracism on OCB-I, and that IPSE moderated the relationship between global self-esteem and OCB-I.

Finally, researchers have explored the idea that workplace ostracism may relate to OCB-I/helping behavior through diminished psychological well-being. For example, based on the COR theory (Hobfoll, 1989), Chung (2018) predicted and found that perceived stress explained the relationship between workplace ostracism and helping behavior, and psychological empowerment moderated the effect of perceived stress on helping behavior. Similarly, Zhang et al. (2017) found that work-family conflict mediated the effect of workplace ostracism on OCB-I. The authors suggested that workplace ostracism can potentially lead to higher work-family conflict by increasing the victims' working time, strains, and negative behaviors at home. Increased work-family conflict can consume the victims' resources and thus limit their ability to engage in OCB-I. The authors also found that the relationship between workplace ostracism and work-family conflict was moderated by rumination, such that this relationship was only significant at high levels of rumination. This is because a higher level of rumination indicates the victims are less likely to unwind from work-related experiences (e.g., ostracism) and have fewer social resources, which can contribute to the increase of work–family conflict.

Lastly, while Scott et al. (2015) found a negative relationship between coworker exclusion and OCB-I, the indirect effect of coworker exclusion on OCB-I through perception of being envied by coworkers was positive. The authors suggest that this occurs because the experience of ostracism promotes self-protective thinking, leading to the perception that the individual is envied by their coworkers. In order to mitigate the perceived envy of their colleagues, the authors predicted and found that participants engage in more OCB-I. This positive indirect effect, accompanied by a negative direct link between coworker exclusion and OCB-I, suggests that the link between coworker exclusion and OCB-I can be explained by multiple mechanisms. Additionally, positive affect was found to moderate the effect of ostracism on perceptions of envy, such that this effect was found to be strongest among those high on positive affect.

Moderators. Researchers have identified several unique moderators of this relationship. For example, drawing on approach/inhibition theory of power (Keltner, Gruenfeld, & Anderson, 2003), Fiset et al. (2017) found a three-way interaction between workplace ostracism, external social support, and ostracizer status on OCB-I, such that individuals that had been ostracized by someone of a higher status and had low external social support were the least likely to engage in OCB-I. This is because these victims not only have more reduced self-worth when ostracized by someone of higher status, but also are less likely to restore lost resources due to low external social support. Based on social exchange theory, Chung (2017) also found that the indirect effect of workplace ostracism on OCB-I was stronger for those perceiving more organizational support.

Drawing on sociometer theory (Leary, 2005), Peng and Zeng (2017) found that 360 feedback (a performance appraisal approach with ratings from sources other than the supervisors, such as peers, subordinates, customers, self) exacerbated the negative relationship between ostracism and helping behaviors through self-esteem. This is because when 360 feedback is used and employees experience workplace ostracism, they are more sensitive to the ostracism experience because their coworkers' opinions will also be part of their final performance review. Thus, their self-esteems are more negatively affected by workplace ostracism and they are likely to engage in fewer helping behaviors.

Balliet and Ferris (2013) examined future orientation, which the authors define as a temporal orientation characterized by a focus on possible future outcomes. The authors found that future orientation buffered the negative relationship between ostracism and helping behaviors because those with higher future orientation are more aware of the potential benefits of engaging in helping behaviors.

Lastly, based on self-verification theory (Swann, 2011), Xu et al. (2017) found a three-way interaction between ostracism, group identification, and tenure, such that ostracism was positively associated with helping behaviors, but only under high group identification and high tenure. The authors argue that this is because workplace ostracism indicates a threat to group identity. As such, those with high group identification and higher tenure are most motivated to engage in helping behaviors to strengthen their group identity. Wu et al. (2016) found that workplace ostracism was more strongly related to OCB-I through organizational identification for those with higher perceived job mobility than for those with lower mobility. The authors suggested that, consistent with social identity theory (Tajfel & Turner, 1979), those with higher job mobilities have more opportunities to achieve the need of belongingness and thus are more likely to reduce organizational identification from the organization in which they experience ostracism.

Proactive Behaviors. Only five studies have examined the relationship between workplace ostracism and proactive behaviors (i.e., taking the initiative to improve one's situation). All of them were conducted in China with multi-wave data except for Liu, Liu, Hui, and Wu (2015) that used cross-sectional data. While Liu et al. (2015) recruited participants from various industries, the other studies' participants were from specific industries such as oil and gas (Wu et al., 2016), hotel industry (Zhu et al., 2017), and IT (Schilpzand & Huang, 2018). The findings generally showed a negative relationship. For example, Schilpzand and Huang (2018) found that ostracism was negatively related to proactive behaviors and Zhu et al. (2017) found that workplace ostracism was negatively related to proactive customer service performance, a specific form of proactive behaviors.

Mediators and Moderators. Organizational identification theory has been used to explain the relationship between workplace ostracism and proactive behaviors. For example, Mok and De Cremer (2016) found that organizational identification explained the effect of ostracism on intentions to engage in proactive behaviors at work. The authors also found that reminders of money, an indication of more resources, buffered the effect of workplace ostracism on this form of prosocial organizational behavior. The previously discussed study by Wu et al. (2016) found that organizational identification mediated the effect of workplace ostracism on proactive behaviors. Perceived job mobility was also found to moderate the indirect effect of ostracism on change-oriented citizenship behaviors (e.g., suggesting ideas for improvement to a supervisor) in the same pattern as was found for OCB-O and OCB-I.

Self-esteem is another major mechanism that explains how workplace ostracism affects proactive work behaviors. Liu et al. (2015) found that organization-based self-esteem mediated the effect of ostracism on employee proactive behavior, and that the negative relationship between ostracism and organization-based self-esteem was stronger among employees higher on neuroticism.

Based on the conservation of resources theory (Hobfoll, 1989), Zhu et al. (2017) examined workplace ostracism in the context of the hotel industry. The authors found that ostracism led to increased job tension that then hindered proactive customer service performance. Zhu and colleagues suggest that this occurs because ostracism depletes an individual's resources—this then leads to psychological tension and makes the employee less willing to be customer-oriented, which ultimately inhibits proactive behaviors. The authors also found that need for affiliation moderated the effect of ostracism on job tension, such that this relationship is stronger among employees high in need for affiliation due to their tendency to perceive more personal and social loss than those low in need for affiliation.

Additional moderators were examined in addition to neuroticism and need for affiliation described above. For example, based on sociometer theory (Leary, 2005), Schilpzand and Huang (2018) found that a self-concept oriented toward individual identity, or an individual identity orientation, moderated the effect of ostracism on proactive behaviors such that having a low individual identity orientation weakened the negative relationship between ostracism and proactive behaviors. This is because those with a low individual identity orientation care more about the collective achievements, and thus will be less likely to withhold proactive behaviors when experiencing workplace ostracism.

Workplace Ostracism and Antisocial Organizational Behaviors

Theoretical Frameworks

Need to belong theory (Baumeister & Heatherton, 1996) has been used to study the effects of workplace ostracism on antisocial organizational behaviors (e.g., Fatima, 2016; Hitlan & Noel, 2009; Thau, Aquino, & Poortvliet, 2007). Need to belong theory argues that individuals have the inherent tendency to be connected or belong to a group. When this need to belong is threatened by workplace ostracism, employees tend to experience negative emotions and react in a negative way, such as engaging in more antisocial organizational behaviors. An example mediator examined based on this theory is job satisfaction (Fatima, 2016).

The transactional stress model (Lazarus & Folkman, 1984) has also been adopted to examine the relationships of workplace ostracism and antisocial organizational behaviors. The transitional stress model suggests that a negative situational stimulus is evaluated based on whether this is a threat to one's well-being (primary appraisal) and whether one has the resources to cope with the threat (secondary appraisal). Once the stimulus is appraised as a threat and one does not have the resources to effectively cope with it, the individual is likely to experience strain reactions including negative behaviors. This framework has been used to explain the antisocial organizational behavioral reactions to workplace ostracism experience (e.g., Jahanzeb & Fatima, 2018; Yang & Treadway, 2016). An example mediator examined based on this theory is emotional exhaustion (Jahanzeb & Fatima, 2018).

Social exchange theory (Blau, 1964) and reciprocity theory (Cropanzano & Mitchell, 2005) have been used to examine the effect of workplace ostracism on employees' antisocial organizational behaviors (e.g., Chung, 2017; Fatima, 2016; Hitlan & Noel, 2009; Xu et al., 2017; Zhao, Peng, & Sheard, 2013). Social exchange theory posits that employees are likely to engage in behaviors similar to those they experience, while the reciprocity theory suggests that employees of negative experiences might hold negative reciprocity beliefs and behave in a negative way to the perpetrators of the negative experiences. Thus, when employees perceived to be ostracized, they are more likely to engage in similar or escalated antisocial organizational behaviors as retaliation.

Self-verification theory (Swann, 2011) has been used to study the effects of workplace ostracism on both prosocial and antisocial organizational behaviors (e.g., Ferris et al., 2015; Xu et al., 2017). Specifically, people are motivated to maintain their self-view in that they prefer others to see them as they see themselves. Thus, workplace ostracism as a negative interpersonal experience might lead employees to engage in negative self-verification behaviors such as reduced prosocial organizational behaviors and increased antisocial organizational behaviors. Self-esteem was proposed to mediate the relationship between workplace ostracism on both prosocial organizational behaviors and antisocial organizational behaviors (Ferris et al., 2015).

Empirical Findings

The majority of research reveals that the relationship between workplace ostracism and antisocial organizational behavior is positive (e.g., Peng & Zeng, 2017; Yan, Zhou, Long, & Ji, 2014; Yang & Treadway, 2016), providing empirical support for the above theories. However, some researchers have found that this effect differs depending on the type of antisocial organizational behavior being considered. For CWB-O/organizational deviance, all ten studies we located found that this relationship was positive. For CWB-I/interpersonal deviance, seven studies found that this relationship was positive, and one study found that this relationship was non-significant. For social loafing, two studies have found that this relationship was negative. Furthermore, several moderators and mediators of these relationships have been identified, including organizational factors (e.g., 360 feedback), social factors (e.g., high team identification), and individual differences (e.g., personality, self-esteem). As such, we will summarize empirical findings for each type of antisocial organizational behavior that has been examined, namely CWB-O and organizational deviance, CWB-I and interpersonal deviance, and social loafing.

CWB-O and Organizational Deviance. The majority of research regarding workplace ostracism and CWB-Os were conducted in non-US countries such as China and Korea. While three of them used cross-sectional designs, the others used multiple waves of data. While four studies recruited participants from various industries, others recruited participants from specific industries such as manufacturing (Yang & Treadway, 2016), telecommunication (Fatima, 2016), and hotel industry (Zhao et al., 2013). These studies have found that this relationship is positive (e.g., Hitlan & Noel, 2009). However, while Ferris et al. (2008) found a positive relationship between workplace ostracism and CWB-O assessed at the same time, this relationship was not significant at a 5-month follow-up.

Mediators. Prior research has examined several mediators of the relationship between workplace ostracism and CWB-O. For example, Yan et al. (2014) found that employee state self-control, or the amount of self-control someone has at any given time (Baumeister & Heatherton, 1996), fully mediated the effect of ostracism on CWB-O. This is because victims of workplace ostracism experience can potentially deplete the victims' self-control resources, which will lead to more CWB-O. Studies have also explored how this effect of workplace ostracism may be explained by organizational attitudes. Specifically, researchers have found that job satisfaction partially mediated the effect of workplace ostracism on CWB-O (Fatima, 2016). Finally, based on social exchange theory (Blau, 1964), Chung and Yang (2017) found that organization-based self-esteem (OBSE), or self-evaluations of one's worth to their organization (Pierce, Gardner, Cummings, & Dunham, 1989), partially mediated the relationship between workplace ostracism and organizational deviance.

Moderators. Individual differences have been found to moderate the effect of workplace ostracism on this form of antisocial organizational behavior. For example, Hitlan and Noel (2009) found that the effect of supervisor exclusion on CWB-O was moderated by neuroticism, agreeableness, conscientiousness, and openness to experience, such that individuals with personality traits that involve stronger behavioral constraints (e.g., high agreeableness and conscientiousness), were less likely to engage in this form of CWB. Additionally, Zhao et al. (2013) found a three-way interaction between proactive personality, political skill, and workplace ostracism on CWB-O. Specifically, the authors found that the relationship between ostracism and CWB-O was weakest for those with high proactive personality and high political skill. This is because those with high political skill and high proactive personality tend to know the best approach to act proactively after experiencing workplace ostracism instead of engaging in more CWB-O. In contrast, the relationship between ostracism and CWB-O was strongest for those with low proactive personality and low political skill. In contrast with the previously reviewed research on CWB-O and organizational deviance, Xu (2012) found that under high team identification, ostracism had a negative relationship with organizational deviance.

The author suggests that this occurs because, when an employee identifies with their team, ostracism reduces antisocial behaviors because the employee wishes to restore their previous level of belongingness.

CWB-I and Interpersonal Deviance. While three studies were conducted in North America, two studies were conducted in China and two were conducted in Pakistan. Three of them recruited participants from various industries, while others recruited participants from specific industries such as telecommunication (Fatima, 2016) and service industry (Jahanzeb & Fatima, 2018). While four studies used cross-sectional designs, five studies used data collected from at least two waves. These studies have found that workplace ostracism is positively related to interpersonal deviance (Ferris et al., 2015; Fiset et al., 2017). For CWB-I, most studies have found a positive relationship between workplace ostracism and this form of CWB (Zhao et al., 2013). However, Hitlan and Noel (2009) found that workplace ostracism was not significantly related to CWB-I. Furthermore, Ferris et al. (2008) found a positive relationship between workplace ostracism and CWB-I, but this relationship was not significant at a 5-month follow-up.

Mediators. Several variables have been found to explain the relationship between workplace ostracism and interpersonal deviance. For example, based on the transactional stress model (Lazarus & Folkman, 1984), Jahanzeb and Fatima (2018) examined the idea that this effect occurs by impacting psychological well-being. The authors found that the relationship between workplace ostracism and interpersonal deviance was partially explained by emotional exhaustion, which is defined as feeling strained and fatigued by one's work (Wright & Cropanzano, 1998). Self-esteem has also been examined as a mediator of this relationship. Using self-verification theory (Swann, 2011), Ferris et al. (2015) found that global self-esteem mediated the effect of workplace ostracism on interpersonal deviance. The authors also found that the effect of global self-esteem on this form of deviance was moderated by contingent self-esteem—the extent to which one's self-worth is based on outcomes in a given domain (Crocker & Wolfe, 2001). Finally, the previously discussed study by Yan et al. (2014) found that employee state self-control fully mediated the effect of ostracism on CWB-I.

Moderators. Several moderators of this relationship have been examined. For example, Fiset et al. (2017) found a three-way interaction between workplace ostracism, external social support, and ostracizer status on interpersonal deviance, such that individuals who had been ostracized by a high-status individual and had low external social support were the most likely to engage in interpersonal deviance. Additionally, Peng and Zeng (2017) found that the use of 360 feedback exacerbated the positive relationship between ostracism and interpersonal deviance. The authors provided similar rationales for the moderating effects as mentioned above for prosocial organizational behaviors such that victims of ostracism are more sensitive to the ostracism experience because their coworkers' opinions will also be part of their final performance review. Thus, their self-esteems are more negatively affected by workplace ostracism and they are likely to engage in more interpersonal deviance.

Several moderators of the effect of workplace ostracism on CWB-O were also found to mediate the effect of ostracism on CWB-I. For example, Hitlan and Noel (2009) found that extraversion moderated the relationship between coworker exclusion and CWB-I, following the same pattern as was observed for CWB-O. Additionally, the previously discussed study by Zhao et al. (2013) found a three-way interaction between proactive personality, political skill, and workplace ostracism on CWB-I, once again following the same pattern observed for CWB-O.

Social Loafing. Existing research has also examined the impact of workplace ostracism on social loafing, defined as employees' decreased motivation and efforts as a member of a group. Prior work on this topic has found that the effect of ostracism on social loafing was moderated by group identification such that, under high group identification, ostracism was negatively associated with social loafing (Xu, 2012; Xu et al., 2017). One of the reasons for this relationship is that victims of workplace ostracism might be motivated to engage in less social loafing due to a desire to restore social capital.

Potential Directions for Future Research

With a few exceptions, the majority of the reviewed studies found that workplace ostracism was negatively related to employee prosocial organizational behaviors and positively related to employee antisocial organizational behaviors. A variety of mediators and moderators have been examined to explain how and when these relationships occur. While these findings provide strong empirical evidence for this line of research, we believe a few directions can be further explored.

Use of Other Research Designs. While many of the above-reviewed studies used cross-sectional designs, many also collected data with multiple waves, which can help address concerns about common method variance in cross-sectional designs (Podsakoff, MacKenzie, Lee, & Podsakoff, 2003). We believe the literature on this topic can benefit from studies using other types of research designs such as experience sampling methods, cross-lagged panel designs, and experimental designs. First, while experience sampling methods such as diary studies have been used in the workplace ostracism literature (Pereira, Meier, & Elfering, 2013), more studies using this method can help us better understand employees' short-term emotional, attitudinal, and cognitive reactions that can affect their prosocial and antisocial organizational behaviors. For example, on days employees experience workplace ostracism, they are likely to experience increased negative emotions, impaired self-identity, and depleted resources, and thus engage in fewer prosocial organizational behaviors and more antisocial organizational behaviors on the same day or next day. Second, cross-lagged panel designs might be used to explore the potentially reciprocal relationship between workplace ostracism experience and employees' prosocial/antisocial organizational behaviors. For example, employees who engage in fewer prosocial organizational behaviors and more antisocial organizational behaviors might experience more workplace ostracism because they are targeted by coworkers or supervisors, which can further contribute to their engagement in prosocial/antisocial organizational behaviors. Third, studies in social psychology using experimental designs have demonstrated the potential causal relationships of ostracism with prosocial and antisocial behaviors. For example, Twenge, Baumeister, DeWall, Ciarocco, and Bartels (2007) found that social exclusion led to decreased prosocial behaviors, while others found that social exclusion led to increased antisocial behaviors (Buckley, Winkel, & Leary, 2004; Chow, Tiedens, & Govan, 2008; Warburton, Williams, & Cairns, 2006). These findings, despite the use of laboratory manipulation of social exclusion and non-work operationalization of prosocial and antisocial behaviors, provide initial evidence for the causal relationships between workplace ostracism and prosocial/antisocial organizational behaviors. Thus, future studies on workplace ostracism can adopt similar designs to simulate workplace ostracism in work-related settings (e.g., Fiset et al., 2017; Mok & De Cremer, 2016) and examine their effects prosocial/antisocial organizational behaviors and the underlying mechanisms.

Workplace Ostracism from Different Sources. Except for a few exceptions (e.g., Ferris et al., 2015; Hitlan & Noel, 2009; Peng &

Zeng, 2017), most studies did not specify the source of workplace ostracism. Yet, workplace ostracism can come from one's coworkers (e.g., Ferris et al., 2015; Hitlan & Noel, 2009; Peng & Zeng, 2017) or supervisors (Hitlan & Noel, 2009) and might have differential effects on different types of prosocial/antisocial organizational behaviors. For example, workplace ostracism from supervisors might be more predictive of prosocial/antisocial behaviors against organizations (e.g., OCB-O and CWB-O) than prosocial/antisocial behaviors against the supervisor. This is because victims are less likely to target the supervisors for retaliation because of supervisors' higher power status and possession of resources needed by the victims; meanwhile, since supervisors are more likely to be considered as the representatives of the organizations, victims of supervisor ostracism might retaliate the organizations by withdrawing extra efforts and engaging in deviance behaviors toward organizations. On the other hand, workplace ostracism from coworkers might be more predictive of prosocial/antisocial organizational behaviors against individuals (e.g., OCB-I and CWB-I). This is because victims and ostracizers share the similar social identity and power status. Thus, victims are likely to directly withdraw efforts and engage in harmful retaliatory behaviors toward the ostracizers.

Differentiation of Targets for Interpersonal Prosocial/Antisocial Behaviors. While many of the above studies differentiate between prosocial/antisocial behaviors toward individuals and organizations, it can also be meaningful to differentiate the targets (e.g., ostracizers vs. non-ostracizers) of interpersonal prosocial/antisocial behaviors. For example, victims of supervisor ostracism might be more likely to engage in fewer prosocial behaviors and more antisocial behaviors toward coworkers (non-ostracizer). This may not affect their prosocial/antisocial organizational behaviors toward the supervisor (ostracizer) given the power and hierarchy difference. Meanwhile, victims of workplace ostracism from some coworkers might engage in more prosocial behaviors and fewer antisocial behaviors toward *other* coworkers (non-ostracizer) to fulfill their needs to belong; meanwhile, they are likely to engage in fewer prosocial and more antisocial behaviors toward the perpetrators (ostracizer). Lastly, employees' prosocial/antisocial behaviors toward customers might also be affected by their workplace ostracism experiences. Given victims of workplace ostracism might experience more negative emotions and fewer self-control resources, it is likely that they will have less motivation and fewer resources to engage in prosocial behaviors toward customers and meanwhile engage in more antisocial behaviors.

The Role of Witnessed Workplace Ostracism. While *experienced* workplace ostracism has been found to predict prosocial and antisocial organizational behaviors, whether *witnessed* workplace ostracism might have the same effect is unclear. Within the same working environment, employees' interactions can be witnessed by others. Thus, workplace ostracism might be perceived by the victims and witnessed by others who are neither victims nor perpetrators, and the witnesses' prosocial/antisocial organizational behaviors can also be affected. For example, research on witnessed incivility shows that witnesses of workplace incivility tend to engage in less OCB (Porath & Erez, 2009). Further, witnessed workplace ostracism might also affect the relationship between experienced workplace ostracism and employees' prosocial/antisocial organizational behaviors, such that the effects might be weaker when the victims witness that the ostracism experience is shared by other coworkers. Indirect evidence can be drawn from the finding that the effect of workplace incivility experience is weaker when this experience is shared by the victims and other targets (Porath & Erez, 2009).

The Role of Attribution. Attribution is an important factor affecting employees' appraisals and reactions to workplace incivility (Schilpzand, De Pater, & Erez, 2016). Similarly, attribution might also be an important factor to affect how one might react to workplace ostracism. For example, hostile attribution bias might strengthen the negative effects of workplace ostracism on employees' prosocial/antisocial organizational behaviors because victims are more likely to believe the perpetrators' exclusion behaviors are intentional and hostile (Zhou, Yan, Che, & Meier, 2015). On the other hand, those with internal attribution style, compared to those with external attribution style, are more likely to believe their ostracism experiences are caused by their own characteristics or behaviors and thus have weaker reactions in terms of prosocial/antisocial organizational behaviors.

The Spiral Effect of Workplace Ostracism. Workplace ostracism experience might escalate to more harmful antisocial organizational behaviors through the spiral process (Andersson & Pearson, 1999). For example, Taylor and Kluemper (2012) found that experienced workplace incivility positively predicts enacted workplace aggression. Thus, when employees perceive that they have been ostracized by coworkers or supervisors, they are likely to experience more negative emotions and lost self-control resources, and are more likely to engage in more severe behaviors such as workplace aggression or workplace violence intentionally in retaliation.

Incorporation of New Theories for Potential Mediators and Moderators. Additional theories can be fruitful to propose new mediators and moderators. For example, the theories of rumination (Smith & Alloy, 2009) suggest that goal failure can activate negative ruminations that can further affect employee prosocial/antisocial organizational behaviors. Because workplace ostracism can impair employees' social identity and need to belong, it can be appraised as a failure to achieve the goal of establishing a favorable social identity or belongingness to the group. Thus, workplace ostracism can potentially predict more negative rumination and lead to subsequently fewer prosocial organizational behaviors and more antisocial organizational behaviors. Further, it might also be meaningful to explore potential moderators on the relationship between workplace ostracism and negative rumination. An example can be trait mindfulness (Brown, Ryan, & Creswell, 2007), which can help employees better cope with workplace ostracism experiences in a nonjudgmental way and thus lead to less negative rumination.

Conclusion

In summary, the existing literature generally suggests that workplace ostracism has a negative relationship with prosocial organizational behaviors and a positive relationship with antisocial organizational behaviors, although the direction of these relationships might change under unique boundary conditions (e.g., Xu et al., 2017). Several well-established theories have been used to explain these relationships as well as potential mediators and moderators, helping us gain a more in-depth understanding of how and when these relationships occur. Yet, we believe future studies in this line of research can continue to explore these relationships in a few new directions.

References

Andersson, L. M., & Pearson, C. M. (1999). Tit for tat? The spiraling effect of incivility in the workplace. *Academy of Management Review, 24*(3), 452–471.

Balliet, D., & Ferris, D. L. (2013). Ostracism and prosocial behavior: A social dilemma perspective. *Organizational Behavior and Human Decision Processes, 120*(2), 298–308.

Baumeister, R. F., & Heatherton, T. F. (1996). Self-regulation failure: An overview. *Psychological Inquiry, 7*(1), 1–15.

Belschak, F. D., & Den Hartog, D. N. (2010). Pro-self, prosocial, and pro-organizational foci of proactive behaviour: Differential antecedents and consequences. *Journal of Occupational and Organizational Psychology, 83*(2), 475–498.

Bennett, R. J., & Robinson, S. L. (2000). Development of a measure of workplace deviance. *Journal of Applied Psychology, 85*(3), 349–360.

Berry, C. M., Carpenter, N. C., & Barratt, C. L. (2012). Do other-reports of counterproductive work behavior provide an incremental contribution over self-reports? A meta-analytic comparison. *Journal of Applied Psychology, 97*(3), 613–636.

Blau, P. (1964). *Exchange and power in social life*. London and New York: Routledge.

Brief, A. P., & Motowidlo, S. J. (1986). Prosocial organizational behaviors. *Academy of Management Review, 11*(4), 710–725.

Brown, K. W., Ryan, R. M., & Creswell, J. D. (2007). Addressing fundamental questions about mindfulness. *Psychological Inquiry, 18*(4), 272–281.

Buckley, K. E., Winkel, R. E., & Leary, M. R. (2004). Reactions to acceptance and rejection: Effects of level and sequence of relational evaluation. *Journal of Experimental Social Psychology, 1*(40), 14–28.

Chow, R. M., Tiedens, L. Z., & Govan, C. L. (2008). Excluded emotions: The role of anger in antisocial responses to ostracism. *Journal of Experimental Social Psychology, 44*(3), 896–903.

Chung, Y. W. (2015). The mediating effects of organizational conflict on the relationships between workplace ostracism with in-role behavior and organizational citizenship behavior. *International Journal of Conflict Management, 26*(4), 366–385.

Chung, Y. W. (2017). The role of person–organization fit and perceived organizational support in the relationship between workplace ostracism and behavioral outcomes. *Australian Journal of Management, 42*(2), 328–349.

Chung, Y. W. (2018). Workplace ostracism and workplace behaviors: A moderated mediation model of perceived stress and psychological empowerment. *Anxiety Stress and Coping, 31*(3), 304–317.

Chung, Y. W., & Yang, J. Y. (2017). The mediating effects of organization-based self-esteem for the relationship between workplace ostracism and workplace behaviors. *Baltic Journal of Management, 12*(2), 255–270.

Crocker, J., & Wolfe, C. T. (2001). Contingencies of self-worth. *Psychological Review, 108*(3), 593–623.

Cropanzano, R., & Mitchell, M. S. (2005). Social exchange theory: An interdisciplinary review. *Journal of Management, 31*(6), 874–900.

Fatima, A. (2016). Impact of workplace ostracism on counter productive work behaviors: Mediating role of job satisfaction. *Abasyn Journal of Social Sciences, 9*(2), 388–408.

Ferris, D. L., Brown, D. J., Berry, J. W., & Lian, H. (2008). The development and validation of the workplace ostracism scale. *Journal of Applied Psychology, 93*(6), 1348–1366.

Ferris, D. L., Chen, M., & Lim, S. (2017). Comparing and contrasting workplace ostracism and incivility. *Annual Review of Organizational Psychology and Organizational Behavior, 4,* 315–338.

Ferris, D. L., Lian, H., Brown, D. J., & Morrison, R. (2015). Ostracism, self-esteem, and job performance: When do we self-verify and when do we self-enhance? *Academy of Management Journal, 58*(1), 279–297.

Fiset, J., Al Hajj, R., & Vongas, J. G. (2017). Workplace ostracism seen through the lens of power. *Frontiers in Psychology, 8,* 1528. https://doi.org/10.3389/fpsyg.2017.01528.

Greenberg, J., & Giacalone, R. A. (1997). *Antisocial behavior in organizations.* Thousand Oaks, CA: Sage.

Halbesleben, J. R. B., Neveu, J.-P., Paustian-Underdahl, S. C., & Westman, M. (2014). Getting to the "COR": Understanding the role of resources in conservation of resources theory. *Journal of Management, 40*(5), 1334–1364.

Hitlan, R. T., & Noel, J. (2009). The influence of workplace exclusion and personality on counterproductive work behaviours: An interactionist perspective. *European Journal of Work and Organizational Psychology, 18*(4), 477–502.

Hobfoll, S. E. (1989). Conservation of resources: A new attempt at conceptualizing stress. *American Psychologist, 44*(3), 513–524.

Howard, M. C., Cogswell, J. E., & Smith, M. B. (2020). The antecedents and outcomes of workplace ostracism: A meta-analysis. *Journal of Applied Psychology, 105*(6), 577–596.

Jahanzeb, S., & Fatima, T. (2018). How workplace ostracism influences interpersonal deviance: The mediating role of defensive silence and emotional exhaustion. *Journal of Business and Psychology, 33*(6), 779–791.

Keltner, D., Gruenfeld, D. H., & Anderson, C. (2003). Power, approach, and inhibition. *Psychological Review, 110*(2), 265–284.

Lazarus, R. S., & Folkman, S. (1984). Coping and adaptation. In *The Handbook of Behavioral Medicine* (pp. 282–325). New York: Guilford Press.

Leary, M. R. (2005). Sociometer theory and the pursuit of relational value: Getting to the root of self-esteem. *European Review of Social Psychology, 16*(1), 75–111.

Leary, M. R., & Baumeister, R. F. (2000). The nature and function of self-esteem: Sociometer theory. In *Advances in Experimental Social Psychology* (Vol. 32, pp. 1–62). San Diego, CA: Elsevier.

Liu, X., Liu, J., Hui, C., & Wu, R. (2015). The Effect of workplace ostracism on proactive behavior: The self-verification theory perspective. *Acta Psychologica Sinica, 47*(6), 826–836.

Mok, A., & De Cremer, D. (2016). The bonding effect of money in the workplace: Priming money weakens the negative relationship between ostracism and prosocial behaviour. *European Journal of Work and Organizational Psychology, 25*(2), 272–286.

Organ, D. W., & Konovsky, M. (1989). Cognitive versus affective determinants of organizational citizenship behavior. *Journal of Applied Psychology, 74*(1), 157–164.

Peng, A. C., & Zeng, W. (2017). Workplace ostracism and deviant and helping behaviors: The moderating role of 360 degree feedback. *Journal of Organizational Behavior, 38*(6), 833–855.

Pereira, D., Meier, L. L., & Elfering, A. (2013). Short-term effects of social exclusion at work and worries on sleep. *Stress and Health, 29*(3), 240–252.

Pierce, J. L., Gardner, D. G., Cummings, L. L., & Dunham, R. B. (1989). Organization-based self-esteem: Construct definition, measurement, and validation. *Academy of Management Journal, 32*(3), 622–648.

Podsakoff, P. M., MacKenzie, S. B., Lee, J.-Y., & Podsakoff, N. P. (2003). Common method biases in behavioral research: A critical review of the literature and recommended remedies. *Journal of Applied Psychology, 88*(5), 879–903.

Porath, C. L., & Erez, A. (2009). Overlooked but not untouched: How rudeness reduces onlookers' performance on routine and creative tasks. *Organizational Behavior and Human Decision Processes, 109*(1), 29–44.

Robinson, S. L., O'Reilly, J., & Wang, W. (2013). Invisible at work: An integrated model of workplace ostracism. *Journal of Management, 39*(1), 203–231.

Rotundo, M., & Sackett, P. R. (2002). The relative importance of task, citizenship, and counterproductive performance for supervisor ratings of overall performance: A policy capturing study. *Journal of Applied Psychology, 87*(1), 66–80.

Schilpzand, P., De Pater, I. E., & Erez, A. (2016). Workplace incivility: A review of the literature and agenda for future research. *Journal of Organizational Behavior, 37*(S1), S57–S88.

Schilpzand, P., & Huang, L. (2018). When and how experienced incivility dissuades proactive performance: An integration of sociometer and self-identity orientation perspectives. *Journal of Applied Psychology, 103*(8), 828–841.

Scott, K. L., Tams, S., Schippers, M. C., & Lee, K. (2015). Opening the black box: Why and when workplace exclusion affects social reconnection behaviour, health, and attitudes. *European Journal of Work and Organizational Psychology, 24*(2), 239–255.

Smith, J. M., & Alloy, L. B. (2009). A roadmap to rumination: A review of the definition, assessment, and conceptualization of this multifaceted construct. *Clinical Psychology Review, 29*(2), 116–128.

Spector, P. E., & Fox, S. (2002). An emotion-centered model of voluntary work behavior—Some parallels between counterproductive work behavior and organizational citizenship behavior. *Human Resource Management Review, 2*(12), 269–292.

Swann, W. B., Jr. (2011). Self-verification theory. In P. A. M. Van Lange, A. W. Kruglanski, & E. T. Higgins (Eds.), *Handbook of theories of social psychology* (pp. 23–42). Sage Publications Ltd.

Tajfel, H., & Turner, J. C. (1979). An integrative theory of intergroup conflict. In W. G. Austin & S. Worchel (Eds.), *The social psychology of intergroup relations* (pp. 33–47). Monterey, CA: Brooks/Cole.

Taylor, S. G., & Kluemper, D. H. (2012). Linking perceptions of role stress and incivility to workplace aggression: The moderating role of personality. *Journal of Occupational Health Psychology, 17*(3), 316–329.

Thau, S., Aquino, K., & Poortvliet, P. M. (2007). Self-defeating behaviors in organizations: The relationship between thwarted belonging and interpersonal work behaviors. *Journal of Applied Psychology, 92*(3), 840–847.

Twenge, J. M., Baumeister, R. F., DeWall, C. N., Ciarocco, N. J., & Bartels, J. M. (2007). Social exclusion decreases prosocial behavior. *Journal of Personality and Social Psychology, 92*(1), 56–66.

Warburton, W. A., Williams, K. D., & Cairns, D. R. (2006). When ostracism leads to aggression: The moderating effects of control deprivation. *Journal of Experimental Social Psychology, 42*(2), 213–220.

Whiting, S. W., Podsakoff, P. M., & Pierce, J. R. (2008). Effects of task performance, helping, voice, and organizational loyalty on performance appraisal ratings. *Journal of Applied Psychology, 93*(1), 125–139.

Wright, T. A., & Cropanzano, R. (1998). Emotional exhaustion as a predictor of job performance and voluntary turnover. *Journal of Applied Psychology, 83*(3), 486–493.

Wu, C.-H., Liu, J., Kwan, H. K., & Lee, C. (2016). Why and when workplace ostracism inhibits organizational citizenship behaviors: An organizational identification perspective. *Journal of Applied Psychology, 101*(3), 362–378.

Xu, E. (2012). *How am I supposed to live without you: An investigation of antecedents and consequences of workplace ostracism* [Unpublished doctoral dissertation]. The Hong Kong Polytechnic University.

Xu, E., Huang, X., & Robinson, S. L. (2017). When self-view is at stake: Responses to ostracism through the lens of self-verification theory. *Journal of Management, 43*(7), 2281–2302.

Yan, Y., Zhou, E., Long, L., & Ji, Y. (2014). The influence of workplace ostracism on counterproductive work behavior: The mediating effect of state self-control. *Social Behavior and Personality: An International Journal, 42*(6), 881–890.

Yang, J., & Treadway, D. C. (2018). A social influence interpretation of workplace ostracism and counterproductive work behavior. *Journal of Business Ethics, 148*(4), 879–891.

Zhang, R., Ye, C., & Ferreira-Meyers, K. (2017). Linking workplace ostracism to interpersonal citizenship behavior: A moderated mediation model of work-to-family conflict and rumination. *International Journal of Stress Management, 24*(3), 293–320.

Zhao, H., Peng, Z., & Sheard, G. (2013). Workplace ostracism and hospitality employees' counterproductive work behaviors: The joint moderating effects of proactive personality and political skill. *International Journal of Hospitality Management, 33*, 219–227.

Zhou, Z. E., Yan, Y., Che, X. X., & Meier, L. L. (2015). Effect of workplace incivility on end-of-work negative affect: Examining individual and organizational moderators in a daily diary study. *Journal of Occupational Health Psychology, 20*(1), 117–130.

Zhu, H., Lyu, Y., Deng, X., & Ye, Y. (2017). Workplace ostracism and proactive customer service performance: A conservation of resources perspective. *International Journal of Hospitality Management, 64*, 62–72.

CHAPTER 6

Performance Consequences of Workplace Ostracism

Sharon Glazer, Sally D. Farley, and Tannaz T. Rahman

Humans are a profoundly social species. Sociality provided our ancestral relatives distinct reproductive and protection benefits, which resulted in a deeply ingrained, immutable, powerful need to belong (Baumeister & Leary, 1995). Thus, the experience of ostracism, being socially excluded and/or ignored by others (Williams, 2007, 2009: Williams & Nida, 2011), results in innumerable deleterious consequences, such as pain, depression, loneliness, a sense of worthlessness, a loss of a sense of meaningfulness in one's life, and poor performance (Eisenberger, 2012; Leary,

The authors wish to thank Laina Serrer and Paris Wilson for preparing annotated bibliographies for a couple dozen articles integrated into this chapter.

S. Glazer (✉) · S. D. Farley
University of Baltimore, Baltimore, MD, USA
e-mail: sglazer@ubalt.edu

T. T. Rahman
IMPAQ International, LLC, Columbia, MD, USA

C. Liu and J. Ma (eds.), *Workplace Ostracism*,
Palgrave Explorations in Workplace Stigma,
https://doi.org/10.1007/978-3-030-54379-2_6

1990; O'Reilly, Robinson, Berdahl, & Banki, 2015; Türkmen, Doğan, & Karaeminoğulları, 2016; Williams & Nida, 2011).

Ostracism is one example of relational devaluation, a perception of asymmetry in the value and importance of a relationship, whereby one partner senses that the other cares less about the relationship than s/he does (Leary, Springer, Negel, Ansell, & Evans, 1998; Wesselmann et al., 2016). Different programs of research have utilized different terminology to capture types of relational devaluation, such as being "out of the loop" (Jones, Carter-Sowell, Kelly, & Williams, 2009; Jones & Kelly, 2010), organizational shunning (the systematic exclusion of an individual in the workplace from the "everyday rites and rituals that signify organizational membership," Anderson, 2009, p. 36), and social rejection (when one's attempts to form a connection with someone else are denied; Blackhart, Nelson, Knowles, & Baumeister, 2009). Although Williams' definition of ostracism subsumes the experience of social rejection (negative attention) with the experience of being ignored (no attention; Williams & Nida, 2011), increasingly, researchers are calling for a differentiation of these important constructs (Riva & Eck, 2016). For the purposes of this chapter, workplace ostracism is conceptualized as purposefully or passively ignoring others, treating others as if they were invisible, or failing to include them in workplace and everyday activities (Ferris, Brown, Berry, & Lian, 2008).

Although ostracism is pervasive and comes in many different forms—starting from the silent treatment and the cold shoulder to being shunned and banished (Williams, Forgas, & von Hippel, 2005), the bulk of ostracism research has investigated short-term responses to experimental manipulations of ostracism (Bernstein, 2016). Because workplace relationships tend to be enduring, consequences of long-term ostracism will be of particular import in organizational settings. According to the temporal need-threat model (Williams, 2007, 2009), individuals' reactions to ostracism may proceed in a series of stages. In the first *reflexive stage*, individuals experience threats to four fundamental needs: belongingness, self-esteem, control, and meaningful existence (Williams & Nida, 2011). Regardless of context or individual differences, individuals who are ostracized experience pain and other negative emotions (Williams & Nida, 2011). In fact, scholars have determined that psychosocial stressors (a category that includes workplace ostracism) are more harmful to employee health and well-being than physical work demands (e.g., lifting heavy items; Cooper & Smith, 1986). Further, fMRI research has revealed that the experience of ostracism presents neural signatures that are analogous to that of physical pain (Eisenberger, Lieberman, & Williams, 2003).

In the subsequent *reflective stage*, ostracized individuals engage in attributional processing and attempt to understand the meaning behind the ostracism. If ostracized individuals perceive that they can redress their thwarted self-esteem or belongingness needs, then they will engage in prosocial reconnection behaviors, such as mimicry (Lakin & Chartrand, 2003), ingratiation (Scott, Tams, Schippers, & Lee, 2015), effort production (Williams & Sommer, 1997), social compliance (Carter-Sowell, Chen, & Williams, 2008), and cooperation (Walasek, Juanchich, & Sirota, 2019). But, if those who are ostracized anticipate failure at reconnection, they may lash out and engage in greater antisocial behavior, such as aggression (Twenge, Baumeister, Tice, & Stucke, 2001), in an attempt to restore their sense of control or meaningful existence (Walasek et al., 2019; Williams & Nida, 2011). Given the intensity of pain associated with ostracism, and the coping resources dedicated to attempts at re-inclusion, individuals who are chronically ostracized enter the final stage of the need-threat model (*resignation*) quite depleted (Williams, 2007). It is at this final stage where "alienation, depression, helplessness, and unworthiness" may set in (Williams & Nida, 2011, p. 71). It is also during this chronic stage that individuals who feel slighted due to lack of eye contact during program meetings (Wirth, Sacco, Hugenberg, & Williams, 2010), being repeatedly not asked to lunch, or being kept out of the loop on workplace-related emails and threads, may engage in more withdrawal behaviors (Ferris et al., 2008; Gamian-Wilk & Madeja-Bien, 2018), including withdrawal from an organization (O'Reilly et al., 2015).

Almost every person has been both a victim and knowingly or unknowingly a perpetrator of workplace ostracism at various points in their lives (Williams & Nida, 2011). The experience of social exclusion can spiral to reduced work effort (Xia, Wang, Song, Zhang, & Qian, 2019) and subsequent poor performance on work tasks (Gamian-Wilk & Madeja-Bien, 2018; Leung, Wu, Chen, & Young, 2011; O'Reilly et al., 2015; Robinson & Schabram, 2016). Importantly, experiencing workplace ostracism is meaningfully different and *more* harmful than experiencing explicit workplace harassment (e.g., bullying), despite perpetrators' and bystanders' inclination to think otherwise (O'Reilly et al., 2015). In addition, ostracism is considerably more ambiguous than other harmful workplace behaviors (Williams, 2001). Particularly pernicious compared to other forms of workplace mistreatment (e.g., workplace incivility, antisocial behavior, workplace harassment, workplace aggression, and sexual harassment), workplace ostracism is a major contributor to worker burnout, including professional inefficacy (Sulea, Filipescu, Horga, Ortan, & Fischmann, 2012). Unfortunately, employees view excluding someone as generally acceptable, whereas almost all other forms of workplace ill-treatments (e.g., harassment and abuse) are considered unacceptable under most circumstances (O'Reilly et al., 2015). This could mean that people are unlikely to intervene on behalf of the victims of ostracism. The victims themselves may also be less likely to seek help or advice. Thus, specifically studying performance-related implications of workplace ostracism on victims, a generally silent group, is of utmost importance.

Situating Workplace Ostracism as Antecedent to Workplace Outcomes

Workplace exclusion is often categorized as a psychosocial stressor. Stressors, when appraised as a threat (per the appraisal theory, Lazarus, 1991) often result in strain or unfavorable or adverse outcomes, including poor psychological (e.g., depression and anxiety) and physiological (e.g., tension headaches, backaches) health, as well as deviant behaviors (e.g., over- or under-eating, stealing, absence from work) that affect the person and the organization (Beehr & Glazer, 2001). As the review below presents, factors associated with the environment and the person often serve as boundary conditions for when workplace ostracism results in unfavorable outcomes, such as negative performance-related outcomes—the focus of this chapter. The remaining sections dive deeply into the performance-related outcomes of workplace ostracism on effort, job performance, creativity/innovation, and job withdrawal behaviors. The chapter concludes with recommendations for future research.

Performance Outcomes of Workplace Ostracism

Effort

The relationship between workplace ostracism and effort. As is often the case in the ostracism literature, the relationship between ostracism and effort is paradoxical, with some theories positing that the experience of ostracism results in increased task motivation and effort, and other theories suggesting that ostracism results in reductions of effort. According to Baumeister, DeWall, Ciarocco, and Twenge (2005), ostracism is costly to effort and performance due to an impairment in self-regulation. In other recent work, Walasek, Juanchich, and Sirota (2019) attempted to disentangle four competing hypotheses as to the relationship between ostracism and cooperative behavior. Two seemingly inconsistent hypotheses were gleaned from the need-threat model, and hinge on which needs were most threatened as a result of the ostracism experience. According to the *reconnection hypothesis*, the motivation to repair esteem and belongingness needs relate to general prosocial tendencies. In contrast, if the dominant response to ostracism is thwarted feelings of self-control and meaningful existence, people will respond to social exclusion by a general withdrawal of cooperative tendencies (the *aggression hypothesis*). The *cognitive depletion hypotheses* argue that decrements in cooperation are the result of a decreased cognitive abilities, based on the assumption that ostracism depletes resources. Finally, the parsimonious *revenge hypothesis* posits that individuals are selectively uncooperative (and potentially less motivated to expend effort with) perpetrators of ostracism.

In support of the reconnection hypothesis, some research finds that people who are ostracized increase their prosocial tendencies, through ingratiation (Scott et al., 2015), social compliance (Carter-Sowell et al., 2008), expressing their liking of others (Maner, DeWall, Baumeister, & Schaller, 2007), doing more for others (i.e., organizational citizenship behaviors; Walasek et al., 2019), and increasing effort (i.e., in-role performance; Williams & Sommer, 1997). Aside from Williams and Sommer's classic (1997) study, experimental support for compensatory effort as a response to ostracism is scant. In this seminal study, women who were ostracized redoubled their efforts in subsequent tasks, but men who were ostracized loafed. Given that men engage in greater self-enhancement than women do (Magee & Upenieks, 2019), resulting in consistent gender differences in self-esteem (Bleidorn et al., 2016; Magee & Upenieks, 2019), we suspect that this interesting gender difference in compensatory effort may be due to attributional differences. Men may have a greater tendency to deflect negative feedback related to ostracism by making external attributions ("The group is a fault"), whereas women may be more likely to internalize the negative feedback ("This is my fault"), which explains their greater task motivation.

In support of the other theories mentioned above (aggression, cognitive depletion, and revenge), much of the organizational literature finds negative associations between ostracism and effort. In a recent study of higher education professionals, workplace ostracism was strongly negatively correlated with self-reported effort, and this relationship was mediated by negative affect (Anjum, Liang, Durrani, & Ahmen, 2019). Participants experiencing high rates of ostracism expressed difficulty in persisting at their work tasks, a finding echoed in Baumeister et al.'s (2005) experimental work. Similarly, among Australian employees, workplace ostracism was associated with withdrawal of work-related effort (Penhaligon, Louis, & Restubog, 2013). Moreover, after accounting for supervisor mistreatment and workgroup mistreatment, perceived workplace ostracism accounted for an additional 12% of variance in withdrawal of effort. A cross-cultural study comparing Turkish and Azerbaijani participants also found significant negative relationships between self-reported workplace ostracism and workplace effort (Türkmen et al., 2016). In an experimental study, ostracism decreased both men and women's efforts on a subsequent motor task (holding one's arms straight out without dropping them; Kerr, Seok, Poulsen, Harris, & Messe, 2008), a finding which seems to lend support to the self-regulatory failure account of ostracism.

Walasek et al.'s (2019) research offers potentially the greatest insight into the perplexing relationship between ostracism and prosocial versus antisocial behavior. In three experiments, the authors found little evidence for generalized prosocial *or* antisocial tendencies following social ostracism—excluded participants were neither more cooperative nor more selfish with novel partners. Rather, the research was most supportive of the revenge hypothesis: Excluded participants were selectively uncooperative (and revenge-oriented) toward the ostracizers. An older study reported parallel effects—there were no differences in effort between participants who were ignored or controls, but those who were ignored were less cooperative when paired with their ostracizers in subsequent tasks, behaving less generously with their perpetrators than others (Geller, Goodstein, Silver, & Sternberg, 1974). Although these findings are not terribly surprising, they go against the prevailing logic of the dominant theoretical ostracism framework, the need-threat model. Moreover, ostracized participants were capable of altering their decisions, which casts some doubt on the cognitive depletion hypothesis.

Associated mediators. Putative mediators between ostracism and effort include negative affect, reduced self-regulation, and decrements in self-awareness. As mentioned above, Anjum et al. (2019) found that workplace ostracism was strongly correlated with negative affect, which was associated with decreased effort. Thus, negative affect was implicated as a mediator of the ostracism—effort relationship. However, in their summary of experimental work, Baumeister et al. (2005) challenge the notion that negative emotional states mediate the relationship between ostracism and behavioral outcomes. Rather, they highlight decrements in self-regulation as a mediator. In six experiments, Baumeister et al. (2005) demonstrated that being excluded or rejected caused impaired self-regulation on a variety of tasks: the ability to make a healthy, but unpalatable diet choice, to resist a high-caloric snack food, to persist on a frustrating task, and to selectively attend to relevant information in a dichotic listening task. It is reasonable to conclude that experiencing caustic social experiences at work reduces one's ability to cope with resource demands and direct energy toward workplace goals.

Furthermore, in one of Baumeister et al.'s (2005) experiments, participants completed a dichotic listening task either in front of a mirror (high self-awareness) or with the mirror facing backwards (low self-awareness). Results showed that making people self-aware successfully mitigated performance decrements after ostracism. The implication of this research for the workplace is that the very state that is necessary for effective self-regulation—self-awareness—is quite aversive after ostracism, but self-awareness also prompts people to be self-reflective about their shortcomings. Thus, workplace conditions that promote self-awareness, such as frequent 360-feedback, developing a coaching culture, and encouraging frequent self-reflection may ameliorate negative effort and poor performance-related outcomes typically associated with ostracism.

Associated moderators. Although additional research is warranted to ferret out moderating variables, two factors that explain when workplace ostracism results in reduced or increased work efforts include motivation (a person-centered factor) and workplace incivility (a work environment factor). There is some evidence that given a financial incentive for performance, targets of ostracism are *capable* of self-regulation, thus suggesting that the likely culprit of decreased effort following ostracism is decreased motivation (Baumeister et al., 2005). In other words, individuals who experience ostracism are less inclined to expend energy/effort, potentially in retaliation against the perpetrators of the ostracism, and potentially, the organizations that implicitly condone such behavior. In addition, in Anjum et al.'s (2019) research, workplace incivility was implicated as a moderator of the ostracism-effort association. The relationship between ostracism and negative affect was stronger in conditions of high workplace incivility than those of low workplace incivility. This suggests that the combination of high ostracism, high workplace incivility, and high negative affect is particularly problematic in workplace environments.

Performance

The relationship between workplace ostracism and performance. Someone who is ostracized in an organization is likely to be deprived of important information and resources required to perform tasks in the job and as a result the person's job performance may suffer (Jones et al., 2009). Additionally, according to the norm of reciprocity (Cialdini, 2001), a victim of mistreatment would be expected to negatively react to the experience, especially when self-esteem is low, per sociometer theory (Leary, 2005; Wu, Wei, & Hui, 2011). The negative relationship between the experience of workplace ostracism and performance has been repeatedly corroborated in other studies.

Most studies examined the relationship between workplace ostracism and performance from the lenses of a number of psychosocial theories. For example, following the temporal need-threat model (Williams, 2009), Lustenberger and Jagacinski (2010) found that students who were ostracized from an online ball tossing game (i.e., Cyberball) performed worse on a word search task than those who felt included. They contended that when a person is ostracized, their cognitive resources are re-allocated (from performing cognitively challenging tasks) to deal with the negative experience. Other studies have considered social identity and self-categorization theories when examining the relationship between workplace ostracism and task performance. According to Chung (2015), the social identity perspective, including social identity theory (i.e., the group with which one best identifies) and self-categorization theory (i.e., people assign themselves a social category of in-group or out-group), suggests that excluded individuals view themselves as part of the out-group and dissimilar to other group members and this perception instigates interpersonal conflict. The "absence of shared identity," in turn, would reduce sharing of work resources and information, which causes task conflict. For example, in a two-wave study, workplace ostracism measured at Time 1 correlated with greater coworker, supervisor, and task conflict, but with lower in-role behavior measured two months later (Chung, 2015). Moreover, coworker conflict mediated the relationship between workplace ostracism and task performance. Chung suggested that coworker conflict increases negative psychological outcomes (e.g., antagonism) which in turn diverts cognitive resources from performing tasks to addressing the psychosocial conflicts.

Cottingham, Erickson, Diefendorff, and Bromley (2013) also found a reduction in quality of patient care as a result of manager-induced exclusion of nurses, after accounting for generational cohort, sex, race, and tenure. Their findings, like Chung (2015), suggest that cognitive resources are diverted from performing tasks to coping with the experience of exclusion. Schilpzand and Huang (2018) extend on the pathway from the experience of exclusion through interpretation of workplace ostracism to a subsequent performance outcome. In a study of 733 employees of an IT service company in China, they found that team member incivility indirectly negatively related to supervisor-rated proactive performance through feelings of ostracism. Moreover, drawing on sociometer and self-identity orientation theoretical perspectives, Schilpzand and Huang (2018) found that collective identity (i.e., pride in the group) and relational identities (i.e., closeness with another person) served as resources that buffered the effects of team member incivility on supervisor rated proactive performance, and intensified the effects of team member incivility on perceived workplace ostracism. In contrast, self-identity orientation (i.e., construing one's identity as unique to others), intensifies the negative relationship between team incivility and proactive performance. Schilpzand and Huang (2018) explained that experiences of incivility, appraised as a signal for potential exclusion, decrease proactive performance, because "proactive" performance can be considered non-normative and because victims are being excluded, their proactive performance is believed to go unnoticed and not acknowledged.

Although researchers typically consider performance to be an outcome measure, results of Howard, Cogswell, and Smith's (2020) meta-analysis suggest that the relationship could be reversed; performance might predict ostracism. Thus, performance issues could drive coworkers to ostracize the victim. This line of research presents an alternative perspective in that the victim's poor performance may be mobilizing coworkers to attempt to change the poor performer's behaviors, as ostracism may be used to exert social control over the behaviors of colleagues (Feinberg, Willer, & Schultz, 2014). A concern of this perspective is a possible "blame the victim" mentality that wrongly justifies treating another person poorly.

Associated mediators and moderators. Several process variables, as mediators and/or moderators, are associated with the relationship between workplace ostracism and performance. For example, the negative relationship between perceived threat of workplace ostracism and performance is stronger for those who have a high need for affiliation and weaker for those high on self-compassion (Ma & Liu, 2020), but the relationship can be buffered by political skill too (Yang & Treadway, 2018). In this section, we focus on properties of the person (e.g., self-esteem, conscientiousness and openness to experience, need to belong, and sense of self) and the environment (e.g., empowerment, work engagement, physical strength and emotional energy, customer orientation, sense of self, and family support) that would increase or decrease the likelihood by which workplace ostracism would relate to performance.

Self-esteem. Per sociometer theory (Leary, 2005), workplace ostracism can impede an individual's self-esteem. According to self-verification theory (Swann, 2012), people have a tendency to act in a way that is consistent with their perception of self. Thus, when a victim's self-esteem is lowered, the victim would try to verify the negative perceptions of self by decreasing job performance. Research has demonstrated that workplace ostracism undermined job performance indirectly via threatening self-esteem (Ferris, Lian, Brown, & Morrison, 2015; Peng & Zeng, 2017). Moreover, although workplace ostracism accounted for a significant 3% of variance in job performance after accounting for conscientiousness and openness to experience, when introducing organizational-based self-esteem, the beta weight for workplace ostracism became non-significant, thus indicating that workplace ostracism threatens self-esteem, which then causes one to disengage as evident in reduced job performance. Huertas-Valdivia, Braojos, and Lloréns-Montes (2019), in a study of hotel workers in Spain, also found that self-esteem mediates the relationship between workplace ostracism and customer service performance. Drawing on self-determination theory (which asserts that people have innate needs for competence, autonomy, and relatedness; Deci & Ryan, 2008), Huertas-Valdivia et al. further found that empowering employees (a property of the work environment) mitigated the negative effects of ostracism on self-esteem and subsequent performance. Moreover, per the sociometer theory and need to belong theory, ostracized individuals, when given an opportunity to socially affiliate with others who had initially excluded them (i.e., fulfill their need for self-esteem and belonging), were motivated to perform better on cognitive ability tasks (Jamieson, Harkins, & Williams, 2010).

Self-esteem can also moderate the relationship between workplace ostracism and performance outcomes (Ferris et al., 2015; Peng & Zeng, 2017). To account for the inconsistent findings regarding the relationship between workplace ostracism and job performance via self-esteem, Ferris et al. (2015) examined the moderating effect of contingent self-esteem (i.e., whether one's self-esteem is context-dependent, in this case performance at work) and found that when someone's self-esteem is contingent on their performance at work, one has a tendency to try and self-enhance (i.e., try to improve their performance) instead of self-verify.

Work engagement and resource-related mediators. In a study of Chinese employees at 19 hotels, work engagement fully mediated the relationship between self-reported workplace ostracism and poor supervisor ratings of (customer) service performance (Leung et al., 2011). Leung et al. (2011) utilized COR theory and the need-threat model to explain why work engagement mediates the relationship. They contend that experience of ostracism threatens fundamental needs and depletes resources which causes the victim to try and conserve the limited resources and re-allocate the limited resources to address the threat to the fundamental needs (Leung et al., 2011). Another study, on a sample in China of 671 subordinates and 121 supervisors, showed that self-reported workplace ostracism negatively correlated with self-reported performance, as well as with supervisor reported task performance and the relationship was mediated by physical strength and emotional energy (Xia et al., 2019). Employing the same two theoretical bases as Xia et al. (2019), in a longitudinal study, job tension and customer orientation fully mediated the relationship between workplace ostracism and customer service orientation (rated by supervisors; Zhu, Lyu, Deng, & Ye, 2017). Zhu et al. (2017) surmised that workplace ostracism lowers personal and social resources by threatening fundamental needs and coping with workplace ostracism, thus requiring utilization of personal and social resources. They argued that scarcity of resources makes it exceedingly difficult for one to fulfill the demands at work and meet all the expectations. This inability to fulfill expectations then causes job tension which reduces customer orientation and ultimately has a negative effect on performance (in terms of proactive customer service performance). Further, drawing on COR theory, as well as self-esteem theory, Wu et al. (2011) found that as self-reported workplace ostracism increased, supervisor ratings of the employees' performance decreased. They explain that performance may suffer as a result of reduced or no information needed to perform well, as well as due to diversion and depletion of resources.

Mitigating moderators. There are also other boundary and process conditions that would help mitigate the negative consequences of workplace ostracism on performance (Ferris et al., 2015; Huertas-Valdivia et al., 2019). Ferris et al. (2015) contend, via self-enhancement and self-verification theory, that people with a strong sense of self, via social reconnection (Maner et al., 2007), might try to improve their performance, whereas those with a poor sense of self might perform poorly. Steinbauer, Renn, Chen, and Rhew (2018), who drew on social exclusion, self-determination, and self-regulation theories to study 101 full-time U.S. manufacturers and resellers, found that self-leadership strategies (i.e., deliberate behaviors a person takes to manage stressors, e.g., goal-setting and self-reward) mediated the ostracism-performance relationship when intrinsic motivation was high, but no mediation was found when intrinsic motivation was low or at the mean level.

Consistent with COR Theory (Hobfoll, 1989), job demands-resources model (Bakker & Demerouti, 2014), and the transactional framework of stress (Lazarus & Folkman, 1984), environmental variables, such as support, sometimes mitigate the relationship between workplace ostracism and performance. In a study of 523 Chinese employees, Xia and colleagues (2019) found that low spousal support intensified the negative relationship between workplace ostracism and emotional energy, but the relationship was mostly mitigated when spousal support was high, which protects against decreased supervisor-rated task performance (Xia et al., 2019). Feng, Li, Feng, and Jiang (2019), in their two-wave study on 727 Chinese hospital workers, found that workplace ostracism negatively related to innovative job performance (i.e., fulfillment or achievement of new and advanced performance indicators) and in-role performance. Moreover, family support buffered the negative relationship between workplace ostracism and innovative job performance. Other work environment variables that have been investigated include psychological empowerment (Chung, 2018; Huertas-Valdivia et al., 2019) and social networking services for work-related purposes (Chung & Kim, 2017).

Creativity/Innovation

The relationship between workplace ostracism and creativity/innovation. Experiencing ostracism has been associated with lower levels of creativity in some studies (e.g., Kwan, Zhang, Liu, & Lee, 2018) and divergent, innovative thinking in others (e.g., Ashton-James & Chartrand, 2009). The dynamic componential theory of creativity argues that creativity is moderated by both social factors within the organization (e.g., through leadership behaviors and coworker interactions) and social factors external to the organization (Amabile & Pratt, 2016). This theory contends that ostracism negatively impacts creativity through reduced access to task resources and decreased creative process engagement. Moreover, when people feel they are not valued, they are likely to decrease engagement and redirect attention to ameliorating their social experiences (per engagement theory; Kwan et al., 2018). Consistent with these theories, Kwan et al. (2018) found that when employees perceived their supervisors were ostracizing them, supervisor-rated creativity of the employee decreased. Supervisor ostracism was also associated with reduced employee access to required task resources, which decreased creativity as rated by the supervisor.

Associated moderators. As elaborated below, we propose that the implications of workplace ostracism on creativity should be considered in terms of perceived organizational support, an individual's sense of social self-efficacy, the subtlety of the ostracism, and cultural context and individual values.

Perceived organizational support (POS). Perceived organizational support (POS) can be operationalized as experiences associated with receiving help or special favor from the organization, as well as resources to support one's well-being, and being valued for one's contribution to the organization, including voicing one's own opinions (Chung, 2017). POS is often associated with one's work context (Beehr & Glazer, 2001), which can help to mitigate consequences of stressors on strains. Kwan et al. (2018) concluded that POS buffered the workplace ostracism—creativity relationship via task resources and creative engagement. In other words, when POS was high, the otherwise negative effects of workplace ostracism on both access to task resources and creative engagement process were not as strong so as to protect individual's creativity.

Therefore, POS has ameliorative implications on helping creative engagement and low POS likely reinforces disengagement per componential and engagement theories.

Social self-efficacy. Another resource that can help people cope with the experience of workplace ostracism is social self-efficacy. Together with COR theory (Hobfoll, 1989), self-efficacy theory (Maddux, 1995) suggests that the effects of workplace ostracism on a person's sense of creativity would be affected by the extent to which one believes in his or her own ability to cope with ostracism. In an experiment, Dotan-Eliaz, Sommer, and Rubin (2009) grouped study participants with two confederates. In one condition, confederates spoke with each other in Russian, thus creating a language exclusion situation. In the second condition, the confederates, although recognizing Russian as a common language between them, did not speak it in front of the study participant, thus creating a language inclusion situation. The researchers found that when participants with *high* social self-efficacy were told they would reconvene with their group to share independently developed ideas, those who were ostracized generated more ideas than those who were included (Dotan-Eliaz et al., 2009). In contrast, those with low social self-efficacy performed worse in the ostracism condition than the inclusion condition. The researchers posit that this difference in behavior is due to conflicting expectations about the likelihood of social reward. Those high in social self-efficacy expect that strong performance will incur social reward (the affiliation hypothesis), whereas those low in social self-efficacy are less optimistic, thus ostracism prompts withdrawal. Thus, social self-efficacy serves as an important moderator of the relationship between ostracism and creativity.

Subtlety of the ostracism experience. Behavioral mimicry (i.e., non-consciously replicating others' facial expressions and gestures, Farley, 2020) is normative in conversations, signals affiliative intent and cooperative motives (Ashton-James & Chartrand, 2009), and elicits conformity (Leander, Chartrand, & Wood, 2010). Thus, the absence of behavioral mimicry is often experienced as social rejection and is more typical of individuals' experiences with out-group members. Because creativity relies upon innovative and divergent thinking, for example, going against the norm, creativity is predicted to be greater in conditions where behavioral mimicry is lacking. In line with this logic, Ashton-James and Chartrand (2009) found that participants in their experiment were more creative and demonstrated greater divergent thinking when they were not mimicked by an experimenter and greater convergent thinking when they were mimicked. In contrast, in their experiment using business students, Fan and Wang (2015) found that being ignored, compared to purposeful rejection, reduced motivation to participate in creativity tasks. Thus, type of social rejection moderated creativity outcome. These studies highlight an important consideration of ostracism's effects. Generally, overt ostracism can function to decrease access to important resources to engage in creative work, and/or harm motivation to engage in creative tasks, thus suppressing creativity. However, subtle nonconscious ostracism (in the form of lack of mimicry or averted eye gaze, Wirth et al., 2010) may stimulate creative thought by signaling independence, autonomy, and non-conformity.

Cultural contexts. Increases in creativity following ostracism were found to be related to self-construal and sense of group belongingness. Kim, Vincent, and Gancalo (2013) argued that when people with an interdependent self-construal are socially rejected, they might be less creative, as they might be utilizing their resources to repair social relationships. Indeed, Park and Kitayama (2014) found that task performance decreased and emotional/defensive responses increased when people with an interdependent self-construal felt that their social self was threatened. This finding might explain why Japanese students who focused more on rejection avoidance (compared with those focused on harmony seeking or those with an independent self-construal) had greater salivary amylase (a physiological indicator of "stress"; Hashimoto & Yamagishi, 2013). Research also shows that creativity is sometimes stifled by excessive stress (Rich, 2016). Together, these findings help to explain why, in Kim et al.'s study, socially rejected individuals primed for interdependent self-construal were less creative than socially included individuals. In contrast, when participants were primed with an independent self-construal, socially rejected participants were more creative and had a higher need for uniqueness than socially included participants (Kim et al., 2013).

As further evidence of the importance of the role of cultural context and interdependence, Tu, Cheng, and Liu (2019) found that in China, telecommunications workers who experienced workplace ostracism had reduced creativity. Moreover, the relationship was stronger when individuals self-reported having greater (individual-level) collectivistic values rather than low collectivistic values. Similarly, Jahanzeb and Fatima

(2018) discussed the harmful implications of ostracism in collectivistic societies, considering the amplification of ostracism on negative outcomes.

Withdrawal Behaviors

The relationship between workplace ostracism and withdrawal behaviors. Absenteeism, turnover intention, and actual turnover are example withdrawal behaviors that might result from workplace ostracism. For example, following the temporal need-threat model of ostracism in a longitudinal study, Liu (2019) found that workplace ostracism positively correlated with self-reported absenteeism. Other studies found that workplace ostracism has a stronger positive correlation with turnover intention than actual turnover, but the correlation with the latter is still significant (Howard et al., 2020; O'Reilly et al., 2015). Renn, Allen, and Huning (2013) also found a significant correlation between workplace ostracism and turnover intention, but not actual turnover (based on actual data gathered seven months post-survey administration) among a sample of U.S. counselors and educators. However, their structural equations model showed a direct effect between workplace ostracism and turnover intention, as well as actual turnover.

When managers were a source of exclusion (or ostracism), turnover intention was high in a sample of US nurses, adding 9.4% of additional significant variance in intention to leave, after accounting for generational cohort, sex, race, and tenure (Cottingham et al., 2013). In another study, workplace ostracism and turnover intention positively correlated among a sample of Chinese employees (Lyu & Zhu, 2017). Workplace ostracism accounted for a significant 11% of additional variance in Australians' turnover intention after several variables, including supervisor mistreatment, workgroup mistreatment, and supportive norms, were taken into account (Penhaligon et al., 2013). Ferris et al. (2008) showed that the positive relationship between workplace ostracism and turnover intention continued to be strong even when the latter was measured five months later.

Associated moderators. Like with other outcome variables, a few studies have presented boundary conditions of the workplace ostracism-withdrawal behavior outcomes. In a study of Chinese employees, Zheng, Yang, Ngo, Liu, and Jiao (2016) found that the positive correlation between workplace ostracism and turnover intention was stronger for those low (vs. high) on psychological capital. However, in a sample of US employees, the relationship between coworker exclusion (operationalized as perceived envy) and turnover intention was stronger for employees high (vs. low) in positive affectivity, though still positive for both (Scott, Tams, Schippers, & Lee, 2015). Scott et al. (2015) explained that for participants high on positive affectivity, but experiencing that they are envied, intention to leave probably increases because they have difficulty socially reconnecting with others (who envy them).

Similarly, Fiset, Al Hajj, and Vongas (2017) found that external social support (from non-work contacts, such as family, friends, significant other) moderated the relationship between workplace ostracism and turnover intention. In their first study (of full-time working adults in the USA, with data collected via Mechanical Turk), ostracized individuals were less likely to consider leaving their organization when external support was high, but in their second study (of full-time working adults in Canada solicited through snowball sampling), external support intensified the workplace ostracism-turnover intention relationship. The authors speculated that cultural factors, such as gender of the ostracizer, temporal orientation, power distance, and individualism-collectivism, might explain some of the divergent findings, but clearly more research is needed.

Future Research Opportunities

Our review of the literature on performance-related outcomes associated with workplace ostracism quietly revealed a potential challenge in the literature, namely, clearly articulating what kind of variable workplace ostracism represents. We also identified that although factors of the person or the environment were identified as boundary conditions that intensify or buffer effects of workplace ostracism on performance-related outcomes, there is little research on how people cope with either the perception of workplace ostracism, or worse, the feeling of workplace ostracism.

Workplace Ostracism as Outcome, Stressor, or Appraisal. Social psychological literature typically studies factors that elicit the experience of ostracism (e.g., Hales, Kassner, Williams, & Graziano, 2016; Rudert, Keller, Hales, Walker, & Greifeneder, 2020). Much of the IO psychology literature attempts to examine the implications of workplace ostracism. However, in so doing, IO psychology scholars will often ignore the antecedents of workplace ostracism. In other words, we need to begin asking what factors in the workplace environment caused one to experience social exclusion as workplace ostracism? In order to rectify problems associated with workplace ostracism, it behooves researchers to delve more deeply into the causes of it. It is the causes of workplace ostracism that need to be examined carefully in order to redress the insidious implication on performance.

This need further sheds light on another problem, which is where workplace ostracism should be situated in the nomological net? This call for clarity is not new. A recent meta-analysis indicates that ostracism's placement in the nomological net is still unclear (Howard et al., 2020). Using the transactional framework of stress, which presents a flow from stressor to appraisal of stressor to strain or outcome, the literature we reviewed sometimes conceptualized workplace ostracism as a psychosocial stressor (i.e., the stimulus or the noxious environmental situation stemming from interpersonal issues) and sometimes as the appraisal of the workplace environment (i.e., appraising social exclusion as ostracism; e.g., O'Reilly et al., 2015; Wesselmann & Dvir, (2020). The effects of workplace ostracism on work performance are, therefore, a result of interpreting workplace exclusion as a threat—as ostracism. However, drawing on both cognitive appraisal theory and temporal need-threat model (Williams, 2009), it is the direct experience of workplace ostracism that creates psychological discomfort that requires adaptive coping (Robinson et al., 2013). Such a toxic workplace may lead to reduced physical and psychological well-being (Wu, Yim, Kwan, & Zhang, 2012). In this example, workplace ostracism is the psychosocial stressor.

Coping. The threat of being ignored or feeling like one is missing out on important information that one's social network or role set normally provides (Robinson et al., 2013; Sparrowe, Liden, Wayne, & Kraimer, 2001; Wu et al., 2012) leads a person to determine if coping resources are available (Lazarus & Folkman, 1984; Williams, 2009). People who are ostracized often ruminate over events during which they felt ostracized and expend resources to try to figure out how to reduce such experiences or identify alternative explanations (Lustenberger & Jagacinski, 2010). By ruminating over the experience, one's coping resources begin to drain, and it becomes increasingly difficult for the employee to fulfill performance expectations, which then creates job tension and ill feelings toward the organization (Wu et al., 2011, 2012). Considering the conservation of resource (COR) Theory (Hobfoll, 1989), people who feel ostracized struggle to feel motivated and excited to engage in other events. When coping resources are insufficient, the threat intensifies to the point that task performance (fulfilling work-related duties), proactivity (future-oriented behaviors that stimulate more opportunities or reduce barriers to goal fulfillment), and adaptive performance (adaptive behaviors with changing organizational processes and requirements) decrease (Ma & Liu, 2020). However, what exactly constitutes coping? Is it the mere presence of resources or the actual use of the resources that enables people to deal with workplace ostracism?

Social support. Social support is a resource (in the environment) that, when perceived to be given, might help reduce the positive relationship between workplace ostracism and performance. For example, Sakurai and Jex (2012) found that supervisor social support buffered the effects of negative emotions that result from workplace incivility on work effort (i.e., attentional resources devoted to fulfilling work tasks). Additionally, Neves and Pina e Cunha (2018) found that employees with abusive supervisors experienced lower levels of ostracism when coworker support through humor was high (vs. low). These results suggest that supervisor or coworker social support could help reduce the threat that incivility or abusive supervision creates, but a lack of social support might threaten one's well-being (Sakurai & Jex, 2012), thereby intensifying the consequences of workplace ostracism. Still, if ostracism is perceived as coming from peers and supervisors, their support would *un*likely yield ameliorative effects, but instead, support from one's life partner appears to help (Xia et al., 2019). Thus far, there is little research on the effects of support on outcomes due to workplace ostracism. Further exploration regarding the role of a person's work and non-work environment on the effects of workplace ostracism on well-being and performance-related outcomes is needed.

Social support: A conundrum. An important point to recall is that part of the operationalization of workplace ostracism includes feeling that support from one's colleagues or supervisor(s) is withheld (Wu et al., 2012). Unfortunately, often people who experience ostracism also have poor interactions with colleagues and supervisors in the workplace (Xia et al., 2019). In fact, it is possible that the target of ostracism might be a threat to the perpetrators and, therefore, might be perceived as burdens to the organization's social order, costing the perpetrators time, reputation, and money (Neves & Pina e Cunha, 2018). Therefore, sometimes a person's demeanor repels support, such as if the person is behaving in an emotionally unstable manner (Bowling, Beehr, & Swader, 2005;

Tulin, Lancee, & Volker, 2018). When a person's personality repels support, it is likely that the individual feeling socially excluded, who is already not perceived favorably, will continue to experience workplace ostracism, which will spiral into poor performance and turnover intention. Looked at from a different lens, people who attract social support from coworkers and supervisors are likely to experience less workplace ostracism, as evident in the coworker "humor as support" study (Neves & Pina e Cunha, 2018; see also Howard et al., 2020, meta-analysis).

Concluding Remarks

The findings summarized in this chapter suggest that workplace ostracism, a ubiquitous human behavior, is a painful experience (Williams, 2007). In addition to its psychological implications, workplace ostracism also creates a noxious experience that resonate as behavioral performance-related outcomes, such as reduced work effort (Xia et al., 2019), poorer task performance (Gamian-Wilk & Madeja-Bien, 2018; Leung et al., 2011; O'Reilly et al., 2015; Robinson & Schabram, 2016), reduced creativity/innovation (Ashton-James & Chartrand, 2009; Kwan et al., 2018), and increased absenteeism, turnover intention, and actual turnover (Howard et al., 2020; Liu, 2019; O'Reilly et al., 2015; Renn et al., 2013). Managers should further diagnose the antecedents of workplace ostracism and find constructive interventions to prevent the antecedents or, at least, introduce resources to help mitigate its subsequent performance consequences.

Still, going to foundational research on ostracism, we cannot forget scholarly findings that ostracism serves an adaptive purpose (Lustenberger & Jagacinski, 2010). "People who are unreliable, who act on selfish impulses, who break moral or legal rules, who fail to keep promises, who subject others to emotional outbursts, who exhibit inappropriate aggressive actions, and who in other ways fail at self-regulation are often rejected or excluded by others" (Baumeister et al., 2005, p. 601).

There is no denying that ostracism is painful and extremely punitive and, sadly, often high performers get away with being workplace ostracizers (Quade, Greenbaum, & Petrenko, 2017). However, people do ***not*** typically ostracize likeable people who are performing to the groups' normative expectations (i.e., high- but not overly high-performers; Jensen, Patel, & Raver, 2014). People are more likely to ostracize (i.e., covertly victimize) unlikable overachievers (i.e., proactive victims;

Howard et al., 2020) and overtly victimize people who don't perform or contribute to the organization (Jensen et al., 2014). In other words, being a victim of ostracism feels terrible and being a passive victim (i.e., someone who is positionally weak, passive, insecure, and often rejected) is even harder as the victim rarely stands up for him or herself. However, having to work with an aggressive, hostile, and generally unlikable person, whose performance does not fit the group's norms also feels terrible (Renn et al., 2013) and both parties' feelings are personal (Howard et al., 2020).

Furthermore, as presented earlier, the causal direction of workplace ostracism and performance is not clearly established (Feinberg et al., 2014; Howard et al., 2020). It is just as likely that workplace ostracism causes poor performance for the victim, as much as the victim's poor (or non-normative) performance causes the victim to experience workplace ostracism. Establishing the possibility of a reverse causal effect, we assert that although at no time would an organization want to condone ostracism, inevitably ostracism can have outcomes that benefit the organization. Examples of benefits to the organization include when a person increases his or her work efforts (to perform better), becomes increasingly creative, and changes behaviors to align with organizational norms. From an evolutionary lens (Lustenberger & Jagacinski, 2010), ostracism can also benefit the organization when an ostracized individual, who did not fit the organization or job (i.e., did not conform to organizational norms), voluntarily leaves. It is hoped that leaving the organization also benefits the individual feeling ostracized, as the person seeks employment somewhere s/he is comfortable and fits in.

This chapter addressed several theories for studying different angles of workplace ostracism, including cognitive appraisal theory, the temporal need-threat model, sociometer theory, self-esteem theory, self-verification theory, attribution theory, job demands-resources theory, and COR theory. Several theories consider the role of individual differences (aspects of the person), such as self-esteem, self-efficacy, and conscientiousness. Other theories address situational factors (aspects of the environment), such as supervisor social support, perceived organizational support, and perhaps even culture (as studies reviewed were from East Asia and Anglo/European countries). Both person and environment variables provide boundary conditions, serving as mediators or moderators of the relationship between workplace ostracism and outcomes. It is clear that workplace ostracism has pragmatic impacts on performance, including creativity (Kwan et al., 2018), however research on the boundary conditions of workplace ostracism are limited. Future studies would benefit from discerning types of workplace ostracism, as well as employing the transactional framework of stress to identify conditions under which workplace ostracism is experienced, aspects of the person (i.e., personality of both victim and perpetrator) and environment (including cultural context and sources of support) which increase or mitigate ostracism and its consequences, and assess the causal direction of workplace ostracism and performance-related variables.

References

Amabile, T. M., & Pratt, M. G. (2016). The dynamic componential model of creativity and innovation in organizations: Making progress, making meaning. *Research in Organizational Behavior, 36*, 157–183. https://doi.org/10.1016/j.riob.2016.10.001.

Anderson, J. W. (2009). Organizational shunning: The disciplinary functions of "non-sense". *Atlantic Journal of Communication, 17*(1), 36–50. https://doi.org/10.1080/15456870802506140.

Anjum, M., Liang, D., Durrani, D., & Ahmed, A. (2019). Workplace ostracism and discretionary work effort: A conditional process analysis. *Journal of Management & Organization*, Advance online publication, 1–18. https://doi.org/10.1017/jmo.2019.14.

Ashton-James, C. E., & Chartrand, T. L. (2009). Social cues for creativity: The impact of behavioral mimicry on convergent and divergent thinking. *Journal of Experimental Social Pscyhology, 45*(4), 1036–1040. https://doi.org/10.1016/j.jesp.2009.04.030.

Bakker, A. B., & Demerouti, E. (2014). Job demands-resources theory. In P. Y. Chen & C. L. Cooper (Eds.), *Wellbeing: A complete reference guide. Vol. III: Work and wellbeing* (pp. 37–64). Chichester, UK: Wiley. https://doi.org/10.1002/9781118539415.wbwell019

Baumeister, R. F., DeWall, C. N., Ciarocco, N. J., & Twenge, J. M. (2005). Social exclusion impairs self-regulation. *Journal of Personality and Social Psychology, 88*(4), 589–604. https://doi-org.proxy-ub.researchport.umd.edu/10.1037/0022-3514.88.4.589.

Baumeister, R. F., & Leary, M. R. (1995). The need to belong: Desire for interpersonal attachments as a fundamental human motivation. *Psychological Bulletin, 117*(3), 497–529.

Beehr, T. A., & Glazer, S. (2001). A cultural perspective of social support in relation to occupational stress. In P. Perrewé, D. C. Ganster, & J. Moran

(Eds.), *Exploring theoretical mechanisms and perspectives: Vol. 1. Research in occupational stress and well-being* (pp. 97–142). Bingley, UK: Emerald Group.

Bernstein, M. J. (2016). Research in social psychology: Consequences of short- and long-term social exclusion. In P. Riva & J. Eck (Eds.), *Social exclusion: Psychological approaches to understanding and reducing its impact* (pp. 51–72). Cham, Switzerland: Springer. https://doi.org/10.1007/978-3-319-33033-4_3.

Blackhart, G. C., Nelson, B. C., Knowles, M. L., & Baumeister, R. F. (2009). Rejection elicits emotional reactions but neither causes immediate distress nor lowers self-esteem: A meta-analytic review of 192 studies on social exclusion. *Personality and Social Psychology Review, 13*(4), 269–309. https://doi.org/10.1177/1088868309346065.

Bleidorn, W., Arslan, R. C., Denissen, J. J. A., Rentfrow, P. J., Gebauer, J. E., Potter, J., & Gosling, S. D. (2016). Age and gender differences in self-esteem—A cross-cultural window. *Journal of Personality and Social Psychology, 111*(3), 396–410. https://doi.org/10.1037/pspp0000078.

Bowling, N. A., Beehr, T. A., & Swader, W. M. (2005). Giving and receiving social support at work: The roles of personality and reciprocity. *Journal of Vocational Behavior, 67*(3), 476–489. https://doi.org/10.1016/j.jvb.2004.08.004.

Carter-Sowell, A. R., Chen, Z., & Williams, K. D. (2008). Ostracism increases social susceptibility. *Social Influence, 3*(3), 143–153. https://doi.org/10.1080/15534510802204868.

Chung, Y. W. (2015). The mediating effects of organizational conflict on the relationships between workplace ostracism with in-role behavior and organizational citizenship behavior. *International Journal of Conflict Management, 26*(4), 366–385. https://doi.org/10.1108/IJCMA-01-2014-0001.

Chung, Y. W. (2017). The role of person-organization fit and perceived organizational support in the relationship between workplace ostracism and behavioral outcomes. *Australian Journal of Management, 42*(2), 328–349. https://doi.org/10.1177/0312896215611190.

Chung, Y. W. (2018). Workplace ostracism and workplace behaviors: A moderated mediation model of perceived stress and psychological empowerment. *Anxiety, Stress & Coping: An International Journal, 31*(3), 304–317. https://doi.org/10.1080/10615806.2018.1424835.

Chung, Y. W., & Kim, T. (2017). Impact of using social network services on workplace ostracism, job satisfaction, and innovative behaviour. *Behaviour & Information Technology, 36*(12), 1235–1243. https://doi.org/10.1080/0144929X.2017.1369568.

Cialdini, R. B. (2001). *Influence: Science and practice*. Needham Heights, MA: Allyn & Bacon.

Cooper, C. L., & Smith, M. J. (1986). *Job stress and blue collar work*. Chichester: Wiley.

Cottingham, M. D., Erickson, R. J., Diefendorff, J. M., & Bromley, G. (2013). The effect of manager exclusion on nurse turnover intention and care quality. *Western Journal of Nursing Research, 20*(10), 1–16. https://doi.org/10.1177/0193945913483880.

Deci, E. L., & Ryan, R. M. (2008). Self-determination theory: A macrotheory of human motivation, development and health. *Canadian Psychology, 49*(3), 182–185. https://doi.org/10.1037/a0012801.

Dotan-Eliaz, O., Sommer, K. L., & Rubin, Y. S. (2009). Multilingual groups: Effects of linguistic ostracism on felt rejection and anger, coworker attraction, perceived team potency, and creative performance. *Basic and Applied Social Psychology, 31*(4), 363–375. https://doi.org/10.1080/01973530903317177.

Eisenberger, N. I. (2012). The pain of social disconnection: Examining the shared neural underpinnings of physical and social pain. *Nature Reviews Neuroscience, 13*(6), 421–434. https://doi.org/10.1038/nrn3231.

Eisenberger, N. I., Lieberman, M. D., & Williams, K. D. (2003). Does rejection hurt? An fMRI study of social exclusion. *Science, 302*(5643), 290–292. https://doi.org/10.1126/science.1089134.

Fan, Z., & Wang, J. (2015). How social interactions demotivate customer participation in creativity tasks: From the perspective of social exclusion theory. Presented at the *2015 International Conference on Service Science (ICSS)*, Weihai, China (pp. 75–78). https://doi.org/10.1109/icss.2015.20.

Farley, S. D. (2020). Introduction to the special issue on nonconscious mimicry: History, applications, and theoretical and methodological innovations. *Journal of Nonverbal Behavior, 44*(1), 1–4. https://doi.org/10.1007/s10919-019-00323-0.

Feinberg, M., Willer, R., & Schultz, M. (2014). Gossip and ostracism promote cooperation in groups. *Psychological Science, 25*(3), 656–664. https://doi.org/10.1177/0956797613510184.

Feng, L., Li, J., Feng, T., & Jiang, W. (2019). Workplace ostracism and job performance: Meaning at work and family support as moderators. *Social Behavior and Personality: An International Journal, 47*(11), 1–13. https://doi.org/10.2224/sbp.8244.

Ferris, D. L., Brown, D. J., Berry, J. W., & Lian, H. (2008). The development and validation of the workplace ostracism scale. *Journal of Applied Psychology, 93*(6), 1348–1366. https://doi.org/10.1037/a0012743.

Ferris, D. L., Lian, H., Brown, D. J., & Morrison, R. (2015). Ostracism, self-esteem, and job performance: When do we self-verify and when do we self-enhance? *Academy of Management Journal, 58*(1), 279–297. https://doi.org/10.5465/amj.2011.0347.

Fiset, J., Al Hajj, R., & Vongas, J. G. (2017). Workplace ostracism seen through the lense of power. *Frontiers in Psychology*, 8, 1-19. https://doi.org/10.3389/fpsyg.2017.01528.

Gamian-Wilk, M., & Madeja-Bien, K. (2018). Ostracism in the workplace. In P. D'Cruz, E. Noronha, L. Keashly, & S. Tye-Williams (Eds.), *Special topics and particular occupations, professions and sectors: Handbooks of workplace bullying, emotional abuse, and harrassment* (Vol. 4, pp. 1–30). Singapore: Springer Nature. https://doi.org/10.1007/978-981-10-5154-8_2-1.

Geller, D. M., Goodstein, L., Silver, M., & Sternberg, W. C. (1974). On being ignored: The effects of the violation of implicit rules of social interaction. *Sociometry, 37*, 541–556. https://doi.org/10.2307/2786426.

Hales, A. H., Kassner, M. P., Williams, K. D., & Graziano, W. G. (2016). Disagreeableness as a cause and consequence of ostracism. *Personality and Social Psychology Bulletin, 42*(6), 782–797. https://doi.org/10.1177/0146167216643933.

Hashimoto, H., & Yamagishi, T. (2013). Two faces of interdependence: Harmony seeking and rejection avoidance. *Asian Journal of Social Psychology, 16*(2), 142–151.

Hobfoll, S. E. (1989). Conservation of resources: A new attempt at conceptualizing stress. *American Psychologist, 44*(3), 513–524.

Howard, M. C., Cogswell, J. E., & Smith, M. B. (2020). Antecedents and outcomes of workplace ostracism: A meta-analysis. *Journal of Applied Psychology, 105*(6), 577–596. http://dx.doi.org/10.1037/apl0000453.

Huertas-Valdivia, I., Braojos, J., & Lloréns-Montes, F. J. (2019). Counteracting workplace ostracism in hospitality with psychological empowerment. *International Journal of Hospitality Management, 76*(Part A), 240–251. https://doi.org/10.1016/j.ijhm.2018.05.013.

Jahanzeb, S., & Fatima, T. (2018). How workplace ostracism influences interpersonal deviance: The mediating role of defensive silence and emotional exhaustion. *Journal of Business and Psychology, 33*(6), 779–791. https://doi.org/10.1007/s10869-017-9525-6.

Jamieson, J. P., Harkins, S. G., & Williams, K. D. (2010). Need threat can motivate performance after ostracism. *Personality and Social Psychology Bulletin, 36*(5), 690–702. https://doi.org/10.1177/0146167209358882.

Jensen, J. M., Patel, P. C., & Raver, J. L. (2014). Is it better to be average? High and low performance as predictors of employee victimization. *Journal of Applied Psychology, 99*(2), 296–309.

Jones, E. E., Carter-Sowell, A. R., Kelly, J. R., & Williams, K. D. (2009). "I'm out of the loop": Ostracism through information exclusion. *Group Processes and Intergroup Relations, 12*(2), 157–174. https://doi.org/10.1177/1368430208101054.

Jones, E. E., & Kelly, J. R. (2010). "Why am I out of the loop?" Attributions influence responses to information exclusion. *Personality and Social Psychology Bulletin, 20*(10), 1–16. https://doi.org/10.1177/0146167210380406.

Kerr, N. L., Seok, D. H., Poulsen, J. R., Harris, D. W., & Messe, L. A. (2008). Social ostracism and group motivation gain. *European Journal of Social Psychology, 38*(4), 736–746.

Kim, S. H., Vincent, L. C., & Goncalo, J. A. (2013). Outside advantage: Can social rejection fuel creative thought? *Journal of Experimental Psychology: General, 142*(3), 605–611. https://doi.org/10.1037/a0029728.

Kwan, H. K., Zhang, X., Liu, J., & Lee, C. (2018). Workplace ostracism and employee creativity: An integrative approach incorporating pragmatic and engagement roles. *Journal of Applied Psychology, 103*(12), 1358–1366. https://doi.org/10.1037/apl0000320.

Lakin, J. L., & Chartrand, T. L. (2003). Using nonconscious behavioral mimicry to create affiliation and rapport. *Psychological Science, 14*(4), 334–339. https://doi.org/10.1111/1467-9280.14481.

Lazarus, R. S. (1991). *Emotion and adaptation*. New York, NY: Oxford University Press.

Lazarus, R. S., & Folkman, S. (1984). *The handbook of behavioral medicine*. New York, NY: Guilford.

Leary, M. R. (1990). Responses to social exclusion: Social anxiety, jealousy, loneliness, depression, and low self-esteem. *Journal of Social and Clinical Psychology, 9*(2), 221–229. https://doi.org/10.1521/jscp.1990.9.2.221.

Leary, M. R. (2005). Sociometer theory and the pursuit of relational value: Getting to the root of self-esteem. *European Review of Social Psychology, 16*(1), 75–111.

Leary, M. R., Springer, C., Negel, L., Ansell, E., & Evans, K. (1998). The causes, phenomenology, and consequences of hurt feelings. *Journal of Personality and Social Psychology, 74*(5), 1225–1237.

Leung, A. S. M., Wu, L. Z., Chen, Y. Y., & Young, M. N. (2011). The impact of workplace ostracism in service organizations. *International Journal of Hospitality Management, 30*(4), 836–844. https://doi.org/10.1016/j.ijhm.2011.01.004.

Liu, C. (2019). Ostracism, attributions, and their relationships with international students' and employees' outcomes: The moderating effect of perceived harming intent. *Journal of Occupational Health Psychology, 24*(5), 556–571. https://doi.org/10.1037/ocp0000130.

Lustenberger, D. E., & Jagacinski, C. M. (2010). Exploring the effects of ostracism on performance and intrinsic motivation. *Human Performance, 23*(4), 283–304. https://doi.org/10.1080/08959285.2010.501046.

Lyu, Y., & Zhu, H. (2017). The predictive effects of workplace ostracism on employee attitudes: A job embeddedness perspective. *Journal of Business Ethics, 158*(4), 1083–1095. https://doi.org/10.1007/s10551-017-3741-x.

Ma, Y., & Liu, C. (2020). *Workplace ostracism and appraisal: The moderating effects of the need for affiliation and self-compassion*. Manuscript in preparation.

Maddux, J. E. (1995). Self-efficacy theory. In J. E. Maddux (Ed.), *Self-efficacy, adaptation, and adjustment* (pp. 3–33). The plenum series in social/clinical psychology. Boston, MA: Springer.

Magee, W., & Upenieks, L. (2019). Gender differences in self-esteem, unvarnished self-evaluation, future orientation, self-enhancement and self-derogation in a U.S. national sample. *Personality and Individual Differences, 149*, 66–77.

Maner, J. K., DeWall, C. N., Baumeister, R. F., & Schaller, M. (2007). Does social exclusion motivate interpersonal reconnection? Resolving the "porcupine problem". *Journal of Personality and Social Psychology, 92*(1), 42–55. https://doi.org/10.1037/0022-3514.92.1.42.

Neves, P., & Pina e Cunha, M. (2018). Exploring a model of workplace ostracism: The value of coworker humor. *International Journal of Stress Management, 25*(4), 330–347.

O'Reilly, J., Robinson, S. L., Berdahl, J. L., & Banki, S. (2015). Is negative attention better than no attention? The comparative effects of ostracism and harassment at work. *Organization Science, 26*(3), 774–793. https://doi.org/10.1287/orsc.2014.0900.

Park, J., & Kitayama, S. (2014). Interdependent selves show face-induced facilitation of error processing: Cultural neuroscience of self-threat. *Social Cognitive and Affective Neuroscience, 9*(2), 201–208. https://doi.org/10.1093/scan/nss125.

Peng, A. C., & Zeng, W. (2017). Workplace ostracism and deviant and helping behaviors: The moderating role of 360 degree feedback. *Journal of Organizational Behavior, 38*(6), 833–855. https://doi.org/10.1002/job.2169.

Penhaligon, N. L., Louis, W. R., & Restubog, S. L. D. (2013). Feeling left out? The mediating role of perceived rejection on workgroup mistreatment and affective, behavioral, and organizational outcomes and the moderating role of organizational norms. *Journal of Applied Social Psychology, 43*(3), 480–497. https://doi.org/10.1111/j.1559-1816.2013.01026.x.

Pereira, D., Meier, L. L., & Elfering, A. (2013). Short-term effects of social exclusion at work and worries on sleep. *Stress and Health, 29*(3), 240–252. https://doi.org/10.1002/smi.2461.

Quade, M. J., Greenbaum, R. L., & Petrenko, O. V. (2017). "I don't want to be near you, unless…": The interactive effect of unethical behavior and performance onto relationship conflict and workplace ostracism. *Personnel Psychology, 70*(3), 675–709.

Renn, R., Allen, D., & Huning, T. (2013). The relationship of social exclusion at work with self-defeating behavior and turnover. *Journal of Social Psychology, 153*(2), 229–249. https://doi.org/10.1080/00224545.2012.723642.

Rich, S. (2016). A brief examination of occupational stress on creativity and innovation. *The Psychologist-Manager Journal, 19,* 107–121.

Riva, P., & Eck, J. (2016). The many faces of social exclusion. In P. Riva & J. Eck (Eds.), *Social exclusion: Psychological approaches to understanding and reducing its impact* (pp. ix–xv). Cham, Switzerland: Springer International Publishing.

Robinson, S., & Schabram, K. (2016). Workplace ostracism. In K. D. Williams & S. A. Nida (Eds.), *Ostracism, exclusion, and rejection* (pp. 224–239). New York, NY: Routledge.

Robinson, S. L., O'Reilly, J., & Wang, W. (2013). Invisible at work: An integrated model of workplace ostracism. *Journal of Management, 39*(1), 203–231. https://doi.org/10.1177/0149206312466141.

Rudert, S. C., Keller, M. D., Hales, A. H., Walker, M., & Greifeneder, R. (2020). Who gets ostracized? A personality perspective on risk and protective factors of ostracism. *Journal of Personality and Social Psychology, 118*(6), 1247–1268. https://doi.org/10.1037/pspp0000271.

Sakurai, K., & Jex, S. M. (2012). Coworker incvility and incivility targets' work effort and counterproductive work behaviors: The moderating role of supervisor social support. *Journal of Occupational Health Psychology, 17*(2), 150–161. https://doi.org/10.1037/a0027350.

Schilpzand, P., & Huang, L. (2018). When and how experienced incivility dissuades proactive performance: An integration of sociometer and self-identity orientation perspectives. *Journal of Applied Psychology, 103*(8), 828–841. https://doi.org/10.1111/peps.12164.

Scott, K. L., Tams, S., Schippers, M. C., & Lee, K. (2015). Opening the black box: Why and when workplace exclusion affects social reconnection behaviour, health, and attitudes. *European Journal of Work and Organizational Psychology, 24*(2), 239–255. https://doi.org/10.1080/1359432X.2014.894978.

Sparrowe, R. T., Liden, R. C., Wayne, S. J., & Kraimer, M. L. (2001). Social networks and the performance of individuals and groups. *Academy of Management Journal, 44*(2), 316–325.

Steinbauer, R., Renn, R. W., Chen, H. S., & Rhew, N. (2018). Workplace ostracism, self-regulation, and job performance: Moderating role of intrinsic work motivation. *The Journal of Social Psychology, 158*(6), 767–783. https://doi.org/10.1080/00224545.2018.1424110.

Sulea, C., Filipescu, R., Horga, A., Ortan, C., & Fischmann, G. (2012). Interpersonal mistreatment at work and burnout among teachers. *Cognition, Brain, Behavior: An Interdisciplinary Journal, 16*(4), 553–570.

Swann, W. B., Jr. (2012). Self-verification theory. In P. A. M. Van Lange, A. W. Kruglanski, & E. T. Higgins (Eds.), *Handbook of theories of social psychology* (Vol. 2, pp. 23–42). Sage. https://doi.org/10.4135/9781446249222.n27.

Tu, M., Cheng, Z., & Liu, W. (2019). Spotlight on the effect of workplace ostracism on creativity: A social cognitive perspective. *Frontiers in Psychology, 10*(Article 1215), 1–9. https://doi.org/10.3389/fpsyg.2019.01215.

Türkmen, E., Doğan, A., & Karaeminoğulları, A. (2016). The impact of ostracism on work effort: A comparison between Turkish and Azerbaijani employees. *International Journal of Human Resource Studies, 6*(4), 110–128. https://doi.org/10.5296/ijhrs.v6i4.10300.

Tulin, M., Lancee, B., & Volker, B. (2018). Personality and social capital. *Social Psychology Quarterly, 81*(4), 295–318. https://doi.org/10.1177/0190272518804533.

Twenge, J. M., Baumeister, R. F., Tice, D. M., & Stucke, T. S. (2001). If you can't join them, beat them: Effects of social exclusion on aggressive behavior. *Journal of Personality and Social Psychology, 81*(6), 1058–1069. https://doi.org/10.1037//0022-3514.81.6.1058.

Walasek, L., Juanchich, M., & Sirota, M. (2019). Adaptive cooperation in the face of social exclusion. *Journal of Experimental Social Psychology, 82*, 35–46. https://doi.org/10.1016/j.jesp.2018.11.005.

Wesselmann. E. D., & Dvir, M. (2020 forthcoming). "Exploring the Overlap Among Workplace Ostracism, Mistreatment, and Related Constructs." In C. Liu and J. Ma (Eds.), *Workplace Ostracism*. London: Palgrave Macmillan.

Wesselmann, E. D., Grzybowski, M. R., Steakley-Freeman, D. M., DeSouza, E. R., Nezlek, J. B., & Williams, K. D. (2016). Social exclusion in everyday life. In P. Riva & J. Eck (Eds.), *Social exclusion: Psychological approaches to understanding and reducing its impact* (pp. 3–23). https://doi.org/10.1007/978-3-319-33033-4.

Williams, K. D. (2001). *Ostracism: The power of silence (emotions and social behavior)*. New York, NY: Guilford.

Williams, K. D. (2007). Ostracism. *Annual Review of Psychology, 58*, 425–452. https://doi.org/10.1146/annurev.psych.58.110405.085641.

Williams, K. D. (2009). Ostracism: A temporal need-threat model. In P. Z. Mark (Ed.), *Advances in experimental social psychology* (Vol. 41, pp. 275–314). San Diego, CA: Elsevier Academic Press.

Williams, K. D., Forgas, J. P., & von Hippel, W. (Eds.). (2005). *The social outcast: Ostracism, social exclusion, rejection, and bullying*. New York, NY: Psychology Press.

Williams, K. D., & Nida, S. A. (2011). Ostracism: Consequences and coping. *Current Directions in Psychological Science, 20*(2), 71–75. https://doi.org/10.1177/0963721411402480.

Williams, K. D., & Sommer, K. L. (1997). Social ostracism by coworkers: Does rejection lead to loafing or compensation? *Personality and Social Psychology Bulletin, 23*(7), 693–706. https://doi.org/10.1177/0146167297237003.

Wirth, J. H., Sacco, D. F., Hugenberg, K., & Williams, K. D. (2010). Eye gaze as relational evaluation: Averted eye gaze leads to feelings of ostracism and relational devaluation. *Personnel and Social Psychology Bulletin, 36*(7), 869–882. https://doi.org/10.1177/0146167210370032.

Wu, L., Wei, L., & Hui, C. (2011). Dispositional antecedents and consequences of workplace ostracism: An empirical examination. *Frontiers of Business Research in China, 5*(1), 23–44. https://doi.org/10.1007/s11782-011-0119-2.

Wu, L.-Z., Yim, F. H.-k., Kwan, H. K., & Zhang, X. (2012). Coping with workplace ostracism: The roles of ingratiation and political skill in employee psychological distress. *Journal of Management Studies, 49*(1), 178–199. https://doi.org/10.1111/j.1467-6486.2011.01017.x.

Xia, A., Wang, B., Song, B., Zhang, W., & Qian, J. (2019). How and when workplace ostracism influences task performance: Through the lens of conservation of resource theory. *Human Resource Management Journal, 29*(3), 353–370. https://doi.org/10.1111/1748-8583.12226.

Yang, J., & Treadway, D. C. (2018). A social influence interpretation of workplace ostracism and counterproductive work behavior. *Journal of Business Ethics, 148*(4), 879–891. https://doi.org/10.1007/s10551-015-2912-x.

Zheng, Z., Yang, J., Ngo, H.-Y., Liu, Z.-Y., & Jiao, W. (2016). Workplace ostracism and its negative outcomes: Psychological capital as a moderator. *Journal of Personnel Psychology, 15*(4), 143–151. https://doi.org/10.1027/1866-5888/a000147.

Zhu, H., Lyu, Y., Deng, X., & Ye, Y. (2017). Workplace ostracism and proactive customer service performance: A conservation of resources perspective. *International Journal of Hospitality Management, 64*, 62–72. https://doi.org/10.1016/j.ijhm.2017.04.004.

CHAPTER 7

Ostracism in the Diverse Workplace: Experiences of Different Racial/Ethnic Groups and Immigrant Employees

Adrienne R. Carter-Sowell, Asha Ganesan, Myia S. Williams, and Carla A. Zimmerman

The U.S. labor force is becoming increasingly diverse. In 2017, the demographic profile of the U.S. workforce consisted of 62.78% non-Hispanic

The co-authors are listed in alphabetical order and the contributions are equally shared in the submission of the final chapter.

A. R. Carter-Sowell (✉)
Department of Psychological & Brain Sciences and Africana Studies Program, Texas A&M University, College Station, TX, USA
e-mail: acsowell@tamu.edu

A. Ganesan
Department of Psychological & Brain Sciences, Texas A&M University, College Station, TX, USA

M. S. Williams
Department of Medicine, Northwell Health, New Hyde Park, NY, USA

C. Liu and J. Ma (eds.), *Workplace Ostracism*,
Palgrave Explorations in Workplace Stigma,
https://doi.org/10.1007/978-3-030-54379-2_7

Whites, 17% Hispanic/Latinx workers, 13% African American/Blacks, and 6% Asians, with the remaining 1.22% consisting of other, unspecified ethnic and racial groups (U.S. Bureau of Labor Statistics, Division of Labor Force Statistics, 2018). Further diversification is expected, reflecting changes in the demographic profile of the population at large. For example, Hispanic/Latinx workers' representation in the workforce is expected to grow to 18% by 2024 as their share of the population increases (Bureau of Labor Statistics, U.S. Department of Labor, 2016). Similarly, the expected growth of the Asian and African American segment of the workforce is likely to outpace that of non-Hispanic Whites. These changes are also attributable in part to the aging of non-Hispanic White workers and the lower birthrates of this demographic group in the overall population. Such dramatic changes are likely to continue in the foreseeable future for the U.S. workforce (Flynn, 2014).

As baby boomers (individuals born after World War II and before 1965) retire, a rise in death rates coupled with low birth rates will also produce a decline in the number of U.S.-born working-age adults. Furthermore, as more U.S.-born employees become college educated, fewer are likely to work in low-skilled jobs requiring a high school education or lower (Buckley & Bachman, 2017; Kosten, 2018; Passel & Cohn, 2017). As a result, between now and the year 2035, an increase in immigrant and foreign-born employees will drive growth for the U.S. workforce (Buckley & Bachman, 2017; Flynn, 2014; Passel & Cohn, 2017).

With this increase in diversity of workers come challenges to workplace cohesion. Commonly, the growth of organizational diversity is an antecedent to workplace ostracism—feelings of being ignored or excluded on the job (Ferris, Brown, Berry, & Lian, 2008; Robinson, O'Reilly, & Wang, 2013; Williams, 1997). Studies indicate that experiences of workplace ostracism are more often reported by employees of color (e.g., Carter-Sowell & Zimmerman, 2015) and ostracized employees link their experiences to their demographic characteristics (O'Reilly & Robinson, 2009). Even differences related to the language used in the workplace can lead people to feel ignored and excluded at work (Hitlan, Kelly,

---

C. A. Zimmerman
Department of Psychology, Colorado State University—Pueblo, Pueblo, CO, USA

Schepman, Schneider, & Zárate, 2006), negatively affecting attitudes toward the workplace.

In this chapter, we will provide an overview of perceived ostracism patterns among members of minority groups. We begin by describing the U.S. labor force in terms of its demographic profile across different groups and sectors. Then, we review laws and company policies that may impact the experience of workplace mistreatment with particular relevance to ostracism. We then describe research on experiences of workplace ostracism, focusing on minority and immigrant workers, and we conclude by discussing directions for future research.

Characteristics of Diversity and Ostracism in the Workplace

The Hispanic/Latinx labor force has grown quickly—from approximately 12% in 2000 to 17% in 2017 (U.S. Bureau of Labor Statistics, Division of Labor Force Statistics, 2018). The largest group of Hispanic/Latinx workers identifies as Mexican American (61%); however, growth in representation in the labor force is seen primarily among Latinx individuals with family origins outside of Mexico, Puerto Rico, and Cuba—i.e., the Dominican Republic, South American, or Central American countries. Since 2008, Hispanic/Latinx workers have shown consistent gains across all categories of occupations, with minor decreases in the proportion of executives and managers (U.S. Equal Employment Opportunity Commission, 2015). However, they appear to be particularly concentrated in certain sectors, representing a majority of workers in agriculture, construction, painting, other home maintenance work, and domestic work. In fact, nearly half of workers employed as maids, housekeepers, and cleaners identify as Hispanic or Latinas (U.S. Bureau of Labor Statistics, Division of Labor Force Statistics, 2018).

African American/Black workers, over time, have also increased representation in the labor force (Rolen & Toossi, 2018) but, surprisingly, even those who are able and eligible to work are underemployed and unemployed at rates disproportionate to their percentage in the U.S. population. Representation of African Americans/Blacks in executive and management positions was on a steady climb, but growth has halted since 2008 (U.S. Equal Employment Opportunity Commission, 2015).

Compared to African American workers, Asian American employees occupy a distinct niche in the labor force, with the highest rates of college education (61%) out of all groups (Bureau of Labor Statistics, 2019). The U.S.' Asian workforce is diverse—consisting predominantly of Indian (23%), Chinese (22%), and Filipino/a (16%) workers, with the remaining subset including at least eight other nationalities. The majority of Asian American employees work in management or professional occupations, a higher proportion than all other racial/ethnic groups, but they also represent a majority in appearance-related occupations (e.g., nail technicians). Asian American employees have gained representation over time in all occupational categories, with growth stalling since 2008 in office, clerical, and sales work (U.S. Equal Employment Opportunity Commission, 2015).

The U.S. labor force currently has 17.4% foreign-born employees (52% female; U.S. Bureau of Labor, 2019a). This number includes legally-admitted immigrants, refugees, temporary residents, and undocumented immigrants. Altogether, foreign-born workers make up nearly one-fifth of the U.S. workforce. These workers are predominantly Hispanic or Latinx (47.7%) and Asian (25.1%). Compared to their U.S.-born counterparts, foreign-born workers include a higher proportion of workers without high school degrees (21.2% foreign-born; 4.1% native-born), but similar percentages of college graduates (36.9% foreign-born; 41.4% native-born). Foreign-born workers are more likely to be employed in service occupations, construction, production, and transportation occupations compared to native-born workers (U.S. Bureau of Labor, 2019b). According to the Pew Research Center, undocumented immigrants consist of 3.2% of the U.S. population. The total number of undocumented immigrants has dropped since 2007, which includes a 10% decrease in the proportion of undocumented immigrants from Mexico, but increases in unauthorized immigrants from Central America and Asia (Krogstad, Passel, & Cohn, 2019).

Sanctioning Workplace Ostracism with Employment Law and Organizational Policies

Title VII of the Civil Rights Act prohibits discrimination based on race, color, and national origin. However, the efficacy of the Equal Employment Opportunity Commission in addressing blatant experiences of discrimination is low, making enforcement of laws related to more subtle forms of discrimination like workplace ostracism unlikely. A report by the Center for Public Integrity found that while reports of discrimination have increased over time, the EEOC suffers from limited resources, and 87% of cases are closed without relief (Jameel, 2019).

Further, when employees report experiencing discrimination at work, they find that the legal standards for discrimination are high. For example, a group of African American workers reported seeing racially offensive graffiti and nooses at their workplace, but were told that they did not present enough evidence of "frequent, severe, physically threatening, humiliating, demeaning, and/or unreasonably interfered" with their ability to work (Jameel & Yerardi, 2019). The legal standard for pervasiveness is difficult to meet, with the focus being on the frequency of incidents rather than the psychological harm caused.

Workplace ostracism is different from other forms of workplace mistreatment in that it involves a lack of interaction with the victim, rather than overtly negative behaviors toward the victim (Robinson et al., 2013). This creates ambiguity in terms of motive that would make it difficult to prosecute workplace ostracism as discrimination. As the current legal interpretations of pervasiveness focus on frequency of negative behaviors rather than harm, it is likely that workplace ostracism would be perceived as fairly harmless, despite research indicating a greater psychological impact than workplace bullying (O'Reilly, Robinson, Berdahl, & Banki, 2014).

Company Policies and Procedures—Workplace Ostracism as a Gray Area

Company policies show variable effectiveness in improving diversity or ensuring that minoritized workers do not experience discrimination, sexual harassment, or bullying. For example, affirmative action programs and the creation of designated diversity staff positions or task forces are linked to increased organizational diversity at management levels (Kalev, Dobbin, & Kelly, 2006). However, the success of these programs comes with the potential for ostracism directed toward minoritized employees. Additionally, strong policies against overt forms of mistreatment, such as harassment or discrimination, may actually increase the likelihood of workplace ostracism as a more acceptable alternative to behaviors banned by the organization (Robinson et al., 2013). Organizational leaders should consider the experiences of minority workers beyond increasing representation or reducing overt discrimination to create an inclusive climate for all. This can include steps to reduce the incidence of workplace ostracism as well as interventions to lessen the negative effects of workplace ostracism for targets.

To reduce the incidence of workplace ostracism, organizational climate, the availability of resources, and the level of goal competition or interdependence can be considered. Organizational norms of inclusion may reduce the likelihood of unintentional ostracism (Robinson et al., 2013). This can be accomplished by creating a strong organizational culture that promotes inclusion and acknowledgment of all employees. Furthermore, workplace ostracism is promoted by competition between employees for resources needed to accomplish their goals; therefore, the likelihood of ostracism can be reduced by providing adequate resources to reduce competition and enhancing cooperation and interdependence between employees. In environments where the level of competition is difficult to change, social skills trainings may reduce the incidence of workplace ostracism by promoting positive interactions (Wu et al., 2015).

In addition to creating policies and procedures to reduce the occurrence of ostracism, organizations can take steps to reduce the negative impact of ostracism on targeted employees. Creating supportive workplace environments through collaborative, cooperative performance evaluations, rewarding employees for supportive behaviors, and holding employees at all levels accountable for unsupportive behaviors can help buffer targets of ostracism by increasing a sense of organizational support (Scott, Zagenczyk, Schippers, & Purvis, 2017). Additionally, employees may be ostracized due to uncooperative or disruptive behaviors (Scott, Restubog, & Zagenczyk, 2013) which may result from earlier workplace ostracism (Hitlan & Noel, 2009). To prevent a potential cycle of exclusion, efforts to foster organizational identification should be considered. Strong organizational identification promotes prosocial responses to ostracism which should in turn reduce the likelihood of future ostracism (Xu, Huang, & Robinson, 2017; Wu, Liu, Kwan, & Lee, 2016). While these efforts might have a larger impact on minority employees due to their increased risk of workplace ostracism, fostering organizational identification, increasing perceived organizational support, and promoting positive interactions between employees can have benefits across the entire organization.

Overview of Workplace Ostracism Experiences—Multiple Viewpoints and Meanings

Workplace ostracism (WOS) is an everyday occurrence and may be just as painful as physical pain and even more negative than other deviant behavior in the workplace (e.g., sexual harassment and bullying; Williams, 1997). In recent decades, there has been growing research on workplace ostracism in relation to identity-based characteristics such as gender (McGraw, 2016; Stout & Dasgupta, 2011), race/ethnicity (Carter-Sowell & Carter, 2016; DelCampo, Jacobson, Van Buren III, & Blancero, 2011; Goodwin, Williams, & Carter-Sowell, 2010; Umaña-Taylor, Vargas-Chanes, Garcia, & Gonzales-Backen, 2008), and religion (Parry & Urwin, 2011; Wesselmann & Williams, 2010). Researchers have identified three features of workplace ostracism: motive, social appropriateness, and acts of omission (Robinson et al., 2013). We describe these next.

Motives Behind Workplace Ostracism

The *motive* behind acts of ostracism can be purposeful or malicious intent, or non-purposeful, unaccountable intentions (Robinson et al., 2013; Williams, 2009). Workplace ostracism is often ambiguous in that the actor may or may not have the intent to hurt the victim, which leaves the victim wondering whether they had been ostracized. For instance, purposeful ostracism occurs when the actor is fully aware that he or she is ostracizing an individual or group but does so to protect themselves or the group. One of the most common examples of purposeful ostracism is "silent treatment." Alternatively, an example of non-purposeful ostracism is being left off a list of email recipients by accident and not consciously.

Social Appropriateness of Ostracism on the Job

Acts of ostracism are dependent upon the *social appropriateness* of a situation (Liu, 2019; Robinson et al., 2013), whereby excluding individuals from social interactions is considered ostracism only when the victims perceive that based on social norms, they *should* be acknowledged in the situation. Usually, organizations have unwritten rules about who should be paid attention to and who should be ignored. Ostracism on the job occurs when social rules are not adhered to or when there are disagreements on the social rules (Robinson et al., 2013). For example, when immigrant employees enter a new work environment, they do not always know the unspoken rules or the documented social norms, values, and rules of the organization (Bhagat & London, 1999). They may be more likely to "perceive" being ignored and excluded, based on their own understanding of the social norm.

Workplace Ostracism and Commonplace Acts of Omission

Ostracism often presents as an act of omission rather than an act of commission (Robinson et al., 2013). Although an ostracizer may not necessarily engage in rude interpersonal behavior toward a co-worker, they can withdraw from engaging in social interactions with the co-worker (Liu, 2019; Robinson et al., 2013). For such instances, Jones, Carter-Sowell, Kelly, and Williams (2009) coined the term *out-of-the-loop* ostracism, which occurs when individuals are excluded from certain group information, tasks, and activities. As an act of omission, workplace ostracism is rife with ambiguity, leading the target to wonder if and why they have been omitted and/or overlooked (Liu, 2019; Robinson et al., 2013).

Workplace Ostracism Among Different Racial Groups: A Workplace Diversity Perspective

Various individual and contextual factors contribute to workplace ostracism (Mao, Liu, Jiang, & Zhang, 2018; Uskul & Over, 2017), but generally research suggests that having a stigmatized identity leads to workplace exclusion and incivility (Cortina, Kabat-Farr, Magley, & Nelson, 2017). These experiences also overlap with the psychological literature grounded in social identity threat theory (Steele, 1997). The theory suggests that members of social groups who are in shared spaces can experience them in psychologically distinct ways (Emerson & Murphy, 2014). For employees (mainly ethnic minorities) experiencing negative interpersonal interactions, the theory suggests that the negative experiences are often covert or subtle, interfering with their overall professional life (see Steele, Spencer, & Aronson, 2002).

When a workplace status quo that empowers majority groups (i.e., White Americans) is maintained over successive generations of the organization (Elliott & Smith, 2004), its enforcement can have twofold effects. First, minority group members are often considered non-prototypical of such organizations (Rosette, Koval, Ma, & Livingston, 2016), leading to negative workplace experiences, including ostracism. Second, majority group members feel threatened by the increasing representation of minority group members, which affects their workplace interactions (Craig, Rucker, & Richeson, 2018).

Thus far, the majority of research focuses on workplace ostracism broadly (e.g., Robinson et al., 2013; Thompson, Carlson, Kacmar, & Vogel, 2020), and there is limited research on workplace ostracism across all three ethnic groups. Thus, we draw on findings from workplace incivility, where elements of social exclusion are assessed. We also draw from evidence on more general workplace experiences related to experiences of racial and ethnic minorities, particularly in highlighting how they shape broader workplace culture that results in workplace ostracism. Relevant research on workplace experiences of Muslim Americans is also included in this section, as approximately 28% of the 3.45 million Muslims in the U.S. are of South Asian descent (Mohammed, 2018). We discuss both shared and diverse workplace ostracism experiences of the three groups.

Shared Dynamics for Minority Populations in the Workforce

Research shows that 23% of the ethnic minority respondents, recruited via non-governmental organizations representing ethnic minority professionals, had experienced some form of social exclusion from social interactions based on their race or ethnicity (Fox & Stallworth, 2005). Minorities are more likely to be exposed to workplace incivility compared to their White colleagues (Cortina, Kabat-Farr, Leskinen, Huerta, & Magley, 2013). Meta-analytic work further supports these ideas, where data drawn from over 58,000 ethnic minority employees show that all three groups (Latinx, African American, and Asian American) report experiencing workplace mistreatment (including ostracism), albeit with small effect sizes (McCord, Joseph, Dhanani, & Beus, 2018). These trends also extend to ethnic minorities in academia, who report more information-based exclusion, regardless of gender, compared to their White colleagues (Zimmerman, Carter-Sowell, & Xu, 2016). These experiences can add up, given that people spend a significant portion of their daily life at the workplace, and some may not have opportunities to work with individuals or teams who are better at workplace interactions.

Even when there is some diversity in workplace representation, ethnic minority professionals—African American men (Wingfield & Wingfield, 2014) and African American women (Dickens, Womack, & Dimes, 2019)—as well as faculty members of color (Settles, Buchanan, & Dotson, 2019) all report feeling tokenized. For some, this experience may impel them to forge forward nevertheless. However, for most, the need to belong to the workgroup or organization may likely lead them to downplay their unique attributes. Optimistically, other research drawing on nationally representative data suggests that workplace satisfaction of African Americans and Hispanic Americans is positively associated with more diverse workplace demographics (termed "racioethnic dissimilarity"), with a negative association shown among White Americans who are higher on prejudice (Avery, Lerman, & Volpone, 2010).

Strategies to address the shared experiences among minority populations should involve not just providing support to minorities, but also challenging stereotypical assumptions of individuals from majority groups. Research suggests that diversity-related policies are usually more effective when they are supported by the employees (Dobbin, Schrage, & Kalev, 2015). In such situations, individuals are more likely to support policies framed as rectifying discrimination compared to policies framed as increasing diversity (Scarborough, Lambouths, & Holbrook, 2019).

Diverging Experiences Among Racially and/or Ethnically Diverse Employees

Race- or ethnicity-based ostracism experiences are theorized to diverge in certain aspects, based on the social identity threat theory and the model of workplace ostracism. The specific stereotypes associated with particular ethnic groups can lead to different workplace outcomes for each group. African Americans/Black and Hispanic/Latinx Americans are more likely to be subjected to negative stereotypes (e.g., unrefined, poor) whereas most Asian Americans are subjected to positive ones (e.g., intelligent). Both these types of stereotypes contribute to the salience of ethnicity-based hierarchies in the workplace, resulting in different kinds of social exclusion and ostracism for various ethnic minorities (see Hagendoorn, 1993; Robinson et al., 2013). For instance, Asian Americans may experience social exclusion by co-workers because the positive stereotypes associated with Asian Americans make them competitive threats. African Americans/Blacks, who are evaluated based on negative stereotypes, might be systematically excluded by the organization itself, such as being passed over for professional development opportunities. Conversely, Asian Americans and Hispanic/Latinx Americans are also more likely to be perceived as foreigners or less "American" compared to African Americans/Black (Zou & Cheryan, 2017). As ethnic minorities in the U.S. are evaluated by different types of cultural stereotypes (Ghavami & Peplau, 2013), these stereotypes likely influence the kind of ostracism ethnic minorities face at work. Despite the growing interest in addressing workplace ostracism, the diversity in experiences and reactions to workplace ostracism among ethnic minorities is still an emerging field of research.

Much of research on workplace experiences of ethnic minorities suggests that each group faces specific unique barriers throughout the various stages of employment, starting with hiring. Job applications with Muslim names elicit more negative evaluations than other ethnicities (Park, Malachi, Sternin, & Tevet, 2009; Widner & Chicoine, 2011). Applicants with East Asian names are rated more negatively than applicants with White names, but more positively than applicants with African American/Black names (Kang, DeCelles, Tilcsik, & Jun, 2016; King, Madera, Hebl, Knight, & Mendoza, 2006). Other research suggests that beyond workplace skills, evaluators form first impressions of job applicants based on their documentation, which also influences perceived interpersonal skills, where African American/Black and Asian applicants are judged as being less personable than White applicants (Bavishi, Madera, & Hebl, 2010). These findings, overall, suggest that stereotypes about ethnic minorities influence who is perceived as being a good fit early in the employment process.

Once hired, in the workplace, African Americans/Blacks do not benefit from co-worker social support in the face of workplace problems as much as other ethnic minorities do (Attell, Brown, & Treiber, 2017). Furthermore, Hispanic/Latinx American men report higher levels of workplace incivility than Hispanic/Latinx American women (Welbourne, Gangadharan, & Sariol, 2015). However, overall, Hispanic/Latinx employees show more resilience when faced with adverse outcomes at work compared to other ethnic minorities and White women (Welbourne et al., 2015). Hagelskamp and Hughes (2014) found that when African American/Black and Hispanic/Latina women reported more negative workplace experiences (including unfair treatment), their adolescent children reported experiencing more messages about ethnic pride and cultural knowledge at home. Chinese American families showed the opposite trend, where increased negative workplace experiences were associated with fewer such messages (Hagelskamp & Hughes, 2014). The researchers theorize that these experiences may be due to the differing historical trajectories of the three ethnic groups. Historical and current experiences with mistreatment in the U.S. may shape Blacks'/African Americans' and Hispanic/Latinx Americans' views of American life. Chinese Americans, who are more likely to experience positive stereotypes than other minority groups, may attempt to minimize being viewed as a perpetual foreigner by sharing messages that include both ethnic and national pride.

Differences are also shown when intersectional identities are considered. For example, Muslim American women who wear hijabs are more likely to experience negative interactions as job applicants than non-Muslim women (King & Ahmad, 2010). Furthermore, in data drawn from a large police department, African American women, followed by African American/Black men and Hispanic/Latina women, report experiencing more workplace incivility and problems compared to White men and women, and Hispanic/Latino men (Hassell & Brandl, 2009). The problem most frequently experienced was reported as a lack of support, influence, or feedback (Hassell & Brandl, 2009). In other research, ethnic minority women also report experiencing more workplace sexual and ethnic harassment compared to majority men, minority men, and majority women (Berdahl & Moore, 2006).

Focusing on intersectional identities can also help identify issues that occur within predominantly ethnic minority work environments, though research concerning predominantly nonwhite workplaces is limited. For instance, African American/Black women in a racially diverse workplace may experience sexism and colorism, the latter being a form of intraracial prejudice that could result in social exclusion (Muhammad, 2018). Other studies report that differences by race or ethnicity in ostracism and social exclusion experiences are minimal, though notably, these studies drew their data from populations where ethnic minorities were highly represented (e.g., Aquino & Bradfield, 2000; Schneider, Hitlan, & Radhakrishnan, 2000). These findings suggest that some representation of ethnic minorities may provide a buffer to ostracism experiences by creating a space where ostracized minorities feel they belong. For instance, if a Hispanic/Latinx American employee was excluded from receiving vital information because of their ethnicity, the presence of other Hispanic/Latinx Americans may lessen the feeling that they do not belong. Alternatively, the presence of diverse individuals creates an avenue for the acceptance of diverse social identities. Thus, even if ethnic minorities lack social support, the presence of diverse others may meet short-term belongingness needs, following an ostracism experience.

It is also notable that research on Asian and Hispanic/Latinx Americans mostly refers to them using pan-ethnic terms, even though there are distinct subgroups within the two ethnic groups. Many of the subgroups have been affected by distinct historical and modern experiences in the U.S., such as the internment of Japanese Americans in the 1940s, and the anti-Muslim and general anti-"brown" sentiments experienced by South Asian and Muslim Americans following the September 11, 2001, terrorist attacks. Similarly, Cuban Americans historically migrated to the U.S. following the Cuban Revolution under Fidel Castro in the 1950s and were accepted as refugees, in contrast to Mexican Americans, who have been subjected to anti-Mexican sentiment in the U.S. from the early 1900s to the present times. A review of 332 Asian American studies in the psychological literature, including qualitative and mixed-method approaches, showed that Chinese and Korean Americans (88.2%) are the predominant focus of research, with an increasing trend of studies that include Taiwanese and Southeast Asian (e.g., Laotian, Hmong, and Thai) Americans (Kiang, Cheah, Huynh, Wang, & Yoshikawa, 2016). Approximately 10% of the papers describe their samples using pan-ethnic terms, as do studies using nationally representative samples of Asian Americans (Kiang et al., 2016). Research also suggests that the use of pan-ethnic terms by Asians and Hispanic/Latinx Americans is associated with higher socioeconomic status of individuals from those groups (Masuoka, 2006). The researcher suggests these economically-stable individuals, who are more likely to be in predominantly White spaces, use pan-ethnic identities to increase feelings of belongingness with other individuals who also identify as "Asian" or "Hispanic"/"Latinx", but are not necessarily of the same national heritage (Masuoka, 2006).

In the workplace, ethnic subgroup differentiation could help identify the various professional trajectories of the subgroups. For example, South Asian Americans (such as Indian Americans) are more likely than East Asian Americans (e.g., Chinese Americans) to hold leadership positions in large U.S. organizations. This difference may be attributable to the perceived incompatibility between the leadership styles of East Asian Americans and the prototypical "American" leadership (Lu, Nisbett, & Morris, 2020). Researchers also theorize that the use of a pan-ethnic term for Latinx Americans in faculty recruitment studies obscures identity-based factors that may help in understanding hiring and retention rates (Delgado-Romero, Manlove, Manlove, & Hernandez, 2007). Thus, future research in workplace ostracism would benefit from considering workplace ostracism that goes beyond the use of pan-ethnic terms and acknowledges finer-grained distinctions within the broad ethnic categories and considers intersectional identities.

Why Foreign-Born, Immigrant, and International Co-workers Are Often Ostracized

In research, employees who are not U.S.-born are often examined as a monolithic population to be contrasted with native-born employees. There has been a more of a focus on gender and race/ethnicity as fundamental dimensions of diversity and interpersonal conflicts in the workplace, resulting in immigration status and acculturation being thrown by the wayside (Gheorghiu & Stephens, 2016). For example, a workplace with a certain percentage of African Americans/Blacks may appear similarly diverse with a workplace where there are employees with African American, Afro-Caribbean background, and first-generation ancestry. Workplace ostracism has received little if any attention as a unique experience for immigrant employees, despite a vast body of work in related fields (migration studies, cultural psychology). The lack of empirical research on perceived workplace ostracism experiences for foreign-born and immigrant employee populations may result in the false assumption that excluding or ignoring members of these groups at work is relatively similar to excluding or ignoring a native-born employee of the same race/ethnicity. However, the intersectionality of race-ethnicity and immigrant status/national culture can create a more complex dynamic and implicit workplace ostracism-generating mechanism (Gheorghiu & Stephens, 2016), particularly compared to the myriad of stressors which the immigrant employee has to face in not only the working environment but the broader milieu (Pasca & Wagner, 2011).

The process of migration has been painted as a rational choice that immigrants make in search of better education, career, and life opportunities, making adaptation to the host and organizational culture a smooth transition (Gheorghiu & Stephens, 2016; Mayda, 2006; Maynard & Ferdman, 2009; O'Connell, 2011). In reality, acculturation, the process of change which occurs when immigrants from different cultural backgrounds come into continuous contact with the local culture, presents a major life event that threatens the psychological and physical well-being of immigrant employees (Berry, 1997; Sam & Berry, 2010).

During acculturation, the foreign-born and immigrant employees experience acculturation demands/stressors (Berry, 1970), which is largely responsible for the negative psychological, psychosomatic, and behavioral reactions to this major life-changing event. Acculturation stress/strain is, therefore, a response to both the positive and negative events which are present during intercultural contact in the host culture (Berry, 2006; Bhagat, Davis, & London, 2009). Acculturation demands/stressors occur when the immigrant experiences the challenges arising from new opportunities, while simultaneously appreciating the demands and constraints which are now present in the new organizational and host cultures. For example, an IT engineer from India who travels to the U.S. in the hopes of finding a new job might be surprised to learn that his professional qualifications from her home country are not accepted in the new host culture. As such, acculturation demands stem from a reduced level of professional status and unfamiliarity with the qualifications system in the new culture. The psychological, social, cognitive, and physical responses to these acculturation demands may set precedents to workplace ostracism.

Negative Attitudes Toward Foreign-Born, Immigrant, and International Employees

As the population of immigrants and immigrant employees grows, the public opinions and perceptions held by the native-born majority will shape the ostracism experiences of immigrant employees in the workplace. Native-born employees are likely to purposefully ostracize immigrant employees if the majority attitude toward immigrants is generally negative. In recent years, attitudes toward immigrant employees have been more openly hostile and xenophobic, leading to more incidents of workplace ostracism (Hainmueller & Hopkins, 2015; Kosic, Mannetti, & Sam, 2005; Sniderman, Peri, de Figueiredo, Jr., & Piazza, 2000). Generally, members of a group are likely to ostracize another group or a member itself if they perceive that group or member to be burdensome

(Robinson et al., 2013). Some native-born employees tend to ostracize, treat badly, and exclude low-skilled immigrant employees. These behaviors are rooted in the belief that low-skilled immigrants are lazy and unambitious (Hainmueller & Hopkins, 2015; Helbling & Kriesi, 2014; Mayda, 2006).

Perceived Job Shortages Influences Ostracism of Immigrants

Native-born employees might engage in ostracism as a way to protect themselves or the groups they belong to. An example is in the area of job opportunities. According to a 2017 Pew Research Center survey, at least one in five working Americans say that the growing number of working immigrants in the U.S. negatively affects their own jobs or careers (Graf, 2018; Horowitz, Parker, & Stepler, 2017). Previous research has shown that native-born employees exclude or oppose individuals who share similar skills and job opportunities as themselves. For example, highly-skilled employees are likely to ostracize high-skilled immigrant employees, while low-skilled native-born employees are likely to ostracize low-skilled employees (Facchini & Mayda, 2012; Hainmueller & Hopkins, 2015; Helbling & Kriesi, 2014; Hello, Scheepers, & Sleegers, 2006; Mayda, 2006).

When native-born employees perceive that foreign-born and immigrant employees are "here to take our jobs," they will withhold certain vital information (i.e., out of the loop), which is necessary for the immigrant employee to function adequately in the working environment (Bhagat & London, 1999). For example, native-born employees might keep immigrant employees out of the loop on the politics of career management. Highly-skilled immigrant employees might need mentors who could help advance their careers, but native-born employees, even when they serve as mentors, might not provide highly-skilled immigrant employees with the right information (Bhagat & London, 1999).

Perceived Demand of Skills Influences Ostracism of Immigrants

According to the welfare state model (Helbling & Kriesi, 2014), native employees generally prefer high-skilled immigrants to low-skilled ones because of the perception that low-skilled immigrants are more likely to use public services (e.g., health care and welfare) at a higher rate than their contribution in terms of paying taxes. Hence, native-born employees are more likely to ostracize low-skilled employees by implementing policy programs which hinder them from getting access to healthcare and work-related services (Berry, 2006; Bhagat et al., 2009; Cuéllar, 2000). Conversely, they are more likely to be inclusive of highly-skilled immigrants when their contributions are thought to be benefiting society as a whole (Facchini & Mayda, 2012; Hainmueller, Hiscox, & Margalit, 2015; Hainmueller & Hopkins, 2015; Helbling & Kriesi, 2014; Hello et al., 2006; Mayda, 2006).

Perceived Dissimilarities Influences Ostracism of Immigrants

The more dissimilar or "foreign" the social norms of the new working environment in the host culture are from the heritage culture, the more likely the immigrant employee will be ostracized by others. For example, foreign-born workers may be used to have public holidays during their religious or cultural occasions (e.g., Eid-ul-Fitr, Diwali, or Chinese New Year). In Western workplaces, these occasions are rarely recognized public holidays, which may exacerbate feelings of being excluded from the host culture that already feels foreign.

Based on the features of the out-of-the-loop form of ostracism, when foreign-born and immigrant workers are excluded from group activities, they may spend their cognitive resources questioning the motivations behind their co-workers' "forgetting" to include them. Such a situation is likened to "tokenism," where the individual is accepted into the working environment only because they are "different" from other members of the minority group they belong to. Despite being viewed as being different, they may still be considered a threat, resulting in information being withheld (Bhagat & London, 1999; Bhagat et al., 2009; de Castro, Gee, & Takeuchi, 2008; Jackson, Thoits, & Taylor, 1995; Lawless & Yea-Wen, 2014; Wingfield, 2010).

Why Foreign-Born, Immigrant, and International Co-workers Experience Ostracism

Race, Ethnicity, and Xenophobia

In the U.S., support for immigrants varies considerably by the immigrants' heritage culture and country of origin (Dustmann & Preston, 2007; Hainmueller & Hangartner, 2013; Hainmueller & Hopkins,

2015). As such, it is reasonable to state that, similar to racial views, individuals' race or ethnicity determines the level and frequency at which immigrant employees experience workplace ostracism from native-born employees (Hainmueller & Hopkins, 2015). Native-born employees who hold negative stereotypes about immigrants (Burns & Gimpel, 2000) and have implicitly biased associations (Pérez, 2010) are more likely to ostracize immigrant employees. As an extension of this racial viewpoint, racial identifiers such as skin tone and hair are precursors to determining whether the immigrant employee will experience workplace ostracism (Campbell, Keith, Gonlin, & Carter-Sowell, 2020). For example, Hispanic immigrant employees are more likely than White/European immigrant employees to be ostracized by native-born employees (DelCampo et al., 2011).

Language and Accent Differences and Ostracism—It's What You Say and How You Say It

When one's native language is other than English, it serves as the basis for real or perceived workplace ostracism and exclusion from native-born employees. Language-based workplace ostracism can be subtle because it involves workplace conversations in a language that an immigrant employee may not fully understand (Hitlan et al., 2006). It can also be explicit, such as when a supervisor reprimands/ostracizes a subordinate for his or her inability to speak proper English (de Castro, Fujishiro, Sweitzer, & Oliva, 2006; Dotan-Eliaz, Sommer, & Rubin,2009; Kulkarni & Sommer, 2015; Newman, Hartman, & Taber, 2012). Language can serve as an antecedent to workplace ostracism based on two interrelated sources: cultural stereotypes about languages and perceptions of competence given one's linguistic proficiency (Kulkarni & Sommer, 2015).

Native-born employees assess immigrant employees according to their adherence to the norms and values related to American identity (Hainmueller & Hopkins, 2015; Newman et al., 2012; Schildkraut, 2011). One important source of American identity is language (Newman et al., 2012). Therefore, it is often hypothesized that immigrant employees who are not fluent in English, or even if fluent, speak English with a distinct accent, are more likely to be ostracized by native-born employees (DelCampo et al., 2011; Dotan-Eliaz et al., 2009; Kulkarni & Sommer, 2015; Masgoret & Ward, 2006; Newman et al., 2012).

Previous studies have identified a reciprocal relationship between language proficiency and social interactions—competency of the native language of the host culture leads to greater participation in the host culture and thus increases proficiency in the native language (Clement, Noels, & Deneault, 2001; Masgoret & Ward, 2006; Newman et al., 2012). Consequently, language skills provide the immigrant employee an avenue to establish and maintain positive interpersonal relationships and social support, which have been shown to improve psychological well-being and adaptation (Masgoret & Ward, 2006; Ng et al., 2013; Ward, 1997; Ward & Kennedy, 1994).

Native-born employees hold cultural stereotypes about the various languages spoken by immigrant employees such that some languages are considered more dominant and powerful than others (Kulkarni & Sommer, 2015; Ng, 2007). For example, English is often viewed positively as a language of progress, whereas Cantonese may be viewed as unimportant and unsuited for functioning in the working environment for certain jobs and workplace tasks (Kulkarni & Sommer, 2015; Phillipson, 1997).

Command of the native language of the host culture is often linked to one's level of competency in the workplace (DelCampo et al., 2011; Kulkarni & Sommer, 2015). Immigrant employees who do not speak English are often viewed as incompetent and incapable of completing various workplace tasks—resulting in being ostracized compared to those who can speak English fluently. For the same reason, high-skilled immigrants are likely to have a good command of the English language, which would lead to them experiencing less ostracism (DelCampo et al., 2011).

Nevertheless, even high-skilled immigrants who are highly proficient in English, but who speak it with an accent that differs from the American accent, may experience subtle forms of ostracism. As a result of their accents, immigrant employees may be denied jobs, excluded, ostracized, or mistreated in the workplace (Kulkarni & Sommer, 2015). Having a foreign accent typically is a marker of immigrant status, at least for first-generation immigrants. In such cases, the accents create the perception of a weak command of the host country's language and cultural norms. As a result, having an "accent" leads particularly low-skilled immigrants to be ostracized and excluded in the workplace (Kulkarni & Sommer, 2015; Masgoret & Ward, 2006; Newman et al., 2012; Ng, 2007). For example, studies have shown that immigrants with non-native languages (e.g., Spanish) are often made to feel inferior in the workplace and are often more likely to be ostracized because of the negative stereotypes associated with "accents" (Arbona et al., 2010; DelCampo et al., 2011; Dotan-Eliaz et al., 2009; Kulkarni & Sommer, 2015; Ng, 2007).

Acculturation Strategies—Making a Plan to Survive and Succeed

Immigrant employees may adopt a variety of strategies in response to the challenges posed by the immigrant experience (Berry, 1997, 2006, 2007). Chosen acculturation strategies may also predict the acculturation outcomes and frequency of workplace ostracism experiences. Berry (1997) developed a framework of acculturation strategy based on two underlying issues: (1) the degree to which one wishes to maintain their heritage culture (e.g., language and identity) and (2) the degree of contact and participation the immigrant employee aims to establish and maintain with members of the host culture. When these two issues cohere, four acculturation strategies are expected: (1) *Assimilation*—the immigrant employee does not wish to maintain aspects of their heritage culture and would like to engage in all aspects of the host culture fully; (2) *Integration*—the immigrant employee maintains all aspects of their heritage culture while actively seeking and maintaining contact and participation in the host culture; (3) *Marginalization*—neither does the immigrant employee want to maintain his/her heritage culture nor to interact with members from the host culture; (4) *Separation*—the immigrant employee maintains his/her heritage culture and does not maintain any interactions in the heritage culture (Berry, 1997).

While exploring the relationship between majority attitudes toward out-group perceptions of acculturation strategies, Kosic et al. (2005) found negative behaviors toward immigrants who chose separation and marginalization strategies. Using vignettes of different immigrant acculturation strategies, *assimilation, marginalization, integration, and separation*, participants reported limiting interpersonal encounters with immigrants who adopted separation and marginalization strategies than those who adopted assimilation and integration strategies.

Theoretical predictions concerning the different assimilation and integration strategies, such as the "exchange hypothesis" (Curtis & Miller, 1986), could explain the reactions of native-born employees. Per the exchange hypothesis, when immigrants adopt assimilation and integration strategies, this serves as social cues that they are interested in learning more about the host culture. In such cases, native-born employees are more inclined to show them the ropes, teach them how to navigate within the new culture, and possibly invite them to social gatherings. On the other hand, separation and marginalization strategies indicate that the immigrant employee is uninterested in the host culture and unengaged in interpersonal interactions with the native-born, who, in turn, may then withhold interpersonal interactions as a form of ostracism (Van Acker & Vanbeselaere, 2012).

Studies have shown that native-born employees prefer immigrant employees to adopt assimilation and integration acculturation strategies (Bourhis, Moïse, Perreault, & Senécal, 1997; Jasinskaja-Lahti, Liebkind, Jaakkola, & Reuter, 2006; Kosic et al., 2005; van Oudenhoven, Prins, & Buunk, 1998; Zagefka & Brown, 2002). For example, in a study of Turkish immigrants in Belgium, Van Acker and Vanbeselaere (2012) found native-born Belgians reported more positive affect when Turkish immigrants adopted assimilation and integration strategies, but negative affect for immigrants with separation strategies. With assimilation and integration strategies, immigrant employees actively seek and maintain positive interpersonal relationships with native-born employees, complimenting native-born employees who are welcoming and are likely to accept immigrant employees into their social environments (Van Acker & Vanbeselaere, 2012). In contrast, immigrant employees who adopt separation strategies do not seek to maintain positive relationships with the native-born employees, who, in turn, are not welcoming and are likely to ostracize immigrant employees (Van Acker & Vanbeselaere, 2012). When immigrant employees adopt separation and marginalization acculturation strategies, native-born employees perceive this as a rejection and disinterest in their culture. As such, native-born employees may exclude immigrant employees from social events and limit their interpersonal interactions (López-Rodríguez, Zagefka, Navas, & Cuadrado, 2014; Van Acker & Vanbeselaere, 2012). Inherent in the discussion of acculturation strategies is that native-born employees hold a privileged position compared to immigrant employees (see Fiset, Al Hajj, & Vongas, 2017). During a time where immigrant employees are attempting to navigate a new cultural context and new workplace norms, experiencing stress resulting from their migration (e.g., immigration and visa paperwork), and acquiring various new skills, they are also expected to exhibit social cues indicating that they intend to assimilate and integrate. In the absence of social support outside of the workplace, it may prove difficult for immigrant employees to avoid feeling ostracized (Fiset et al., 2017). Future research should endeavor to explore this issue further, particularly in how immigrant employees can feel they belong while they are navigating the host culture.

Downsizing the Effects of Workplace Ostracism

Since workplace ostracism negatively affects the well-being of employees, it is imperative that researchers examine potential factors that can help reduce its harmful effects. We suggest the following three factors as relevant: heritage cultural identity salience, social support, and harmony enhancement.

Heritage Cultural Identity Salience—An Ideology for Overcoming Perceived Isolation

Research shows that having a strong racial/ethnic identity potentially buffers the effects of a negative workplace experience (Williams, Spencer, & Jackson, 1999). An immigrant employee's cultural identity (Berry, 2007) refers to the degree to which an immigrant identifies with the host or heritage cultures (Berry, 2006; Berry, Phinney, Sam, & Vedder, 2006; Phinney, 2004; Sam & Berry, 2010). *Heritage cultural identity* is the extent to which an immigrant holds their heritage culture with more considerable importance than the host culture (Mohammadi, 2013; Samnani, Boekhorst, & Harrison, 2013; Ting-Toomey et al., 2000).

While an important aspect of heritage cultural identity is that it captures the degree to which an immigrant employee desires to maintain his/her heritage culture, another important factor is the extent to which the heritage culture is deeply rooted in one's overall social identity (Samnani et al., 2013). *Identity salience* refers to the degree to which an individual's identity is central to their goals and core sense of self (Ashforth & Mael, 1989; Petriglieri, 2011). *Cultural identity salience* (CIS) is the degree to which an individual's culture is an integral part of their identity relative to other social roles. For immigrants with a high degree of CIS, their cultural identity is deeply rooted in their self-view and beliefs. In contrast, for immigrants low in CIS, cultural identity is secondary to who they are as an individual (Mohammadi, 2013). *Heritage cultural identity salience* (HCIS) is the extent to which an immigrant employee considers his/her heritage culture as an integral component of his/her identity in comparison with other social roles. Identity salience buffers the relationship between acculturation demands and workplace ostracism, as well as the relationship between workplace ostracism and negative outcomes.

According to the sociometer theory set forth by Baumeister and Leary (1995), one's self-esteem serves as a sociometer for individuals that seek to establish and maintain positive interpersonal relationships (Leary, Tambor, Terdal, & Downs, 1995). For immigrant employees with low HCIS, they may be motivated to embody some if not all aspects of the host culture and rely heavily on the native-born employees to fulfill their fundamental need to belong and boost their self-esteem. In contrast, for immigrant employees with high HCIS, they are likely to attribute possible ostracism experiences as something external and turn to the cultural identity as a source of self-worth and boost to their self-esteem (Williams, 2017).

This is similar to research in the race/ethnicity domain which has shown that when individuals from minority groups experience stressors, their group identity (e.g., cultural or ethnic identity) is more salient and serves as a way to protect their self-worth and self-esteem (Phinney, Horenczyk, Liebkind, & Vedder, 2001; Tajfel & Turner, 1986; Umaña-Taylor et al., 2008). For example, Goodwin et al. (2010) found individuals who attributed ostracism to racism based on their group membership felt less distress. Likewise, according to the approach-orientation of individuals with high self-esteem or high core self-evaluation (Chang, Ferris, Johnson, Rosen, & Tan, 2012), HCIS of immigrant employees is positively related to self-esteem (Phinney, 1991; Ting-Toomey et al., 2000; Umaña-Taylor et al., 2008), which makes them more approachable and less likely to be ostracized.

When a minority employee draws on the sense of belonging from their own racial/ethnic identity, workplace ostracism experiences may be less likely to affect them. Future research could examine how the adverse effects of workplace ostracism experiences affect biracial individuals, as biracial individuals experience significant identity-based threats (in some situations more so than non-biracial individuals), which in turn affects their sense of belonging (Albuja, Sanchez, & Gaither, 2019).

Social Support Buffers Workplace Ostracism Experiences and Negative Outcomes

Perceived social support from organizations, supervisors, and co-workers is crucial for immigrant employees and has been included in multiple studies examining adaptation into the new working environment (Amason, Allen, & Holmes, 1999; Jian, 2012; Kosic, 2004; Kosic et al., 2005; Ng et al., 2013; Ng & Sorensen, 2008; Williams, 2017). Social support buffers the effects of chronic ostracism by increasing feelings of belongingness (Williams, 2007).

Immigrant employees need social networks to be able to thrive and adapt to the new working environment. Results on acculturation strategies have shown that immigrant employees who adopt an integration strategy (i.e., aiming to get social support from members of both the heritage and host cultures) do far better in the host culture than those who adopt other acculturation strategies (Kosic, 2004; Lieber, Chin, Nihira, & Mink, 2001; Lu, Samaratunge, & Hartel, 2011; Ng et al., 2013; Williams, 2017). With a strong support network in the workplace, any attempts to ostracize the individual will be thwarted as the employee can rely on their network to counteract the mistreatment (Ng et al., 2013; Lu et al., 2011; Williams, 2017).

Moreover, having social support from the organization, co-workers, and supervisors can discourage rather than encouraging workplace ostracism of immigrant workers. In cooperative environments where inclusion is encouraged, immigrant employees are provided with the necessary tools and information needed to function and thrive in the working environment (Williams, 2017). Previous studies have found that when immigrants are provided with support such as sponsorship for jobs, language proficiency classes, and legal support they feel more included and are less likely to be faced with ostracism (Amason et al., 1999; Au, Garey, Bermas, & Chan, 1998; de Castro et al., 2006; Lu et al., 2011; Williams, 2017). On the other hand, in toxic work environments, immigrant employees who have visible surface-level characteristics (e.g., race, gender, or accent) are more likely to be ostracized than those who do not. Low-skilled immigrant employees are more likely to experience workplace ostracism particularly in environments where they lack social support from co-workers, supervisors, and leaders (Amason et al., 1999; Au et al., 1998; de Castro et al., 2006; Naumann, Stoetzer, & Pietrantuono, 2018). In the long term, the formation of workplace friendships or at the least, a friendly work team, may help individuals cope with ostracism challenges.

Harmony Enhancement Bolsters Workplace Inclusion Experiences and Positive Outcomes

Ostracism is an act of omission which threatens an individual's fundamental belongingness need (Robinson et al., 2013). Baumeister and Leary (1995) posited the need to belong theory, which states that human beings have a fundamental need to maintain and establish long-lasting positive interpersonal relationships. In such instances, an important cultural value that reflects people's relationship orientation and need to maintain positive relationships is interpersonal harmony (Leung, 1997). Leung (1997) presented a dualistic view of harmony based on two different harmony motives of an individual: *disintegration avoidance* and *harmony enhancement*. Disintegration avoidance is defined as "avoiding action that will strain a relationship and lead to its weakening and dissolving," while harmony enhancement (HE) is defined as "engaging in behaviors presumed to strengthen the relationships among the parties involved" (Leung, Brew, Zhang, & Zhang, 2011, p. 796).

Williams (2017) examined the moderating effect of HE on the relationship between acculturation demand and workplace ostracism. HE reflects the unique way in which immigrant employees socially interact with native employees (Williams, 2017). During acculturation, immigrant employees with high HE are likely to seek and establish positive interpersonal relationships and minimize interpersonal conflicts with native-born employees.

Marginalized employees low in HE are less likely to spend time and effort in establishing and sustaining interpersonal relationships; as such, majority group employees are likely to form their own prejudices and uphold stereotypes (e.g., immigrants are anti-social, lazy, and incompetent). On the contrary, marginalized employees with high HE seek out and maintain positive relationships and are likely to dispel any stereotypes which majority group employees hold regarding their group, which makes them less likely to be ostracized.

Individuals who are highly anxious and very aggressive are likely to experience hostile and exclusive behaviors from others (e.g., victim precipitation theory, Lasky, 2020). For instance, marginalized employees high in HE are likely to establish positive interpersonal relationships in an attempt to minimize conflict and perform behaviors that will strengthen relationships and help minimize workplace ostracism. This reaction means that individuals high in HE may also exhibit agreeableness, compliance, friendliness, and conforming (Leung, Wu, Chen, & Young, 2011). In contrast, marginalized employees low in HE are likely to be confrontational, unkind, and aggressive—as research shows disagreeable individuals engage in more interpersonal conflicts (Graziano & Eisenberg, 1997; Howard, Cogswell, & Smith, 2020; Jensen-Campbell, Graziano, & Hair, 1996; Tobin, Graziano, Vanman, & Tassinary, 2000; Wu, Wei, & Hui, 2011). Consequently, based on the premise of the victim precipitation theory, disagreeable employees are the ones who may respond to situations in a hostile manner, resulting in their ostracism in the workplace (Howard et al., 2020; Jensen-Campbell et al., 1996; Olweus, 1978; Wu et al., 2011).

Conclusion

Workplace ostracism based on social identity (e.g., different racial groups; immigrant workers) is a multifaceted, complex experience. The majority of research has addressed this matter broadly, and tailored research focusing on ostracism experiences based on the social identities of employees is scarce. For instance, there is a dearth of research focusing on the ostracism experiences of Asian Americans. The changing political climate worldwide, particularly toward immigration, impacts workplace experiences of recent immigrants or international employees, as shown in European studies (e.g., Harrison, Harrison, & Shaffer, 2019; van der Linden, Hooghe, de Vroome, & Van Laar, 2017). Further expansion in this area of research is needed to provide a more nuanced and complete picture of experiences of workplace ostracism among ethnic minorities in North America.

The research findings on workplace ostracism may also be industry dependent and exploration of how being an ethnic minority in different types of workplaces would be beneficial to build on existing workplace ostracism models. For instance, the experiences of ethnic minority employees in the education sector could be different from those in the business and medical sectors. However, some researchers caution that the lack of data available on whether individuals left their previous jobs because of ostracism experiences may skew findings that seem promising (McCord et al., 2018). Empirical studies on workplace ostracism are instructive but their applications in increasingly diverse workplaces are less clear without knowing in which populations certain dynamics are most apparent. Participant demographics for marginalized groups are under-reported routinely (see Sojo, Wood, & Genat, 2016). More studies with detailed reporting of participant demographics are needed in order to detect diverging experiences of workplace ostracism based on social identities.

Additionally, organizations and managers should work on creating an inclusive culture for immigrant employees. Awareness training can help sensitize immigrant experiences through a series of role-plays, open and honest discussions, as well as case testimonies from immigrants (Bhagat & London, 1999). In organizations with a substantial number of immigrant employees, education on cultural expectations can be provided as well as opportunities to perform new cultural behaviors in a non-judgmental/unsafe environment (Bhagat & London, 1999). Lastly, the organization and managers can educate all employees on the harmful effects of workplace ostracism and create a culture that discourages workplace ostracism. Managers should have open-door policies that encourage open discussions among employees and provide advice on how to solve interpersonal issues as they arise.

Finally, the COVID-19 global pandemic has laid bare preexisting inequities and prejudices and brought into the forefront instances of ostracism against Asians in particular, but also African American/Black, Hispanic/Latinx, foreign-born, immigrant, and international workers. This new normal also threatens to solidify inequalities for members of the traditionally marginalized groups in the U. S. labor force. Specifically, "essential workers" are often women of color in such jobs as care-giving. They are required to go to work but do not qualify for hazard pay (Gonzalez, 2020). Therefore, these workers are excluded from proper compensation in light of well-documented exposures to on-the-job risks. Moreover, seasonal and dairy farmworkers, along with meatpacking plants across the U.S., employ mostly foreign-born and immigrant workers. These vital, but invisible workers are being excluded from workplace protections, including social distance workspaces, testing for COVID-19 infections, sick leave options, access to soap and water for hand washing, availability of proper face masks and body gear, as well as installed shields and guards while working (Ura, 2020). Unquestionably, these foreign-born and immigrant workers must risk life and death to earn a paycheck. Lastly, as schools, colleges, and university campuses remain closed to prevent the spread of the COVID-19 virus, many international students have lost their campus jobs and visa restrictions bar them from seeking off-campus employment to replace lost wages (Dickerson, 2020). The concerns of international status, student workers are being mostly ignored and remain a low priority for administrators compared to attention paid to student athletes, incoming student cohorts, and disgruntled class of 2020 graduates.

In sum, past and present workplace dynamics produce intentional and unintentional circumstances for the reoccurring exclusion of members from prototypically disenfranchised groups. The changing conditions of the workplace, during this global pandemic, may also change the strained paths of inclusion for a growing and diverse workforce.

Funding Funds used in this research were provided by the National Science Foundation (NSF) The Texas A&M System AGEP Alliance: A Model to Advance Historically Underrepresented Minorities, Grant # 1723255.

References

Albuja, A. F., Sanchez, D. T., & Gaither, S. E. (2019). Identity denied: Comparing American or White identity denial and psychological health outcomes among bicultural and biracial people. *Personality and Social Psychology Bulletin, 45*(3), 416–430. https://doi.org/10.1177%2F0146167218788553.

Amason, P., Allen, M. W., & Holmes, S. A. (1999). Social support and acculturative stress in the multicultural workplace. *Journal of Applied Communication Research, 27*(4), 310–334. https://doi.org/10.1080/00909889909365543.

Aquino, K., & Bradfield, M. (2000). Perceived victimization in the workplace: The role of situational factors and victim characteristics. *Organization Science, 11*(5), 525–537. http://dx.doi.org/10.1287/orsc.11.5.525.15205.

Arbona, C., Olvera, N., Rodriguez, N., Hagan, J., Linares, A., & Wiesner, M. (2010). Acculturative stress among documented and undocumented Latino immigrants in the United States. *Hispanic Journal of Behavioral Sciences, 32*(3), 362–384. https://doi.org/10.1177/0739986310373210.

Ashforth, B. E., & Mael, F. (1989). Social identity theory and the organization. *Academy of Management Review, 14*(1), 20–39. https://doi.org/10.5465/amr.1989.4278999.

Attell, B. K., Brown, K. K., & Treiber, L. A. (2017). Workplace bullying, perceived job stressors, and psychological distress: Gender and race differences in the stress process. *Social Science Research, 65*, 210–221. https://doi.org/10.1016/j.ssresearch.2017.02.001.

Au, A., Garey, J., Bermas, N., & Chan, M. M. (1998). The relationship between acculturation and job satisfaction among Chinese immigrants in the New York city restaurant business. *International Journal of Hospitality Management, 17*(1), 11–21. Retrieved from https://www.sciencedirect.com/science/article/pii/S0278431997000406.

Avery, D. R., Lerman, B., & Volpone, S. D. (2010). Investigating the racioethnic differences in the link between workplace racioethnic dissimilarity and life satisfaction. *Cultural Diversity and Ethnic Minority Psychology, 16*(3), 307–312. https://doi.org/10.1037/a0018669.

Baumeister, R., & Leary, M. (1995). The need to belong: Desire for interpersonal attachments as a fundamental human motivation. *Psychological Bulletin, 117*(3), 497–529. https://doi.org/10.1037/0033-2909.117.3.497.

Bavishi, A., Madera, J. M., & Hebl, M. R. (2010). The effect of professor ethnicity and gender on student evaluations: Judged before met. *Journal of Diversity in Higher Education, 3*(4), 245–256. https://doi.org/10.1037/a0020763.

Berdahl, J. L., & Moore, C. (2006). Workplace harassment: Double jeopardy for minority women. *Journal of Applied Psychology, 91*(2), 426–436. https://doi.org/10.1037/0021-9010.91.2.426.

Berry, J. (1997). Immigration, acculturation, and adaptation. *Applied Psychology, 46*(1), 5–34. https://doi.org/10.1111/j.1464-0597.1997.tb01087.x.

Berry, J., Phinney, J., Sam, D., & Vedder, P. (2006). Immigrant youth: Acculturation, identity, and adaptation. *Applied Psychology, 55*(3), 303–332. https://doi.org/10.1111/j.1464-0597.2006.00256.x.

Berry, J. W. (1970). Marginality, stress and ethnic identification in an acculturated aboriginal community. *Journal of Cross-Cultural Psychology, 1*(3), 239–252. https://doi.org/10.1177/135910457000100303.

Berry, J. W. (2006). Acculturative stress. In P. T. P. Wong & L. C. J. Wong (Eds.), *International and cultural psychology series: Handbook of multicultural perspectives on stress and coping* (pp. 287–298). Dallas, TX, US: Spring Publications. http://dx.doi.org/10.1007/0-387-26238-5_12.

Berry, J. W. (2007). Acculturation strategies and adaptation. In L. E. Lansford, M. H. Deater-Deckard, & K. Bornstein (Eds.), *Duke series in child development and public policy: Immigrant families in contemporary society* (pp. 69–82). New York, NY: Guilford Press.

Bhagat, R. S., Davis, C. A., & London, M. L. (2009). Acculturative stress in professional immigrants: Towards a cultural theory of stress. In A.-S. G. Antoniou, C. L. Cooper, G. P. Chrousos, C. D. Spielberger, & M. W. Eysenck

(Eds.), *New horizons in management: Handbook of managerial behavior and occupational health* (pp. 345–361). Northampton, MA, US: Edward Elgar Publishing. http://dx.doi.org/10.4337/9781848447219.00035.

Bhagat, R. S., & London, M. (1999). Getting started and getting ahead: Career dynamics of immigrants. *Human Resource Management Review, 9*(3), 349–365. https://doi.org/10.1016/S1053-4822(99)00024-8.

Bourhis, R. Y., Moïse, L. C., Perreault, S., & Senécal, S. (1997). Towards an interactive acculturation model: A social psychological approach. *International Journal of Psychology, 32*(6), 369–386. https://doi.org/10.1080/002075997400629.

Buckley, P., & Bachman, D. (2017, July 31). Meet the U.S. workforce of the future: Older, more diverse, and more educated. *Deloitte Review*, Issue 21. https://www2.deloitte.com/us/en/insights/deloitte-review/issue-21/meet-the-us-workforce-of-the-future.html.

Bureau of Labor Statistics, U.S. Department of Labor. (2016). *The Economics Daily, 26.8 million Hispanics or Latinos in the U.S. labor force in 2016.* Retrieved from https://www.bls.gov/opub/ted/2017/26-point-8-million-hispanics-or-latinos-in-the-u-s-labor-force-in-2016.htm.

Bureau of Labor Statistics, U.S. Department of Labor. (2019a). The Employment Situation—September 2019. *USDL-19-1735.* Retrieved from https://www.bls.gov/news.release/pdf/empsit.pdf.

Bureau of Labor statistics, U.S. Department of Labor. (2019b). Labor force characteristics of foreign-born workers summary. *USDL-19-0812.* Retrieved from https://www.bls.gov/news.release/forbrn.nr0.htm.

Bureau of Labor Statistics. (2019). *Foreign born workers: Labor force characteristics 2018.* Bureau of Labor Statistics. Retrieved from https://www.bls.gov/news.release/forbrn.nr0.htm/labor-force-characteristics-of-foreign-born-workers-summary.

Burns, P., & Gimpel, J. G. (2000). Economic insecurity, prejudicial stereotypes, and public opinion on immigration policy. *Political Science Quarterly, 115*(2), 201–225. https://doi.org/10.2307/2657900.

Campbell, M. E., Keith, V. M., Gonlin, V., & Carter-Sowell, A. R. (2020). Is a picture worth a thousand words? An experiment comparing observer-based skin tone measures. *Racs and Social Problems*. https://doi.org/10.1007/s12552-020-09294-0.

Carter-Sowell, A. R., & Carter, J. E. M. (2016). Examining bullying, ostracism, and pervasive stereotypes of black immigrants from the Caribbean living in the United States. *Journal of Black Sexuality and Relationships, 2*(3), 25–48. https://doi.org/10.1353/bsr.2016.0011.

Carter-Sowell, A. R., & Zimmerman, C. A. (2015). Hidden in plain sight: Locating, validating, and advocating the stigma experiences of women of color. *Sex Roles: A Journal of Research, 73*(9–10), 399–407. https://doi.org/10.1007/s11199-015-0529-2.

Chang, C.-H. (Daisy), Ferris, D. L., Johnson, R. E., Rosen, C. C., & Tan, J. A. (2012). Core self-evaluations. *Journal of Management, 38*(1), 81–128. https://doi.org/10.1177/0149206311419661.

Clement, R., Noels, K. A., & Deneault, B. (2001). Interethnic contact, identity, and psychological adjustment: The mediating and moderating roles of communication. *Journal of Social Issues, 57*(3), 559–577. https://doi.org/10.1111/0022-4537.00229.

Cortina, L. M., Kabat-Farr, D., Leskinen, E. A., Huerta, M., & Magley, V. J. (2013). Selective incivility as modern discrimination in organizations: Evidence and impact. *Journal of Management, 39*(6), 1579–1605. https://doi.org/10.1177/0149206311418835.

Cortina, L. M., Kabat-Farr, D., Magley, V. J., & Nelson, K. (2017). Researching rudeness: The past, present, and future of the science of incivility. *Journal of Occupational Health Psychology, 22*(3), 299–313. https://doi.org/10.1037/ocp0000089.

Craig, M. A., Rucker, J. M., & Richeson, J. A. (2018). The pitfalls and promise of increasing racial diversity: Threat, contact, and race relations in the 21st century. *Current Directions in Psychological Science, 27*(3), 188–193. https://doi.org/10.1177/0963721417727860.

Cuéllar, I. (2000). Acculturation and mental health: Ecological transactional relations of adjustment. In I. Cuéllar & F. A. Paniagua (Eds.), *Handbook of multicultural mental health* (pp. 45–62). San Diego, CA, US: Academic Press. http://dx.doi.org/10.1016/B978-012199370-2/50004-3.

Curtis, R. C., & Miller, K. (1986). Believing another likes or dislikes you: Behaviors making the beliefs come true. *Journal of Personality and Social Psychology, 51*(2), 284–290. https://doi.org/10.1037/0022-3514.51.2.284.

de Castro, A. B., Fujishiro, K., Sweitzer, E., & Oliva, J. (2006). How immigrant workers experience workplace problems: A qualitative study. *Archives of Environmental & Occupational Health, 61*(6), 249–258. https://doi.org/10.3200/AEOH.61.6.249-258.

de Castro, A. B., Gee, G. C., & Takeuchi, D. T. (2008). Job-related stress and chronic health conditions among Filipino immigrants. *Journal of Immigrant and Minority Health, 10*(6), 551–558. https://doi.org/10.1007/s10903-008-9138-2.

DelCampo, R. G., Jacobson, K. J., Van Buren III, H. J., & Blancero, D. M. (2011). Comparing immigrant and US born Hispanic business professionals: Insights on discrimination. *Cross Cultural Management: An International Journal, 18*(3), 327–350. https://doi.org/10.1108/13527601111152851.

Delgado-Romero, E. A., Manlove, A. N., Manlove, J. D., & Hernandez, C. A. (2007). Controversial issues in the recruitment and retention of Latino/a faculty. *Journal of Hispanic Higher Education, 6*(1), 34–51. https://doi.org/10.1177/1538192706294903.

Dickens, D. D., Womack, V. Y., & Dimes, T. (2019). Managing hypervisibility: An exploration of theory and research on identity shifting strategies in the workplace among Black women. *Journal of Vocational Behavior, 113*, 153–163. https://doi.org/10.1016/j.jvb.2018.10.008.

Dickerson, D. (2020, April 25). 'My world is shattering': Foreign students stranded by Coronavirus. *The New York Times*. https://www.nytimes.com/2020/04/25/us/coronavirus-international-foreign-students-universities.html.

Dobbin, F., Schrage, D., & Kalev, A. (2015). Rage against the Iron Cage: The varied effects of bureaucratic personnel reforms on diversity. *American Sociological Review, 80*(5), 1014–1044. https://doi.org/10.1177/0003122415596416.

Dotan-Eliaz, O., Sommer, K. L., & Rubin, Y. S. (2009). Multilingual groups: Effects of linguistic ostracism on felt rejection and anger, coworker attraction, perceived team potency, and creative performance. *Basic and Applied Social Psychology, 31*(4), 363–375. https://doi.org/10.1080/01973530903317177.

Dustmann, C., & Preston, I. P. (2007). Racial and economic factors in attitudes to immigration. *The B.E. Journal of Economic Analysis & Policy, 7*(1). https://doi.org/10.2202/1935-1682.1655.

Elliott, J. R., & Smith, R. A. (2004). Race, gender, and workplace power. *American Sociological Review, 69*(3), 365–386. https://doi.org/10.1177/000312240406900303.

Emerson, K. T. U., & Murphy, M. C. (2014). Identity threat at work: How social identity threat and situational cues contribute to racial and ethnic disparities in the workplace. *Cultural Diversity and Ethnic Minority Psychology, 20*(4), 508–520. https://doi.org/10.1037/a0035403.

Facchini, G., & Mayda, A. M. (2012). Individual attitudes towards skilled migration: An empirical analysis across countries. *The World Economy, 35*(2), 183–196. https://doi.org/10.1111/j.1467-9701.2011.01427.x.

Ferris, D. L., Brown, D. J., Berry, J. W., & Lian, H. (2008). The development and validation of the Workplace Ostracism Scale. *Journal of Applied Psychology, 93*(6), 1348–1366. Retrieved from https://doi.org/10.1037.a0012743.

Fiset, J., Al Hajj, R., & Vongas, J. G. (2017). Workplace ostracism seen through the lens of power. *Frontiers in Psychology, 8*, 1528. https://doi.org/10.3389/fpsyg.2017.01528.

Flynn, M. A. (2014, June). Safety and the diverse workforce: Lessons from NIOSH's work with Latino immigrants. *Professional Safety, 59*(6), 52–57.

Fox, S., & Stallworth, L. E. (2005). Racial/ethnic bullying: Exploring links between bullying and racism in the US workplace. *Journal of Vocational Behavior, 66*(3), 438–456. http://dx.doi.org/10.1016/j.jvb.2004.01.002.

Ghavami, N., & Peplau, L. A. (2013). An intersectional analysis of gender and ethnic stereotypes: Testing three hypotheses. *Psychology of Women Quarterly, 37*(1), 113–127. http://dx.doi.org/10.1177/0361684312464203a.

Gheorghiu, E., & Stephens, C. S. (2016). Working with "The Others": Immigrant academics' acculturation strategies as determinants of perceptions of conflict at work. *The Social Science Journal, 53*(4), 521–533. https://doi.org/10.1016/J.SOSCIJ.2016.08.002.

Gonzalez, S. (2020, May 1). About that hazard pay (No. 996). [Audio podcast episode]. *Planet Money*. Washington, DC: NPR. https://www.npr.org/2020/05/01/849390745/episode-996-about-that-hazard-pay.

Goodwin, S. A., Williams, K. D., & Carter-Sowell, A. R. (2010). The psychological sting of stigma: The costs of attributing ostracism to racism. *Journal of Experimental Social Psychology, 46*(4), 612–618. https://doi.org/10.1016/J.JESP.2010.02.002.

Graf, N. (2018). *Trends changing the US workplace seen as both positive, negative*. Pew Research Center. Retrieved September 5, 2018, from http://www.pewresearch.org/fact-tank/2018/01/23/americans-see-both-good-and-bad-in-trends-that-are-changing-the-workplace/.

Graziano, W. G., & Eisenberg, N. (1997). Agreeableness: A dimension of personality. In R. Hogan, J. A. Johnson, & S. R. Briggs (Eds.), *Handbook of personality psychology* (pp. 795–824). San Diego, CA, US: Academic Press. http://dx.doi.org/10.1016/B978-012134645-4/50031-7.

Hagelskamp, C., & Hughes, D. L. (2014). Workplace discrimination predicting racial/ethnic socialization across African American, Latino, and Chinese families. *Cultural Diversity and Ethnic Minority Psychology, 20*(4), 550–560. https://doi.org/10.1037/a0035321.

Hagendoorn, L. (1993). Ethnic categorization and outgroup exclusion: Cultural values and social stereotypes in the construction of ethnic. *Ethnic and Racial Studies, 16*(1), 26–51. https://doi.org/10.1080/01419870.1993.9993771.

Hainmueller, J., & Hangartner, D. (2013). Who gets a Swiss passport? A natural experiment in immigrant discrimination. *American Political Science Review, 107*(1), 159–187. https://doi.org/10.1017/S0003055412000494.

Hainmueller, J., Hiscox, M. J., & Margalit, Y. (2015). Do concerns about labor market competition shape attitudes toward immigration? New evidence. *Journal of International Economics, 97*(1), 193–207. https://doi.org/10.1016/J.JINTECO.2014.12.010.

Hainmueller, J., & Hopkins, D. J. (2015). The hidden American immigration consensus: A conjoint analysis of attitudes toward immigrants. *American*

Journal of Political Science, 59(3), 529–548. https://doi.org/10.1111/ajps.12138.

Harrison, D. A., Harrison, T., & Shaffer, M. A. (2019). Strangers in strained lands: Learning from workplace experiences of immigrant employees. *Journal of Management, 45*(2), 600–619. https://doi.org/10.1177%2F0149206318790648.

Hassell, K. D., & Brandl, S. G. (2009). An examination of the workplace experiences of police patrol officers: The role of race, sex, and sexual orientation. *Police Quarterly, 12*(4), 408–430. https://doi.org/10.1177/1098611109348473.

Helbling, M., & Kriesi, H. (2014). Why citizens prefer high-over low-skilled immigrants: Labor market competition, welfare state, and deservingness. *European Sociological Review, 30*(5), 595–614. https://doi.org/10.1093/esr/jcu061.

Hello, E., Scheepers, P., & Sleegers, P. (2006). Why the more educated are less inclined to keep ethnic distance: An empirical test of four explanations. *Ethnic and Racial Studies, 29*(5), 959–985. https://doi.org/10.1080/01419870600814015.

Hitlan, R. T., Kelly, K. M., Schepman, S., Schneider, K. T., & Zárate, M. A. (2006). Language exclusion and the consequences of perceived ostracism in the workplace. *Group Dynamics: Theory, Research, and Practice, 10*(1), 56–70. https://doi.org/10.1037/1089-2699.10.1.56.

Hitlan, R. T., & Noel, J. (2009). The influence of workplace exclusion and personality on counterproductive work behaviours: An interactionist perspective. *European Journal of Work and Organizational Psychology, 18*(4), 477–502. https://doi.org/10.1080/13594320903025028.

Horowitz, J., Parker, K., & Stepler, R. (2017). *Methodology*. Retrieved September 5, 2018, from http://www.pewsocialtrends.org/2017/10/18/methodology-12/.

Howard, M. C., Cogswell, J. E., & Smith, M. B. (2020). The antecedents and outcomes of workplace ostracism: A meta-analysis. *Journal of Applied Psychology, 105*(6), 577–596. https://doi.org/10.1037/apl0000453.

Jackson, P. B., Thoits, P. A., & Taylor, H. F. (1995). Composition of the workplace and psychological well-being: The effects of tokenism on America's Black elite. *Social Forces, 74*(2), 543–557. https://doi.org/10.1093/sf/74.2.543.

Jameel, M. (2019). *More and more workplace discrimination cases are closed before they're even investigated*. The Center for Public Integrity. Retrieved from https://publicintegrity.org/business/workers-rights/workplace-inequities/injustice-at-work/more-and-more-workplace-discrimination-cases-being-closed-before-theyre-even-investigated/.

Jameel, M., & Yerardi, J. (2019). *Despite legal protections, most workers who face discrimination are on their own*. Center for Public Integrity. Retrieved from https://publicintegrity.org/business/workers-rights/workplace-inequities/injustice-at-work/workplace-discrimination-cases/.

Jasinskaja-Lahti, I., Liebkind, K., Jaakkola, M., & Reuter, A. (2006). Perceived discrimination, social support networks, and psychological well-being among three immigrant groups. *Journal of Cross-Cultural Psychology, 37*(3), 293–311. https://doi.org/10.1177/0022022106286925.

Jensen-Campbell, L. A., Graziano, W. G., & Hair, E. C. (1996). Personality and relationships as moderators of interpersonal conflict in adolescence. *Merrill-Palmer Quarterly, 42*(1), 148–164. https://doi.org/10.2307/23090524.

Jian, G. (2012). Does culture matter? An examination of the association of immigrants' acculturation with workplace relationship quality. *Management Communication Quarterly, 26*(2), 295–321. https://doi.org/10.1177/0893318912440178.

Jones, E. E., Carter-Sowell, A. R., Kelly, J. R., & Williams, K. D. (2009). 'I'm out of the loop': Ostracism through information exclusion. *Group Processes & Intergroup Relations, 12*(2), 157–174. https://doi.org/10.1177/1368430208101054.

Kalev, A., Dobbin, F., & Kelly, E. (2006). Best practices or best guesses? Assessing the efficacy of corporate affirmative action and diversity policies. *American Sociological Review, 71*(4), 589–617. https://doi.org/10.1177/000312240607100404.

Kang, S. K., DeCelles, K. A., Tilcsik, A., & Jun, S. (2016). Whitened résumés: Race and self-presentation in the labor market. *Administrative Science Quarterly, 61*(3), 469–502. https://doi.org/10.1177/0001839216639577.

Kiang, L., Cheah, C., Huynh, V., Wang, Y., & Yoshikawa, H. (2016). Annual review of Asian American psychology, 2015. *Asian American Journal of Psychology, 7*(4), 219–255. http://dx.doi.org/10.1037/aap0000055.

King, E. B., & Ahmad, A. S. (2010). An experimental field study of interpersonal discrimination toward Muslim job applicants. *Personnel Psychology, 63*(4), 881–906. https://doi.org/10.1111/j.1744-6570.2010.01199.x.

King, E. B., Madera, J. M., Hebl, M. R., Knight, J. L., & Mendoza, S. A. (2006). What's in a name? A multiracial investigation of the role of occupational stereotypes in selection decisions. *Journal of Applied Social Psychology, 36*(5), 1145–1159. https://doi.org/10.1111/j.0021-9029.2006.00035.x.

Kosic, A. (2004). Acculturation strategies, coping process and acculturative stress. *Scandinavian Journal of Psychology, 45*(4), 269–278. https://doi.org/10.1111/j.1467-9450.2004.00405.x.

Kosic, A., Mannetti, L., & Sam, D. L. (2005). The role of majority attitudes towards out-group in the perception of the acculturation strategies of immigrants. *International Journal of Intercultural Relations*, *29*(3), 273–288. Retrieved from https://doi.org/10.1016/j.ijintrel.2005.06.004.

Kosten, D. (2018). *Immigrants as economic contributors: Immigrant Entrepreneurs*. National Immigration Forum. Retrieved from https://www.immigrationresearch.org/report/other/immigrants-economic-contributors-immigrant-entrepreneurs.

Krogstad, J. M., Passel, J. S., & Cohn, D. (2019, February). *5 Facts about illegal immigration in the U.S.* Pew Research Center. Retrieved from https://www.pewresearch.org/fact-tank/2019/06/12/5-facts-about-illegal-immigration-in-the-u-s/.

Kulkarni, M., & Sommer, K. (2015). Language-based exclusion and prosocial behaviors in organizations. *Human Resource Management, 54*(4), 637–652. https://doi.org/10.1002/hrm.21637.

Lasky, N. V. (2020). Victim precipitation theory. In F. P. Bernat & K. Frailing (Eds.), *The encyclopedia of women and crime* (pp. 1–5). https://doi.org/10.1002/9781118929803.ewac0517.

Lawless, B., & Yea-Wen, C. (2014). Immigrant women, academic work, and agency: Negotiating identities and subjectivities with/in the Ivory Tower. *International Journal of Diversity in Organisations, Communities & Nations: Annual Review, 14,* 39–50. https://doi.org/10.18848/1447-9532/CGP/v14/40143.

Leary, M. R., Tambor, E. S., Terdal, S. K., & Downs, D. L. (1995). Self-esteem as an interpersonal monitor: The sociometer hypothesis. *Journal of Personality and Social Psychology, 68*(3), 518–530. https://doi.org/10.1037/0022-3514.68.3.518.

Leung, A. S. M., Wu, L. Z., Chen, Y. Y., & Young, M. N. (2011). The impact of workplace ostracism in service organizations. *International Journal of Hospitality Management, 30*(4), 836–844. https://doi.org/10.1016/J.IJHM.2011.01.004.

Leung, K. (1997). Negotiation and reward allocations across cultures. In P. C. Early & M. Erez (Eds.), *New perspectives on international industrial and organizational psychology* (pp. 640–675). San Francisco, CA: New Lexington.

Leung, K., Brew, F. P., Zhang, Z.-X., & Zhang, Y. (2011). Harmony and conflict: A cross-cultural investigation in China and Australia. *Journal of Cross-Cultural Psychology, 42*(5), 795–816. https://doi.org/10.1177/0022022110363474.

Lieber, E., Chin, D., Nihira, K., & Mink, I. T. (2001). Holding on and letting go: Identity and acculturation among Chinese immigrants. *Cultural Diversity and Ethnic Minority Psychology, 7*(3), 247–261. Retrieved from https://psycnet.apa.org/buy/2001-07566-005.

Liu, C. (2019). Ostracism, attributions, and their relationships with international students' and employees' outcomes: The moderating effect of perceived harming intent. *Journal of Occupational Health Psychology, 24*(5), 556–571. https://doi.org/10.1037/ocp0000130.

López-Rodríguez, L., Zagefka, H., Navas, M., & Cuadrado, I. (2014). Explaining majority members' acculturation preferences for minority members: A mediation model. *International Journal of Intercultural Relations, 38*, 36–46. https://doi.org/10.1016/J.IJINTREL.2013.07.001.

Lu, J. G., Nisbett, R. E., & Morris, M. W. (2020). Why East Asians but not South Asians are underrepresented in leadership positions in the United States. *Proceedings of the National Academy of Sciences, 117*(9), 4590–4600. https://doi.org/10.1073/pnas.1918896117.

Lu, Y., Samaratunge, R., & Hartel, C. E. (2011). Acculturation strategies among professional Chinese immigrants in the Australian workplace. *Asia Pacific Journal of Human Resources, 49*(1), 71–87. https://doi.org/10.1177/1038411110391709.

Mao, Y., Liu, Y., Jiang, C., & Zhang, I. D. (2018). Why am I ostracized and how would I react?—A review of workplace ostracism research. *Asia Pacific Journal of Management, 35*(3), 745–767. https://doi.org/10.1007/s10490-017-9538-8.

Masgoret, A.-M., & Ward, C. (2006). Culture learning approach to acculturation. In D. L. Sam & J. W. Berry (Eds.), *The Cambridge handbook of acculturation psychology* (pp. 58–77). New York, NY, US: Cambridge University Press. https://doi.org/10.1017/CBO9780511489891.008.

Masuoka, N. (2006). Together they become one: Examining the predictors of panethnic group consciousness among Asian Americans and Latinos. *Social Science Quarterly, 87*(5), 993–1011. https://doi.org/10.1111/j.1540-6237.2006.00412.x.

Mayda, A. M. (2006). Who is against immigration? A cross-country investigation of individual attitudes toward immigrants. *Review of Economics and Statistics, 88*(3), 510–530. https://doi.org/10.1162/rest.88.3.510.

Maynard, D., & Ferdman, B. (2009). The marginalized workforce: How IO psychology can make a difference. *The Industrial-Organizational Psychologist, 46*(4), 25–29.

McCord, M. A., Joseph, D. L., Dhanani, L. Y., & Beus, J. M. (2018). A meta-analysis of sex and race differences in perceived workplace mistreatment. *Journal of Applied Psychology, 103*(2), 137–163. https://doi.org/10.1037/apl0000250.

McGraw, K. (2016). Gender differences among military combatants: Does social support, ostracism, and pain perception influence psychological health? *Military Medicine, 181*(1S), 80–85. https://doi.org/10.7205/MILMED-D-15-00254.

Mohammadi, M. R. (2013). Effect of acculturation strategies and cultural diversity on human resource management. *International Journal of Research in Organizational Behaviour and Human Resource Management, 1*(4), 46–57. Retrieved from https://tinyurl.com/y69h2csb.

Mohammed, B. (2018). *New estimates show U.S. Muslim population continues to grow*. Pew Research Center. Retrieved from http://pewrsr.ch/2lP2MKc.

Muhammad, R. (2018). *African American women managers' experiences in predominantly Black work environments*. Doctoral dissertation, Walden University, Walden Dissertations and Doctoral Studies.

Naumann, E., Stoetzer, L., & Pietrantuono, G. (2018). Attitudes towards highly skilled and low-skilled immigration in Europe: A survey experiment in 15 European countries. *European Journal of Political Research, 57*(4), 1009–1030. https://doi.org/10.1111/1475-6765.12264.

Newman, B. J., Hartman, T. K., & Taber, C. S. (2012). Foreign language exposure, cultural threat, and opposition to immigration. *Political Psychology, 33*(5), 635–657. https://doi.org/10.1111/j.1467-9221.2012.00904.x.

Ng, S. H. (2007). From language acculturation to communication acculturation. *Journal of Language & Social Psychology, 26*(1), 75–90. https://doi.org/10.1177/0261927X06296471.

Ng, T. K., Tsang, K. K., & Lian, Y. (2013). Acculturation strategies, social support, and cross-cultural adaptation: A mediation analysis. *Asia Pacific Education Review, 14*(4), 593–601. https://doi.org/10.1007/s12564-013-9285-6.

Ng, T. W. H., & Sorensen, K. L. (2008). Toward a further understanding of the relationships between perceptions of support and work attitudes. *Group & Organization Management, 33*(3), 243–268. https://doi.org/10.1177/1059601107313307.

O'Connell, M. (2011). How do high-skilled natives view high-skilled immigrants? A test of trade theory predictions. *European Journal of Political Economy, 27*(2), 230–240. https://doi.org/10.1016/J.EJPOLECO.2010.11.002.

Olweus, D. (1978). *Aggression in the schools: Bullies and whipping boys*. Toronto, ON: Wiley.

O'Reilly, J., & Robinson, S. L. (2009, August). The negative impact of ostracism on thwarted belongingness and workplace contributions. In *Academy of Management Proceedings* (Vol. 2009, No. 1, pp. 1–7). Academy of Management. https://doi.org/10.5465/ambpp.2009.44243707.

O'Reilly, J., Robinson, S. L., Berdahl, J. L., & Banki, S. (2014). Is negative attention better than no attention? The comparative effects of ostracism and harassment at work. *Organizational Science, 26*(3), 774–793. https://doi.org/10.1287/orsc.2014.0900.

Park, J., Malachi, E., Sternin, O., & Tevet, R. (2009). Subtle bias against Muslim job applicants in personnel decisions. *Journal of Applied Social Psychology, 39*(9), 2174–2190. https://doi.org/10.1111/j.1559-1816.2009.00520.x.

Parry, E., & Urwin, P. (2011). Generational differences in work values: A review of theory and evidence. *International Journal of Management Reviews, 13*(1), 79–96. https://doi.org/10.1111/j.1468-2370.2010.00285.x.

Pasca, R., & Wagner, S. L. (2011). Occupational stress in the multicultural workplace. *Journal of Immigrant and Minority Health, 13*(4), 697–705. https://doi.org/10.1007/s10903-011-9457-6.

Passel, J. S., & Conn, D. (2017, March 8). *Immigration projected to drive growth in U.S. working-age population through at least 2035*. Pew Research Center's Fact Tank: News in the Numbers. https://www.pewresearch.org/fact-tank/2017/03/08/immigration-projected-to-drive-growth-in-u-s-working-age-population-through-at-least-2035/.

Pérez, E. O. (2010). Explicit evidence on the import of implicit attitudes: The IAT and immigration policy judgments. *Political Behavior, 32*(4), 517–545. https://doi.org/10.1007/s11109-010-9115-z.

Petriglieri, J. L. (2011). Under threat: Responses to and the consequences of threats to individuals' identities. *Academy of Management Review, 36*(4), 641–662. https://doi.org/10.5465/amr.2009.0087.

Phillipson, R. (1997). Realities and myths of linguistic imperialism. *Journal of Multilingual and Multicultural Development, 18*(3), 238–248. https://doi.org/10.1080/01434639708666317.

Phinney, J. S. (1991). Ethnic identity and self-esteem: A review and integration. *Hispanic Journal of Behavioral Sciences, 13*(2), 193–208. https://doi.org/10.1177/07399863910132005.

Phinney, J. S. (2004). Ethic identity and acculturation. In *Acculturation: Advances in theory, measurement, and applied research.* (pp. 63–81). Washington: American Psychological Association. https://doi.org/10.1037/10472-006.

Phinney, J. S., Horenczyk, G., Liebkind, K., & Vedder, P. (2001). Ethnic identity, immigration, and well-being: An interactional perspective. *Journal of Social Issues, 57*(3), 493–510.

Robinson, S. L., O'Reilly, J., & Wang, W. (2013). Invisible at work. *Journal of Management, 39*(1), 203–231. https://doi.org/10.1177/0149206312466141.

Rolen, E., & Toossi, M. (2018). *Blacks in the labor force*. U.S. Bureau of Labor Statistics. Retrieved from https://www.bls.gov/careeroutlook/2018/article/blacks-in-the-labor-force.htm?view_full.

Rosette, A. S., Koval, C. Z., Ma, A., & Livingston, R. (2016). Race matters for women leaders: Intersectional effects on agentic deficiencies and penalties. *The Leadership Quarterly, 27*(3), 429–445. https://doi.org/10.1016/j.leaqua.2016.01.008.

Sam, D. L., & Berry, J. W. (2010). Acculturation: When individuals and groups of different cultural backgrounds meet. *Perspectives on Psychological Science, 5*(4), 472–481. https://doi.org/10.1177/1745691610373075.

Samnani, A.-K., Boekhorst, J. A., & Harrison, J. A. (2013). The acculturation process: Antecedents, strategies, and outcomes. *Journal of Occupational and Organizational Psychology, 86*(2), 166–183. https://doi.org/10.1111/joop.12012.

Scarborough, W. J., Lambouths, D. L., & Holbrook, A. L. (2019). Support of workplace diversity policies: The role of race, gender, and beliefs about inequality. *Social Science Research, 79,* 194–210. https://doi.org/10.1016/j.ssresearch.2019.01.002.

Schildkraut, D. J. (2011). National identity in the United States. In S. J. Schwartz, K. Luyckx, & V. L. Vignoles (Eds.), *Handbook of identity theory and research* (pp. 845–865). New York, NY: Springer Science + Business Media. https://doi.org/10.1007/978-1-4419-7988-9-36.

Schneider, K. T., Hitlan, R. T., & Radhakrishnan, P. (2000). An examination of the nature and correlates of ethnic harassment experiences in multiple contexts. *Journal of Applied Psychology, 85*(1), 3–12. https://doi.org/10.1037/0021-9010.85.1.3.

Scott, K. L., Restubog, S. L. D., & Zagenczyk, T. J. (2013). A social exchange-based model of the antecedents of workplace exclusion. *Journal of Applied Psychology, 98*(1), 37–48. https://doi.org/10.1037/a0030135.

Scott, K. L., Zagenczyk, T. J., Schippers, M. C., & Purvis, R. L. (2017). Coworker exclusion and employee outcomes: Moderating roles of organizational and social support. *Academy of Management Proceedings.* https://doi.org/10.5465/ambpp.2014.14594abstract.

Settles, I. H., Buchanan, N. T., & Dotson, K. (2019). Scrutinized but not recognized: (In)visibility and hypervisibility experiences of faculty of color. *Journal of Vocational Behavior, 113,* 62–74. https://doi.org/10.1016/j.jvb.2018.06.003.

Sniderman, P., Peri, P., de Figueiredo, Jr., R., & Piazza, T. (2000). *The outsider: Politics and prejudice in Italy.* Princeton, NJ: Princeton University Press.

Sojo, V. E., Wood, R. E., & Genat, A. E. (2016). Harmful workplace experiences and women's occupational well-being: A meta-analysis. *Psychology of Women Quarterly, 40*(1), 10–40. http://dx.doi.org/10.1177/0361684315599346.

Steele, C. M. (1997). A threat in the air: How stereotypes shape intellectual identity and performance. *American Psychologist, 52*(6), 613–629. https://doi.org/10.1037/0003-066X.52.6.613.

Steele, C. M., Spencer, S. J., & Aronson, J. (2002). Contending with group image: The psychology of stereotype and social identity threat. *Advances in Experimental Social Psychology, 34*, 379–440. https://doi.org/10.1016/S0065-2601(02)80009-0.

Stout, J. G., & Dasgupta, N. (2011). When he doesn't mean you: Gender-exclusive language as ostracism. *Personality and Social Psychology Bulletin, 37*(6), 757–769. https://doi.org/10.1177/0146167211406434.

Tajfel, H., & Turner, J. C. (1986). The social identity theory of intergroup behavior. In S. Worschel & W. Austin (Eds.), *Psychology of intergroup relations*. Chicago: Nelson-Hall.

Thompson, M. J., Carlson, D. S., Kacmar, K. M., & Vogel, R. M. (2020). The cost of being ignored: Emotional exhaustion in the work and family domains. *Journal of Applied Psychology, 105*(2), 186–195. https://doi.org/10.1037/apl0000433.

Ting-Toomey, S., Yee-Jung, K. K., Shapiro, R. B., Garcia, W., Wright, T. J., & Oetzel, J. G. (2000). Ethnic/cultural identity salience and conflict styles in four US ethnic groups. *International Journal of Intercultural Relations, 24*(1), 47–81. https://doi.org/10.1016/S0147-1767(99)00023-1.

Tobin, R. M., Graziano, W. G., Vanman, E. J., & Tassinary, L. G. (2000). Personality, emotional experience, and efforts to control emotions. *Journal of Personality and Social Psychology, 79*(4), 656–669. https://doi.org/10.1037/0022-3514.79.4.656.

U.S. Bureau of Labor Statistics, Division of Labor Force Statistics. (2018). Labor force characteristics by race and ethnicity, 2017. *Report 1076*. Retrieved from https://www.bls.gov/opub/reports/race-and-ethnicity/2017/home.htm.

U.S. Equal Employment Opportunity Commission. (2015). *American experiences versus American expectations*. Retrieved from https://www.eeoc.gov/eeoc/statistics/reports/american_experiences/.

Umaña-Taylor, A. J., Vargas-Chanes, D., Garcia, C. D., & Gonzales-Backen, M. (2008). A longitudinal examination of latino adolescents' ethnic identity, coping with discrimination, and self-esteem. *Journal of Early Adolescence, 28*(1), 16–50. https://doi.org/10.1177/0272431607308666.

Ura, A. (2020, April 27). Meatpacking workers in Texas panhandle have little power to avoid the coronavirus. *The Texas Tribune*. https://www.texastribune.org/2020/04/27/meatpacking-texas-coronavirus-panhandle/ https://www.npr.org/2020/05/01/849390745/episode-996-about-that-hazard-pay.

Uskul, A. K., & Over, H. (2017). Culture, social interdependence, and ostracism. *Current Directions in Psychological Science, 26*(4), 371–376. https://doi.org/10.1177/0963721417699300.

Van Acker, K., & Vanbeselaere, N. (2012). Heritage culture maintenance precludes host culture adoption and vice versa. *Group Processes & Intergroup Relations, 15*(1), 133–145. https://doi.org/10.1177/1368430211417263.

van der Linden, M., Hooghe, M., de Vroome, & Van Laar, C. (2017). Extending trust to immigrants: Generalized trust, cross-group friendship and anti-immigrant sentiments in 21 European societies. *PLoS One, 12*(5), e0177369. https://doi.org/10.1371/journal.pone.0177369.

van Oudenhoven, J. P., Prins, K. S., & Buunk, B. P. (1998). Attitudes of minority and majority members towards adaptation of immigrants. *European Journal of Social Psychology, 28*(6), 995–1013. https://doi.org/10.1002/(SICI)1099-0992(199811 0)28:6<995::AID-EJSP908>3.0.CO;2-8.

Ward, C. (1997). Culture learning, acculturative stress, and psychopathology: Three perspectives on acculturation. *Applied Psychology, 46*(1), 58–62. https://doi.org/10.1111/j.1464-0597.1997.tb01094.x.

Ward, C., & Kennedy, A. (1994). Acculturation strategies, psychological adjustment, and sociocultural competence during cross-cultural transitions. *International Journal of Intercultural Relations, 18*(3), 329–343. https://doi.org/10.1016/0147-1767(94)90036-1.

Welbourne, J. L., Gangadharan, A., & Sariol, A. M. (2015). Ethnicity and cultural values as predictors of the occurrence and impact of experienced workplace incivility. *Journal of Occupational Health Psychology, 20*(2), 205–217. https://doi.org/10.1037/a0038277.

Wesselmann, E. D., & Williams, K. D. (2010). The potential balm of religion and spirituality for recovering from ostracism. *Journal of Management, Spirituality & Religion, 7*(1), 31–49. https://doi.org/10.1080/14766080903497623.

Widner, D., & Chicoine, S. (2011). It's all in the name: Employment discrimination against Arab Americans. *Sociological Forum, 26*(4), 806–823. https://doi.org/10.1111/j.1573-7861.2011.01285.x.

Williams, D. R., Spencer, M. S., & Jackson, J. S. (1999). Race, stress, and physical health: The role of group identity. In R. J. Contrada & R. D. Ashmore (Eds.), *Rutgers series on self and social identity, Vol. 2: Self, social identity, and physical health: Interdisciplinary explorations* (pp. 71–100). New York, NY, US: Oxford University Press.

Williams, K. (2009). Ostracism: A temporal need-threat model. In M. P. Zanna (Ed.), *Advances in Experimental Social Psychology*, *41*, 275–314. https://doi.org/10.1016/S0065-2601(08)00406-1.

Williams, K. D. (1997). Social ostracism. In R. M. Kowalski (Ed.), *The Plenum series in social/clinical psychology: Aversive interpersonal behaviors* (pp. 133–170). New York, NY: Plenum Press.

Williams, K. D. (2007). Ostracism: The kiss of social death. *Social and Personality Psychology Compass, 1*(1), 236–247. https://doi.org/10.1111/j.1751-9004.2007.00004.x.

Williams, M. S. (2017). *Acculturation and immigrants: The moderating effect of cultural identity salience and harmony enhancement and the mediating effect of social support and ostracism on the relationship between acculturation demands and employee outcomes* (Doctoral dissertation). Hofstra University, Long Island, New York.

Wingfield, A. H. (2010). Are some emotions marked “Whites Only”? Racialized feeling rules in professional workplaces. *Social Problems, 57*(2), 251–268. https://doi.org/10.1525/sp.2010.57.2.251.

Wingfield, A. H., & Wingfield, J. H. (2014). When visibility hurts and helps: How intersections of race and gender shape Black professional men’s experiences with tokenization. *Cultural Diversity and Ethnic Minority Psychology, 20*(4), 483–490. https://doi.org/10.1037/a0035761.

Wu, C. H., Liu, J., Kwan, H. K., & Lee, C. (2016). Why and when workplace ostracism inhibits organizational citizenship behaviors: An organizational identification perspective. *Journal of Applied Psychology, 101*(3), 362. https://psycnet.apa.org/buy/2015-49213-001.

Wu, L., Wei, L., & Hui, C. (2011). Dispositional antecedents and consequences of workplace ostracism: An empirical examination. *Frontiers of Business Research in China, 5*(1), 23–44. https://doi.org/10.1007/s11782-011-0119-2.

Wu, L. Z., Ferris, D. L., Kwan, H. K., Chiang, F., Snape, E., & Liang, L. H. (2015). Breaking (or making) the silence: How goal interdependence and social skill predict being ostracized. *Organizational Behavior and Human Decision Processes, 131*, 51–66. https://doi.org/10.1016/j.obhdp.2015.08.001.

Xu, E., Huang, X., & Robinson, S. L. (2017). When self-view is at stake: Responses to ostracism through the lens of self-verification theory. *Journal of Management, 43*(7), 2281–2302. https://doi.org/10.1177/0149206314567779.

Zagefka, H., & Brown, R. (2002). The relationship between acculturation strategies, relative fit and intergroup relations: Immigrant-majority relations in Germany. *European Journal of Social Psychology, 32*(2), 171–188. https://doi.org/10.1002/ejsp.73.

Zimmerman, C. A., Carter-Sowell, A. R., & Xu, X. (2016). Examining workplace ostracism experiences in academia: Understanding how differences in the faculty ranks influence inclusive climates on campus. *Frontiers in Psychology, 7*, Article 753. https://doi.org/10.3389/fpsyg.2016.00753.

Zou, L. X., & Cheryan, S. (2017). Two axes of subordination: A new model of racial position. *Journal of Personality and Social Psychology, 112(5)*, 696–717. https://doi.org/10.1037/pspa0000080.

CHAPTER 8

Workplace Ostracism Among Gender, Age, and LGBTQ Minorities, and People with Disabilities

Yisheng Peng and Nicholas P. Salter

Introduction

In the past decades, the workforce is becoming increasingly diverse. For example, the labor workforce participation of females has increased from 29.6% in 1950 (Toossi, 2002) to 56.8% by 2016 (U.S. Department of Labor, 2019). And it has been projected that by 2024 almost one in four workers will be 55 or older (Toossi & Torpey, 2017). Additionally, organizational scholars pointed out that more attention should be allocated to employees from certain groups, such as those with disabilities and lesbian, gay, bisexual, transgender, and queer (LGBTQ) employees (Ruggs et al., 2013). The results of the U.S. census found that over 56 million Americans—nearly one in five—have a disability (Brault, 2012), with 29 million of them are between the working ages of 21 and 64

Y. Peng (✉)
George Washington University, Washington, DC, USA

N. P. Salter
Hofstra University, Hempstead, NY, USA

C. Liu and J. Ma (eds.), *Workplace Ostracism*,
Palgrave Explorations in Workplace Stigma,
https://doi.org/10.1007/978-3-030-54379-2_8

(Hyland & Rutigliano, 2013). It has also been estimated that there are 8.8 million LGBTQ adults living in the United States (Ramos, Badgett, & Sears, 2008), suggesting a potential significant portion of the workforce (Webster, Adams, Maranto, Sawyer, & Thoroughgood, 2018). In all, the diversity of the workforce is increasingly reflected in the makeup of employees in the current labor workforce, leading to new challenges for organizations to better manage diversity at work.

A particular challenge in the context of an increasingly diverse workforce is ostracism (Oyet, Dupré, & Arnold, 2013; Robinson, O'Reilly, & Wang, 2013), which could occur across various social contexts including the workplace. Workplace ostracism refers to the degree to which an individual "perceives that he or she is ignored or excluded by others" (Ferris, Brown, Berry, & Lian, 2008, p. 1348). As people may naturally tend to develop bonds with people who are more similar to themselves (e.g., O'Reilly & Robinson, 2009), people who are dissimilar from other organizational members might experience ostracism at work simply due to the differences (e.g., gender, etc.) between them and other people (e.g., Jackson, Barth, Powell, & Lochman, 2006; Robinson et al., 2013). For instance, people can be ostracized simply because of speaking a language different from other people's native language (Dotan-Eliaz, Sommer, & Rubin, 2009). Particularly relevant to the current chapter, Robinson et al. (2013) proposed a model of workplace ostracism in which they suggested that workplace diversity could be an important antecedent of ostracism. That is, because people tend to exclude others who are different from them, workplace ostracism is more likely to occur in a diverse work environment. But why people are likely to ostracize minority employees? And how minority employees perceive and react to workplace ostracism? The structure of this chapter will look at ostracism from both the perpetrator and victim's perspectives. In the following section, we will first introduce social categorization theory (SCT; also called as self-categorization theory; Turner & Oakes, 1989; Turner & Reynolds, 2012) as an overarching framework to discuss the perpetrator's perspective as to why people ostracize minorities. Then, we will discuss the victim's perspective on ostracism, covering four different minorities' statuses (gender, age, sexual and gender orientation, and disability status).

Theoretical Foundations

In the field of social psychology, SCT is an influential theory that has been frequently used to explain a variety of interpersonal interactions and intergroup relations (e.g., Turner & Oakes, 1989; Turner & Reynolds, 2012). SCT has originated from the social identity theory (e.g., Tajfel & Turner 1979, 1986), which proposes that individuals' self-identities are shaped by their group memberships (Tajfel, 1978). Furthermore, people are motivated to strengthen their self-concept by searching for a positively valued distinctiveness for those groups. As a result, they conduct social comparisons to distinguish between their ingroups (i.e., the groups to which they belong) and relevant outgroups (i.e., the groups to which they do not belong), which emphasizes similarities within individuals sharing group memberships and differences among those from different groups. Self-categorization refers to the process by which people identify with those groups due to self-perceived similarities (Turner, 1985). According to the social identity theory (Tajfel & Turner, 1986), demographic characteristics (e.g., age, gender, race, etc.) may serve as the foundations for people to gauge the degree to which they are similar or different in those demographic attributes when compared with their ingroups and outgroups. SCT (Turner, 1987) further suggests that people may use demographic characteristics such as age, gender, or race to classify themselves and others into different social categories. As people tend to identify themselves with groups in which they are similar, they also tend to value members of the same group as similar to each other. Accordingly, people are likely to favor members from their ingroups over those from outgroups (i.e., ingroup bias), and, thus, may tend to be untrusting, aggressive toward those from outgroups perceived as threatening (see Abrams & Hogg, 2006; Brewer, 1979; Hogg & Terry, 2000). Indeed, as salient cues for social categorization (Turner, 1987), demographic characteristics (e.g., age, gender) can induce prejudice and discrimination (e.g., North & Fiske, 2012). The ingroup bias could further play a role in determining whom is likely to be the target of ostracism (Scott & Duffy, 2015).

SCT (Turner, 1985, 1987) also posits that when those social categories become salient, individuals' cognitive structures will experience significant shifts in that they will change to depersonalize their identities and regard themselves more as representatives of social categories than as unique individuals. Correspondingly, intergroup differentiation becomes more significant as similarities within ingroup members and differences from outgroup members are amplified, which sustains individuals' own self-esteem (Turner, 1987). This differentiation also leads to higher levels of trust for, and affective reactions to, their ingroup members, which finally may be expressed as a differential regard, or even bias, for people with whom they share group membership as opposed to those in outgroups (Tajfel & Turner, 1986; Turner, Hogg, Oakes, Reicher, & Wetherell, 1987). Accordingly, SCT offers insight into interpersonal behaviors (e.g., workplace ostracism) and intergroup relations (Roberson, 2019; Roberson, Ryan, & Ragins, 2017).

SCT provides explanation as to why people are likely to ostracize minority employees (i.e., the perpetrator's perspective). Specifically, differences (e.g., gender, disability status, etc.) between majority and minority group employees could lay down the foundation for individuals' identification with ingroups and outgroups (e.g., Gómez, Morales, Hart, Vázquez, & Swann, Jr., 2011; Tajfel & Turner 1979). Majority group employees tend to favor members from their ingroups over those from minority groups (i.e., ingroup bias), and, thus, may ostracize people from minority groups perceived as threatening. For instance, it has been argued that people may display prejudicial attitudes and behaviors directed toward people with disabilities (Park, Faulkner, & Schaller, 2003). People identify themselves as members of minority groups, such as people with visible disabilities, physical illnesses (Wynne & McAnaney, 2009) or mental illnesses (Marr, Thau, Aquino, & Barclay, 2012) are often likely to be ostracized (Gamian-Wilk & Madeja-Bien, 2018).

SCT further provides another possible explanation as to why minority employees tend to perceive more ostracism (i.e., the victim's perspective). According to SCT (Turner, 1985, 1987), people may develop a salient social identity based on the similarities and differences across different social categories. Because people generally have a fundamental need to develop and maintain stable and meaningful interpersonal relationships with others (Leary, 2005; Leary & Baumeister, 2000), minority employees with salient social identities with their own groups (e.g., employees with disabilities) may tend to have a sensitive "alert" system which enables them to perceive more ostracism episodes. By its nature, ostracism is highly subjective (Ferris, Chen, & Lim, 2017) because it is an act of omission rather than commission (Robinson et al., 2013). Thus, when an act of omission happens to a minority employee with a salient social identity with his or her own group (e.g., not invited for a work meeting), he or she may be more likely to perceive being ostracized in this ambiguous situation due to the minority status.

Furthermore, attributing ostracism to one's minority status can be particularly detrimental to the victim. Research has found ostracism is more upsetting to people when it results from an internal attribute (Liu, 2019; Robinson et al., 2013), when it is based on something non-temporary (Wirth & Williams, 2009), and when it has finality (Scott & Thau, 2013). When people believe they are being ostracized because of their minority status, all three of these conditions are fulfilled. Specifically, minority identity is an internal attribute, it is certainly not temporary, and therefore this attribution has a feeling of finality to it (i.e., "I can't change being a minority, so therefore the ostracism will not change"). Therefore, believing that you are being ostracized due to being a minority can be very upsetting.

In conclusion, SCT not only provides theoretical explanations for why minority employees might be the target of ostracism but also offers insights into explanations for why minority employees may perceive and react differently to ostracism. In each of the following four minority group sections, in addition to briefly discussing the current literature following the perpetrator's perspective, we will mainly take the victim's perspective to review the existing literature and discuss the effects of gender, age, LGBTQ status, and disability status on employees' experiences of and reactions to ostracism.

Literature Review

Gender and Ostracism

Women comprise over half of the population (U.S. Department of Labor, 2019) and yet are still regarded as minorities in the workplace due to the historical discrimination they have and continue to receive (Karsten, 2016; Lewis, 2018). As minorities, this population may be especially susceptible to being ostracized and excluded at work. Research (both in and out of the workplace) has therefore examined ostracism among women in order to answer this question. As will be seen, though, the relationship between gender and ostracism is still unclear. Below, this line of research is discussed in terms of women's experiences of and reactions to ostracism.

Gender as a Predictor of Ostracism

Research that explicitly studies gender in the context of ostracism suggests that women experience higher levels of workplace ostracism than men do. For instance, in an academic context, Settles and O'Connor (2014) found that women experienced higher levels of exclusion than men at a conference on the history of science. Similarly, Maranto and Griffin (2011) found that women in academia reported more ostracism in their institutions than men, and they found that the effect was larger when there was a smaller proportion of women in the department. However, Zimmerman, Carter-Sowell, and Xu (2016) found that women perceived more ostracism regardless of the proportion of women in their departments; in other words, ostracism still occurred even if there were many women in the department. It should be noted that race can also intersect with gender in this area; Arar (2018) argued that Arab females in particular face exclusion in academia. Although much research in this area has been conducted within academia, this trend could be generalized to other industries. For example, it has also been found that female nurses experienced more workplace ostracism than males (Cottingham, Erickson, Diefendorff, & Bromley, 2013).

Although studies that explicitly seek to determine if men or women experience more ostracism in the workplace consistently suggest women do, a recent meta-analysis contradicts this. Howard, Cogswell, and Smith (2020) analyzed 63 different samples (N = 18,006 participants) that examined ostracism and gender and found a small but significant relationship. However, rather than women reporting higher levels of ostracism than men (as would be expected from the literature on ostracism and gender), their analysis found men to report higher levels than women. This suggests that although studies that explicitly examine gender in the context of ostracism (such as the research previously discussed) suggest women report higher levels of being ostracized, research that merely includes gender as a demographic variable or covariate suggests the opposite. For instance, some studies that included gender but did not explicitly hypothesize about it found men reported more workplace exclusion than women (Hitlan, Clifton, & DeSoto, 2006; Wu et al., 2015), though it should be noted some studies also found no significant relationship between gender and ostracism (Quade, Greenbaum, & Mawritz, 2019; Quade, Greenbaum, & Petrenko, 2017).

To further complicate our understanding of the relationship between gender and ostracism, the related field of research on workplace incivility finds that female employees report more uncivil treatment than their male counterparts (Cortina, 2008; Cortina, Kabat-Farr, Leskinen, Huerta, & Magley, 2013; Miner, Pesonen, Smittick, Seigel, & Clark, 2014). As noted by Zimmerman et al. (2016), ostracism is conceptually different from workplace incivility or other type of workplace mistreatment, such as abusive supervision or social undermining. Still, there is much conceptual overlap between the constructs, and measures of mistreatment often include items or a sub-scale measuring ostracism or exclusion (e.g., Anthony, Yastik, MacDonald, & Marshall, 2014; Ferris et al., 2017; Martin & Hine, 2005). Therefore, it is especially surprising that women report less ostracism than men as this is opposite of how women experience workplace incivility. More research is needed to explore this nuance.

What might explain these contradictions? The theoretical rationale as to why men might experience more ostracism is unclear. Although this clearly suggests more research should be done, there are a number of possible explanations. For instance, Howard et al. (2020) suggested that men may experience more ostracism than women due to gender norms. Specifically, society typically expects women to exhibit qualities such as empathy and communality but men are expected to be assertive and agentic (Eagly & Johannesen-Schmidt, 2001). Howard et al. suggested that people may be less likely to ostracize women for this reason (and possibly more comfortable ostracizing men for this same reason). However, they did not test this proposition, so further research is needed. Furthermore, the unexpected findings might be found only in certain samples. For instance, many of the studies discussed earlier that do support women experiencing more ostracism than men were all measured among academic samples (e.g., Maranto & Griffin, 2011; Settles & O'Connor, 2014; Zimmerman et al., 2016); perhaps academia is more male-oriented and therefore encourages more ostracism against women. Therefore, it may be plausible that the unexpected gender difference in ostracism may exist in more female-oriented occupations.

Studies such as these suggest that there may be factors in the workplace that contribute to ostracism against women out of the perpetrators' awareness. However, without further study, it is difficult to draw conclusions as to why data suggests that men experience more ostracism than women (Howard et al., 2020) even though there are theoretical reasons to believe it would operate in the opposite direction. We encourage future research to examine these questions.

Outcomes of Ostracism Against Men and Women

As can be seen, it appears that women experience less workplace ostracism than men do (although the rationale for this appears to be unclear so should therefore be studied more). Similarly, it is unclear whether women react differently to ostracism than men do. In this section, we outline research addressing this question. It should be noted that most of the research discussed in this section is not conducted in the work context (and specifically often lab studies), pointing to the paucity of workplace ostracism research in general and with regard to minority groups in specific.

Previous research on the outcomes of ostracism (specifically, emotional outcomes, as these are the dependent variables typically examined in these studies) shows somewhat conflicting results. For instance, Hales, Dvir, Wesselmann, Kruger, and Finkenauer (2018) found that being ostracized when having a conversation with a person (operationalized as the other person checking their cellphones) resulted in women feeling worse than men did when they were ostracized. On the other hand, other research found men to report lower well-being due to exclusion than women (Hitlan et al., 2006). Yet another perspective suggests no gender difference in reactions to ostracism. Bozin and Yoder (2008) had male and female participants play Cyberball, a computer game commonly used in research to evoke ostracism. They found no significant differences between male and female participants in their reactions to ostracism.

One nuance to the relationship between ostracism and gender is that it may not be that women react better or worse to ostracism than men, but just differently. Williams and Sommer (1997) manipulated if participants were ostracized or not (also using the Cyberball manipulation) and found that men and women's reactions were different. Specifically, ostracized women worked harder at the game in an effort to become more involved. The authors suggested that ostracism threatens women's sense of belongingness; ostracized women felt that they didn't belong so they worked harder to try to make others accept them into the group. Men, on the other hand, did not respond to ostracism by increasing their effort. Instead, they socially loafed and withdrew from the game. The authors explained that for men ostracism threatens their ego needs such as control and self-esteem. In other words, when men were ostracized, they chose to mentally withdraw in an effort to preserve their ego. These explanations are supported by research on self-construals, which has found that women hold interdependent self-construals (corresponding with a need to belong) but men hold independent self-construals (corresponding with ego needs; Cross & Madson, 1997; Guimond, Chatard, Martinot, Crisp, & Redersdorff, 2006). However, this explanation should be interpreted cautiously as this was an experimental study and field research on the topic shows inconsistent findings regarding how ostracized employees respond behaviorally (see Chapters 4, 5, and 6 of this book for more on this).

Another important distinction to consider when examining gender differences in reactions to ostracism is if a person is being ostracized by people of the same gender (i.e., ingroup ostracism) or by people of a different gender (i.e., outgroup ostracism). Generally, research suggests that with regard to gender, ingroup ostracism is more upsetting than outgroup ostracism (Wittenbaum, Shulman, & Braz, 2010). One study found that women reacted negatively only when they were ostracized by other women; outgroup ostracism by men had no effect on them (Cursan, Bernstein, Pascual, & Félonneau, 2017). It should be noted that this may also be influenced by other minority statuses, such as race. For instance, Hayman, McIntyre, and Abbey (2015) found that ingroup ostracism was worse than outgroup ostracism in that African-American women responded worse to being ostracized by women of their same race (i.e., ingroup members) than by Caucasian women (i.e., ingroup in the context of gender, but outgroup in the context of race). Interestingly, although it appears that women react differently to being ostracized by men compared to women, one study found that rates of ingroup versus outgroup ostracism did not differ (Schaffer & Riordan, 2013)

Age and Ostracism

There are a handful of empirical studies that specifically examined age differences in the experience of or reaction to ostracism, though few of them were conducted in the work context. In a sample of nearly 200 Maine workers aged 62 and above, Blackstone (2013) found that workplace isolation is one of the most common harassment experiences among older workers. In the following, we will discuss different propositions based on existing theoretical frameworks.

Age as a Predictor of Ostracism

Older workers are more likely to be ostracized at work. According to SCT (Turner, 1987), employee age can be used as a salient cue for social categorization. Younger workers are likely to favor those from the relatively similar age group and dislike people from a different age group (i.e., older workers). Indeed, age has been found to induce prejudice and discrimination (North & Fiske, 2012). Such age bias is present in the workplace. For instance, it has been found that young raters tend to be prejudiced toward older workers (Finkelstein, Burke, & Raju, 1995; Gordon & Arvey, 2004). Older workers are also more likely to experience workplace ostracism stemming from ageism compared to younger workers. Ageism refers to systematic stereotypes and discrimination against older people because of their age (Butler, 1989). Age stereotypes typically consist of beliefs and expectations people have about older workers that are usually inaccurate and negative (Fiske & Neuberg, 1990). The negative age stereotypes about older workers are common in organizations and are often viewed as the cause of age discrimination (Finkelstein & Farrell, 2007; Shore & Goldberg, 2005). Related to this, Adams, DeArmond, Jex, and Webster (2013) suggested that older workers are more likely to experience mistreatment based on ageism. Another related perspective is that older workers may experience ostracism due to resource tension between generations (North & Fiske, 2015). For instance, in a series of experimental studies, North and Fisk (2016) found that resource scarcity exaggerated the tendency of younger participants to subtly disregard older workers. This intergenerational—tension ageism perspective provides another unique framework to understand older workers' experiences of ostracism at work (North, in press).

However, an opposite view is that older workers are less likely to experience workplace ostracism. Ng (2017) has argued that older workers might be less likely to be targets of ostracism because they may receive more respect and esteem due to their richer work experiences and seniority (Armstrong-Stassen & Lee, 2009). Furthermore, socioemotional selectivity theory (Carstensen, Isaacowitz, & Charles, 1999) suggests that older people may experience less ostracism at work. SST categorizes human goals into two categories: knowledge acquisition and emotion regulation. An individual's perception of time influences how he/she places importance to these goals. Specifically, because older people tend to perceive their future as limited, they tend to value emotional goals more than other goals compared to younger people. As older adults place more emphasis on emotional goals (e.g., experiencing positive emotions and building up social connectedness) than other goals (e.g., knowledge acquisition, recognition, and achievement), they would focus more on social-emotionally meaningful goals and relationships and try to maximize positive emotional experiences. On the one hand, to gain positive emotions, older workers may tend to interact more with people whom they have close relationships (e.g., emotionally close social partners; Hommelhoff, Müller, & Scheibe, 2017). As such, it is likely that they will experience less ostracism at work. On the other hand, the salience of social-emotional goals may increase older workers' sensitivity to ostracism episodes. In other words, as they place more emphasis on social-emotional meaningful goals and relationships, they may become sensitive to ostracism episodes (e.g., not invited to a social event) and thus are more likely to perceive ostracism in those ambiguous situations. It is likely that these two opposite forces cancel out each other and result in non-significant relationship between age and ostracism, as found a recent meta-analytic study (Howard et al., 2020).

Outcomes of Ostracism Against Older People
From the victim's perspective, employee age not only can relate to workplace ostracism directly, but also may moderate the impact people's reaction to workplace ostracism. On the one hand, older employees may react more negatively to workplace ostracism. Specifically, older employees may attribute their experiences of workplace ostracism to their age category (i.e., older workers); a non-temporary (Wirth & Williams, 2009) and an internal attribute (Robinson et al., 2013). Such attribution is internal, non-temporary, and out of one's control (Weiner, 1985). When people attribute negative events (e.g., workplace ostracism) to something internal, stable, and uncontrollable, they would experience worse outcomes such as depression (Liu, 2019).

On the other hand, according to socioemotional selectivity theory (Carstensen et al., 1999), older employees tend to place more emphasis on social-emotional goals and tend to focus more on positive rather than negative information (age-related positivity effect; Mather & Carstensen, 2005). They may have stronger motivation to regulate their emotions and may be better able to do so (Blanchard-Fields, Mienaltowski, & Seay, 2007; Carstensen, 2006). Consistently, it has been found that with age people tend to engage in more frequent use of cognitive reappraisal (Yeung, Wong, & Lok, 2011), a typical antecedent-focused emotion regulation strategy that can effectively regulate negative emotions and is beneficial to one's health and well-being (e.g., Gross & John, 2003). Even for emotional suppression, one consequence-focused emotion regulation strategy that is usually less helpful or even harmful to one's health and well-being (Gross & John, 2003), it has been found to be effective and can lead to a variety of work and well-being benefits among older workers but not among younger workers (Peng, Tian, Jex, & Chen, 2017; Yeung & Fung, 2012; Yeung & Wong, 2020). Older workers may also have more experiences and are more effective in coping with workplace mistreatment (e.g., ostracism). For instance, research has found that older workers use more effective emotion regulation strategies (e.g., cognitive reappraisal) when they are experiencing interpersonal mistreatment (Peng, Xu, & Matthews, 2020). Age-related improvement in emotion regulation (e.g., Doerwald, Scheibe, Zcher, & Van Yperen, 2016) may help older workers cope with interpersonal stressors (Blanchard-Fields, 2007), such as ostracism. Furthermore, older adults tend to place more emphasis on positive over negative information in attention and memory (Mather & Carstensen, 2005) and make more positive appraisals over negative appraisals of the source of the hurtful comments (Charles & Carstensen, 2008; Hawkley, Williams, & Cacioppo, 2011). These positive focuses in memory, attention, and appraisals would thus enable older workers to be less concerned about being ostracized by others (Hawkley et al., 2011).

Taken together, social-emotional goals, age-related positivity effect, and social network (Peng, Jex, & Wang, 2018) may help older workers react less negatively to workplace ostracism. Supporting this argument, it has been found that compared with their younger counterparts, older adults report diminished negative responses to social rejection and exclusion (Hawkley et al., 2011; Löckenhoff, Cook, Anderson, & Zayas, 2013). However, other scholars have argued that age differences were only observed under mild ostracism but not under severe ostracism (Cheng & Grühn, 2015; Löckenhoff et al., 2013). When ostracism are explicit and severe, older adults could eventually experience more negative reactions. As such, age differences in reactions to workplace ostracism may also depend on the severity of ostracism. Future research may need to specify the severity level of ostracism. Again, most of the research discussed in this section were not conducted in the work context, suggesting a strong need of research on age and workplace ostracism.

LGBTQ Status and Ostracism

LGBTQ employees have historically been marginalized and discriminated against in the workplace (Barron & Hebl, 2011; Herek, 2007). However, Velez, Moradi, and Brewster (2013) pointed out that not all anti-LGBTQ discrimination is overt; instead, it can be subtle at times. For this reason, ostracism might be particularly relevant to LGBTQ employees: ostracism can be a subtle form of discrimination against this group. As pointed out by DeSouza, Wesselmann, and Ispas (2017), very little research has focused on this topic in a workplace context, though some research on this population outside of the workplace has been conducted.

LGBTQ Status as a Predictor of Ostracism
Some research suggests that LGBTQ employees experience ostracism. Much of the empirical research on this topic has been qualitative; case studies have shown that ostracism and exclusion is a consistent theme that arises among LGBTQ employees (Colgan, Creegan, McKearney, & Wright, 2008; Embrick, Walther, & Wickens, 2007), even in organizations that consider themselves "inclusive" (Priola, Lasio, De Simone, & Serri, 2014). However, some research has been quantitative in nature; for instance, Hoel, Lewis, and Einarsdottir (2017) found that LGBTQ employees were more likely to perceive being excluded than their heterosexual counterparts. In fact, between 22 and 26% of LGBTQ employees report feeling excluded at work (Eliason, Dibble, & Robertson, 2011; Lloren & Parini, 2017). These studies suggest this phenomenon occurs among this population, though clearly the topic is understudied so results should be interpreted with caution.

Although there has not been an extensive amount of empirical research on this topic among LGBTQ people, scholars agree that ostracism and exclusion is a common (and in some cases, daily) occurrence among LGBTQ people (DeSouza et al., 2017; Fish, 2010). Many have highlighted the presence of ostracism against transgender people in particular (Hargie, Mitchell, & Somerville, 2017; Scheim, Bauer, & Shokoohi, 2017) as this population faces even more discrimination than other sexual minorities. Similarly, it is likely that bisexuals also face extra ostracism for similar reasons, though this population is understudied. In general, many would argue that ostracism is a regular occurrence for LGBTQ people (and LGBTQ employees in particular), suggesting that more empirical research should be conducted.

Why ostracism against LGBTQ people might be especially likely to occur? In addition to the issues raised at the start of this chapter, there are other reasons that are particularly relevant to LGBTQ people. First, society holds certain norms about how different genders are expected to act (Eagly, Nater, Miller, Kaufmann, & Sczesny, 2019), but LGBTQ people are seen as breaking these gender norms. For instance, Salter and Liberman (2016) found that gay males were seen as more similar to heterosexual females than to heterosexual males, and lesbians were seen as having characteristics similar to both heterosexual males and females; in other words, gay male and lesbians were not seen as neatly fitting into the norm of how people of their gender are "supposed" to act. Norms are an expectation of how people "should" behave; if people do not behave in this manner, it can make others feel uncomfortable, which may lead them to exclude and ignore the offending parties.

Second, societal barriers erected against LGBTQ people may create structural exclusion toward LGBTQ employees. Typically, ostracism is thought of as the actions of one person in particular, however it may be the case that people can be ostracized by society in general. For instance, Lee (2018) suggested that undocumented workers are an excluded population due to the legal and structural barriers enacted by society and the government; an argument could be made that this population is ostracized as a whole. Relevant to LGBTQ people, there are many structures built into society that normalize discrimination and ostracism against this population, such as the lack of employment discrimination protections (Fish, 2010). Until recently, gay and lesbian people could not legally marry or serve in the military (due to the policy of Don't Ask Don't Tell). Although these have been rectified in recent years, they have permeated culture and influenced how LGBTQ people are viewed, resulting in them being seen as second-class citizens by some (Bell, Özbilgin, Beauregard, & Sürgevil, 2011; Hammack & Cohler, 2011). Structures such as these can be seen as relegating this population to "second-class citizenship" and therefore can make them vulnerable to ostracism.

Outcomes of Ostracism Against LGBTQ People

As can be seen, there has been less empirical research on this topic but extensive rationale as to why it may be particularly prevalent for this population. Furthermore, there is also reason to believe that ostracism may be especially problematic for this population. As stated in the start of this chapter, if a person attributes ostracism against them to their minority status, they see being excluded as due to an external, non-temporary aspect of themselves that has finality, all of which has been shown to lead to people reacting even more negatively to ostracism (Liu, 2019; Robinson et al., 2013; Scott & Thau, 2013; Wirth & Williams, 2009). Being LGBTQ qualifies as all of these, so perceived ostracism due to one's sexual or gender orientation can be particularly painful.

However, it is likely that being LGBTQ results in unique challenges with regard to responding to ostracism that other minorities may not face in the same way. This is because in addition to being ostracized by individuals, LGBTQ people are also excluded by society in general. As discussed earlier, an argument can be made that society has structures in place (historically as well as currently) that promote the widespread exclusion of LGBTQ people, and this has many implications for how LGBTQ people react to being ostracized. For instance, Williams (2007) argued that it is important to consider the effects of ostracism over time (instead of solely considering specific instances); if LGBTQ people feel a general sense of not being included by society in general then they may chronically feel ostracized. Research suggests that chronic ostracism can have particularly negative mental and physical health outcomes (Robinson et al., 2013; Williams, 2007) so LGBTQ people chronically feeling ostracized may therefore be especially affected by it.

One study did examine ostracism against transgender people and suggests that long-term chronic ostracism against this population may indeed have unique negative outcomes (Mueller, Wierckx, Boccador, & T'Sjoen, 2018). In their study, both transgender and cisgender participants were first ostracized (through the use of the aforementioned CyberBall manipulation) but were then reincluded within the group. As expected, psychosocial stress (as measured with an fMRI) was reduced when participants were no longer ostracized—but this occurred only among the cisgender participants. Among the transgender participants, on the other hand, psychosocial stress did not diminish after they were reincluded within the group. The authors suggest that transgender people may have an inability to recover from ostracism; this may be due to chronically feeling ostracized by society in general.

It should be noted that although a few studies have examined whether or not ostracism occurs against LGBTQ people (such as those discussed previously), we are not aware of any studies (except Mueller et al., 2018) that examines the outcomes of ostracism against LGBTQ people. Therefore, although there is theoretical rationale as to why this phenomenon may be particularly problematic in this population, it has yet to be empirically studied as of yet. We encourage future research to analyze these unanswered questions.

Disability Status and Ostracism

The Americans with Disabilities Act (ADA) defines disability as a physical or mental impairment that substantially limits one or more major life activities of an individual, for example, walking, talking, hearing, or caring for oneself (United States Department of Justice, 1990).[1] Employees with disabilities are prone to experience more ostracism (e.g., Keller & Galgay, 2010; Marr et al., 2012; Wynne & McAnaney, 2009; Zhang, Ye, & Ferreira-Meyers, 2017). As reviewed by Vornholt, Uitdewilligen, and Nijhuis (2013), there are a number of different factors affecting the acceptance of people with disabilities at work. It should be noted, though, very little research has examined how employees with disabilities perceive or react different to ostracism.

Disability Status as a Predictor of Ostracism

From the perpetrator's perspective, the SCT (Turner, 1987) framework suggests that people may form different social categorizations based on a salient cue (i.e., disability status). As people may perceive that those with disabilities are different from themselves, they are likely to develop stigma, stereotypes, and biases toward disabled employees. For example, it has been found that people with physical disabilities and those with psychological disabilities experience both public and self-stigma (Kowalski & Peipert, 2019). Individuals tend to perceive individuals with disabilities but not those without as dependent, incompetent, unemployable, passive, and weak (Louvet, 2007; Louvet, Rohmer, & Dubois, 2009; Nario-Redmond, 2010; Rohmer & Louvet, 2018; Ozawa & Yaeda, 2007). And people may lean on their stereotypes to perceive employees with disabilities as poor performers, frequently absent and as bringing along a sense of unease to people who are around (Kaye, Jans, & Jones, 2011). Critcher and Zayas (2014) suggested that people would perceive threats not merely when exposed to infectious stimuli that may impact them immediately but also when considering abstract threats related

[1] The Americans with Disabilities Amendments Act of 2008 further clarifies and expands components of the legal definition of disability to allow more individuals with coverage.

to distal social groups (Inbar, Pizarro, Knobe, & Bloom, 2009; Park et al., 2003), such as people with disabilities. These perceptions of threat may further contribute to the development of negative stereotypes and attitudes toward employees with disabilities. Indeed, it has been recognized that people with disabilities is one of the typically socially excluded groups (Lenoir, 1974). Compared with their non-disabled counterparts, they are more likely to experience more overt and subtle discrimination, more procedural injustice (Snyder, Carmichael, Blackwell, Cleveland, & Thornton, 2010), and more prejudice and exclusion from interpersonal interactions with others (Hu, 2008).

It has been found that stereotypes toward people with disabilities can influence inclusive behavior through attitudes toward the employment of people with disabilities (Nelissen, Hülsheger, van Ruitenbeek, & Zijlstra, 2016). Related to this, Vornholt et al. (2013) found that many people possess a biased view of the capacities of employees with disabilities. In addition to perceiving a coworker with disabilities as someone whom has poor performance and causes increased job difficulty and a higher workload (Burge, Ouellette-Kuntz, & Lysaght, 2007; Scherbaum, Scherbaum, & Popovich, 2005), people may also be less likely to work with coworkers with disabilities if the performance of employees with disabilities has direct consequence for them (Colella, DeNisi, & Varma, 1998; Vornholt et al., 2013).

Furthermore, employees with disabilities may also experience workplace ostracism due to social (e.g., poor communication with disabled employees) and physical (e.g., disabled employees do not have easy access to the location of a social event) barriers, and such barriers could be driven either by the intention to hurt another person or driven without a clear intent (Naraine & Lindsay, 2011; O'Reilly & Banki, 2016). On the one hand, employees may perceive accommodations especially made for a coworker with a disability as unfair and thus have less acceptance of the employee with a disability (Paetzold et al., 2008). On the other hand, employers may have negative attitudes toward employees with disabilities (Harlan & Robert, 1998; Scheid, 2005) because employers could be concerned about the costs of accommodations and the legal liability (Kaye et al., 2011; Vornholt et al., 2013). Employers could also have concerns about safety when hiring an employee with a disability (Hand & Tryssenaar, 2006; Morgan & Alexander, 2005), and such concerns may actually originate from stereotypes or stigmas employers hold toward employees with disabilities (Vornholt et al., 2013). As such, it comes no surprise that employees with disabilities may find it difficult to integrate into the work environment and may experience workplace ostracism (e.g., Marr et al., 2012; Wynne & McAnaney, 2009; Zhang et al., 2017).

Outcomes of Ostracism Against Employees with Disabilities

As noted, there has been little empirical research on this topic but potential rationale as to why it may be particularly problematic for this group of employees. As discussed in the beginning of this chapter, attributing one's experience of ostracism to disability status can be especially harmful to the victim. According to previous research (Liu, 2019; Robinson et al., 2013), ostracism may be more psychologically threatening to employees with disabilities when they attribute their experiences of ostracism to something non-temporary and internal to them (Wirth & Williams, 2009), such as chronological physical disabilities. Furthermore, it is likely that individuals' attribution of ostracism to disabilities has a feeling of finality (e.g., I cannot change the physical or mental disabilities). Thus, perceiving that one is being ostracized because of one's disability status could be very upsetting.

Within the few studies that have specifically examined consequences of ostracism-related experiences (e.g., bullying) among individuals with disabilities, findings generally suggest that people with disabilities are not only at higher risk of bullying victimization (e.g., being ostracized), but the negative outcomes (e.g., depression, physical symptoms) of being bullied tend to be more pronounced (e.g., Gausel & Thørrisen, 2014; Kowalski, Morgan, Drake-Lavelle, & Allison, 2016). For instance, Kowalski and Peipert (2019) found that people with psychological disabilities would experience more negative outcomes than those with physical disabilities (i.e., increased depression, social anxiety, as well as decreased levels of self-esteem). Importantly, they also found that more ostracism were experienced among people with psychological disabilities than those with physical disabilities. The authors explained that the higher levels of public stigma, self-stigma, and stigma consciousness observed among people with psychological disabilities relative to those with physical disabilities may contribute to these findings. These results suggest an interesting direction for future research is to further examine the differences between people with different types of disabilities, and importantly, the underlying mechanisms. Again, it should be noted that so far we are not aware of any empirical studies that examined the different consequences of ostracism between people with disabilities and those without disabilities in the work context, and we strongly encourage future research to study these remaining questions.

Practical Implications

Overall, a major message from this chapter is that workplace ostracism may disproportionately target against minority employees. As such, in addition to prevent and eradicate workplace ostracism, we suggest that management should give more care to these minorities who are likely to experience ostracism at work due to their minority group memberships. First, we encourage organizations to implement and enforce equal employment opportunity laws that prevent discrimination against minority employees (e.g., Civil Rights Act, CRA; Age Discrimination in Employment Act, ADEA; Americans with Disabilities Act, ADA) and increase their employment-related opportunities. Such legislation should be implemented well in all relevant organizational practices (e.g., hiring, interviewing, job design). For instance, employers should make a "reasonable accommodations" for older employees or employees with disabilities to perform major job functions. Organizational policies could also consider including such legislation information in order to explicitly reinforce employees and managers' perceptions of and appropriate behaviors and attitudes toward minority employees. Overall, legal interventions can prevent minority employees from unfair treatment and can supply them with legal protection.

Second, a potential way to reduce workplace ostracism is to create a fair and open work environment (Zhang et al., 2017) and improve interactions/communications (and perhaps mutual understanding and relationship ties) between minority and majority employees. Organizational policies should incorporate employee equality/justice items and more attention shall be allocated to protect minorities (e.g., a complaint system that can stop unfair treatment timely) who are prone to experience ostracism (Zhang et al., 2017). Team-building and interpersonal understanding among employees from different groups should also be encouraged. For instance, organizations may encourage minority workers to interact more with other employees and can even mentor others and pass on their knowledge and experience in the workplace. For instance, such generativity opportunities could promote high-quality contact at work between younger and older employees (Henry, Zacher, & Desmette, 2015). In addition to open and clear communication, retaining one's job, and the provision of ergonomic modification, job accommodations such as time flexibility and working from home shall also be incorporated into disability management practices and procedures (Westmorland, Williams,

Amick III, Shannon, & Rasheed, 2005; Vornholt et al., 2013). Organizations shall recognize that making accommodations for employees with disabilities can actually benefit employers in various aspects (Hartnett, Stuart, Thurman, Loy, & Batiste, 2011), such as the retention of quality employees, increased company profitability, workplace diversity, and avoidance of costs in hiring and training new employees (Vornholt et al., 2013). Such job accommodation can also have indirect benefits including improved interactions with coworkers, enhanced company morale, and overall productivity (Solovieva, Dowler, & Walls, 2011).

Third, organizations can also strive to create pro-diversity work climate perceptions (McKay et al., 2007), which may help reduce ostracism or discriminations toward minority employees. Specifically, management practices could be tailored to suit the needs of employees with different minorities' statuses (e.g., age, gender, disabilities, or sexual/gender orientation minorities). Organizational efforts in this regard could take the form of increased input from minority employees on work-related issues, supportive workplace environments (Ciampa & Chernesky, 2013), age-friendly organizations (Appannah & Biggs, 2015), access to development and training opportunities, and emphasis on the value of diversity at the firm and organizational-level (McKay & Avery, 2005; Roberson & Stevens, 2006). Furthermore, Oyet et al. (2013) suggested that organizations can strive to enhance employees' identification with organization by creating and implementing human resource policies and practices. Organizational identity may mitigate the effects of demographically dissimilarity on workplace ostracism by promoting employee in-role and extra-role behaviors that can include and show the acceptance of minority employees.

Directions for Future Research

Based on the current literature, we would like to add that the current research regarding workplace ostracism in minority employees is quite sparse. More research is needed to document the potential group differences (e.g., gender, age, etc.) in workplace ostracism. We have following suggestions to future research. First, research should aim to better understand the prevalence of workplace ostracism among these workgroups. Second, more research should be conducted to understand the antecedents of workplace ostracism among gender, age, and LGBTQ minorities, and people with disabilities. Third, different reactions and outcomes should be further examined. Fourth, interventional studies should be conducted to improve the work environment and ultimately the health and well-being for all employees.

First, although scholars have called for more studies examining the prevalence of ostracism (Liu, 2019), we would like to further emphasize that future research should examine its prevalence among different populations and why it happens at the first place. With findings from prevalence research, researchers can better identify at-risk groups of employees and help raise practitioners' awareness of workplace ostracism among these groups of employees.

Second, future research should explore the idea of structural ostracism against minorities. We discussed this as a potential issue for LGBTQ people (i.e., societal structures that normalize ostracism against this population). However, it is likely that this may also exist for other minorities (e.g., female employees) as well. To our knowledge, this idea of larger-scale ostracism (rather than only from one person) has not yet been explored, but may be particularly relevant to the study of minorities and ostracism.

Given that the workforce is becoming more diverse in many aspects (e.g., age, gender, race, sexual and gender orientation, etc.), another direction for future research would be to investigate the interactive effects of various employee demographic characteristics (Adams et al., 2013). For instance, it is likely that age may co-vary with gender in that older females may experience more and react more negatively to workplace ostracism than other groups. Studies of intersectionality "simultaneously consider the meaning and consequences of multiple categories of identity, difference, and disadvantage" (Cole, 2009, p. 170). Based on this intersectional perspective, researchers have suggested that women of color may be most at risk for uncivil treatment (e.g., being ignored at work; Kabat-Farr & Cortina, 2012). Accordingly, taking an intersectional perspective enables researchers to simultaneously consider multiple demographic characteristics (e.g., age, gender, race/ethnicity, sexuality, etc.) when studying workplace ostracism, rather than focusing on the analysis of one single factor and neglecting others.

Third, research should not only examine the *vulnerability* of employees from these populations, but should also examine ways in which they may be more or less resilient to ostracism than their counterparts. For instance, while older workers may exhibit stronger reactions to workplace ostracism because it is harmful when people attribute the unpleasant treatment to their age, a stable (Wirth & Williams, 2009) and internal attribute (Liu, 2019; Robinson et al., 2013), they might also cope well with workplace ostracism due to their age-related advantages in emotion regulation (Blanchard-Fields, 2007; Doerwald et al., 2016). Other researchers argued that older workers may or may not react more negatively to workplace ostracism, depending on the severity of the negative experience (Cheng & Grühn, 2015; Löckenhoff et al., 2013). Given the complexities of the issue, we strongly recommend that more empirical studies are needed to test these speculations.

Another area future research could explore is sensitivity to ostracism among minorities. We have posited that minorities might be particularly likely to be ostracized and may react poorly if attributing it to their minority status (Liu, 2019; Robinson et al., 2013; Scott & Thau, 2013; Wirth & Williams, 2009). However, this assumes that the victim attributes the ostracism to their minority status, but this may not always be the case. Perhaps minority status identification could moderate this relationship; if the person highly identifies with their minority status, then they may be more likely to react negatively to ostracism (and vice versa). Future research should consider this as well as other potential moderators.

Fourth, a challenging task is to conduct intervention research. The existing research on workplace ostracism among minority employees in general is somewhat limited. Future research may build upon previous intervention research (Scott & Duffy, 2015) and seek to examine the effectiveness of interventions among minority employees. For instance, Truxillo, Cadiz, and Hammer (2015) conducted a literature review on aging at work, discussed physical, cognitive, personality, and motivational changes, as well as many other important lifespan development theories and work issues. They proposed a variety of avenues for intervention research to address age differences at work. Future research may further extend their study to examine interventions that can reduce ostracism toward older workers and help them better cope with workplace ostracism.

References

Abrams, D., & Hogg, M. A. (2006). *Social identifications: A social psychology of intergroup relations and group processes*. London, UK: Routledge.

Adams, G. A., DeArmond, S., Jex, S. M., & Webster, J. R. (2013). Older workers, occupational stress and safety. In J. Field, R. J. Burke, & C. L. Cooper (Eds.), *The Sage handbook of aging, work and society*. London, UK: Sage.

Anthony, M., Yastik, J., MacDonald, D. A., & Marshall, K. A. (2014). Development and validation of a tool to measure incivility in clinical nursing education. *Journal of Professional Nursing, 30,* 48–55.

Appannah, A., & Biggs, S. (2015). Age-friendly organisations: The role of organisational culture and the participation of older workers. *Journal of Social Work Practice, 29,* 37–51. https://doi.org/10.1080/02650533.2014.993943.

Arar, K. (2018). Female Arab faculty staff in the Israeli academy: Challenges and coping strategies. *International Journal of Educational Development, 62,* 313–321.

Armstrong-Stassen, M., & Lee, S. H. (2009). The effect of relational age on older Canadian employees' perceptions of human resource practices and sense of worth to their organization. *The International Journal of Human Resource Management, 20,* 1753–1769. https://doi.org/10.1080/09585190903087156.

Barron, L. G., & Hebl, M. (2011). Sexual orientation: A protected and unprotected class. In M. A. Paludi, C. A. Paludi, & E. R. Desouza (Eds.), *Praeger handbook on understanding and preventing workplace discrimination: Legal management, and social science perspectives* (Vol. 1, pp. 251–273). Santa Barbara, CA: Praeger.

Bell, M. P., Özbilgin, M. F., Beauregard, T. A., & Sürgevil, O. (2011). Voice, silence, and diversity in 21st century organizations: Strategies for inclusion of gay, lesbian, bisexual, and transgender employees. *Human Resource Management, 50,* 131–146.

Blackstone, A. (2013). Harassment of older adults in the workplace. In P. Brownell & J. Kelly (Eds.), *Ageism and mistreatment of older workers: Current reality, future solutions* (pp. 31–47). Dordrecht, The Netherlands: Springer.

Blanchard-Fields, F. (2007). Everyday problem solving and emotion: An adult developmental perspective. *Current Directions in Psychological Science, 16,* 26–31. https://doi.org/10.1111/j.1467-8721.2007.00469.x.

Blanchard-Fields, F., Mienaltowski, A., & Seay, R. B. (2007). Age differences in everyday problem-solving effectiveness: Older adults select more effective strategies for interpersonal problems. *The Journals of Gerontology Series B: Psychological Sciences and Social Sciences, 62,* P61–P64. https://doi.org/10.1093/geronb/62.1.P61.

Bozin, M. A., & Yoder, J. D. (2008). Social status, not gender alone, is implicated in different reactions by women and men to social ostracism. *Sex Roles, 58,* 713–720.

Brault, M. W. (2012). *Americans with disabilities: 2010* (Current Population Report No. P70-131). Washington, DC: U.S. Census Bureau.

Brewer, M. B. (1979). In-group bias in the minimal intergroup situation: A cognitive-motivational analysis. *Psychological Bulletin, 86,* 307–324. https://doi.org/10.1037/0033-2909.86.2.307.

Burge, P., Ouellette-Kuntz, H., & Lysaght, R. (2007). Public views on employment of people with intellectual disabilities. *Journal of Vocational Rehabilitation, 26,* 29–37.

Butler, R. N. (1989). Dispelling ageism: The cross-cutting intervention. *The Annals of the American Academy of Political and Social Science, 503,* 138–147. https://doi.org/10.1177/0002716289503001011.

Carstensen, L. L. (2006). The influence of a sense of time on human development. *Science, 312,* 1913–1915. https://doi.org/10.1126/science.1127488.

Carstensen, L. L., Isaacowitz, D. M., & Charles, S. T. (1999). Taking time seriously: A theory of socioemotional selectivity. *American Psychologist, 54,* 165–181. https://doi.org/10.1037/0003-06.

Charles, S. T., & Carstensen, L. L. (2008). Unpleasant situations elicit different emotional responses in younger and older adults. *Psychology and Aging, 23,* 495–504.

Cheng, Y., & Grühn, D. (2015). Age differences in reactions to social rejection: The role of cognitive resources and appraisals. *Journals of Gerontology: Series B, Psychological Sciences and Social Sciences, 70,* 830–839. https://doi.org/10.1093/geronb/gbu054.

Ciampa, E., & Chernesky, R. (2013). Creating supportive workplace environments for older workers. In P. Brownell & J. Kelly (Eds.), *Ageism and mistreatment of older workers: Current reality, future solutions* (pp. 93–110). Dordrecht: Springer.

Cole, E. R. (2009). Intersectionality and research in psychology. *American Psychologist, 64,* 170–180. https://doi.org/10.1037/a0014564.

Colella, A., DeNisi, A. S., & Varma, A. (1998). The impact of ratee's disability on performance judgments and choice as partner: The role of disability–job fit stereotypes and interdependence of rewards. *Journal of Applied Psychology, 83,* 102–111.

Colgan, F., Creegan, C., McKearney, A., & Wright, T. (2008). Lesbian workers: Personal strategies amid changing organisational responses to "sexual minorities" in UK workplaces. *Journal of Lesbian Studies, 12,* 31–45.

Cortina, L. M. (2008). Unseen injustice: Incivility as modern discrimination in organizations. *Academy of Management Review, 33,* 55–75.

Cortina, L. M., Kabat-Farr, D., Leskinen, E. A., Huerta, M., & Magley, V. J. (2013). Selective incivility as modern discrimination in organizations: Evidence and impact. *Journal of Management, 39,* 1579–1605.

Cottingham, M. D., Erickson, R. J., Diefendorff, J. M., & Bromley, G. (2013). The effect of manager exclusion on nurse turnover intention and care quality. *Western Journal of Nursing Research, 35,* 970–985.

Critcher, C. R., & Zayas, V. (2014). The involuntary excluder effect: Those included by an excluder are seen as exclusive themselves. *Journal of Personality and Social Psychology, 107,* 454–474.

Cross, S. E., & Madson, L. (1997). Models of the self: Self-construals and gender. *Psychological Bulletin, 122,* 5–37.
Cursan, A., Bernstein, M. J., Pascual, A., & Félonneau, M.-L. (2017). Impact of gendered ingroup/outgroup ostracism on women's academic performances. *The Journal of Social Psychology, 157,* 338–351.
DeSouza, E. R., Wesselmann, E. D., & Ispas, D. (2017). Workplace discrimination against sexual minorities: Subtle and not-so-subtle. *Canadian Journal of Administrative Sciences, 34,* 121–132.
Doerwald, F., Scheibe, S., Zacher, H., & Van Yperen, N. W. (2016). Emotional competencies across adulthood: State of knowledge and implications for the work context. *Work, Aging and Retirement, 2,* 159–216. https://doi.org/10.1093/workar/waw013.
Dotan-Eliaz, O., Sommer, K. L., & Rubin, Y. S. (2009). Multilingual groups: Effects of linguistic ostracism on felt rejection and anger, coworker attraction, perceived team potency, and creative performance. *Basic and Applied Social Psychology, 31,* 363–375.
Eagly, A. H., & Johannesen-Schmidt, M. C. (2001). The leadership styles of women and men. *Journal of Social Issues, 57,* 781–797.
Eagly, A. H., Nater, C., Miller, D. I., Kaufmann, M., & Sczesny, S. (2019). Gender stereotypes have changed: A cross-temporal meta-analysis of US public opinion polls from 1946 to 2018. *American Psychologist, 75,* 301–315.
Eliason, M. J., Dibble, S. L., & Robertson, P. A. (2011). Lesbian, gay, bisexual, and transgender (LGBT) physicians' experiences in the workplace. *Journal of Homosexuality, 58,* 1355–1371.
Embrick, D. G., Walther, C. S., & Wickens, C. M. (2007). Working class masculinity: Keeping gay men and lesbians out of the workplace. *Sex Roles: A Journal of Research, 56,* 757–766.
Ferris, D. L., Brown, D. J., Berry, J. W., & Lian, H. (2008). The development and validation of the Workplace Ostracism Scale. *Journal of Applied Psychology, 93,* 1348–1366.
Ferris, D. L., Chen, M., & Lim, S. (2017). Comparing and contrasting workplace ostracism and incivility. *Annual Review of Organizational Psychology and Organizational Behavior, 4,* 315–338.
Finkelstein, L. M., Burke, M. J., & Raju, M. S. (1995). Age discrimination in simulated employment contexts: An integrative analysis. *Journal of Applied Psychology, 80,* 652–663. https://doi.org/10.1037/0021-9010.80.6.652.
Finkelstein, L. M., & Farrell, S. K. (2007). An expanded view of age bias in the workplace. In K. S. Shultz & G. A. Adams (Eds.), *Aging and work in the 21st century* (pp. 73–108). New York, NY: Psychology Press.
Fish, J. (2010). Conceptualizing social exclusion and lesbian, gay, bisexual, and transgender people: The implications for promoting equality in nursing policy and practice. *Journal of Research in Nursing, 15,* 303–312.

Fiske, S. T., & Neuberg, S. L. (1990). A continuum of impression formation, from category-based to individuating processes: Influences of information and motivation on attention and interpretation. *Advances in Experimental Social Psychology, 23,* 1–74. Academic Press. https://doi.org/10.1016/S0065-2601(08)60317-2.

Gamian-Wilk, M., & Madeja-Bien, K. (2018) Ostracism in the workplace. In P. D'Cruz, E. Noronha, L. Keashly, & S. Tye-Williams (Eds.), Special topics and particular occupations, professions and sectors. *Handbooks of workplace bullying, emotional abuse and harassment* (Vol. 4, pp. 1–30). Singapore: Springer.

Gausel, N., & Thørrisen, M. M. (2014). A theoretical model of multiple stigma: Ostracized for being an inmate with intellectual disabilities. *Journal of Scandinavian Studies in Criminology and Crime Prevention, 15,* 89–95.

Gómez, Á., Morales, J. F., Hart, S., Vázquez, A., & Swann, W. B., Jr. (2011). Rejected and excluded forevermore, but even more devoted: Irrevocable ostracism intensifies loyalty to the group among identity-fused persons. *Personality and Social Psychology Bulletin, 37,* 1574–1586.

Gordon, R. A., & Arvey, R. D. (2004). Age bias in laboratory and field settings: A meta-analytic investigation. *Journal of Applied Social Psychology, 34,* 468–492. https://doi.org/10.1111/j.1559-1816.2004.tb02557.x.

Gross, J. J., & John, O. P. (2003). Individual differences in two emotion regulation processes: Implications for affect, relationships, and well-being. *Journal of Personality and Social Psychology, 85,* 348–362.

Guimond, S., Chatard, A., Martinot, D., Crisp, R. J., & Redersdorff, S. (2006). Social comparison, self-stereotyping, and gender differences in self-construals. *Journal of Personality and Social Psychology, 90,* 221–242.

Hales, A. H., Dvir, M., Wesselmann, E. D., Kruger, D. J., & Finkenauer, C. (2018). Cell phone-induced ostracism threatens fundamental needs. *The Journal of Social Psychology, 158,* 460–473.

Hammack, P. L., & Cohler, B. J. (2011). Narrative, identity, and the politics of exclusion: Social change and the gay and lesbian life course. *Sexuality Research & Social Policy: A Journal of the NSRC, 8,* 162–182.

Hand, C., & Tryssenaar, J. (2006). Small business employers' views on hiring individuals with mental illness. *Psychiatric Rehabilitation Journal, 29,* 166–173.

Hargie, O. D. W., Mitchell, D. H., & Somerville, I. J. A. (2017). 'People have a knack of making you feel excluded if they catch on to your difference': Transgender experiences of exclusion in sport. *International Review for the Sociology of Sport, 52,* 223–239.

Harlan, S. L., & Robert, P. M. (1998). The social construction of disability in organizations: Why employers resist reasonable accommodation. *Work and Occupations, 25,* 397–435.

Hartnett, H. P., Stuart, H., Thurman, H., Loy, B., & Batiste, L. C. (2011). Employers' perceptions of the benefits of workplace accommodations: Reasons to hire, retain and promote people with disabilities. *Journal of Vocational Rehabilitation, 34*, 17–23.

Hawkley, L. C., Williams, K. D., & Cacioppo, J. T. (2011). Responses to ostracism across adulthood. *Social Cognitive and Affective Neuroscience, 6*, 234–243. https://doi.org/10.1093/scan/nsq045.

Hayman, L. W., McIntyre, R. B., & Abbey, A. (2015). The bad taste of social ostracism: The effects of exclusion on the eating behaviors of African-American women. *Psychology & Health, 30*, 518–533.

Henry, H., Zacher, H., & Desmette, D. (2015). Reducing age bias and turnover intentions by enhancing intergenerational contact quality in the workplace: The role of opportunities for generativity and development. *Work, Aging and Retirement, 1*, 243–253. https://doi.org/10.1093/workar/wav005.

Herek, G. M. (2007). Confronting sexual stigma and prejudice: Theory and practice. *Journal of Social Issues, 63*, 905–925.

Hitlan, R. T., Cliffton, R. J., & DeSoto, M. C. (2006). Perceived exclusion in the workplace: The moderating effects of gender on work-related attitudes and psychological health. *North American Journal of Psychology, 8*, 217–236.

Hoel, H., Lewis, D., & Einarsdottir, A. (2017). Debate: Bullying and harassment of lesbians, gay men and bisexual employees: Findings from a representative British national study. *Public Money & Management, 37*, 312–314.

Hogg, M. A., & Terry, D. I. (2000). Social identity and self-categorization processes in organizational contexts. *Academy of Management Review, 25*, 121–140. https://doi.org/10.5465/amr.2000.2791606.

Hommelhoff, S., Müller, T., & Scheibe, S. (2017). Experimental evidence for the influence of occupational future time perspective on social preferences during lunch breaks. *Work, Aging and Retirement, 4*, 367–380. https://doi.org/10.1093/workar/wax022.

Howard, M. C., Cogswell, J. E., & Smith, M. B. (2020). The antecedents and outcomes of workplace ostracism: A meta-analysis. *Journal of Applied Psychology, 105*, 577–596.

Hu, B. B. (2008). The research on the problems of the disable persons' social exclusion from the perspective of social justice. *Hubei Social Sciences, 6*, 46–49. https://doi.org/10.13660/j.cnki.42-1112/c.009069.

Hyland, P. K., & Rutigliano, P. J. (2013). Eradicating discrimination: Identifying and removing workplace barriers for employees with disabilities. *Industrial and Organizational Psychology, 6*, 471–475.

Inbar, Y., Pizarro, D. A., Knobe, J., & Bloom, P. (2009). Disgust sensitivity predicts intuitive disapproval of gays. *Emotion, 9*, 435–439.

Jackson, M. F., Barth, J. M., Powell, N., & Lochman, J. E. (2006). Classroom contextual effects of race on children's peer nominations. *Child Development, 77,* 1325–1337. https://doi.org/10.1111/j.1467-8624.2006.00937.x.

Kabat-Farr, D., & Cortina, L. M. (2012). Selective incivility: Gender, race, and the discriminatory workplace. In D. Kabat-Farr & L. M. Cortina (Eds.), *Gender and the dysfunctional workplace* (pp. 120–134). Northampton, MA: Edward Elgar Publishing.

Karsten, M. F. (2016). *Gender, race, and ethnicity in the workplace: Emerging issues and enduring challenges* (M. F. Karsten, Ed.). Santa Barbara, CA: Praeger/ABC-CLIO.

Kaye, H. S., Jans, L. H., & Jones, E. C. (2011). Why don't employers hire and retain workers with disabilities? *Journal of Occupational Rehabilitation, 21,* 526–536. https://doi.org/10.1007/s10926-011-9302-8.

Keller, R. M., & Galgay, C. E. (2010). Microaggressions experienced by people with disabilities in US society. In D. W. Sue (Ed.), *Microaggressions and marginality: Manifestation, dynamics, and impact* (pp. 241–268). New York, NY: Wiley.

Kowalski, R. M., Morgan, C. A., Drake-Lavelle, K., & Allison, B. (2016). Cyberbullying among college students with disabilities. *Computers in Human Behavior, 57,* 416–427.

Kowalski, R. M., & Peipert, A. (2019). Public- and self-stigma attached to physical versus psychological disabilities. *Stigma and Health, 4,* 136–142.

Leary, M. R. (2005). Sociometer theory and the pursuit of relational value: Getting to the root of self-esteem. *European Review of Social Psychology, 16,* 75–111.

Leary, M. R., & Baumeister, R. F. (2000). The nature and function of self-esteem: Sociometer theory. *Advances in Experimental Social Psychology, 32,* 1–62.

Lee, J. J. (2018). Redefining the legality of undocumented work. *California Law Review, 106,* 1617–1656.

Lenoir, R. (1974). *Les Exclus.* Paris, France: Seuil.

Lewis, J. A. (2018). From modern sexism to gender microaggressions: Understanding contemporary forms of sexism and their influence on diverse women. In C. B. Travis, J. W. White, A. Rutherford, W. S. Williams, S. L. Cook, & K. F. Wyche (Eds.), *APA handbook of the psychology of women: History, theory, and battlegrounds* (Vol. 1., pp. 381–397). Washington, DC: American Psychological Association.

Liu, C. (2019). Ostracism, attributions, and their relationships with international students' and employees' outcomes: The moderating effect of perceived harming intent. *Journal of Occupational Health Psychology, 24,* 556–571. https://doi.org/10.1037/ocp0000130.

Lloren, A., & Parini, L. (2017). How LGBT-supportive workplace policies shape the experience of lesbian, gay men, and bisexual employees. *Sexuality Research & Social Policy: A Journal of the NSRC, 14*, 289–299.

Löckenhoff, C. E., Cook, M. A., Anderson, J. F., & Zayas, V. (2013). Age differences in responses to progressive social exclusion: The role of cognition and socioemotional functioning. *Journals of Gerontology: Series B, Psychological Sciences and Social Sciences, 68*, 13–22. https://doi.org/10.1093/geronb/gbs042.

Louvet, E. (2007). Social judgment toward job applicants with disabilities: Perception of personal qualities and competencies. *Rehabilitation Psychology, 52*, 297–303. https://doi.org/10.1037/0090-5550.52.3.297.

Louvet, E., Rohmer, O., & Dubois, N. (2009). Social judgment of people with a disability in the workplace: How to make a good impression on employers. *Swiss Journal of Psychology, 68*, 153–159. https://doi.org/10.1024/1421-0185.68.3.153.

Maranto, C. L., & Griffin, A. E. (2011). The antecedents of a 'chilly climate' for women faculty in higher education. *Human Relations, 64*, 139–159.

Marr, J. C., Thau, S., Aquino, K., & Barclay, L. J. (2012). Do I want to know? How the motivation to acquire relationship-threatening information in groups contributes to paranoid thought, suspicion behavior, and social rejection. *Organizational Behavior and Human Decision Processes, 117*, 285–297.

Martin, R. J., & Hine, D. W. (2005). Development and validation of the Uncivil Workplace Behavior Questionnaire. *Journal of Occupational Health Psychology, 10*, 477–490.

Mather, M., & Carstensen, L. L. (2005). Aging and motivated cognition: The positivity effect in attention and memory. *Trends in Cognitive Sciences, 9*, 496–502. https://doi.org/10.1016/j.tics.2005.08.005.

McKay, P. F., & Avery, D. R. (2005). Warning! Diversity recruitment could backfire. *Journal of Management Inquiry, 14*, 330–336. https://doi.org/10.1177/1056492605280239.

McKay, P. F., Avery, D. R., Tonidandel, S., Morris, M. A., Hernandez, M., & Hebl, M. R. (2007). Racial differences in employee retention: Are diversity climate perceptions the key? *Personnel Psychology, 60*, 35–62. https://doi.org/10.1111/j.1744-6570.2007.00064.x.

Miner, K. N., Pesonen, A. D., Smittick, A. L., Seigel, M. L., & Clark, E. K. (2014). Does being a mom help or hurt? Workplace incivility as a function of motherhood status. *Journal of Occupational Health Psychology, 19*, 60–73.

Morgan, R. L., & Alexander, M. (2005). The employer's perception: Employment of individuals with developmental disabilities. *Journal of Vocational Rehabilitation, 23*, 39–49.

Mueller, S. C., Wierckx, K., Boccadoro, S., & T'Sjoen, G. (2018). Neural correlates of ostracism in transgender persons living according to their gender identity: A potential risk marker for psychopathology? *Psychological Medicine*.

Naraine, M. D., & Lindsay, P. H. (2011). Social inclusion of employees who are blind or low vision. *Disability & Society, 26*, 389–403.

Nario-Redmond, M. R. (2010). Cultural stereotypes of disabled and non-disabled men and women: Consensus for global category representations and diagnostic domains. *British Journal of Social Psychology, 49*, 471–488. https://doi.org/10.1348/014466609X468411.

Nelissen, P. T., Hülsheger, U. R., van Ruitenbeek, G. M., & Zijlstra, F. R. (2016). How and when stereotypes relate to inclusive behavior toward people with disabilities. *The International Journal of Human Resource Management, 27*, 1610–1625. https://doi.org/10.1080/09585192.2015.1072105.

Ng, T. W. (2017). Can idiosyncratic deals promote perceptions of competitive climate, felt ostracism, and turnover? *Journal of Vocational Behavior, 99*, 118–131. https://doi.org/10.1016/j.jvb.2017.01.004.

North, M. S. (in press). Intergenerational resource tensions. In D. Gu & M. E. Dupre (Eds.), *Encyclopedia of gerontology and population aging*. https://doi.org/10.1007/978-3-319-69892-2_599-1.

North, M. S., & Fiske, S. T. (2012). An inconvenienced youth? Ageism and its potential intergenerational roots. *Psychological Bulletin, 138*, 982–997. https://doi.org/10.1037/a0027843.

North, M. S., & Fiske, S. T. (2015). Intergenerational resource tensions in the workplace and beyond: Individual, interpersonal, institutional, international. *Research in Organizational Behavior, 35*, 159–179.

North, M. S., & Fiske, S. T. (2016). Resource scarcity and prescriptive attitudes generate subtle, intergenerational older-worker exclusion. *Journal of Social Issues, 72*, 122–145.

O'Reilly, J., & Banki, S. (2016). Research in work and organizational psychology: Social exclusion in the workplace. In P. Riva & J. Eck (Eds.), *Social exclusion* (pp. 133–155). Cham: Springer.

O'Reilly, J., & Robinson, S. L. (2009). *The negative impact of ostracism on thwarted belongingness and workplace contributions*. Best paper proceedings, Academy of Management meeting, Chicago.

Oyet, M., Dupré, K. E., & Arnold, K. A. (2013, August). The effects of employee dissimilarity on organizational and interpersonal deviance. In *Academy of Management Conference, Lake Buena Vista*, Orlando, FL.

Ozawa, A., & Yaeda, J. (2007). Employer attitudes toward employing persons with psychiatric disability in Japan. *Journal of Vocational Rehabilitation, 26*, 105–113.

Paetzold, R. L., García, M. F., Colella, A., Ren, L. R., Triana, M. D. C., & Ziebro, M. (2008). Perceptions of people with disabilities: When is accommodation fair? *Basic and Applied Social Psychology, 30*, 27–35.

Park, J. H., Faulkner, J., & Schaller, M. (2003). Evolved disease-avoidance processes and contemporary anti-social behavior: Prejudicial attitudes and avoidance of people with physical disabilities. *Journal of Nonverbal Behavior, 27*, 65–87.

Peng, Y., Jex, S. M., & Wang, M. (2018). Aging and occupational health. In K. Shultz & G. Adams (Eds.), *Aging and work in the 21st century* (2nd ed., pp. 213–233). New York: Routledge.

Peng, Y., Tian, B., Jex, S. M., & Chen, Y. (2017). Employees' age moderates relationships of emotional suppression with health and well-being. *Work, Aging and Retirement, 3*, 89–101.

Peng, Y., Xu, X., & Matthews, R. (2020). Older and less deviant reactions to abusive supervision? A moderated mediation model of age and cognitive reappraisal. *Work, Aging and Retirement, 3*, 195-205.

Priola, V., Lasio, D., De Simone, S., & Serri, F. (2014). The sound of silence: Lesbian, gay, bisexual and transgender discrimination in 'inclusive organizations'. *British Journal of Management, 25*, 488–502.

Quade, M. J., Greenbaum, R. L., & Mawritz, M. B. (2019). "If only my coworker was more ethical": When ethical and performance comparisons lead to negative emotions, social undermining, and ostracism. *Journal of Business Ethics, 159*, 567–586.

Quade, M. J., Greenbaum, R. L., & Petrenko, O. V. (2017). "I don't want to be near you, unless…": The interactive effect of unethical behavior and performance onto relationship conflict and workplace ostracism. *Personnel Psychology, 70*, 675–709.

Ramos, C., Badgett, M., & Sears, B. (2008). *Evidence of employment discrimination on the basis of sexual orientation and gender identity: Complaints filed with state enforcement agencies 1999–2007*. Retrieved from http://escholarship.org/.

Roberson, Q., Ryan, A. M., & Ragins, B. R. (2017). The evolution and future of diversity at work. *Journal of Applied Psychology, 102*, 483–499. https://doi.org/10.1037/apl0000161.

Roberson, Q. M. (2019). Diversity in the workplace: A review, synthesis, and future research agenda. *Annual Review of Organizational Psychology and Organizational Behavior, 6*, 69–88. https://doi.org/10.1146/annurev-orgpsych-012218-015243.

Roberson, Q. M., & Stevens, C. K. (2006). Making sense of diversity in the workplace: Organizational justice and language abstraction in employees' accounts of diversity-related incidents. *Journal of Applied Psychology, 91*, 379–391. https://doi.org/10.1037/0021-9010.91.2.379.

Robinson, S. L., O'Reilly, J., & Wang, W. (2013). Invisible at work: An integrated model of workplace ostracism. *Journal of Management, 39,* 203–231. https://doi.org/10.1177/0149206312466141.

Rohmer, O., & Louvet, E. (2018). Implicit stereotyping against people with disability. *Group Processes & Intergroup Relations, 21,* 127–140. https://doi.org/10.1177/1368430216638536.

Ruggs, E. N., Hebl, M. R., Law, C., Cox, C. B., Roehling, M. V., & Wiener, R. L. (2013). Gone fishing: I–O psychologists' missed opportunities to understand marginalized employees' experiences with discrimination. *Industrial and Organizational Psychology, 6,* 39–60.

Salter, N. P., & Liberman, B. (2016). The role of sexual orientation and gender on leadership perceptions. In T. Köllen (Ed.), *Sexual orientation and transgender issues in organizations: Global perspectives on LGBT workforce diversity* (pp. 429–449). New York: Springer.

Schaffer, B. S., & Riordan, C. M. (2013). Relational demography in supervisor-subordinate dyads: An examination of discrimination and exclusionary treatment. *Canadian Journal of Administrative Sciences, 30,* 3–17.

Scheid, T. L. (2005). Stigma as a barrier to employment: Mental disability and the Americans with Disabilities Act. *International Journal of Law and Psychiatry, 28,* 670–690.

Scheim, A. I., Bauer, G. R., & Shokoohi, M. (2017). Drug use among transgender people in Ontario, Canada: Disparities and associations with social exclusion. *Addictive Behaviors, 72,* 151–158.

Scherbaum, C. A., Scherbaum, K. L., & Popovich, P. M. (2005). Predicting job-related expectancies and affective reactions to employees with disabilities from previous work experience. *Journal of Applied Social Psychology, 35,* 889–904.

Scott, K. L., & Duffy, M. K. (2015). Antecedents of workplace ostracism: New directions in research and intervention. In P. L. Perrewe, J. R. B. Halbesleben, & C. C. Rosen (Eds.), *Research in occupational stress and well-being* (Vol. 13, pp. 137–165). Bingley: Emerald Group Publishing Limited.

Scott, K. L., & Thau, S. (2013). Theory and research on social exclusion in work groups. In N. DeWall (Ed.), *Oxford handbook of social exclusion* (pp. 65–76). New York, NY: Oxford University Press.

Settles, I. H., & O'Connor, R. C. (2014). Incivility at academic conferences: Gender differences and the mediating role of climate. *Sex Roles, 71,* 71–82.

Shore, L. M., & Goldberg, C. B. (2005). Age discrimination in the workplace. In R. L. Dipboye & A. Colella (Eds.), *Discrimination at work* (pp. 203–225). Mawhaw, NJ: Lawrence Erlbaum.

Snyder, L. A., Carmichael, J. S., Blackwell, L. V., Cleveland, J. N., & Thornton, G. C. (2010). Perceptions of discrimination and justice among employees with disabilities. *Employee Responsibilities and Rights Journal, 22,* 5–19. https://doi.org/10.1007/s10672-009-9107-5.

Solovieva, T. I., Dowler, D. L., & Walls, R. T. (2011). Employer benefits from making workplace accommodations. *Disability and Health Journal, 4*, 39–45.

Tajfel, H. (1978). *Differentiation between social groups*. London, UK: Academic Press.

Tajfel, H., & Turner, J. C. (1979). An integrative theory of intergroup conflict. In S. Worchel & W. G. Austin (Eds.), *The social psychology of intergroup relations* (pp. 33–47). Monterey, CA: Brooks/Cole.

Tajfel, H., & Turner, J. C. (1986). The social identity theory of intergroup behavior. In S. Worshel & W. Austin (Eds.), *The psychology of intergroup relations* (pp. 7–24). Chicago: Nelson-Hall.

Toossi, M. (2002). A century of change: The US labor force, 1950–2050. *Monthly Labor Review, 125*, 15.

Toossi, M., & Torpey, E. (2017, May). *Older workers: Labor force trends and career options*. U.S. Bureau of Labor Statistics. Retrieved from https://www.bls.gov/careeroutlook/2017/article/older-workers.htm.

Truxillo, D. M., Cadiz, D. M., & Hammer, L. B. (2015). Supporting the aging workforce: A research review and recommendations for workplace intervention research. *Annual Review of Organizational Psychology and Organizational Behavior, 2*, 351–381. https://doi.org/10.1146/annurev-orgpsych-032414-111435.

Turner, J. C. (1985). Social categorization and the self-concept: A social cognitive theory of group behavior. In E. J. Lawler (Ed.), *Advances in group processes* (Vol. 2, pp. 77–122). Greenwich, CT: JAI Press.

Turner, J. C. (1987). A self-categorization theory. In J. C. Turner, M. A. Hogg, P. J. Oakes, S. D. Reicher, & M. S. Wetherell (Eds.), *Rediscovering the social group: A self-categorization theory* (pp. 42–67). Oxford, UK: Blackwell.

Turner, J. C., Hogg, M. A., Oakes, P. J., Reicher, S. D., & Wetherell, M. S. (1987). *Rediscovering the social group: A self-categorization theory*. Oxford, UK: Blackwell.

Turner, J. C., & Oakes, P. J. (1989). Self-categorization theory and social influence. In P. B. Paulus (Ed.), *Psychology of group influence* (2nd ed., pp. 233–275). Hillsdale, NJ: Erlbaum.

Turner, J. C., & Reynolds, K. J. (2012). Self-categorization theory. In P. Van Lange, A. Kruglanski, & T. Higgins (Eds.), *Handbook of theories of social psychology* (pp. 399–417). Thousand Oaks, CA: Sage

United States Department of Justice. (1990). *Americans with Disabilities Act of 1990*. Retrieved February 9, 2020 from http://www.ada.gov/pubs/ada.htm.

U.S. Department of Labor. (2019, September 30). *Labor force participation rates*. Retrieved from https://www.dol.gov/wb/stats/NEWSTATS/latest/laborforce-text.htm#LFPagesex.

Velez, B. L., Moradi, B., & Brewster, M. E. (2013). Testing the tenets of minority stress theory in workplace contexts. *Journal of Counseling Psychology, 60,* 532–542.

Vornholt, K., Uitdewilligen, S., & Nijhuis, F. J. (2013). Factors affecting the acceptance of people with disabilities at work: A literature review. *Journal of Occupational Rehabilitation, 23,* 463–475.

Webster, J. R., Adams, G. A., Maranto, C. L., Sawyer, K., & Thoroughgood, C. (2018). Workplace contextual supports for LGBT employees: A review, meta-analysis, and agenda for future research. *Human Resource Management, 57,* 193–210. https://doi.org/10.1002/hrm.21873.

Weiner, B. (1985). An attributional theory of achievement motivation and emotion. *Psychological Review, 92,* 548–573.

Westmorland, M. G., Williams, R. M., Amick, B. C., III, Shannon, H., & Rasheed, F. (2005). Disability management practices in Ontario workplaces: Employees' perceptions. *Disability and Rehabilitation, 27,* 825–835.

Williams, K. D. (2007). Ostracism. *Annual Review of Psychology, 58,* 425–452. https://doi.org/10.1146/annurev.psych.58.110405.085641.

Williams, K. D., & Sommer, K. L. (1997). Social ostracism by coworkers: Does rejection lead to loafing or compensation? *Personality and Social Psychology Bulletin, 23,* 693–706.

Wirth, J. H., & Williams, K. D. (2009). 'They don't like our kind': Consequences of being ostracized while possessing a group membership. *Group Processes & Intergroup Relations, 12,* 111–127. https://doi.org/10.1177/1368430208098780.

Wittenbaum, G. M., Shulman, H. C., & Braz, M. E. (2010). Social ostracism in task groups: The effects of group composition. *Small Group Research, 41,* 330–353.

Wu, L.-Z., Ferris, D. L., Kwan, H. K., Chiang, F., Snape, E., & Liang, L. H. (2015). Breaking (or making) the silence: How goal interdependence and social skill predict being ostracized. *Organizational Behavior and Human Decision Processes, 131,* 51–66.

Wynne, R., & McAnaney, D. (2009). Preventing social exclusion through illness or disability: Models of good practice. *Work, 32,* 95–103.

Yeung, D. Y., & Fung, H. H. (2012). Impacts of suppression on emotional responses and performance outcomes: An experience-sampling study in younger and older workers. *Journals of Gerontology: Series B, Psychological Sciences and Social Sciences, 67,* 666–676.

Yeung, D. Y., Wong, C. K., & Lok, D. P. (2011). Emotion regulation mediates age differences in emotions. *Aging & Mental Health, 15,* 414–418.

Yeung, D. Y., & Wong, S. (2020). Effects of cognitive reappraisal and expressive suppression on daily work-related outcomes: Comparison between younger and older Chinese workers. *International Journal of Psychology*. https://doi.org/10.1002/ijop.12661.

Zhang, R., Ye, C., & Ferreira-Meyers, K. (2017). Linking workplace ostracism to interpersonal citizenship behavior: A moderated mediation model of work-to-family conflict and rumination. *International Journal of Stress Management, 24*, 293–320. https://doi.org/10.1037/str0000056.

Zimmerman, C. A., Carter-Sowell, A. R., & Xu, X. (2016). Examining workplace ostracism experiences in academia: Understanding how differences in the faculty ranks influence inclusive climates on campus. *Frontiers in Psychology, 7*, 1–9.

CHAPTER 9

Research Methods for Studying Workplace Ostracism

Paul E. Spector and David J. Howard

There is growing awareness that employee mistreatment is a serious problem because it has been linked to a variety of negative outcomes for employees and organizations (Bowling & Beehr, 2006). There are many forms of mistreatment ranging from fairly minor acts of rudeness to bullying and physical violence. Workplace ostracism stands out as a form of mistreatment because it is for the most part the absence of behavior (ignoring someone or failing to include him or her in activities and discussions) rather than actively abusing or insulting someone. The passive nature of ostracism creates special research challenges because it must be inferred from patterns of behavior and what is not done rather than what is done. An employee might report that he or she has experienced ostracism, but linking that purely subjective internal state to something more objective is difficult, and can limit the sorts of inferences that we might draw about the antecedents of ostracism.

P. E. Spector (✉) · D. J. Howard
University of South Florida, Tampa, FL, USA
e-mail: pspector@usf.edu

C. Liu and J. Ma (eds.), *Workplace Ostracism*,
Palgrave Explorations in Workplace Stigma,
https://doi.org/10.1007/978-3-030-54379-2_9

This chapter will explore the methodological issues involved in studying workplace ostracism. Part of our discussion will include an overview of the methods that have been used in this literature. We will include the assessment of ostracism and the research designs utilized in published studies. Much of our discussion will focus on the nature of the inferences that can reasonably be made using the typical methods used to study ostracism in the organizational sciences. We will also make suggestions about the sorts of methodologies that might be applied to be able to more confidently reach the conclusions we generally wish to make about potential antecedents and consequences of workplace ostracism.

How Has Workplace Ostracism Been Studied?

In May 2019, we conducted a literature review of workplace ostracism using the search term "workplace ostracism" in the topic field within the Web of Science database. This search returned 121 articles. Thirteen were unavailable, reducing the number to 108. After reviewing each paper, 35 articles were excluded from further analysis because they were not specifically relevant to workplace ostracism, but rather focused on another construct entirely, or focused on social ostracism and/or global ostracism and did not measure ostracism in the workplace. The remaining 73 articles featured 95 samples (studies). We content analyzed the method sections of those articles and coded for features of the research designs and measures used.

Table 9.1 Research designs used in workplace ostracism studies

Method	*Number of studies*	*Percent*
Longitudinal or time-lagged	42	44
Cross-sectional	26	27
Multiple data sources	25	26
Experimental	14	15
Theoretical papers including reviews	4	4
Daily diary/experience sampling	1	1
Interventions	1	1
Qualitative (Interview)	1	1

Table 9.1 summarizes the number of studies that used various design features to investigate workplace ostracism. Most used survey methods but some of those studies incorporated multiple design features (e.g., time-lagged studies with supervisor-employee dyads). Thus, the number of studies in the table sums to more than 95. As can be seen, the most commonly used design incorporates time, and was either longitudinal (all variables assessed repeatedly) or time-lagged (different variables assessed at different times). Cross-sectional designs were also popular, used in about a quarter of the studies. About a quarter of the studies used more than one source of data, such as self-reports and supervisor reports.

There were more than a dozen studies that used experimental designs. Some of these used computerized simulations (e.g., Cyberball) and did not take place in the workplace or use employees as their participants. We included them in our content analysis because they are written for organizational research journals and are framed in a workplace context (e.g., Kouchaki & Wareham, 2015; Lustenberger & Jagacinski, 2010). Daily diary designs, intervention studies, and qualitative methods were not popular in this area, as we found only a single case of each.

Table 9.2 summarizes the scales used to assess workplace ostracism. As can be seen, almost three-fourths of the studies used the Workplace Ostracism Scale (Ferris, Brown, Berry, & Lian, 2008), with the remaining studies using a variety of ad hoc measures designed for the particular study, or other less used measures. For example, Al-Atwi (2018) categorized some common workplace ostracism behaviors as "negative ties at work" and measured these behaviors using dichotomous (yes/no) items such as "Sometimes people at work don't feel comfortable or easy with

Table 9.2 Measures used in workplace ostracism studies

Scale or manipulation used	*Number of studies*	*Percent*
Workplace Ostracism Scale[a]	68	72
Ad hoc	9	9
Computerized simulation (e.g., Cyberball)	6	6
Scenario vignettes (mostly based on Hitlan 2009)	6	6
WES-R[b]	4	4
Ostracism intervention behavior scale[c]	2	2

[a]Ferris et al. (2008)
[b]Hitlan and Noel (2009)
[c]Fiset and Boies (2018)

us, therefore, they try to avoid interacting with us. Do you perceive that this person avoids interacting with you?" (p. 655).

Ostracism and the Nature of Inference

Ostracism is studied as a form of workplace mistreatment that is assumed to have detrimental effects on people and organizations. There are two fundamental questions that drive much of this research. First, what are the antecedents of workplace ostracism? Included are environmental conditions within organizations that might encourage or fail to discourage this behavior, and characteristics of actors who engage in this behavior, and characteristics of targets. Second, what are the potential consequences of workplace ostracism? This includes the impact of workplace ostracism on individual employees (including targets and observers) and on organizations. The goal of these lines of research is to provide convincing evidence that supports the assumed role of specific factors as antecedents or consequences. Drawing such inferences is challenging using the typical methods applied in this domain, which is unfortunate as knowing what might drive ostracism would be important in designing effective interventions, and knowing what serve as consequences would provide insights about the importance of reducing it.

Assessment of Workplace Ostracism

As with many organizational constructs, the typical methodology for assessing ostracism is to rely on humans as measuring instruments. Given the personal nature of ostracism, and the fact that it is often the absence rather than presence of behavior that is of interest, the most direct way to assess it is with self-reports. For example, Ferris et al. (2008) developed the 10-item Workplace Ostracism Scale, used in most ostracism studies, that is designed as a self-report instrument to assess employee experiences. Respondents indicate on a 7-point scale from "Never" to "Always" how frequently each experience occurs at work, such as being excluded from conversation or ignored. Although the scale is typically used as a self-report instrument, it is also used with alternative sources, such as coworkers or supervisors, to indicate how often they observe each item. Others will certainly not be aware of all interactions (or failed interactions) that occur for a target employee, but they might have a general impression of whether ostracism is occurring.

Another approach to studying ostracism is to view it from the perspective of the actors—employees who engage in ostracism against others. Many measures of mistreatment include ostracism items, but they are combined with other acts so that it is not possible to isolate them in their potential antecedents and consequences. In fact Ferris et al. (2008) noted that they developed much of their item pool for the WOS by adapting items from several mistreatment scales, such as bullying (Fox & Stallworth, 2005) and deviance (Bennett & Robinson, 2000). If the focus is on specific behaviors, the same items can be written to assess behaviors done by actors and behaviors experienced by targets. Few studies have focused on the ostracism behaviors as reported by actors.

It is also possible to study ostracism without the use of questionnaires. Possibilities include interviews of individuals to ask about ostracism from the perspective of actors and targets. Although this approach still relies on people's reports, interviews allow for more in-depth exploration of the sorts of behaviors people say they engage in, and the behaviors they have experienced. This can be important because ostracism can be subtle, and it is patterns of behavior in a particular context that results in someone perceiving themselves to be ostracized. As noted, our review found only a single interview study.

Another possibility is to avoid a self-report study entirely, and look for other ways of getting at ostracism in the workplace. This could involve the analysis of incident reports where employees file grievances about their mistreatment, to look for instances of ostracism. For example, one could look at reports of complaints for ethnic harassment to see the extent to which ostracism is mentioned.

Design and Inference in the Study of Workplace Ostracism

Three Forms of Inference

In the context of health risk factors, Kraemer, Stice, Kazdin, Offord, and Kupfer (2001) suggest three forms of evidence. In our context, we can talk about antecedent conditions that increase an employee's risk of ostracism, and extend that to the connection of ostracism to potential outcomes. A **correlate** is a condition that has been shown to relate to workplace ostracism, perhaps in a cross-sectional survey study. The results of this type of study allow us to infer that that condition is related to workplace ostracism, and that it might be an antecedent, but this method does not allow us to draw firm conclusions beyond association. At best we can say that our results support the possibility that the condition in question is an antecedent, or that we could not rule it out based on our data. A **proxy factor** is a condition that can predict future workplace ostracism or consequences of workplace ostracism. For example, we might find that people who report being ostracized at work in a survey are likely to quit their job at a 6 month follow-up. Thus ostracism assessed at Time 1 predicts future turnover assessed at a subsequent time. The use of this sort of two-wave research design where you can show that something occurring at Time 1 predicts something at Time 2 that had not occurred prior to Time 1 gives an added level of confidence that turnover might have been the outcome of workplace ostracism. The limitation is that we cannot be certain that workplace ostracism was in fact responsible for the turnover. It is feasible that the workplace ostracism—turnover relationship is spurious. In other words, there is some condition at work related to workplace ostracism that is the real driver of turnover. For example, suppose employees are ostracized because they are poor performers. Their failure to adequately complete job tasks puts a burden on coworkers who retaliate with social exclusion. The underperforming individuals might quit their jobs, not because they were ostracized, but because they were getting pressure from supervisors to perform better.

The third form of evidence is a **causal risk factor**. This is a condition that, when manipulated, will lead to the consequence in question. Thus we might introduce an intervention designed to reduce employee mistreatment including ostracism. A pretest-posttest comparison of data collected both before and after an intervention would demonstrate that the intervention had a positive effect on workplace ostracism by employees. Even better would be an experiment in which employees were randomly assigned to the intervention or a control condition. If ostracism declined for the intervention group from pretest to posttest, but did not decline for the control group, one would have some confidence that the intervention was the cause of the decline in ostracism. Although one can conclude that the intervention was effective, it is not entirely certain that the intervention itself, and not something associated with the intervention was the real cause.

Manipulationist Approach to Causality

Philosophers of science have provided a number of approaches to addressing the issue of causal inference. Perhaps the most relevant to the issue of organizational research (Spector, 2019) comes from the manipulationists (Hausman & Woodward, 1999; Illari & Russo, 2014; Woodward, 2017). According to this view, there are four elements to determining causality: a proposed cause (X), a proposed effect (Y), an intervention that manipulates X, and a temporal sequence of:

$$\text{Intervention} \rightarrow X \rightarrow Y.$$

For example, suppose we want to test the idea that supportive supervisor behavior (X) reduces ostracism behavior by subordinates (Y). We can create an intervention to encourage supportive supervisor behavior, although manipulationists note that an intervention does not have to be created by a researcher. It can merely be observed by the researcher as in a naturally occurring experiment. The idea is that X is manipulated through an intervention (e.g., conducting a training intervention to increase consideration), and then subsequent effects (e.g., later levels of ostracism) are observed. There are three additional conditions, however, that must be met in order to draw causal conclusions.

- The change in X is only due to the intervention and not something associated with the intervention. Control groups are used to address this possibility, for example, by offering placebo training to a control group as a means of showing that results were not just due to the fact that the intervention group was trained. However, even with the most carefully conducted randomized experiment, conducted in the field or laboratory, there is the possibility that it was not the content of the training itself that had the effect, but some other unintended factor. For example, in a field experiment suppose that during the supervisor training, the trainer shows a clip from a popular movie, and after seeing the clip, many of the participants decide to watch the movie on their own time, even though doing so was not part of training or suggested by the trainer. Further suppose that the training itself was ineffective, but it was viewing the movie that had the intended effect. In a laboratory study there is the possibility that demand characteristics or experimenter effects are responsible for the results (Rosenthal & Rosnow, 2009).
- The intervention only acts through X and not directly on Y. In this case suppose the employees are aware that supervisors are being

trained to be more supportive, and that knowledge is having a trickle-down effect on subordinates. The intervention is having an effect on the subordinates because they find out that the company values good relationships among employees—values it enough to invest in training. Knowing that supervisors are being trained has an effect on subordinates directly—it has nothing to do with the behavior of supervisors or the training they received.

- There are no causes related to the intervention that are affecting *Y*. In other words, we can rule out that the relationship between the intervention and *Y* is spuriously due to the action of a third (or fourth) variable. This might occur because of something associated with the training that affects subordinates. Suppose the company has limited training resources, and because supervisors are being trained, a subordinate training program was canceled. Subordinates might become aware of the reasons for the diverting of training resources, and decide to be nicer to one another to avoid more loss of resources in the future. The effect on subordinate ostracism was not due to the training affecting supervisor behavior, or due to the effect of that training on subordinates that had nothing to do with supervisors. Rather there was a factor outside of the training that is the causal element.

Even with a randomized experiment, it can be quite challenging to meet the three conditions. The possibility of demand characteristics and experimenter effects (Rosenthal & Rosnow, 2009) is widely known, although often ignored. Blind and double-blind procedures are often used to address such limitations, but they are not always feasible as in many experiments, experimenters know the conditions because they must administer them.

Beyond those problems is the issue of a possible disconnect between the intervention and the *X* variable. Most studies are interested in making connections between theoretical constructs, such as ostracism and potential antecedents and consequences. Constructs are manipulated via interventions by operationalizing varying levels, and it is assumed that those operationalizations are in fact manipulating the construct of interest. It is not necessarily the case that a manipulated variable in fact reflects the intended theoretical construct, particularly as so many organizational constructs are abstract representations of the social environment.

All this is to say that conclusions about causality are always tentative, and that the best we can do is demonstrate that specific interventions might result in desired results in the workplace. Thus we might find in a causal factor sense that providing certain training to supervisors would be expected to reduce ostracism in employees. This does not mean that the content of the training itself is necessarily the causal factor, as other possibilities exist.

The Study of Process

Although it is not often stated explicitly, most of our research and theories are implicitly concerned with investigating process, that is, the sequence of events that occurs within organizations. With ostracism, this might mean conditions and events at work that might lead one or more employees to ostracize one or more colleagues, and the sequence of events leading from being ostracized to employee and organizational outcomes. Process is implied in models of simple mediation chains suggesting X leads to Y, mediated by one or more other variables. It is implied in more complex structural models. Unfortunately, most of the research designs utilized to test hypotheses and theories about process are unable to provide much insight because they fail to include methods that can reasonably do so (Spector & Meier, 2014).

The idea of a process implies a temporal sequence of conditions or events that unfolds in a particular order. One such order would be that an employee who violates group norms is ostracized by the group, and after being ostracized, that employee feels anxious. This statement specifies how one event leads to another—ostracized employee's behavior to ostracism by other employees to emotional state of the ostracized employee. Processes are generally stated as causal flows, although it is possible that events unfold in a sequence without one event necessarily being a cause of another. In other words an event might be a proxy factor in that it precedes another event in time, although some other factor associated with the proxy factor is the actual cause.

Because processes are concerned with temporal precedence of conditions and events, the time frame in which the process unfolds must be built into research designs. That is, one must be able to demonstrate that the elements of the proposed process occurred in the specified order. This means research methods must be chosen that can assess the various elements in the sequence in which they occur. This can be readily accomplished when the elements involve discrete events that occur at specific times, such as having an accident or quitting a job. It is more challenging when the variables of interest involve more chronic conditions or levels, such as job characteristics (e.g., skill variety) or job stressors (e.g., role ambiguity). Designs that estimate relationships among such variables are generally unable to shed much light on when the conditions occurred. In such cases it might be possible to show that certain events led to a change in a condition (e.g., ostracism became more frequent). Most studies, even those with longitudinal designs, fail to illuminate the sequence of change.

Spector, Yang, and Zhou (2015) is an example of a longitudinal study that incorporated temporal features to investigate the direction of the connection between violence prevention climate and mistreatment. They chose newly graduated nurses in their first nursing position and assessed them 6 months and 12 months after graduation. Climate and mistreatment (physical and nonphysical) were assessed at both time periods. Analyzing only those individuals who had not experienced mistreatment at Time 1, they were able to show that climate (Time 1) predicted the first mistreatment event the nurses experienced, thus providing evidence for the climate-mistreatment temporal order. To test the reverse order, they conducted a repeated measures analysis of variance to see if those experiencing their first mistreatment event at Time 2 would have larger reduced climate scores than those who did not experience mistreatment. This analysis was able to rule out that direction of effects. This design and analysis strategy required different analyses to test each direction of effects because of the discrete versus continuous nature of the two variables.

Observational Research Designs

There are a wide variety of observational research designs that can be used to study workplace ostracism. These designs involve the collection of data without any sort of intervention or manipulation of variables. These designs vary mainly in two aspects. First, designs can be static and assess all variables at one point in time, or they can have multiple observations over time. Second, they can collect all data from a single source (e.g., employee self-reports) or from multiple sources (e.g., employee and supervisor reports). They can involve only data from surveys, whether completed by employees or others, or they can incorporate other forms and sources of data.

Cross-Sectional Designs

The most basic observational design is the cross-sectional single-source design when all data are collected from a single source, most typically the employee. This design is the most popular in the job stress and occupational health domains in which the study of mistreatment and ostracism inhabit (Spector & Pindek, 2016), although we found with ostracism itself, more studies incorporated a time element. Most studies in this domain are surveys of employees that can be conducted anonymously using online survey hosting platforms like Qualtrics or Survey Monkey. These surveys can be conducted inexpensively, especially if volunteers are solicited as subjects. Having the resources to compensate subjects can make it easier to recruit specialized populations, and increases response rates.

As typically used, the cross-sectional design is limited to establishing covariation among variables, or showing that a particular variable is a correlate as defined by Kraemer et al. (2001). Such designs can be effective in showing links of ostracism with potential antecedents and consequences, and can be used to explore boundary conditions of those links, for example, that they are stronger for certain groups of people versus others. What they cannot indicate, no matter what complex statistics are applied, is that a particular variable might serve as a proxy factor or a causal factor. Reasonable evidence that a variable serves in those roles requires the introduction into the research design of appropriate temporal features. We will return to those issues later when we discuss the issue of studying processes.

The cross-sectional design can be particularly useful in early stages of research when it is important to efficiently establish linkages among variables of interest. It can be used in an exploratory way to determine which variables are interrelated, and it can be used in a confirmatory way to test theory-based hypotheses about relationships, both additive and interactive. Peng and Zeng (2017) used this approach in the first of two studies, as they examined the relationship of workplace ostracism with self-esteem, helping behavior, interpersonal deviance, and the role 360-degree feedback plays in moderating the strength of those relationships.

Once it is established with cross-sectional designs that variables are related, follow-up research can be conducted to rule in or rule out alternative explanations for results. For example, if an ostracism study shows that the more frequently people report ostracism, the more negative affect they indicate, one might wonder if this relationship is spuriously due to the action of personality, such as neuroticism. A cross-sectional design could be used to see if controlling for a measure of neuroticism will have an impact on the ostracism-negative affect relationship. Finding little difference between analyses controlling versus not controlling for neuroticism helps rule out personality as a confounding variable. Finding that neuroticism can "explain" the relationship between ostracism and affect is inconclusive. The relationship might be spurious, but there might be something more complex going on, such as people who are frequently ostracized are traumatized and become higher in neuroticism. Drawing firm conclusions would require a series of studies using different designs and methodologies to rule in or rule out personality as the driver of ostracism and affect reports.

The cross-sectional design has been much maligned in both the literature and by editors and reviewers in the publication process. Some journals have policies to reject out of hand all submitted manuscripts using this design. Despite the low esteem of the design, it remains the most popular, undoubtedly due to its efficiency and low cost. Critics of the cross-sectional design are often quick to tout the virtues of the longitudinal design that is considered to be a vast improvement. As we will see next, the potential advantages of the longitudinal design are too infrequently realized as they are typically used (Spector, 2019).

Longitudinal Designs

Longitudinal designs involve the repeated assessment of individuals over time through collection of two or more waves of data, and are the most popular design for workplace ostracism research. In many cases all variables in the study are assessed at each wave, but in some cases what is included in each wave varies. Wu, Selig, and Little (2013) distinguish longitudinal from diary designs in terms of the number and timing of waves. Longitudinal designs generally have a handful of waves and a fairly long time frame measured in months or years, whereas diary designs typically have far more measurement occasions over far shorter time frames. A typical diary design might have 2 or more assessments for each of 10 or more days. The diary design will be discussed in a separate section.

The potential advantage of the longitudinal design is the ability to demonstrate that one variable can predict a future variable, or is a proxy factor. However, the ability to demonstrate temporal flow, that is, one variable can predict the other, is not automatic with this design, and depends on the ability to determine when things occurred in relation to one another (Spector, 2019). Most applications of longitudinal designs in the organizational realm fail to include features that would allow for the determination of temporal precedence, and this is true in the workplace ostracism domain, as well. This is because the starting time of the study and the lag between waves are chosen arbitrarily, after many causal processes have achieved steady state, or what Mitchell and James (2001) refer to as equilibration. In the second study published in the aforementioned article, Peng and Zeng (2017) measured ostracism and other variables at two time points one month apart. There is nothing in this study to suggest that a significant event occurred during this time frame that would have led to ostracism or its effects.

To determine causes or effects of ostracism, temporal precedence must be incorporated into the design. Suppose a study were interested in the connection between frequency of ostracism and job satisfaction. The ideal design would be to assess job satisfaction before and after ostracism began occurring to see if those who became ostracized for the first time suffered a reduction in job satisfaction, and those who were not ostracized maintained their level of satisfaction. Finding a difference in job satisfaction from before ostracism occurred until after it happened would establish that ostracism is at least a proxy factor. It can predict change in job satisfaction. It is not a causal factor because we cannot know from just the assessment of the two variables if there is another factor related to ostracism that is the real driver of job satisfaction. For example, perhaps individuals who perform poorly are ostracized by coworkers for not pulling their weight, but fail to enjoy rewards such as bonus pay due to their inadequate productivity. It might well be that the lack of rewards is the driver of job satisfaction. Thus, the ostracism—job satisfaction relationship could be spurious.

However, once the process connecting ostracism to job satisfaction has been completed, assessing both variables at two arbitrary points in time can only establish that they are correlates. It cannot shed much light on whether ostracism leads to job dissatisfaction or the reverse. The use of the longitudinal design does not offer much advantage over the cross-sectional design in this instance.

The ideal way to utilize a longitudinal design is to assess a potential predictor at a meaningful Time 1 before the potential outcome has occurred. The lag before Time 2 assessment would be chosen to follow the occurrence of the outcome so that it could be determined if the proposed predictor could forecast the future outcome. This can most readily be done when the outcome is a discrete event, such as quitting the job. Another strategy would be to study newly hired employees so that a predictors can be gathered prior to or shortly after hiring but before the outcome has occurred (for an example see Schonfeld, 2001). As noted earlier, Spector et al. (2015) utilized this approach when assessing violence prevention climate in a sample of newly graduated nurses who had not yet been assaulted, subsequently finding that climate was a proxy factor in predicting subsequent mistreatment and physical assault. This approach could be used with predictors of ostracism if newly hired employees who had not yet been ostracized were studied. Potential predictors could be assessed at Time 1 early in the employees' tenure in a sample who had not yet experienced ostracism, and ostracism could be assessed at a later wave.

Longitudinal designs are most typically used with traditional summated rating scales completed by employees about their experience with ostracism. One novel approach used in recent work (Yang & Treadway, 2018) was to examine both targets' perceptions of workplace ostracism and their behaviors as a perpetrator of ostracism at two time points three months apart using a social network-type measure (i.e., they asked each individual how often they ostracized each person in their department).

Diary Designs

With the typical diary design, individuals complete assessments multiple times over fairly short periods of time. Most diary studies survey respondents on consecutive work days, often more than once per day. Some studies use fixed times to conduct the survey, such as before work, at lunch (or meal) break, and the end of work, and before bed. For example, Pereira, Meier, and Elfering (2013) investigated the impact of workplace ostracism (measured at the end of the work shift) on worrying (measured before bed) and sleep quality (measured the following morning). Other studies might ask respondents to complete a survey when a certain event occurs (event sampling), such as when a customer is rude. The time frame for these studies is not fixed, as weekly or monthly lags could be chosen.

Diary designs are typically used to assess within-person phenomena. With ostracism they could be used to see if on days a person experiences some form of ostracism (e.g., coworkers went to lunch and didn't invite the target person), the outcomes are different than on days when ostracism did not occur. The advantage of studying within-person effects is that many person-level variables are controlled, since analysis is being done of variability within and not between people. The within-person approach can also be more directly tied to many theories that suggest the effects of organizational experiences, like ostracism, might be immediate and transitory, so that on days the experience happens, outcomes are different than on days when they did not, or conversely, on days that certain events happened, ostracism was more likely to occur.

Although diary designs can indicate an association between a particular experience and outcome, the direction of effects is not always clear. This is because in most cases respondents are asked for retrospective reports of events and experiences such as ostracism, and for outcomes, but the time frame by which these occurred is not captured. For example, one might ask at the end of the workday about ostracism and current mood. Even though the event happened prior to the assessment, and mood is current, this method does not indicate when that mood occurred relative to the ostracism event. Mood might have been assessed after the event, but that does not mean that it began after the event. It is possible that mood drove the ostracism rather than the reverse. Even if a pretest of mood is taken at the beginning of the shift, it still cannot tell us direction of effects because even if mood changes from beginning to end of the shift, we cannot determine if it changed before or after the event of interest. All we can determine is that mood is worse at the end of the day (or changed for the worse) on days certain events occurred. Determining direction of effects would require knowing when mood changed in relation to the ostracism event.

The diary design can also be used to shed light on proxy factors, that is, whether something that occurred at the beginning of the workday could predict an event that happened subsequently. For example, one could ask for reports of how well the person slept the prior night at the beginning of the day to see if it could predict whether or not an ostracism event occurred, assessed at the end of the day. Finding that connection could establish sleep quality as a predictor, but that does not mean that sleep quality was the causal factor. It could be that a third variable might have driven poor sleep and then ostracism. For example, suppose employees who have conflicts with others on day 1 are likely to sleep poorly that night, and are likely to be ostracized by other employees the next day. Disentangling this sort of complex series of events would be difficult with the sorts of methods typically used.

Multiple Data Sources

A concern with studies that use a single source of data such as self-reports is the possibility that relationships among variables are distorted due to common biases or common method variance (Podsakoff, MacKenzie, & Podsakoff, 2012; Spector, Rosen, Richardson, Williams, & Johnson, 2019). For example, it is possible that individuals with certain personality characteristics or people in certain moods are likely to distort their reports of ostracism and other variables within the same survey. One way to control for potential confounding with a survey (or any single data source) is to utilize more than one data source to minimize, although not entirely eliminate (Spector, 1994), this possibility. As we noted, this is a popular strategy in the study of workplace ostracism. Some of these studies surveyed employees and their supervisors about the employees' ostracism experiences and potential antecedents (Quade, Greenbaum, & Petrenko, 2017) and consequences (Xu, Huang, & Robinson, 2017).

With survey research, alternative sources are typically people related to the target employee who complete parallel surveys. Depending upon the purpose of the study, those individuals might be organizational insiders (coworkers, subordinates, or supervisors) or outsiders (customers or significant others). They might be asked to provide data on the ostracism experiences of the employee, or on potential antecedents (e.g., working conditions) or outcomes (e.g., person's affective state). In some cases, the alternative source might complete the same scale as the target employee to show that relationships of ostracism with other variables are not just due to common method variance.

One advantage of using alternative sources is the potential control of method variance and the ability to get convergent validity evidence for self-reports. The main weakness is that alternative sources typically have only limited information upon which to base judgments. Given the passive nature of most ostracism behaviors, they can be difficult to observe. A coworker or supervisor, for example, will not have complete knowledge about all the instances of ostracism the target employee might have experienced. Thus these alternative sources should be considered rough indicators that are likely less accurate than self-reports (Frese & Zapf, 1988).

Most multi-source studies are single-level with the unit of analysis being the employee, even though data are provided by two sources. We located one study that was multi-level with multiple employees nested within supervisors (Liu, Li, Bruk Lee, & Ma, 2019). Employees and supervisors provided data on different variables so that the experiences of employees and supervisors can be considered jointly.

Alternative sources of data do not have to come from surveys. Depending upon the variable of interest, there might be a number of other types of measures to use. Some might be available from organization records, for example, absenteeism or turnover. Others might be physiological measures, such as blood pressure or heart rate. Some organizational variables might be assessed objectively, such as organization size or structure. Financial performance of individual units might be tied to levels of ostracism. The use of a variety of data sources can expand the sorts of questions that are addressed, and can provide additional confidence in conclusions when results converge across sources.

Designs to More Directly Address Process

The traditional designs that rely on survey methodology are valuable tools for establishing correlation, sometimes proxy factors, and in rare cases causal factors. There are other methods, however, that need more extensive use in order to shed light on the processes underlying ostracism and its effects. They include archival studies, direct observations, experiments, qualitative studies, retrospective event histories, and sequence analysis (Spector & Meier, 2014) that enable the researcher to more closely identify the time frame by which a phenomenon unfolds.

Intervention Studies

To say we need intervention studies in the published literature is quite cliché because it is a suggestion frequently made, but rarely followed. The reasons for this are certainly complex, but publishing intervention studies is not currently in favor. We found only a single workplace ostracism intervention study (Ramsey & Jones, 2015) that investigated the efficacy of a mindfulness exercise in reducing ostracism behaviors in those trained. This intervention involved a series of discussions about experiences of workplace stress and mistreatment including ostracism, and then mindfulness exercises to deal with those experiences. It included meditation sessions to be performed at home. It is unfortunate that there aren't more intervention studies as they come closest to the manipulationist ideal for drawing causal inferences. With such studies researchers can create interventions in order to produce certain conditions or events, and then follow-up to see the effects on the target and potential organizational outcomes. Although no single intervention study would be conclusive, such studies can provide evidence that manipulating a potential antecedent could have the desired effect. Even if we cannot be certain why the intervention had the effects that it did, such research has practical utility in providing potential solutions to organizational problems.

For example, if the goal of an intervention is reducing ostracism, that intervention might focus on potential drivers of ostracism, for example, poor performance of targets. An intervention could be devised to help raise performance of struggling employees which would be expected to reduce ostracism. Such an intervention might be individualized and involve feedback, mentoring, and training. A pretest-posttest design could be used to show that the intervention did in fact raise performance. At the same time the study could determine if ostracism was reduced from before to after intervention. Of course, an even stronger design would involve a control group that did not receive the intervention, and random assignment to intervention or control conditions would be ideal.

Retrospective Event Histories

Most contemporary research studies typically ask people to rate levels of conditions or incidence frequencies. With ostracism this could mean asking employees to rate how often they are the targets of ostracism behaviors by coworkers, the frequency with which they experience certain emotions, and their current levels of job satisfaction. These studies fail to fully capture the range of data that employees can provide about their experiences and organizations. A retrospective event history (Tuma & Hannan, 1984) asks respondents to recall a series of events, and recall them in order, generally by providing dates. This can be done in an interview during which respondents recall events in order. Events can be discrete instances, for example, of specific ostracism experiences within a particular job, or they could involve a person's work history, indicating in which jobs ostracism occurred or did not occur. Event histories can also rely on archival data, such as organizational records of mistreatment complaints.

One example in the organizational realm was conducted by Glick, Huber, Miller, Doty, and Sutcliffe (1990) who interviewed a group of key informants four times at 6 month intervals. The repeated interviews allowed them to ask informants about the consequences of events asked in prior periods. Although this and other such studies are subject to limitations of human cognition and memory, it is not clear that such data are necessarily less accurate than the typical survey data that are collected.

Qualitative Studies

Qualitative studies can be used to investigate specific ostracism events and experiences that can provide far more depth than is possible with quantitative methods. There are a variety of such methods that can be useful. Some involve employees as informants who can relate experiences with ostracism in their careers or in their current jobs. This can be accomplished through interviews or open-ended surveys. Individuals can be asked about general experiences, or they can be asked to relate the most memorable or most recent incident. This approach is very much like the Stress Incident Record (Keenan & Newton, 1985) that has been used to study stressful work incidents.

When interview or written material is collected, there are two general approaches for analysis. First, the researcher can read the materials and write an analysis based on themes that are noted. Various quotes can be pulled out to illustrate each of the themes. Second, the researcher can conduct a content analysis in which materials are placed into categories, typically mutually exclusive. When there are relatively few respondents, typically the case with interviews, each statement might be placed into a category. Often with open-ended questionnaires there are 100 or more respondents, so that each person's response might be placed into a category. This is likely the case when critical incidents are collected that reflect the topic of interest, such as instances of being ostracized, or instances of ostracizing someone else. Content analysis can be conducted manually through the use of two or more trained raters. It can also be automated and conducted through software that can perform text analysis. An example of a qualitative ostracism study is Waldeck, Tyndall, and Chmiel (2015) who conducted a thematic analysis of semi-structured interviews with 21 participants who reported how they processed and coped with workplace ostracism.

Other approaches are possible, such as ethnographies where the researcher is a participant observer who spends time in an organization and records observations of events. This might involve the researcher spending a week or more in an organization during which he or she can interact with employees during the work day. The researcher would interpret and synthesize what was observed and reach conclusions. Such a study of ostracism, for example, would allow the researcher to detail how employees interacted with one another, and how certain individual were socially excluded from certain activities. This sort of study could provide a rich context by which to understand how an individual might be the target, and how different individuals explained their interactions with various members of their work groups.

Building Better Research Programs

As noted by Spector and Meier (2014), the methods utilized in too much of our research are driven more by convention than by what might best answer our research questions. There is much we do not know about the antecedents, consequences, and boundary conditions of ostracism and other forms of workplace mistreatment. Many of our questions cannot be readily answered with the typical methods that are applied. Too much of our research relies on observational methods that can provide important insights about what relates to ostracism, but not many insights about the processes surrounding ostracism. For example, longitudinal studies are most likely to choose arbitrary time points in an attempt to shed light on variables that might occur prior to or subsequent to ostracism. Those research designs, however, are not very helpful when we want to learn how it is that a person becomes targeted, and how interaction patterns might evolve over time.

A better approach is to think in terms of programs of research, both within research teams and across research teams throughout the field, rather than individual studies. Such programs should involve a diverse set of methods that can, in combination, provide more insights than studies or series of studies that rely on a single approach. This should include qualitative methods to provide a richer view of ostracism at work, and quantitative studies that can investigate relationships. More attention should be paid to events rather than to levels of conditions. Many of our models are really models of individual incidents, yet most studies focus on relative frequencies, that is, employee estimated frequency of ostracism might be related to their reported frequency of negative emotions or physical symptoms.

When relationships are found between two variables in a study, immediate follow-up studies should be conducted to better understand why that relationship was found and what possible boundary conditions might exist. If ostracism is related to an outcome in a self-report study, is it possible that the outcome drove the ostracism? Did the reports of both variables suffer from shared biases and common method variance? Is the relationship moderated by individual differences, or by contextual factors in the workplace? These are the sorts of questions that should be addressed before assuming that the observed relationship means that ostracism drives outcomes.

A programmatic approach can also address the three forms of inference. Cross-sectional and longitudinal designs with arbitrary time frames can be helpful in establishing correlates. Longitudinal designs in which potential antecedents are assessed prior to their presumed outcomes can establish proxy factors. Interventions, whether created by the investigator or naturally occurring, will be needed to shed light on causal factors. Programs can be designed to systematically address these questions in order.

The study of workplace ostracism and broader mistreatment is relatively new, but it has provided important insights into how this phenomenon can be harmful to individuals and organizations. To this point, a relatively narrow range of methodologies have been used to study workplace ostracism, leaving much to be done to more definitely build our understanding of workplace conditions that might lead to or prevent this behavior. Of particular value would be the application of methods that can more definitively indicate the temporal order in which workplace events, including ostracism, occur. Ostracism can be potentially damaging to employees and their organizations, so a better understanding of this phenomenon would provide insights into how best to manage it at work.

References

Al-Atwi, A. A. (2018). Oblivious, paranoid, and disclosed negative ties: An examination of the mechanisms underlying the relationship between negative ties and job performance. *Journal of Organizational Behavior, 39*(5), 648–662. https://doi.org/10.1002/job.2261.

Bennett, R. J., & Robinson, S. L. (2000). Development of a measure of workplace deviance. *Journal of Applied Psychology, 85*(3), 349–360. https://doi.org/10.1037/0021-9010.85.3.349.

Bowling, N. A., & Beehr, T. A. (2006). Workplace harassment from the victim's perspective: A theoretical model and meta-analysis. *Journal of*

Applied Psychology, 91(5), 998–1012. https://doi.org/10.1037/0021-9010.91.5.998.

Ferris, D. L., Brown, D. J., Berry, J. W., & Lian, H. W. (2008). The development and validation of the Workplace Ostracism Scale. *Journal of Applied Psychology, 93*(6), 1348–1366. https://doi.org/10.1037/a0012743.

Fiset, J., & Boies, K. (2018). Seeing the unseen: Ostracism interventionary behaviour and its impact on employees. *European Journal of Work and Organizational Psychology, 27*(4), 403–417. https://doi.org/10.1080/1359432x.2018.1462159.

Fox, S., & Stallworth, L. E. (2005). Racial/ethnic bullying: Exploring links between bullying and racism in the US workplace. *Journal of Vocational Behavior, 66*(3), 438–456. https://doi.org/10.1016/j.jvb.2004.01.002.

Frese, M., & Zapf, D. (1988). Methodological issues in the study of work stress: Objective vs subjective measurement of work stress and the question of longitudinal studies. In C. L. Cooper & R. Payne (Eds.), *Causes, coping and consequences of stress at work* (pp. 375–411). Oxford, England: Wiley.

Glick, W. H., Huber, G. P., Miller, C. C., Doty, D. H., & Sutcliffe, K. M. (1990). Studying changes in organizational design and effectiveness: Retrospective event histories and periodic assessments. *Organization Science, 1*(3), 293–312. https://doi.org/10.2307/2635007.

Hausman, D. M., & Woodward, J. (1999). Independence, invariance and the causal Markov condition. *The British Journal for the Philosophy of Science, 50*(4), 521–583. https://doi.org/10.1093/bjps/50.4.521.

Hitlan, R. T., & Noel, J. (2009). The influence of workplace exclusion and personality on counterproductive work behaviours: An interactionist perspective. *European Journal of Work and Organizational Psychology, 18*(4), 477–502. https://doi.org/10.1080/13594320903025028.

Illari, P., & Russo, F. (2014). *Causality: Philosophical theory meets scientific practice*. Oxford, UK: Oxford University Press.

Keenan, A., & Newton, T. (1985). Stressful events, stressors and psychological strains in young professional engineers. *Journal of Occupational Behaviour, 6*(2), 151–156.

Kouchaki, M., & Wareham, J. (2015). Excluded and behaving unethically: Social exclusion, physiological responses, and unethical behavior. *Journal of Applied Psychology, 100*(2), 547–556. https://doi.org/10.1037/a0038034.

Kraemer, H. C., Stice, E., Kazdin, A., Offord, D., & Kupfer, D. (2001). How do risk factors work together? Mediators, moderators, and independent, overlapping, and proxy risk factors. *The American Journal of Psychiatry, 158*(6), 848–856. https://doi.org/10.1176/appi.ajp.158.6.848.

Liu, C., Li, H., Bruk Lee, V., & Ma, J. (2019, August 9–13). *Supervisor conflict, supervisor ostracism, and employee outcomes: The role of interpersonal harmony*. Paper presented at the Academy of Management, Boston.

Lustenberger, D. E., & Jagacinski, C. M. (2010). Exploring the effects of ostracism on performance and intrinsic motivation. *Human Performance, 23*(4), 283–304. https://doi.org/10.1080/08959285.2010.501046.

Mitchell, T. R., & James, L. R. (2001). Building better theory: Time and the specification of when things happen. *The Academy of Management Review, 26*(4), 530–547. https://doi.org/10.2307/3560240.

Peng, A. C. Y., & Zeng, W. (2017). Workplace ostracism and deviant and helping behaviors: The moderating role of 360 degree feedback. *Journal of Organizational Behavior, 38*(6), 833–855. https://doi.org/10.1002/job.2169.

Pereira, D., Meier, L. L., & Elfering, A. (2013). Short-term effects of social exclusion at work and worries on sleep. *Stress and Health, 29*(3), 240–252. https://doi.org/10.1002/smi.2461.

Podsakoff, P. M., MacKenzie, S. B., & Podsakoff, N. P. (2012). Sources of method bias in social science research and recommendations on how to control it. *Annual Review of Psychology, 63*, 539–569. https://doi.org/10.1146/annurev-psych-120710-100452.

Quade, M. J., Greenbaum, R. L., & Petrenko, O. V. (2017). "I don't want to be near you, unless…." The interactive effect of unethical behavior and performance onto relationship conflict and workplace ostracism. *Personnel Psychology, 70*(3), 675–709. https://doi.org/10.1111/peps.12164.

Ramsey, A. T., & Jones, E. E. (2015). Minding the interpersonal gap: Mindfulness-based interventions in the prevention of ostracism. *Consciousness and Cognition, 31*, 24–34. https://doi.org/10.1016/j.concog.2014.10.003.

Rosenthal, R., & Rosnow, R. L. (2009). *Artifacts in behavioral research*. New York: Oxford University Press.

Schonfeld, I. S. (2001). Stress in 1st-year women teachers: The context of social support and coping. *Genetic, Social, and General Psychology Monographs, 127*(2), 133–168.

Spector, P. E. (1994). Using self-report questionnaires in OB research: A comment on the use of a controversial method. *Journal of Organizational Behavior, 15*(5), 385–392. https://doi.org/10.1002/job.4030150503.

Spector, P. E. (2019). Do not cross me: Optimizing the use of cross-sectional designs. *Journal of Business and Psychology, 34*(2), 125–137. https://doi.org/10.1007/s10869-018-09613-8.

Spector, P. E., & Meier, L. L. (2014). Methodologies for the study of organizational behavior processes: How to find your keys in the dark. *Journal of Organizational Behavior, 35*(8), 1109–1119. https://doi.org/10.1002/job.1966.

Spector, P. E., & Pindek, S. (2016). The future of research methods in work and occupational health psychology. *Applied Psychology: An International Review, 65*(2), 412–431. https://doi.org/10.1111/apps.12056.

Spector, P. E., Rosen, C. C., Richardson, H. A., Williams, L. J., & Johnson, R. E. (2019). A new perspective on method variance: A measure-centric approach. *Journal of Management, 45*(3), 855–880. https://doi.org/10.1177/0149206316687295.

Spector, P. E., Yang, L.-Q., & Zhou, Z. E. (2015). A longitudinal investigation of the role of violence prevention climate in exposure to workplace physical violence and verbal abuse. *Work & Stress, 29*(4), 325–340. https://doi.org/10.1080/02678373.2015.1076537.

Tuma, N. B., & Hannan, M. T. (1984). *Social dynamics Models and methods*. Saint Louis, US: Elsevier.

Waldeck, D., Tyndall, I., & Chmiel, N. (2015). Resilience to ostracism: A qualitative inquiry. *Qualitative Report, 20*(10), 1646–1669.

Woodward, J. (2017). Scientific explanation. In E. N. Zalta (Ed.), *Stanford encyclopedia of philosophy*. Retrieved from https://plato.stanford.edu/archives/fall2017/entries/scientific-explanation.

Wu, W., Selig, J. P., & Little, T. D. (2013). Longitudinal data analysis. In T. D. Little (Ed.), *Oxford handbook of quantitative methods* (Vol. 2, pp. 387–410). New York City: Oxford University Press.

Xu, E., Huang, X., & Robinson, S. L. (2017). When self-view is at stake: Responses to ostracism through the lens of self-verification theory. *Journal of Management, 43*(7), 2281–2302. https://doi.org/10.1177/0149206314567779.

Yang, J., & Treadway, D. C. (2018). A social influence interpretation of workplace ostracism and counterproductive work behavior. *Journal of Business Ethics, 148*(4), 879–891. https://doi.org/10.1007/s10551-015-2912-x.

Appendix

See Tables A.1, A.2, A.3, A.4, A.5, and A.6.

C. Liu and J. Ma (eds.), *Workplace Ostracism*, Palgrave Explorations in Workplace Stigma, https://doi.org/10.1007/978-3-030-54379-2

Table A.1 Workplace Ostracism Questionnaire (WOS) using a 7-point Likert-type response scale

How often has this happened to you in the last year?	*(1)–(7)*
Others ignored you at work	
Others left the area when you entered	
Your greetings have gone unanswered at work	
You involuntarily sat alone in a crowded lunchroom at work	
Others avoided you at work	
You noticed others would not look at you at work	
Others at work shut you out of the conversation	
Others refused to talk to you at work	
Others at work treated you as if you weren't there	
Others at work did not invite you or ask you if you wanted anything when they went out for a coffee break	

Note (1)-Never (2)-Once in a while (3)-Sometimes (4)-Fairly often (5)-Often (6)-Constantly (7)-Always

Source Ferris, D. L., Brown, D. J., Berry, J. W., & Lian, H. (2008). The development and validation of the Workplace Ostracism Scale. *Journal of Applied Psychology, 93,* 1348–1366

Table A.2 Revised Workplace Exclusion Scale (WES-R) using a 5-point Likert-type response scale

How often do you experience these behaviors during the past 12 months at your organization?	*(1)–(5)*
Your boss or supervisor complimenting you on a job well done (Supervisor—R)	
Co-workers giving you the "silent treatment" (Co-worker)	
Co-workers shutting you out of their conversations (Co-worker)	
Co-workers giving you the impression that they enjoy your company (Co-worker—R)	
Co-workers interacting with you only when they are required to do so (Co-worker)	
Feeling accepted by other employees at your organization (Coworker—R)	
Employees updating you about important work-related activities (Co-worker—R)	
Supervisors not replying to your requests/questions within a reasonable period of time (Supervisor)	
Co-workers making you feel like you were not a part of the organization (Co-worker)	
Supervisors inviting you to participate in work related activities (Supervisor—R)	
Co-workers speaking to one another in a language you do not understand (Language)	
Co-workers not speaking English on the job (Language)	
Being unable to interact with others at work due to language communication difficulties (Language)	
Supervisors keeping important work-related information from you (e.g., deadlines) (Supervisor)	
Supervisors interacting with you at work (Supervisor—R)	
Felt as if you were being ostracized by co-workers (Criterion)	
Felt as if you were being ostracized by supervisors (Criterion)	

Note The WES-R includes three subscales: The coworker subscale, the supervisor subscale, and the language subscale. The coworker subscale assesses one's perception of being excluded by coworkers. The supervisor subscale assesses one's perception of being excluded by supervisors. The language subscale assesses ostracism based on language. (1)-Never (2)-Rarely (3)-Sometimes (4)-Often (5)-Most of the time

Source Hitlan, R. T., & Noel, J. (2009). The influence of workplace exclusion and personality on counterproductive work behaviours: An interactionist perspective. *European Journal of Work and Organizational Psychology, 18,* 477–502

Table A.3 Ostracism Experience Scale for Adolescents (OES–A) using a 5-point Likert-type response scale

In general, others	*(1)–(5)*
Being ignored subscale	
… treat me as if I am invisible	
… look through me as if I do not exist	
… have ignored my greetings when we are walking by one another	
… ignore me during conversation	
… ignore me	
Being excluded subscale	
… "hang out" with me at my home	
… invite me to join their club, organization, or association	
… include me in their plans for the holidays	
… make an effort to get my attention	
… invite me to go out to eat with them	
… invite me to join them for weekend activities, hobbies, or events	

Note The OES-A includes two subscales: Being ignored and being excluded. The being ignored subscale assesses the extent to which an adolescent feels he/she has been socially neglected or overlooked by the peer group. The being excluded subscale assesses the extent to which an adolescent feels he/she has been socially rejected and excluded by the peer group. (1)-Never (2)-Rarely (3)-Sometimes (4)-Often (5)-Always

Source Gilman, R., Carter-Sowell, A., Dewall, C. N., Adams, R. E., & Carboni, I. (2013). Validation of the ostracism experience scale for adolescents. *Psychological Assessment, 25*, 319–330

Table A.4 Ostracism Intervention Behavior Scale using a 7-point Likert-type response scale. Estimate the extent to which you have experienced the following behaviors over the past 6 months

My direct supervisor (manager)	*(1)–(7)*
Proactive behavior subscale	
Is proactive in ensuring that the group works together	
Enthusiastically participates in team-building activities	
Takes charge of resolving issues between co-workers	
Social awareness behavior subscale	
Identifies when things are going wrong within my workgroup	
Is aware of the interpersonal landscape of my workgroup	
Recognizes when there is conflict in my workgroup	
Harmony seeking behavior subscale	
Makes group members feel included	
Cares about developing a harmonious work environment	
Displays genuine interest in ensuring that my group works well together	

Note The three subscales were proactive behavior, social awareness behavior, and harmony seeking behavior. Proactive Behavior subscale assesses leadership behaviors that facilitate an overall social engagement of the workgroup. Social Awareness Behavior subscale assesses leadership behaviors that demonstrate conscious attention to the functional and dysfunctional social dynamic of a workgroup. Harmony Seeking Behavior subscale assesses leadership behaviors that show genuine interest in an inclusive and harmonious workgroup. (1)-Strongly agree (2)-Disagree (3)-Some-what disagree (4)-Neither agree or disagree (5)-Some-what agree (6)-Agree (7)-Strongly disagree

Source Fiset, J., & Boies, K. (2018). Seeing the unseen: Ostracism interventionary behaviour and its impact on employees. *European Journal of Work and Organizational Psychology, 27,* 403–417

Table A.5 Temporary Worker Alienation Scale using a 5-point Likert-type response scale

	(1)–(5)
I don't feel like I have much control over my work	
I often don't see the purpose of the tasks I'm asked to do	
I'm often given the work that no one else wants to do	
Coworkers generally ignore me	
I often feel separated from coworkers when doing my work	
I am often included in social conversations among coworkers (reversed)	
On the job, I have been referred to by something other than my name (e.g., "the temp")	
I sometimes don't even feel like a person when I'm at work (e.g., feel more like a machine)	
I often remind myself that I am just a temporary worker	

Note (1)-Never (2)-Rarely (3)-Sometimes (4)-Often (5)-Very often

Source Clark, S. K., Halbesleben, J. R., Lester, S. W., & Heintz, R. (2010). Temporary worker alienation and job performance: The impact of rating source. *Journal of Leadership & Organizational Studies, 17,* 287–297

Table A.6 Interpersonal Workplace Exclusion (IWE) scale using a 5-point Likert-type response scale

	(1)–(5)
Coworker IWE	
Recognized the personal events of others (e.g., birthday) but not mine	
Whispered things to others, from which I am excluded, right in front of me	
Gave sentiments of appreciation to others but not to me	
Walked out of the room when I entered	
Did not encourage me to participate in work-related activities	
Did not invite me to socialize (e.g., lunch, coffee breaks, office pools, etc.)	
Did not introduce me when an introduction would have been appropriate	
Refused to work with me	
Arranged their schedules to avoid working with me	
Arranged their work location so that they sit away from me	
Supervisor IWE	
Refused to give me any work assignments at all	
Did not respond to my greetings	
Whispered things to others, from which I am excluded, right in front of me	
Arranged their schedule to avoid working with me	
Assigned me projects so that I missed important events and activities	
Did not introduce me when an introduction would have been appropriate	
Refused to work with me	
Arranged their work location so that they sit away from me	

Think about the supervisor/coworkers closest to you in your current job, or the most recent job that you have held. Below you will find a list of ways that your supervisor/coworkers may have behaved towards you recently or in the past few months. Read each item carefully and indicate the extent to which you agree or disagree with each item listed

Note (1)-Strongly disagree (2)-Disagree (3)-Neither (4)-Agree (5)-Strongly agree

Source Scott, K. D. (2007). *The development and test of an exchange-based model of interpersonal workplace exclusion*. Doctoral dissertation, University of Kentucky. Retrieved from https://uknowledge.uky.edu/gradschool_diss/534/

Index

C. Liu and J. Ma (eds.), *Workplace Ostracism*, Palgrave Explorations in Workplace Stigma, https://doi.org/10.1007/978-3-030-54379-2